An Anatomy of Criminal Justice

An Anatomy of Criminal Justice

A System Overview

Edited by
Cleon H. Foust
D. Robert Webster
Indiana Lawyers Commission, Inc.

LexingtonBooks
D.C. Heath and Company
Lexington, Massachusetts
Toronto

Library of Congress Cataloging in Publication Data
Main entry under title:

An anatomy of criminal justice.

1. Criminal justice, Administration of—United States—Addresses, essays, lectures. I. Foust, Cleon H. II. Webster, D. Robert.
HV7921.A57 364'.973 79-3908
ISBN 0-669-02854-1

Published simultaneously in Canada.

Printed in the United States of America.

International Standard Book Number: 0-669-02854-1

Library of Congress Catalog Card Number: 79-3908

Contents

Foreword

The criminal justice system in the United States is often described as a failure. That is of course too strong, as Charles Silberman has demonstrated in his book, *Criminal Violence, Criminal Justice.* Serious crimes are taken seriously, and severe sanctions are often imposed. In fact, prison sentences are longer in the United States than in any other Western nation, and the proportion of the population confined to prison is higher than in any of those nations.

It would, however, be equally mistaken to conclude that substantial rates of imprisonment for relatively long terms establish that the criminal justice system works well. In fact, it does not.

Many, perhaps most, crimes are not reported, to an alarming extent because the victims think that little will come of their complaints beyond unwelcome involvement in prosecutorial bureaucracy and possible risk of harm from the alleged wrongdoer.

Apprehension rates are low, especially in assaults, robberies, and burglaries, the crimes most feared by the public.

A high proportion of all arrests result in dismissals. Witnesses, including complainants, frequently will not testify; prosecutors conclude that the evidence is insufficient to convict, or the case is simply not time–worthy in an overcrowded system.

Criminal court dockets are so heavy that prosecutors, defense counsel, and judges take shortcuts to lighten the burden. Plea negotiation is not necessarily an evil, but it is overused, sometimes oppressively by the prosecution, sometimes by an accused who uses the court overburden to his/her advantage.

Disparity in the imposition of sanctions remains a serious problem. When persons convicted of crime cannot understand the basis for sentencing, the resulting feeling of unfairness negates the sense of justice essential to a defensible system.

Jails and prisons, far from being the "country clubs" sometimes claimed by advocates of harsh punishment, often fail to satisfy minimum standards of decency. Many have deserved reputations as breeders of crime rather than places for the correction of wrongdoers.

The criminal justice system in the United States is shaped by four attributes, each of which has implications adverse to fairness and efficiency.

First, at every stage of the process there is a large measure of discretion available to the principal actors. Police officers can arrest or not arrest; prosecutors have discretion to charge or not charge; judges ordinarily have wide choice in the severity of sanctions to be imposed; and parole boards are almost uncontrolled in their determination of the all-important question of release.

Second, the adversary system, which makes the lawyers on both sides the principal agents for investigation and presentation of facts and law, depends for its efficiency and fairness on the assumption of relatively equal talent and resources on both sides. But we all know this is not true, often to the disadvantage of the accused in a criminal trial.

Third, as already noted, prison sentences are imposed on more persons in proportion to population and for longer terms than in any other Western nation. But harshness seems not to have made any significant impact on crime.

Fourth, worst of all is the fact that there is no general agreement whether the purpose of the sanctioning process is to punish, to incapacitate, to deter or to rehabilitate—or perhaps some undetermined combination of these. Neither theoretical nor practical solutions are likely to be agreed on if common purposes cannot be developed.

What makes "An Anatomy of the Criminal Justice System" useful is that the various chapters address these gaps in our knowledge forthrightly. The confessions of present inadequacy are specific, the examples are realistic, and the suggested next steps are pragmatic.

As two of the cooperating sponsors of this endeavor, we are proud to be associated with the project and the book. We congratulate the Indiana Lawyers Commission, which accepted principal responsibility throughout, for this genuinely useful contribution to a troubled area of the law.

B.J. George
President
Southwestern Legal Foundation

Robert B. McKay
Director
Aspen Institute Justice Program

Preface and Acknowledgments

The Anglo-American legal system suffers mightily from lack of specific answers to unadjudicated factual situations. Lawyers are accustomed to and can deal with the uncertainties of litigation prediction, but laymen, unfamiliar with the system and more particularly those who become involved with it, are distressed by the size of legal grey areas. The lack of specifics is almost as omnipresent in the branch of law that deals with the criminal justice system as it is in civil personal-injury cases, for example. However, if one complains that he cannot cope with low-percentage predictability in the application of criminal law to fact situations, my advice would be that he completely abjure the waffling and buzz words of popular criminology. For here, the formulation of any sort of generalization is compounded by human reactions and relationships involving social and economic environments, neurological differences, and many other factors, most of them inadequately explored.

Consequently, in dealing with the criminal justice system, one can talk only so long about improvement of prison conditions, increased appropriations for correction, legislative changes, and correctional fads. Then, it becomes obvious that one must make some effort to dispel some of the uncertainties in management of the judicial aspects of the system, in problems of deterrence and rehabilitation, in early intervention to prevent juvenile delinquency, and in many other problems that remain problems because they are unsolvable or because we have not devoted sufficient time and effort to solutions or partial solutions.

Thus the Indiana Lawyers Commission, in its five plus years of rather intensive application to the improvement of the criminal justice system in Indiana, found itself piling up question marks that served as a barricade against further exploration of the system.

For almost all of us, there is a childhood recollection of an Indian fable of the six blind men who were asked to describe an elephant. One remembers, each blind man was led astray in his description of the animal by the fact that he had examined only one part such as the trunk, an ear, or a leg. If the criminal justice system, like the elephant, were examined by four different persons sent to four different segments of the system, one to the police, one to a prison, one to a felony court, and one to a grand jury, each would produce a similarly distorted description of the system. What seems to be worse in connection with the criminal justice system is that even those in one segment are not aware sometimes that, like an elephant that reacts as a biological system, the criminal justice system will react as a system. When it has a cold in the nose, the whole elephant shivers, and when there is circulatory congestion in a leg, the whole elephant limps. Similarly, what the police do will affect the entire system including courts and correctional facilities. What the courts do likewise affects the correctional facilities and the police and so on.

So while the Lawyers Commission was finding many more questions than answers, it became further convinced that despite segmentation, there really is a criminal justice system, or at least, whatever its name, it reacts as a system. A look at the literature produced a good deal of information from institutes, seminars, and conferences dealing with parts of the system. Many of these conferences were excellent, but none, so far as one could ascertain, had been devoted to the holistic approach—to the system as a system. Further study confirmed the Lawyers Commission belief in the need for at least one attempt to approach the system as a whole. Unless that approach were taken, it would be difficult to set priorities for investigation and research, to allocate resources in the appropriate places, and to assess the functional impacts of one segment on another.

The decision was made, therefore, to begin preparation for an exchange of expert information about all parts of the system. It was hoped that this information would evaluate the state of the art in managing the system as it now is, would recommend improvements, and would set priorities for action.

The purpose of the Indiana Lawyers Commission is to improve the criminal justice system in Indiana and, consequently, the colloquium should be Indiana oriented. However, to the extent that the Indiana criminal justice system presents problems similar to those encountered in most other states, recommendations produced at the colloquium could be applied to a good many other jurisdictions. The decision was thus made late in 1976 to aim for a national colloquium, based on the Indiana milieu for the purposes already mentioned. Obviously, the criminal justice system could not be covered in depth in three or four days and, indeed, the emphasis on interrelationships and priorities in the total system would militate against the examination in depth of any particular part of the system.

Once the decision was made, three questions became apparent: (1) How should the system be subdivided for the holistic approach? (2) who were the experts to be invited? and (3) how would they be informed about Indiana and its criminal justice model?

After discussion with a great number of people, it was decided to break down the system functionally starting with prearrest problems such as prevention and deterrence and ending with correctional problems. This produced fourteen or fifteen topics that were finally approved. The next problem was to find the people to talk about the listed topics. For that we first approached that very able generalist in law, Robert McKay, director of the

Criminal Justice Program of the Aspen Institute For Humanistic Studies, and also another able generalist in the criminal justice discipline, B.J. George, immediate past chairman of the Criminal Justice Section of the American Bar Association and president of the Southwestern Legal Foundation. Their assistance was invaluable not only in managing the holistic approach but in finding participants. It soon became apparent that the Criminal Justice Program of the Aspen Institute and the Criminal Justice Section of the American Bar Association would be very valuable cosponsors, and we were gratified when our request that they act as such was approved by both. Their cosponsorship proved vital not only in preparation but in the management of the colloquium. We are deeply indebted to both cosponsors.

It soon appeared that two of the topics could not be touched even briefly without opening so many more topics that not only would there be inadequate time but also there would be some danger of tangential misdirection of the whole. So at an early state it was decided to eliminate substantially all problems of juvenile deviant behavior and the impact on the system of such behavior, as well as white-collar or corporate crime. Each could well become the subject matter of further colloquia. Also one of the directors of the Indiana Lawyers Commission suggested that for a change of pace and for more appropriate presentation, it would be advisable to adopt a more dramatic vehicle for presentation of violent crime. It was therefore decided to present criminal violence in three theatrical episodes one involving rape, another, assaultive robbery, and a third, homicide. The services of an improvisational theater troupe, Living Stage, A Venture of Arena Stage of Washington, D.C., were obtained to produce the drama for a live audience and also for video taping. After each of the three crimes was presented, a different panel of experts was arranged to discuss the episode. The panel on rape was Edith Flynn and William Fisher; that on robbery was Stanton Samenow and George Beto; and that on homicide, Marvin Wolfgang and Kenneth Moyer. At the conclusion, the three panels joined with the moderator, for a general discussion of criminal violence. No attempt has been made to include those panel discussions since they relate to improvisational situations not reproducible here.

This volume contains presentations at the colloquium, as well as relevant postdinner addresses by Jerome Hall and David L. Bazelon. We are grateful to them and to all the contributors listed elsewhere in this volume.

Beyond the topical presentations at the colloquium, there were, of course, scheduled responses and a substantial amount of participant dialogue. Much of the response and all of the dialogue were informal. It was decided that the response and dialogue where pertinent would be included in this volume as commentary and in the final chapter entitled, "Conclusions."

In addition to the many hours of consultation and assistance from Robert McKay and B.J. George, we wish to acknowledge the assistance of the Indiana Criminal Justice Planning Agency, Lilly Endowment, Inc., Indiana Committee For The Humanities, and the Indiana State Bar Association for their support in funding and producing the conference.

We also want to record our appreciation for the dedicated and skillful assistance of David Metzger as a special consultant, and Christine I. Ward-Hull, Timothy V. Clark, Catherine O'Connor, Pamela Smith, and Anne Haslem.

Finally, we would like to pay special tribute to Constantine Simonidies, vice president, Massachusetts Institute of Technology, who skillfully guided group discussion and served as facilitator of the colloquium.

An Anatomy of Criminal Justice

Part I
Prevention

1 Morality and the Law

David Bazelon

The American people are in deep fear, if not panic, over the violent street crime in the nation. It is not the fear of white-collar crime that makes us put so many locks on our doors; nor is it the organized crime that corrupts our politics and business life; nor is it the crimes of passion. No, what makes us fear for our safety are the random muggings and burglaries, the assaults on our sense of security and repose committed by those people we don't even know, and for reasons we cannot understand. The public is paying us—the hired hands of the criminal justice system—and it demands that we "solve" the problem of street crime. Were it not for the menace of street crime, there would be no Law Enforcement Assistance Administration (LEAA); we would not be debating proposed recodification of the Federal criminal code in Senate Bill 1 and House Bill 1437; and, frankly, many of us might not be so well employed. We certainly cannot ignore critical relationships of public fear to sentencing.

It is important to keep in mind that crime—the kind of crime that produces these fearful reactions, the kind of crime that accounts for the burgeoning of our profession—is a human problem, which can be understood only in its full social context, with an awareness of its human element. In other words, crime is fundamentally a political and moral issue, inseparable from society's notions of social justice.

Because I have recognized the importance of this interrelationship between criminal justice and social justice, I decided to address this topic when I accepted an invitation to deliver the first J. Edgar Hoover Foundation Lecture at the University of Southern California (USC) in November, 1975. Aware of the irony of the occasion, I discussed what I saw as two fundamentally contrasting views of criminal law. My lecture on the role of morality in criminal law sparked an entirely unanticipated dialogue with Stephen Morse, a distinguished young criminal law professor at USC. That dialogue has since been published in the *Southern California Law Review,*[1] and it has deep implications for the criminal justice issues facing the public.

My lecture identified two models of the criminal justice system. Both start from the common premise that the purpose of the criminal law is to create social order. And each asserts that there can be no moral development in a society in which the mighty prey on the weak. What separates the two views is the means used to achieve order and ultimately the type of order sought. The first view holds that achieving order is so important that there is little room for concerns of social justice in devising means; this view explicitly suggests an amoral process, justified by a high moral end. It is thus able to endorse what seems to be the easiest means to achieving order, the imposition of strong external constraints. It demands that the criminal law punish disorder and make the cost of violating the law so great that few will dare to do so. This view and the cluster of beliefs associated with it I called the "law-as-external-constraint" thesis.

Standing against this thesis is the view that the law's aims must be achieved by a moral process. This philosophy sees externally imposed order, that is, repressive order, as suffering from the same basic defect as disorder; both lack moral authority. The philosophy asserts that the moral foundation of order is tenuous at best when people obey the law solely because they fear the consequences of disobedience. The only truly moral order, according to this philosophy, is that based on the internalization of control, that is, on the members' of the society obeying the law because they personally believe that its commands are justified. Thus this view demands that the law facilitate the internalization process by becoming a moral force in the community.

As many of you know, I believe in the second view of the criminal law as it is embodied in the words, "do unto others as you would have them do unto you *if you were in their circumstances.*" That is my definition of morality, and I believe that this concept must infuse every stage in the criminal justice system.

The preceding view of morality is highly relevant to virtually all problems in the administration of criminal justice such as claims of ineffective assistance of counsel for the poor, plea bargaining, sentencing, corrections, and bail. I would follow the teaching of Justice Hugo Black: "There can be no equal justice where the kind of trial a man gets depends on the amount of money he has."[2] The presence of inequality should be a challenge, not a moral inevitability. In the words of Judge Elbert Tuttle, "[T]he only way the law has progressed from the days of the rack, the screw and the wheel is the development of moral concepts... ."[3]

I would like to focus on one question in particular to which the two models that I have described elicit markedly different responses: What should be our standard of criminal responsibility? I chose this question not only because it defines the central issue and marks the starting point for operation of the criminal justice system but also because the answer will determine the responses we must make and even the questions we must ask in every other phase of the system, including police function and prevention, trial procedures, sentencing, and corrections.

My analysis begins with the fundamental moral principle that the sanctions of the criminal law should apply only to the culpable, that is, only to those it can morally condemn. Accordingly, a decision for conviction requires three determinations: (1) that a condemnable *act* was committed by the actor-defendant; (2) that the *actor* can be condemned, that is, that he could reasonably have been expected to have conformed his behavior to the demands of the law; and (3) that society's own conduct in relation to the actor, in other words, society's own responsibility for the multiple deprivations and degradations he has been made to suffer, entitles it to sit in condemnation of him. To some extent the law already inquires into at least the first two of these factors through the element of intent or *mens rea*. But although it has been asserted repeatedly that only a free choice to do wrong will be punished, in practice, the law presumes almost irrebuttably that proscribed behavior is the product of "a free agent confronted with a choice between doing right and doing wrong and choosing freely to do wrong."[4]

Our sense of moral responsibility, however, is far more complex than the foregoing presumption. The purpose of our 1954 opinion in *Durham* v. *United States*[5] was to open the door to the behavioral sciences and to bring into the courtroom information and analysis that might generate more sophisticated insights into the defendant's behavior and might permit a more realistic assessment of individual choice. Learned Hand once told me that although he admired my opinion in *Durham,* he feared that it "created" more problems than it solved. I would say that Judge Hand's assessment was exactly right except for the very important word "creates." *Durham* did not "create" the problems Judge Hand feared; it simply uncovered them. By exposing these bullets that society had always refused to bite, we believed we were giving the community an opportunity to recognize—and thereby more clearly understand—not only the complexity of the criminal responsibility issue but also the societal conditions that generated the criminal act and the actions required to accommodate the interests and needs of both the individual and society.

The expert testimony elicited by *Durham,* however, was sterile and conclusory, thereby covering up the underlying questions of moral attribution and precluding their consideration by the jury. The experts never candidly described what they knew and did not know about an individual or what they could not know considering the state of knowledge in the behavioral sciences. The experts' definitions of *disease* reflected their personal views, as did the behavioral descriptions of the causal relation between mental impairment and a criminal act. Inevitably, this development culminated in the experts'—not the jury's—deciding whether a person was morally blameworthy.

Thus in the 1972 decision of *U.S.* v. *Brawner,*[6] I joined with other members of my court in abandoning the *Durham* rule. But I could not agree with the alternative my colleagues chose, which in my view was little more than a warmed-over amalgam of *M'Naghten*[7] and *Durham* and which failed to resolve the problem of expert dominance. I wrote separately to propose that the jury be instructed

> that a defendant is not responsible *if at the time of his unlawful conduct his mental or emotional processes or behavior controls were impaired to such an extent that he cannot justly be held responsible for his act.*[8]

This proposed instruction is more akin to the minority proposals of the American Law Institute (ALI) Model Penal Code[9] or to one of the recommendations of the British Royal Commission on Capital Punishment.[10] It reflects what I derived from the *Durham* experience: (1) Neither psychiatric experts nor appellate judges have a magic formula to determine how the balance between morality and safety should be struck in individual cases; (2) the community at large, which is both the beneficiary and the victim of these balancing decisions should, through its traditional surrogate the jury assess criminal responsibility in light of the community's moral sense; and (3) the legal rules were restricting the jury's inquiry into the causes of a criminal act and thereby deflecting the jury's attention away from the central moral question. The instruction would freely allow expert and lay testimony on the nature and extent of behavioral impairments and of physiological, psychological, environmental, cultural, educational, economic, and heredity factors. Its ultimate aim, much like *Durham*'s, would be to give all of us a deeper understanding of the causes of human behavior in general and criminal behavior in particular.

Presently, it should be clear that the need to engage the moral perception of the jury, thereby joining the criminal law to the moral sense of the community, should not be limited to what has traditionally been regarded as the domain of the insanity defense. For if blameworthiness were truly to be the prerequisite for criminal sanctions, we would have to consider, to take some contemporary examples from cases that have come before me, whether a free choice to do wrong can be found in the acts of a poverty-stricken and otherwise deprived black youth from the central city who kills a marine who taunted him with a racial epithet,[11] in the act of a modern Jean Valjean who steals to feed his family,[12] in the act of a narcotics addict who buys drugs for his own use,[13] or in the act of a superpatriot steeped in cold war ideology who burglarizes in the name of "national security."[14]

Professor Morse, in response to my lecture, took exception to my view of criminal responsibility. First, he argued that behavior is a matter of choice, and because he saw no reason to believe that people are not responsible for their behavior, Professor Morse suggested that the defense of nonresponsibility should be narrowed rather than broadened. Clearly, he noted, environmental factors are not all determinative since the majority of people in even the most criminolgenic subcultures are law abiding, and since there are some members of the most law abiding subcultures who commit crimes. Even if obeying the law is harder for some than for others, the decision to offend is still the result of the actor's free choice and deserves to be punished on retributive as well as deterrent grounds.

Professor Morse's second argument was that, even assuming that the criminal law must take a broader view of moral culpability, the appropriate institution to measure the moral sense of the community is the legislature, not the jury. Although juries are representatives of the moral standards of the community, he said, each jury is not a totally independent "legislature" free to decide what those moral standards should be. Juries do not create community moral standards; they apply them after being instructed on the law by the judge. If, as I had proposed, juries were free to engage the full moral complexities presented by each individual defendant, they would be without guidance.

Finally, Professor Morse claimed that my assumption that environment affects behavior was ultimately paternalistic and would lead to what he called "the therapeutic state." He suggested that there were only three options for dealing with dangerous defendants whom juries found nonculpable: release, preventive detention, and treatment. Release he rejected as incompatible with the fundamental purpose of the criminal law, the maintenance of order. Preventive detention was undesirable because it would involve massive violations of civil rights. And treatment was inappropriate because it would require an immense stretching of the medical model to cover those who are not conventionally viewed as ill, or even mentally ill. If social conditions have caused a defendant to be dangerous, reasoned Professor Morse, then it would be necessary to "change" the defendant before allowing him to return to society. Society's goal would then be to change who the defendant *is* rather than to punish him for what he has done. The state might thus treat all deviants without regard to blameworthiness. Such a program would lead to disrespect for personal autonomy and to massive invasions of privacy. The conundrum occurs, Professor Morse felt, because the appropriate model of behavior for the criminal law is to assume that most people do choose their behavior and should be held accountable for it.

Professor Morse then went on to discuss my call for social reform as the only moral solution to the crime problem. He labeled the proposal "utopian," a term apparently intended to call for its dismissal. He believed that the elimination of the culture of poverty, if possible at all, could be achieved only by massive redistribution of wealth and intrusive intervention into the family life of the poor, a result that would be "inconsistent with a capitalist and libertarian society."

Perhaps even more damning, however, was Professor Morse's assertion that the liberal social science approach had been tested in the 1960s and had proved ineffective in stemming the rising crime rates. Such welfare programs were doomed to failure, in Professor Morse's eyes, because poverty is neither a sufficient nor a necessary cause of crime. Until the allegedly underlying causes of crime are understood, reasoned Professor Morse, it is better and, indeed, fairer to approach the crime problem by so-called get-tough measures that address the problem directly and effectively. Because a society in which citizens cannot live safely is incapable of moral development and because the social welfare programs of the sixties had failed to brake the upsurge of street violence, more repressive law-enforcement techniques are necessary to ensure greater public safety, even at the cost of increased infringement on liberty and privacy.[15]

Professor Morse's arguments raise some cogent and difficult issues, but I think that ultimately his position is a dangerous and even self-defeating one. I say "dangerous" because the current get-tough programs lull us into a false sense of security that something is being done while diverting our attention and resources away from the social structural changes that are truly needed to combat crime. Ten years ago these programs were justified as temporary expedients while the more intractable problems of crime's causes were slowly being worked through; today we hear nothing about the causes of crime. And I say that Professor Morse's position is self-defeating because if we fail to look to the conditions that breed crime in the first place, we must expect the offender to break the law again when we send him back to those same conditions.

In fact, I would venture to say that Professor Morse's position may even be self-destructive, for applying repression without simultaneously working to eliminate the fundamental causes of crime begins a vicious circle. Repressive tactics only exacerbate the intolerable conditions that engender crime. Inevitably, then, crime will increase. More crime will call fourth more repression, thus completing this hopeless circle of fear and despair.

I can pose this danger no more eloquently than did Anthony V. Bouza, the Bronx borough commander for the New York City Police Department, in questioning the morality of his own role in controlling violent urban crime:

> To the degree that I succeed in keeping the ghetto cool, to the degree that I can be effective—to that degree, fundamentally, am I deflecting America's attention from discovering this cancer? . . . Maybe I'd be better off not being as effective as I presume myself to be.
>
> And that way America would be confronting the problem as it had to do during the urban riots of the '60's and so on. The fact of the matter is that we are manufacturing criminals. We are manufacturing brutality out there. We are very efficiently creating a very volatile and dangerous subelement of our society. And we are doing it simply because we don't want to face the burdens and the problems and the responsibilities that their existence

> imposes on any society with conscience. So rather than awaken your conscience to the problem you're far better off just ignoring it.[16]

I simply cannot accept Professor Morse's assertion that improvement in the economic conditions of poor people does not reduce the level of violent crime. Almost 2,000 years ago, Marcus Aurelius observed that "[p]overty is the mother of crime."[17] Today study after study reveals that the overwhelming majority of the violent street crime is committed by people at the bottom of the socioeconomic cultural ladder: the ignorant, the ill-educated, the unemployed and often unemployable. John Conrad and Simon Dinitz have told me that recent empirical studies in Columbus, Ohio—one of the more affluent northern cities with a relatively low unemployment rate—reveal that over 90 percent of the violent street crime is perpetrated by those from the lowest census tracts.[18] Could anyone rationally believe that this relationship is coincidental?

With all due respect, I do not need criminologists and empirical studies to convince me of the relationship between crime and our unjust social structure. Someone once said that "[p]rison reform will never work until we start sending a better class of people there." There is more than a grain of truth to that statement. My three decades on the bench have firmly convinced me that street crime springs from the anger and resentment of those who have been twisted by a culture of grinding oppression and deprivation—wretched poverty, broken families, malnutrition, mental and physical illness, mental retardation, racial discrimination, and, perhaps most importantly, lack of opportunity. For the most part, these people turn to crime for economic survival, out of a sense of excitement or accomplishment, or as an outlet for their frustration, desperation, and rage. The roots of street crime are thus embedded deep within the inequities of our very social structure. So long as these inequities remain, these roots will be continually refreshed and rejuvenated.

The existence of this culture of poverty cannot be irrelevant to our instinctive sense of moral responsibility. As a society, this places us under an imperative to eradicate, if possible, this root cause of crime. And, as architects of a criminal justice system, it requires us to make systematic use of what information we do possess about the actual causes of crime. Professor Leslie Wilkins has wryly observed, "We refer to a crime as being 'solved' when we have found someone who can be blamed for committing it; this is an odd use of the term 'solved.'"[19]

The fundamental assumption of our criminal justice system, that the causes of behavior reside solely within the individual, is markedly at odds with the theories of contemporary psychology, which have emphasized the degree to which situations, and *not* personalities, control behavior. As Professor Stanley Milgram has concluded, "Under certain circumstances, it is not so much the kind of person a man is as it is the kind of situation in which he is placed that determines his actions."[20] I must question whether the legal system can any longer afford to adhere to a consciously fictional model of human action in which all conduct is viewed as the product of a free and rational choice. And I must question whether it is ethical for the criminal law deliberately to ignore relationships between behavior and environment that we know or have good reason to believe exist.

Space does not allow me to discuss the implications of fully incorporating this broader notion of responsibility into our criminal justice system. For example, it would at a minimum call for a reexamination of the role of the jury. The jury would consider the *why* of behavior, the reasons for the conduct in dispute, and the context in which the crime was committed. It would then determine whether, as society's conscience, it felt entitled to sit in condemnation of the defendant. I do not mean to imply, of course, that I personally would always agree with a jury's moral perspective. I simply believe, lacking any infallible index, that we have no alternative but to trust it. As Thomas Jefferson once wrote,

> I know no safe depository of the ultimate powers of the society but the people themselves; and if we think them not enlightened enough to exercise their control with a wholesome discretion, the remedy is not to take it from them, but to inform their discretion.[21]

The composition of juries might also change if we more fully appreciated the situational determinants of behavior. Greater strides would be taken to ensure that the jury contained a broad cross-section of the community, including those whose situations are similar to that of the defendant.

Sentencing and correctional policies would also reflect this expanded view of criminal responsibility. Pronouncement of a criminal sentence should force the participants in the criminal process to confront anew the moral and political complexities inherent in the criminal act. Thus the same information that was so vital for the jury's determination of responsibility is also needed after conviction. In contrast to the present practice in some courts, defendants' attempts to explain their behaviors and to provide needed contextual information would be encouraged rather than discouraged. The current trend toward automating the sentencing process by categorizing defendants or offenses will be seen as hopeless at best; since no guidelines can possibly encompass the rich complexity of the particular case, their use would deprive us of the educational potential and moral underpinnings of the sentencing process.

Most importantly, perhaps, a theory of criminal responsibility that recognizes the relationship between poverty and crime would force us to reexamine the role of the corrections system in our society. We cannot eliminate the violent street crime that so troubles us merely by imprisoning those who commit crime, no matter how we may try to justify such confinement through elaborate theories of "rehabilitation," "deterrence," or "treatment." We delude society if we see any of these programs as anything more than after-the-fact treatments that never prevent, and only rarely cure, criminal behavior.

When Senator Kennedy introduced S. 1437, he pointed out that the bill was not a cure-all for crime in America, that no one, as he put it, "should labor under the misapprehension that [its] passage will eliminate the violent crime which plagues our local communities."[22] But Senator Kennedy's remarks remain buried on page S15962 of the *Congressional Record.* I cannot help but wonder whether society would support such programs so readily if it were made fully and sharply aware that they will *not* reduce crime significantly, if at all. I do not mean to suggest that the various proposals for sentencing and prison reforms are worthless. If the present debates in corrections are aimed at making sentencing fairer and prisons less brutal, then the effort is commendable. But such programs should be supported for their decency and should not be sold on the promise that they will reduce crime.

I have mentioned to you that Professor Morse feared that acquittal of a large number of defendants under a broad test of nonresponsibility would ultimately lead to a paternalistic "therapeutic state" that would take it upon itself to "treat" the defendant before allowing him to return to society. I agree with Professor Morse that society must take measures to protect itself. But it is in considering the alternative responses to the crime problem that I think he has fallen widest of the mark. The solution lies not only in changing the defendant so that he can return to society but also in changing the society to which he ultimately must return. I do not underestimate the enormity of such a task; it will require an effort that dwarfs the token responses that were offered in the 1960s yet have been all but eliminated by the recent administrations. Professor Morse is correct: The social welfare reforms have failed. But they have failed not because they have produced no reduction in crime rates; they have failed in their primary goal of reducing the inequalities of riches in our society. I could cite statistic after statistic to show that the distribution of wealth in our country remains unchanged. Unemployment for black teenagers has reached an astronomical 37 percent. One need only compare U.S. crime rates to those of comparable European countries where poverty and unemployment are drastically lower to see the results of truly committed and effective social welfare reforms.

Of course, the crime problem cannot be solved simply by throwing money at it. I agree with Professor Morse that we must address and destroy the "culture of poverty," that income redistribution alone is no panacea. For example, one of the few clues we do have to the sources of street crime is that a viable family structure is crucial for social integration. A child needs a family because that is where his roots and his education are. But many poverty parents have less time and energy for their families. They are easily overwhelmed simply by the struggle for survival. A frantic and harassed woman is not an attentive mother, and a failing and desperate man is not a supportive father, and he may not even stay around long enough to try. A parent who cannot put food on the table cannot convey to a child a sense of order, purpose, or self-esteem. It seems to me then that insofar as a "culture of poverty" does exist, it has developed as a response to the economic fact of poverty and will recede only as poverty recedes.

I believe there is a desperate need to inform the nation that there are no nostrums for street crime apart from social reform and that to put social order ahead of social justice is repressive. To choose to eliminate social injustice is to choose a long, painful, and costly process. But the only option I can imagine that is less appealing is not to choose it.

I am sure you all are familiar with the comforting prayer of Reinhold Niebuhr, which reads,

> O God, give us serenity to accept what cannot be changed, courage to change what should be changed, and wisdom to distinguish the one from the other.[23]

I feel sure that Dr. Niebuhr also believes, as I do, that it is easy to concede the inevitability of social injustice and find the serenity to accept it. The far harder task is to feel its intolerability and to seek the strength to change it.

Notes

1. *See:* D. Bazelon, "The Morality of the Criminal Law," *S. Cal. L. Rev.* 49 (1976): 385; S. Morse, "The Twilight of Welfare Criminology: A Reply to Judge Bazelon," *S. Cal. L. Rev.* 49 (1976): 1247; D. Bazelon, "The Morality of the Criminal Law: A Rejoinder to Professor Morse," *S. Cal. L. Rev.* 49 (1976): 1269; S. Morse, "The Twilight of Welfare Criminology: A Final Word," *S. Cal. L. Rev.* 49 (1976): 1275. Used with permission.
2. Griffin v. Illinois, 351 U.S. 12, 19 (1956).
3. Novack v. Beto, 453 F. 2d 661, 672 (5th Cir. 1971) (Tuttle, J., concurring in part and dissenting in part), *cert. denied,* 409 U.S. 968 (1972).
4. R. Pound, "Introduction" to F. Sayre, *Cases on Criminal Law* (Rochester, N.Y., The Lawyers Cooperative Publishing Co., 1927), p. xxxvii.
5. 214 F. 2d 862 (D.C. Cir. 1954).
6. 471 F. 2d 969 (D.C. Cir. 1972).
7. M'Naghten's Case, 8 Eng. Rep. 718 (H.L. 1843).

8. United States v. Brawner, 471 F. 2d at 1032 (Bazelon, C.J., concurring in part and dissenting in part)(emphasis in original).

9. *Model Penal Code* § 4.01(1), Alternative (a) (Tent. Draft No. 4, 1955), quoted in United States v. Brawner, 471, F. 2d at 986–987 n. 24.

10. *Royal Commission on Capital Punishment, Report, Cmd. No.* 8932, ¶ 333(iii), at 116 (1953) (three commissioners dissenting from this recommendation), quoted in United States v. Brawner, 471 F. 2d at 986 n. 23.

11. *See:* United States v. Alexander, 471 F. 2d 923 (D.C. Cir.), *cert. denied,* 409 U.S. 1044 (1973); *cf:* United States v. Robertson, 507 F. 2d 1148 (D.C. Cir. 1974).

12. *Cf:* Everett v. United States, 336 F. 2d 979 (D.C. Cir. 1964).

13. *See:* United States v. Moore, 486 F. 2d 1139 (D.C. Cir.), *cert. denied,* 414 U.S. 980 (1973). *See also:* Easter v. District of Columbia, 361 F. 2d 50 (D.C. Cir. 1966) (*en banc*).

14. *See:* United States v. Barker, 514 F. 2d 208 (D.C. Cir.), *cert. denied,* 421 U.S. 1013 (1975).

15. *See:* S. Morse, "The Twilight of Welfare Criminology: A Reply to Judge Bazelon," *S. Cal. L. Rev.* 49 (1976): 1247.

16. Broadcast excerpt of Chief Anthony v. Boyza from Susan and Alan Raymond's documentary, "The Police Tapes." Reprinted with permission.

17. Aristotle, *Politics* 2. New York: Modern Library, 1946.

18. J. Conrad, S. Dinitz, and S. Miller, *The Career of the Dangerous Criminal* (Lexington, Mass.: Lexington Books, D.C. Heath, forthcoming 1980).

19. L.T. Wilkins, "Crime and Criminal Justice at the Turn of the Century," *Annals of the American Academy of Political & Social Sciences* 408, no. 13 (July 1973), p. 22.

20. S. Milgram, "Some Conditions of Obedience and Disobedience to Authority," *Human Relations* 18, no. 57 (1965): p. 75.

21. T. Jefferson, Letter to William Charles Jarvis, 28 September 1820.

22. 123 *Cong. Rec.* S. 15962 daily ed., 29 September 1977.

23. R. Niebuhr, *Prayer,* 1934.

2 Correlates of Crime: Should the Relation of Unemployment and Crime Be Reconsidered?

Lucy N. Friedman

A high percentage of alleged criminals is poor, undereducated, unemployed, and minorities. While most people who fit this profile do not commit crimes and many who do not fit the profile do commit crimes, the aggregate data from many different sources indicate a strong and consistent relationship between crime and these factors. Efforts to identify other factors that influence criminal activity such as family or personality characteristics have been neither particularly successful nor useful in yielding clear policy directions.

This chapter addresses the relation between crime and only one factor, unemployment. Unemployment, to a greater extent than many factors linked with criminal activity (such as age, sex, or family structure), can be affected by governmental policies and program initiatives. Therefore, increasing employment for certain groups by changing government policies and allocating resources could conceivably reduce the crime rate.

It has almost become conventional wisdom that unemployment is associated with crime. Much of the literature that has led to this belief is based on aggregate data. The Vera Institute of Justice in New York City, however, has derived individual data from a work program developed partially on the assumption that providing employment or employment skills would help reduce crime. Vera's data have raised questions about the relationship between crime and unemployment. These data have proven disappointing for those who have seen employment as a panacea for the crime problem.

The data discussed in this chapter come from a three-year evaluation of Wildcat, a supported (government subsidized) work program established by the Vera Institute in New York City in 1972. Wildcat was designed to test whether supported work affected the lives of participants: their long-term employment, earning, welfare dependency, drug use, life styles, and criminal activities.

Supported employment provides low stress work with the goal of instilling steady work habits and a sense of self-worth in persons with histories of failure in the regular job market. The carefully structured environment offers peer support, graduated stress, and immediate and regular feedback on performance while preparing employees for transition to the regular job market. Employees generally work nine o'clock to five five days a week and are paid a starting salary of $95 a week; they are fired if they do not meet the demands of employment, but those demands are less stringent than in the regular work place. The approximately 900 employees perform a wide range of activities for municipal and nonprofit agencies in New York City. They microfilm for the city's real estate department, perform custodial work in police precincts, file in the public library, deliver meals to the elderly, and translate from Spanish to English in hospitals and courts.

To conduct the research on Wildcat, 500 qualified applicants were randomly assigned to either an experimental or control group. The members of each group were interviewed regularly for three years. In addition, official records from police, corrections, welfare, and the Social Security Administration were obtained. For roughly 80 percent of the sample—401 participants—data was complete for the three years.

The participants were ex-addicts; 90 percent were male, 90 percent were minorities (65 percent black and 25 percent Puerto Rican). They were poorly educated, and only one in five had worked at all during the previous six months. On the average, a participant had been arrested nine times and convicted four times before applying to Wildcat.

The research results indicate that supported work enhanced the earning capacity of its participants (even after they left the program), reduced welfare dependency, and encouraged stable living patterns. In addition, Wildcat reduced arrest rates in the short run. However, the Wildcat program did not appear to affect drug use or drinking habits. A cost-benefit analysis indicates that the taxpayer received $1.12 in services, increaed taxes, reduced welfare, and criminal justice costs for every dollar spent on the program. While these results come from one program in New York City, the supported work program model has been extended to more than twenty jurisdictions with different groups: ex-offenders, out-of-school youth, welfare mothers, and ex-alcoholics. The Manpower Demonstration Research Corporation (MDRC) is orchestrating this national demonstration of supported work and has contracted with Mathematica Policy Research to conduct controlled research. Preliminary data after nine months indicate that the impact of other supported work programs on ex-addicts and ex-offenders is remarkably similar to that of Wildcat.[1] These results suggest that the Wildcat program's results can be generalized beyond New York.

Although arrest rates were lower for experimentals than controls in the short run, the comparisons between the two groups did not provide strong evidence that Wildcat reduced criminal activity. In the design of Wildcat, it was hypothesized that if a reduction in criminal activity occurred, the reduction might be related to one or a combination of factors: improved financial resources, increased pressures toward conformity, and less opportunity to become involved in criminal activity.

Since property crimes may be economically motivated, it was hypothesized that an increase in income might decrease the impetus for such crimes. Supported workers had sporadic employment histories and were on welfare when they came to Wildcat. Therefore, both the increase in income and the overall effects of a regular paycheck might contribute to a reduction in criminal activity.

Further, participants might find employment more reliable than hustling to get money. Thus they might develop new attitudes about the "straight world" of work and discover that work has a less risky cost-benefit ratio than crime. Such a rational-choice model has been proposed by Becker, who suggests that individuals make decisions to engage in illegal activity after weighing the relative returns and risks involved.[2] A study by Ehrlich suggested that this model is most applicable to economically motivated crimes. He found a relatively stronger correlation between income and the rate of property crimes than between income and violent crimes.[3]

In a controlled test of this theory, Lenihan demonstrated that a stipend of $60 per week for thirteen weeks to newly released convicts in Baltimore did not reduce overall criminal activity but did reduce arrests for property crimes.[4] At a maximum, Lenihan's stipends were $780; experimentals in supported work, however, earned an average of $4,400. Therefore, it was hypothesized that supported work might be more effective than Lenihan's stipend in reducing property crimes.

Alternatively, supported work could discourage criminal behavior by creating pressure on employees to conform to "straight" life styles. Piliavin's conforming model suggests that nondelinquent behavior among juveniles depends on the strength of the need to conform. Such a need develops in response to expectations of parents, peers, and schools. If these external constraints are internalized, the theory goes, the individual acquires a self-image as a conformer.[5]

It was hypothesized that by immersing the ex-addict in a legitimate work situation, peers and supervisors in supported work would provide role models that would encourage the development of a conformist self-image. These peers and supervisors might also pressure the employed ex-addicts to be law abiding regardless of internalized self-image. Moreover, the ex-addict's family might pressure him to conform as they came to depend on his stable earnings from work, imposing further constraints on his susceptibility to criminal activity.

Another theory, which predicted a decline in criminal activity assumed that because Wildcat employees were occupied during the day, they would have less unsupervised time available for crime than unemployed persons. They would also be less likely to associate with friends engaged in criminal activity and thus less likely to hear about "easy scores."

In the Wildcat study, arrest rates were used as an indicator of criminal activity. Although arrest rates are not an accurate measure of criminal activity, they were chosen because they are more reliable than self-report data and more easily obtained and interpreted than conviction data. In addition, arrest rates seemed relatively immune to systematic biases between experimentals and controls or working and nonworking participants. In the data that follow, conclusions about relative differences in arrest figures can be more comfortably drawn than conclusions about the absolute amount of criminal activity.[6]

Few members of the Wildcat reseasrch sample were experienced criminals. Rather, many engaged in some criminal activity from time to time, much as they secured legitimate jobs or depended on welfare from time to time. In the year prior to the study, about one third were arrested. During the first year of the study, the proportion of experimentals and controls arrested decreased (see table 2–1). However, the decrease was significantly greater for the experimentals than for the controls.

In the second year the percentage arrested dropped again for both groups; however, the decrease was greater for controls than for experimentals. In the third year, the percentage arrested dropped again for the control group. In contrast, it increased for the experimental group with the result that a higher proportion of experimentals than controls were arrested. This difference, however, was not statistically significant.

The seriousness of the offenses—the proportion of felony, misdemeanor, and violation arrests—with which experimentals and controls were charged was roughly similar; the types of charges were also roughly similar. Although controls had less income, they were not more likely to be arrested for property crimes—burglary and grand larceny—than were experimentals.

An examination of the extent of employment and arrest rates revealed that for both experimentals and controls, arrest rates for the more steadily employed were half those for the less steadily employed (see table 2–2). Arrest rates by type of charge and time employed were also analyzed. The patterns for each type of crime replicated the general pattern: The more steadily a person was employed, the less likely he was to be arrested for violent, property, or drug crimes. These findings strongly suggest a relation between unemployment and crime but do not shed light on the nature of the relationship. The finding that regularly employed participants were less likely than the sporadically employed to engage in drug or violent crimes as well as property crimes indicates that an economic explanation for criminal activity is not adequate.

In an effort to better understand the relation of Wildcat employment and arrest activity, arrest rates and reasons for leaving Wildcat were analyzed. Table 2–3 indicates that Wildcat employees had lower arrest rates than those who graduated, who in turn had lower arrest rates than employees who resigned or were fired.

Table 2-1
Percent of Experimentals and Controls Arrested Before and After Entering Study.

	Experimentals (*n* = *194*)	*Controls* (*n* = *207*)
Year prior to study	31	37
Year 1	19	31
Year 2	17	22
Year 3	24	16
Ever arrested during the 3 years	43	51

Source: L. Friedman, *The Wildcat Experiment* (Washington, D.C.: U.S Government Printing Office, 1978), pp. 80, 83, and 85.

Note: Difference statistically significant at the 95-percent level.

Table 2-2
Arrest Rates per Person-year by Time Employed and Sample Status

	Employed less than 18 Months	*Employed more than 18 Months*	*Total*
Experimentals (*n* = 194)	.50	.23	.31
Controls (*n* = 207)	.47	.22	.39
Total	.48	.22	.35

Source: L. Friedman, *The Wildcat Experiment* (Washington, D.C.: U.S. Government Printing Office, 1978), pp. 80, 83, and 85.

Table 2-3
Arrest per Person-year, by End-of-year Work Status, and Year of Study (*Experimentals Only*)

	Working at Wildcat at End of Year	*Graduated*	*Resigned*	*Fired*
Year 1	.20	.45	.38	.27
Year 2	.09	.18	.46	.49
Year 3	.20	.34	.52	.62

Source: L. Friedman, *The Wildcat Experiment* (Washington, D.C.: U.S. Government Printing Office, 1978), pp. 80, 83, and 85.

The fact that Wildcat employees had lower arrest rates than Wildcat graduates suggests that Wildcat inhibited criminal activity or, alternatively, that nonsubsidized jobs offered criminal opportunities. The fact that those who quit or were fired experienced the highest arrest rates apparently reflects a correlation between failing on the job, or dissatisfaction and lack of motivation, with a relatively high rate of criminal activity.

Unfortunately, it is not possible to make a conclusive determination from the data whether the prolonged stay at Wildcat caused the low arrest rates or, conversely, whether firing an employee caused an increase in criminal activity. The data was not collected in a manner that permitted analysis of the precise sequence between legitimate and illegitimate activity. The relation between employment and low arrest rates may have resulted from the stability that regular employment introduced into the participants' lives, or it may be that continuous employment reduced social alienation, which in turn reduced criminality. Finally, it may be that a third factor was responsible both for the prolonged employment at Wildcat and a decrease in criminality and, in reverse, for failure at Wildcat and a high incidence of arrests.

Since overall arrest rates of Wildcat participants were not lower than that of controls, conclusions need to be approached gingerly. In fact, these data raised more questions than they answered. Perhaps the prickliest question is why hadn't Wildcat been able to achieve a long-range impact on crime as it could on unemployment. As long as employment rates were consistently higher among experimentals than controls, wouldn't crime rates have been consistently depressed?

Perhaps Wildcat peer pressure effectively restrained antisocial behavior. But when an experimental left Wildcat, antisocial feelings that had been building at Wildcat were released, and the Wildcat terminee engaged in an exaggerated amount of criminal activity. Another possible explanation is that an employee terminated from Wildcat felt extraordinarily frustrated or hopeless because he had failed in a situation specially designed for him in which many of his peers were succeeding. Thise sense of anger or futility may have led him to become more involved in criminal activity than he would have if he had not experienced this one—and perhaps in his perspective—most damaging failure.

These findings on arrest rates suggested some program modifications in Wildcat. More importantly, perhaps, they made Vera researchers reconsider the notion that employment would reduce crime. Accordingly, Vera researchers returned to the literature to gain insight into the Wildcat data. They found that research on patterns of criminal behavior has typically linked the incidence of crime—particularly property crime—with poverty, unemployment, and underemployment. Specific connections, however, between individual criminal activities and employment histories have not been well documented, partially because many studies of criminal careers provide few insights into the legitimate work histories of those who commit crimes and partially because most studies of employment expectations and experiences say little about criminal behavior. Because "workers" and "criminals" usually have been segregated for study purposes, the connection between work and crime is not well understood.

This information led Vera to undertake a long-term research project to probe the relation more carefully. This research, funded under the Research Agreements Program of the National Institute for Law Enforcement and Criminal Justice, seeks to explore the connection, if any, between crime and unemployment and to determine if employment reduces certain types of crime for certain groups of people.

Numerous studies report an association; some suggest a causal relation. Gillespie's summary of more than thirty studies published between 1955 and 1975 reports that "statistical results of studies relating unemployment to crime show general, if not uniform, support for a positive correlation between these two variables."[7] Several different studies of prison admissions also indicate that admissions increase following increases in the unemployment rate. Other studies suggest that worsening economic conditions first affect young, lower-class individuals with marginal jobs.[8] Brenner notes that countries with higher unemployment rates also report higher crime rates.[9]

These studies do not disaggregate data and thus do not directly address the issue of whether employment reduces or prevents crime on an individual basis. Part of the problem in interpreting the aggregate data stems from the statistics. Unemployment rates may be a faulty index of the employment and income difficulties experienced by wage-earners, particularly inner-city residents. Furthermore, the difficulties of using arrest rates for any program evaluation are compounded when they depend on aggregate crime data and prison intake rates as an index of criminal activity.

Despite problems in data interpretation, the two fields, criminology and the study of employment, agree that the years between the ages of fourteen to twenty-four are critical in establishing career patterns, legitimate or criminal. This age group makes up the bulk of the reformatory and penitentiary population. Most typically, this age group is charged with property crimes.

During their mid-twenties and early thirties, however, many repeat offenders "mature out," abandoning crime for more legitimate careers.[10] It is not clear, however, which of them will "mature out," what their employment histories are, or how their work and crime careers have interacted.

Glaser points out that today's adolescents, particularly in urban areas, are more independent and have more adult economic needs than did adolescents in past years.[11] Yet they are not able to achieve self-sufficiency as easily or as early as adolescents once did. And the recently imposed higher minimum wage further reduces opportunities for teenage employment. Much property crime appears to be a part-time activity to supplement or replace legitimate income of youth and young adults, especially males. It is tempting to assume that crime becomes employment of last resort, but the multiplicity of possible linkages suggests many other factors in a youth's decision to engage in criminal activity: economic need coupled with lack of legitimate opportunity; neighborhood and family patterns; anger at family, community, or society; need to achieve prestige; and desire to conform to expectations of the youth subculture.

These speculations mainly address careers of young male offenders and prospective offenders. Despite an increase in number and types of studies of female offenders, few address the relationship of unemployment and crime. Looking at the aggregate data in the absence of individual data, we find that as employment rates among women have increased, property crimes among women have also increased.[12] It is not known if these categories—women workers and women property offenders—overlap.

Intervention programs such as Wildcat or Lenihan's Life Project designed to reduce crime through regular stipends allow us to get closer to individual dynamics. But none of these programs have shown a significant or consistent effect on criminal activity of participants.

For example, an evaluation of the Neighborhood Youth Corps found that arrests among youths offered employment were not significantly reduced as a result of program participation.[13] There is evidence, however, that arrest rates did decrease slightly among girls who worked in the program. Girls generally held clerical jobs while boys usually were assigned to janitorial positions. Thus it appears that some types of jobs may be more effective crime deterrents than others.[14]

Concerning diversion programs, about a dozen of approximately 150 have been evaluated, and few show consistent and long-term effects on crime. The Zimring study of the Manhattan Court Employment Project, for example, revealed no clear-cut relationship between program participants and crime reduction.[15]

A review of treatment-evaluation studies (prison rehabilitation programs) indicates that prison educational and vocational programs also have not consistently reduced recidivism.[16] And although Lenihan's initial study in Baltimore indicated that guaranteed weekly stipends reduced property crime, replications in Georgia and Texas have been disappointing.[17]

Why weren't these programs more successful? The answers may lie in the kinds of personal, educational, and vocational services the program provided to participants; in the participants' limited access to the job market; in the types of jobs obtained by participants (clerical, food service, or maintenance, for example); or in other characteristics of the jobs such as salary, work setting, and opportunity for advancement.

This last issue, type of employment, has received little attention but may be an important determinant of choosing illegitimate activity over legitimate opportunities. Three separate studies suggest that a young adult's first job experience—particularly the degree of potential mobility in that job—is important in determining his future as a productive worker.[18] And a study underway at the Hoover Institution suggests preliminarily:

> ...only to the extent that those engaging in criminal activity consider the effect on increased employment opportunities on the costs of imprisonment will such changes be associated with substantial changes in property crime rates. Moreover, changes in current employment rates will be associated with significant changes in crime rates only if these weigh heavily in the individual's projection of future opportunities.[19]

What emerged most clearly from this welter of often contradictory studies was the need to chart on an individual basis the sequency of participation in and out of legitimate and illegitimate activity. Having traveled from the assumption that employment would reduce crime, we found ourselves entertaining the notion that some types of employment may cause crime; or that a successful criminal career may lead to unemployment. This is not to deny that on the aggregate levels some relation can be demonstrated: Unskilled people are disproportionately among those charged with crimes and disproportionately among the unemployed; minorities experience higher arrest rates and lower employment rates than the population as a whole; and the young are more likely to be arrested and less likely to be employed. However, on the individual level, the evidence that unemployment causes crime or correspondingly, employment reduces crime is scanty, and the evidence that unemployment is associated with crime is abundant but not conclusive. We do not know whether and under what conditions an unemployed person is more likely than when employed to engage in criminal activity.

The Research Agreement Program has taken a first look at this question through preliminary analysis of interviews with sixty inmates at Riker's Island.[20] These interviews revealed several connections between legitimate and illegitimate activities: The most commonly reported pattern fit the stereotype, and about a fourth of the inmates interviewed said they refrained from illegitimate activities when they were working. Illustrating the economic model, one respondent remarked, "If you're working and you see something your want, you wonder how you're going to save to buy it. If you're not working and you see something you want, you wonder how you're going to take it." Other inmates reported that the fact of having a wife and children encouraged them to try employment rather than crime as a way of life.

Other respondents, however, comfortably mixed legitimate and illegitimate activities. One respondent, who worked in the Wall street area, would go out once a week at lunch hour and pick pockets. Some of these respondents reported that they would hustle more if they lost their jobs. For these, more or better work might effectively deter crime.

Work provided an opportunity for expanding or enriching criminal activities for some Riker Island inmates. Work was sometimes used as a cover for crime. A numbers banker who had worked his way up from a runner used a gypsy cab operation and a bogus bike shop as a front for his real business. One respondent said a job was a good cover for selling drugs. "If you're stopped on the street by the police with $1,700 in your pocket, it looks bad if you're not working."

Other respondents reported intermingling work and crime in order to get an economic stake for either legitimate or illegitimate businesses. One inmate said he had engaged in petty crime in order to finance a licensed t-shirt selling operation. Another planned to use legitimate employment to earn $500 for a pound of marijuana to "get back on his feet."

Some inmates viewed employment as a way to expand connections and numbers policies. Other respondents reported quasi-legal enterprises on the job, selling socks, hats, watches. It was not clear whether these items were being fenced or whether they were legitimate purchases being resold without a peddlar's license.

One respondent saw work as an opportunity for theft. When asked how much he was making at this last job, he responded, "$100 and all I can steal." Another respondent was intrigued by a recent series of successful hotel robberies and hypothesized that they might have been "inside jobs." People like him, he said, did not have the contacts for that high-class, profitable kind of crime. He saw himself as a petty street thief, stuck at the lower level of the illegitimate economy. For some of the inmates interviewed, work and crime did not appear to be related.

The bewildering data on crime and unemployment seem to make it premature to recommend policy changes in the manpower field with the expectation that such changes would reduce crime. The Wildcat data, corroborated by evaluations of other data, suggest that employment programs, as valuable as they probably are for the individual or society, may not significantly and permanently discourage participants from committing crimes. The long-range recommendations for modification in the labor market or criminal justice system would better follow increased understanding of employment's relations to and possible impact on crime rates.

The data, however, suggest some tentative recommendations for short-term improvements even if the conclusion from future studies turned out to be that on the individual level legitimate and illegitimate activities operate relatively independently from each other:

1. More jobs should be excluded from the minimum-wage requirements or federal subsidies should be developed so that fewer young and marginally employed people are prevented from entering the labor market.

2. More programs such as Wildcat should be developed that provide a low stress work environment for ex-offenders and youth; such programs appear to be cost beneficial, increase earning capacity, and reduce crime rates in the short run.

3. The data from Wildcat indicating particularly high crime rates among those who failed at supported work suggest that employment programs should attempt to screen out applicants who may fail because failure in such a program may be more damaging than not entering at all, and supported work programs should develop procedures to soften the separation process.

4. The barriers to obtaining jobs should be reduced by limiting the many licensing requirements that restrict ex-offenders from obtaining a variety of jobs.

5. The policies of those working in employment and criminal justice should be coordinated so that the efforts compliment each other if research indicates an association between crime and unemployment.

Rather than synthesizing these often confusing, counterintuitive, and sometimes contradictory data into a neat package, this chapter posits no definite conclusions about the relationship of legitimate and illegitimate activity and thus can make no major recommendations for substantial policy changes or program initiatives. The clearest need that emerges is for an increased understanding of the connection between crime and unemployment.[21]

Notes

1. *Manpower Demonstration Research Corporation,* Second Annual Report on the National Supported Work Demonstration, New York, 1978.

2. Gary S. Becker, "Crime and Punishment: An Economic Approach," *Journal of Political Economy* 76 (March/April 1968):2.

3. Issac Ehrlich, "Participation in Illegitimate Activities: An Economic Analysis," in *Essays in Economics of Crime and Punishment,* eds. Becker and Landes (Washington, W.D.C.: National Bureau of Economic Research, 1974).

4. Kenneth J. Lenihan, "When Money Counts: An Experimental

Study of Providing Financial Aid and Job Placement Services to Released Prisoners," Bureau of Social Science Research, Washington, D.C., January 1976.

5. I. Piliavin, A.C. Vadum, and J.A. Hardyck, "Delinquency, Personal Costs, and Parental Treatment: A Test of a Reward/Cost Model of Juvenile Delinquency," *Journal of Criminal Law* 60 (1969):pp. 165–175.

6. Some of the following comparisons are based on the proportion of experimentals and controls arrested during a particular year. A percent-arrested figure, however, does not take account of periods during which members of the sample were incarcerated and therefore not "at risk" of being arrested; and it does not differentiate between sample members arrested once and more than once. To remedy this artifact and provide a fair basis of comparison, arrest rates per person year have also been calculated.

7. Robert W. Gillespie, *Economic Factors in Crime and Delinquency: A Critical Review of the Empirical Evidence* (Washington, D.C.: National Institute of Law Enforcement and Criminal Justice. September 1975).

8. U.S. Bureau of Prisons, "Correlation of Unemployment and Federal Prison Population" (Washington, D.C.: U.S. Bureau of Prisons Report, March 1975); George H. Cox, and Timothy S. Carr, "Unemployment and Prison Population Trends in Georgia: 1967–1974." (Atlanta, Ga.: Georgia Department of Corrections/Offender Rehabilitation, 5 March, 1975); and William H. Robinson, Phylis Smith, and Jean Wolf, "Prison Population and Costs: Illustrative Projections to 1980" (Washington, D.C.: Congressional Research Service, Library of Congress, 24 April 1974 (HV 8442 74–95 ED), cited Ralph Swisher in *Unemployment and Crime,* Office of Planning and Management, Law Enforcement Assistance Administration, September 1975.

9. Harvey M. Brenner, *Effects of the Economy on Criminal Behavior and the Administration of Criminal Justice: A Multinational Study,* John Hopkins University, unpublished manuscript. Used with permission.

10. Daniel Glaser, *Adult Crime and Social Policy* (Englewood Cliffs, N.J.: Prentice-Hall, 1972), p. 20.

11. Ibid., and Richard Quinney, *Criminology Analysis and Critique of Crime in America* (Boston: Little, Brown, 1970).

12. Rita James Simon, *The Contemporary Women and Crime* (Washington, D.C.: National Institute of Mental Health, Crime and Delinquency Issues, 1975).

13. Steven H. Clark, "Juvenile Offender Programs and Delinquency Prevention," *Crime and Delinquency Literature* 36 (September 1974):390–392 and U.S. Department of Labor, Manpower Administration, "The Neighborhood Youth Corps: Review of Research," Manpower Research Monograph No. 13, (Washington, D.C.: U.S. Government Printing Office, 1970).

14. Personal communication, Tom Joyce, ORD, Department of Labor, 6 January 1977. Used with permission.

15. Franklin E. Zimring, "Measuring the Impact of Pretrial Diversion from the Criminal Justice System," *University of Chicago Law Review* 41 (1974):224.

16. Douglas Lipton, et al., *The Effectiveness of Correctional Treatment: A Survey of Treatment Evaluation Studies* (New York: Praeger, 1975).

17. Kenneth J. Lenihan, "A Report on the Transitional Aid Research Project," forthcoming.

18. Christopher Jencks, et al., *Inequality* (New York: Basic Books, 1972); Marcia Freedman, *The Process of Work Establishment* (New York: Columbia University Press, 1969); and James Morgan, et al., *Five Thousand American Families: Patterns of Economic Progress* (Ann Arbor, Mich.: Survey Research Center, Institute for Social Research, University of Michigan, 1974).

19. Michael K. Block, et al., *Preliminary Estimates of the Effect of Unemployment on Crime Rates,* Center for Econometric Studies of the Criminal Justice System, Hoover Institution, January 1978, p. 18; (Reprinted with permission); Personal communication from Michael K. Block to author, 6 January 1978; Michael K. Block, et al., *Property Crime and the Returns to Legitimate and Illegitimate Activities* (first draft), March 1978, pp. 28–31. It must be emphasized that the Hoover findings are preliminary. (Cited in Richard A. Tropp, "Suggested Policy Initiatives for Employment and Crime Problems," mimeographed).

20. Anonymous, Vera Institute of Justice research memorandum, New York, undated.

21. The Wildcat Experiment is documented in L. Friedman, *The Wildcat Experiment* (Washington D.C.: U.S. Government Printing Office, 1978).

Commentary

Marvin Wolfgang

It is interesting to me that the Vera Institute Wildcat study revealed that employment support for ex-offenders seemed to be good for the short term but showed no significant differences in the long term. Friedman's paper reminded me of a program that the Pennsylvania Prison Society studied a couple of years ago involving people released from the county prisons in Philadelphia. What was interesting relative to employment was that over 50 percent of those who did get jobs said that they attributed their acquisition of the jobs to friends; another 20 percent to family and relatives and very, very few (about 5 percent of them, as I recall) to the support agencies.

Another point I would like to make about the Friedman paper is that it is not surprising to me that se many were arrested both in the experimental and control group after a three-year period. As the paper indicated, the average number of arrests for offenses the individuals had was around eight. With that number of per-capita offenses, the odds are greatly in favor of repetition of offenses. For example, we found in the longitudinal study in Phildelphia of 10,000 boys born in 1945 whom we followed up to age thirty that after four or five offenses (these are official-arrests offenses), the probability of continuing on with another arrest is about .80. This figure was constant whether the four or five offenses began during the juvenile years before age eighteen or began in the adult years from eighteen to thirty.

Relative to employment, too, I should mention that Professor McClintock, now a professor of criminology at Edinburgh, Scotland, has conducted some studies on employment among postprison populations in England and Scotland. He found that employment reduced recidivism; however, the population McClintock studied is not the same hard-core population that the Vera Institute dealt with in the Wildcat program.

In her paper Dr. Friedman refers to M. Harvey Brenner at Johns Hopkins who had been studying certain economic conditions in crime in the United States, Canada, Scotland, England, and Wales between 1900 and 1972. Brenner found an inverse relationship between employment and crime rates. Now a rise in employment, I should hasten to add, does not necessarily mean a reduction of unemployment. Though I have not seen all of Dr. Brenner's materials, some of them simply refer to employment rather than unemployment.

I cannot avoid referring to my mentor, Dr. Celini, because in 1937 he was responsible for summarizing most of the work that had been done in the relationship of crime and economic conditions, employment and business cycles. He wrote a research memorandum on crime in the Depression for the Social Science Research Council. In summarizing the work that had been done in this area over a period of more than a hundred years, he could not find evidence of any definitely consistent relationship between economic conditions and the state of crime. Nevertheless, one seems to exist, but there are inconsistencies throughout the studies. We seem to have a paradoxial finding that although the crime rate has a socioeconomic status in geographical areas in a city or country, the areas vary in an inverse relationship, but no such variation has been discernible when the socio-economic status of individuals within an area changes with fluctuations of the business cycle.

Many theories have suggested that social disorganization is a cause of crime. These hypotheses are premised on the notion that crime is not the product of poverty or economic need but rather of the social situation that accompanies poverty under certain conditions. And most of the authors who maintain this view have said that it is the breakdown of the agencies of social control and the disappearance of intimate conventional social types that breed crime. I do not know how much direction that theory provides us, but as Dr. Friedman said, there is a need to disaggregate data and to look more intimately at the individual and his relationship to the low employment problem and perhaps types of employment as well as types of crime.

In all of the data in Friedman's paper, the age distribution is important. More disaggregate data on the age-specific distribution of the Wildcat group would have been useful to me. I am also thinking of disaggregation and the demographic changes in Dr. Brenner's data found in the United States and England from 1900 to the 1970s.

As we all know, according to the uniform crime report statistics, since 1960 crimes of violence, for example, have increased about 180–200 percent. Explanations for the assumed increase vary and embrace such issues as unemployment, broken homes, inadequate eduation, housing, racial injustice, relative deprivation, lack of law enforcement, and leniency in the courts. Most of these factors are very difficult to measure.

What we do know is that there has been a significant demographic change directly related to change in crime rates. The high fertility rates right after World War II known as the "baby boom" produced a significant alteration in the age composition of the U.S. population so that there was a swelling of the age group between fifteen and twenty-four in the early 1960s. And it was in the early 1960s that the rapid rise in crime, particularly crimes of violence, was first noted. For example, in 1940 and 1950 the fifteen- to twenty-four-year-olds constituted only 14 percent of the total population. But in 1960, 1965, and 1970, the proportion of this same age group went from 14 percent to 16 percent to 18 percent, and because this age group contributes the most heavily to crime in general and crimes of violence in particular, it is certain that the increase in this age group has been the major contributor to the increase of crimes of violence.

No matter what the social interventions may have been to control, prevent, or deter crime, it seems the changing age composition of population has been significantly responsible for the increase of crime and violence.

Some Indiana data given to me may give you a bit of optimism. As I looked at the Indiana male population by age specifics (I am ignoring females for the moment because it is the male, at least officially, who is making the major contribution to crimes of violence, as well as property crimes), in 1960 this age group, eighteen to twenty-four, in Indiana constituted 14 percent of the population. In terms of violence the juvenile-delinquency and crime rates in general were relatively low. In 1970 the same age group constituted 20 percent of the population of Indiana, and if you have seen an increase in the crimes of violence in Indiana, I would assert that some contribution comes from this swelling of that particular segment of the age composition of population. In looking at the projections of 1995 to the year 2000, I find that there will be an apparent drop in this same age group to about 15 percent in 1995 and 16 percent in the year 2000. Thus if the population forecast is correct, you probably have a more optimistic picture to look forward to in Indiana than the United States does as a whole.

Sociological explanations of crime have dominated much of the American terminology of the past thirty years. The cultural diversities—plurality of norms and values—have been the major theme within the sociological literature, a theme recognizing that people who become delinquents and criminals should no longer be viewed as pathological; their responses are commonly normal responses to the norms and values of behavior in their immediate environment. This has been the general sociological position, and I think it has dominated criminological explanations. But at the same time, I should hasten to add that sociology within the criminological discipline increasingly wants to proceed in a multi- and an interdisciplinary way because increasing recognition is being given to the interactions between the internal and the external environments of all behavior, regardless of whether it is conforming or in violation of law.

The last point I would make is that governmental intervention on the criminal justice system cannot impact many of the primary-level sociological and psychological variables that have been studied in the past generations. For example, it is asserted that we cannot by governmental intervention increase affection in the family or improve supervision of children; but on a second level, we may be able to promote better housing or housing policy. We may be able to have some effect on inflation, and certainly these steps should be taken for purposes other than crime reduction.

That leads us to the third level of governmental intervention directly to the criminal justice system. There has not been a preponderance of evidence in the past that changes in the operation of the criminal justice system affect the crime rates. But there is increasing belief, perhaps just hope, that through continued research, some of the expectations of reducing crime, by concentrating resources and penal sanctions with more certainty and celerity but not increased severity upon the chronic career offender is an area of possible improvement.

Commentary

Cleon H. Foust and
D. Robert Webster

Lucy Friedman's discussion of the Wildcat project provoked comment from other conferees. For example, Robert McKay noted that the offender participants in Wildcat already had substantial records of criminality and suggested that perhaps if intervention had been tried at an earlier point in their careers, it might have been more successful, on the theory that those who commit crimes once or twice are less habituated to criminal activity. Dr. Friedman replied that they broke down the Wildcat data by age. There was no indication that younger people (eighteen- and nineteen-year-olds) who came into the program and by necessity had shorter criminality records than the older people were more affected by the program.

Nicholas Kittrie suggested that in the rehabilitation context, much of the traditional benefit of work is not totally that it pays the bills, although that is important, but that it also can provide direction and meaning to an otherwise rudderless existence. On the other hand, for some personalities, some jobs can be frustrating and counterproductive, "So I am not really sure that a job per se is the answer." But, in any event, he did not think that, pragmatically, there is time to do the extensive research to find what sort of jobs should be provided offenders. "It seems to me," he said, "for those who want work and seek ways to be trained for satisfying work, we have to find ways to meet that particular need, regardless of whether we can directly show that this reduces criminality by 1 percent, 10 percent, or whatever."

Stanton Samenow commented that if he were asked whether to supply offenders with the opportunity to learn job skills, he would say, "yes, of course." But the only sure result of job-skills training for criminals is that society now has criminals with job skills. The majority are still criminals. Further, he suggested that individual prescriptions for rehabilitative work are only theorizing until the offender's perception of work is stabilized. Generally, the criminal mind perceives that he will be successful overnight in any job, and success to him means being Number One. The consequence is fault-finding frustration. So, after supplying a job skill, the really critical next step is to alter his work attitudes and help him to function on the job.

Ernest van den Haag adopted a different perspective. He said that it is not employment that prevents criminal behavior or unemployment that leads to it. As long as the net benefit from crime exceeds the net benefit from available employment, many people will prefer crime. It follows then that the search for crime reduction should focus primarily on reduction of the net benefit from crime.

3 Brain Mechanisms and Crime

Kenneth E. Moyer

In meetings on criminology that I have attended recently, there has been considerable concern and discussion of the organic bases of criminal behavior. This chapter will address two aspects of that problem.[1]

It is of course true that all criminal behavior like all other behavior has an organic or a physiological basis. Behavior is controlled by the brain, which reflects an individual's past experience. A mother's love, a father's scorn, punishment, reward, and solitary confinement in a prison all affect, and relatively permanently, the brain. When we teach a child to say, "Please may I have a cookie," instead of "Hey you, gimme a cookie," we are making a relatively permanent change in his brain, which will last the rest of his life and which will determine his behavior. When a child is rewarded for hitting another child in order to get what he wants, his brain is also changed. This kind of aggressive behavior used to gain specific ends is frequently referred to as *instrumental aggression,* and I will say more about it later.

These changes occur, in general, in the cerebral cortex and involve primarily the neural processes concerned with learning. These are the kinds of brain mechanisms that may help determine whether an individual will tend to emulate General Patton, or Saint Francis of Assisi. They are probably not the primary mechanisms that might turn him into a Charles Whitman.

There are processes in other parts of the brain that contribute to and help determine other types of behavior. When certain neural systems in the lower brain are active, one has an internal sensation of hunger, and the probability of eating behavior is increased. When other neural systems in that portion of the brain are active, feelings associated with sexual responses are reported. There are also neural systems in the lower brain that result in feelings of anger or irritability. When they are active, the probability of aggressive behavior is increased.

I have suggested a dichotomy between the two parts of the brain, cerebral cortex, and the lower portion. It must be pointed out that such a distinction is drawn only with the license of an author to clarify, to highlight, and to promote understanding of the different kinds of mechanisms. In actual fact, the different levels and different parts and systems of the brain always interact to determine behavior. The brain processes that control learning and memory are constantly interacting with those processes that control basic motivational and feeling processes. However, the distinction is a useful one for the purposes of discussion.

Our concern will be with the second mechanism, which is primarily responsible for certain types of crime, that is, aggressive, destructive, or violent behavior. More is known about these brain processes, and we now have some idea about how to alter their functioning. This chapter will present a model that will provide some of the details on the underlying mechanisms for crimes of this nature. I will also cover the potential for altering these brain mechanisms and suggest ways in which such alterations might contribute to the control of this kind of aggression. Finally, we will consider the limitations of the physiological approaches to criminal behavior.

It should be pointed out first that aggression is not a unitary construct. There are a number of different kinds of aggressive behavior.[2] In other words, it is not possible to construct a single model that will fit all kinds in detail. However, we can deal with the mechanisms or the kinds of mechanisms that are common to some, if not most, of the different kinds of aggressive behavior. The basic premise of this model is that there are in the brains of animals and humans neural systems that when fired in the presence of a relevant target result in aggressive or destructive behavior toward that target. In the case of humans, the actual aggressive behavior may be controlled while individuals will still have the appropriate feelings of hostility. There is now abundant evidence to support that premise.

Neural Systems for Aggression

Some of the most fundamental work in this area has been done by John Flynn at Yale. He has worked with cats and has enlarged on techniques that were developed in the early 1940s. It is possible to implant an electrode in specific areas deep in an animal's brain. The electrode can then be attached to a plug that is cemented to the skull. The plug can then be attached to a stimulation source, and it is possible to stimulate the depths of the brain of an animal that is awake and free to move around. When the experiment is finished for the day, the subject can be returned to its home cage none the worse for the experience.

The cats Flynn used were nonpredatory and would not normally attack rats. Some in fact would live with a rat for months and not molest it. But when an electrode implanted in the cat's lateral hypothalamus was electrically activated, the animal ignored the experimenter standing there and immediately attacked and killed an available rat. The kill was quite precise resulting from a bite in the cervical region of the spinal cord, in typical predatory behavior of the feline. However, when the electrode was located in the medial hypothalamus and the cat was stimulated in the presence of the rat, it ignored the rat and turned and attacked the experimenter. The attack on the experimenter was highly directed. It was not similar to the random attacks of a decerebrate animal. The cat intends to do the experimenter harm, and in fact, it did.[3]

One particularly interesting experiment was done by Robinson and his colleagues.[4] They implanted an electrode in the anterior hypothalamus of a small Rhesus monkey. They then put the animal in a primate chair, activated the electrode, and showed that the monkey did not become aggressive toward inanimate objects, nor did it become aggressive toward the experimenter. It was then put in a cage with two other monkeys, one of whom was larger and dominant to the experimental animal and the other of whom was the dominant monkey's female consort. When stimulated in this situation, the experimental monkey vigorously and immediately attacked the dominant monkey. It did not attack the female. It attacked only the dominant male monkey. This appeared to be a valid primate attack because the dominant monkey reacted by counterattacking just as viciously as it usually would if attacked by a submissive animal. This scenario was repeated a number of times and although the result is quite unusual, Robinson, et al., found that the dominance relationship changed. The stimulation-induced attacks were so intense that the formerly dominant animal ultimately became submissive to the experimental monkey.

This experiment shows first that the particular brain stimulation used resulted in one specific kind of aggression, which I have called "intermale," that is, the specific tendency for one male to attack another. Second, the experiment demonstrates that aggressive behavior is stimulus bound. In the absence of the relevant stimulus, that monkey, even though stimulated time and again, showed no irritability or increased tendency to attack other targets. The essential results of these experiments have been repeated in many laboratories.

It is important not to generalize too quickly from one species to another. One must be particularly cautious in generalizing from animals to humans. However, we now have good evidence that man, for all of his encephalization, has not escaped from the neutral determinants of his aggressive behavior. There are now several hundred people who have electrodes implanted in their brains. The wires are attached to small sockets cemented to the skull. These patients can be brought into the laboratory, plugged in, and precise areas deep in the brain can be electrically stimulated.

A case reported by King is particularly instructive.[5] This patient was a very mild-mannered woman who was a generally submissive, kind, friendly person. An electrode was implanted in the area of her brain called the *amygdala*. Dr. King stimulated this patient in the amygdala with a current of 4 milliamperes, and there was no observable change in her behavior. (One cannot tell when one's brain is stimulated; there are no receptors that can indicate it, and thus she was unaware of the stimulation.) When the amperage was increased to 5 milliamperes, she became hostile and aggressive. She said such things as, "Take my blood pressure. Take it now." Then she said, "If you're going to hold me, you'd better get five more men." Whereupon she stood up and started to strike the experimenter. He then wisely turned down the current.

It was possible to turn this woman's anger on and off with a simple flick of the switch because the electrode was located in a part of the neural system for hostility. She indicated having felt anger. She also reported having been concerned about the fact that she was angry. She did not report pain or other discomfort. She was simply "turned on" angry. Similar findings have been reported by other investigators.[6]

Brain Dysfunctions Relating to Aggression

There are a number of pathological processes in the human brain that result in the activation of the neural systems for feelings of hostility. Tumors with an irritative focus frequently result in increased irritability and rage attacks if they are located in particular portions of the brain. It is important to note that all brain tumors do not produce pathological aggression. Many in fact produce apathy and somnolence. However, if they develop in such a way as to impinge upon and activate the neural systems for aggressive behavior, the syndrome of pathological aggressivity may appear. Tumors in the septal region, the temporal lobe, and the frontal lobe have produced this reaction. In 1962 Sano reported on 1,800 cases of brain tumor and found the irritability syndrome in those that involved the temporal lobe and the anterior hypothalamus.

The literature contains many cases of pathological aggressiveness induced by brain tumors. Only a few examples are cited. Two violent patients with tumors of the temporal lobe are described by Sweet, et al.[7] One man, a powerful individual, attempted to kill his wife and daughter with a butcher knife. When brought to the hospital, he was in a full-blown rage reaction, during which he snarled, showed his teeth, and attempted to hit or kick anyone who came close enough. History-taking revealed that over a period of six months, his personality had gradually changed and he had complained of blurred vision and intense headaches. When the tumor pressing on the anterior temporal lobe was removed, his symptoms rapidly abated.

Another patient who had shown hyperirritability for years began to show serious destructive rages. He drove his car recklessly and began to direct his outbursts of rage against his wife and son. Although intellectually capable as a chemist, he was unable to hold a position for longer than a few months because of his volatile and irritable behavior patterns. After the removal of a slow-growing tumor that had evidently been invading the temporal lobe over a period of several years, his symtoms disappeared. He became more stable, more placid, and functioned adequately as a chemist during the nineteen-month follow-up.

There are a variety of disorders that involve generalized damage to the central nervous system including cerebral arteriosclerosis, senile dementia, Korsakoff's syndrome, and Huntington's chorea. These dysfunctions frequently present a common symptomatology referred to as *chronic brain syndrome,* which is characterized by memory deficit, orientation loss, and affective disturbances. There are wide fluctuations of mood and a general emotional instability, but the affective pattern is dominated by anger, rage, and increased irritability.[8]

Epilepsy

Another neurological disorder that may result in an increase in aggressive tendencies is epilepsy, particularly temporal lobe epilepsy. It is certainly true that temporal lobe epilepsy is not necessarily accompanied by an increased tendency to impulsiveness and hostility, but the evidence indicates that the probability of that behavior's occurring is increased.

Ictal aggression (that occurring during the seizure) is relatively rare. However, there is abundant evidence that uncontrolled, impulsive, assaultive behavior is not uncommon as an interictal behavior pattern, particularly among temporal lobe epileptics.[9] Falconer, et al.,[10] reporting on fifty patients, indicated that 38 percent of them showed spontaneous outbursts of aggression. About half of the psychomotor epileptic patients studied by Schwab, et al.,[11] developed destructive behavior and paroxysmal bursts of anger as a part of a behavior disorder. Other investigators have reported similar results.[12]

It is important to emphasize that the subjects in the preceding studies were from a highly selected population of individuals with epilepsy. They were, in general, people who had been committed to an institution or who were candidates for surgery. There are of course thousands of epileptics who are making an adequate adjustment in the real world and do not suffer from personality disturbances, impulsiveness, or uncontrolled aggressive tendencies. Behavior pathology occurs only when certain specific neural systems are involved.

There is also evidence from several sources that, like many other systems in the brain, there are suppressor systems that are antagonistic to the aggression systems. Bernstein and I showed several years ago that if you remove the olfactory bulbs from a rat, you turn a peaceful laboratory rat into a vicious animal that will attack other rats, mice, or experimenter.[13]

Wheatley showed many years ago that if the medial hypothalamus of the cat is lesioned, a tame cat is turned into a wild cat.[14] It appears that these suppressor systems inhibit the activity in the neural systems for aggression. It should be pointed out that lesion experiments by themselves are not conclusive evidence of suppressor activity. However, much additional evidence for aggression–suppressor systems is available and will be discussed later in this chapter.

Aggression Thresholds

It is fortunate that in neither humans nor animals is aggression very frequent. It is relatively uncommon. Thus in order to understand the physiology of aggression, we must understand what it is that turns on these neural systems and what it is that turns them off. Perhaps one of the best ways to think about this is in terms of thresholds for the systems. In certain circumstances the threshold for the firing of the neural systems for aggression is very high. In that case it takes a great deal of provocation to activate them. There are other circumstances in which the threshold is very low, and relatively little provocation will result in the activation of the neural systems with the result that an individual has an increased tendency to behave aggressively.

Heredity

Some of the variables that influence the thresholds of the neural systems for aggression appear to be hereditary. For example, we have shown in my laboratory that some strains of rats behave aggressively toward small chickens in significantly greater numbers than do other strains.[15]

It is also possible, as Dr. Lagerspetz of Finland has shown, to take a large population of mice and select from them the aggressive and nonaggressive animals.[16] Within relatively few generations, if the very aggressive animals are mated, it is possible to develop a highly aggressive strain in which mice will attack immediately when they are put together. If the nonaggressive animals are bred, a strain can be developed that will not fight no matter what you do to them.

Dr. Wolpy at Earlham College in Indiana tells me that he is raising an extremely aggressive strain of rabbits. These rabbits will attack other rabbits or the experimenter. If some of these animals get out into the Indiana countryside, there are going to be some surprised hunting dogs. Obviously, we do not have any comparable data on human beings. However, if this model has any validity and if there are specific neural systems for different kinds of aggressive behavior, it must be that different thresholds for aggression are inherited. Neurological differences must be inherited in the same way that differences in the shapes of noses are.

Blood Chemistry

Another significant variable that contributes to differences in the aggression threshold level is blood chemistry. It has been known for centuries, of course, that one can take the raging bull and convert it into a gentle steer by the operation of castration, which reduces the level of testosterone in the blood stream. The formal work on this problem was done in 1947 by Elizabeth Beeman.[17] It has been repeatedly confirmed in many laboratories. Dr. Beeman worked with a strain of mice that would fight when put together. She castrated the animals of the experimental group prior to puberty. After maturity when those mice were put together, they did not fight at all. The control group showed the usual amount of aggression characteristic of that strain. She then carried the experiment a step further and implanted pellets of testosterone subcutaneously in the castrated mice. When the testosterone became effective, they fought at the same level as the control animals had. She then surgically removed the pellets of testosterone whereupon the mice once again became docile. It was possible to manipulate the aggressive behavior of these mice simply by changing the testosterone level.

There are a variety of other blood-chemistry changes that influence the thresholds for aggression. For example, we know that frustration and stress are important variables in inducing aggressive behavior, particularly if the frustration and stress are prolonged. It seems likely that this occurs because the stressors change the hormonal status and thus change the thresholds for the neural systems for aggression. Although we do not yet have experimental evidence to support this conjecture, there are a number of people working on the problem.

It is also true, as many women have found, that there is a period during the week before menstruation when a significant percentage of women feel irritable, hostile, and easily aroused to anger.[18] Those who have had inadequate training in impulse control sometimes behave and act on those impulses. In fact, one study that was conducted on 249 female prison inmates showed that 62 percent of the crimes of violence were committed in the premenstrual week, whereas only 2 percent of the crimes of violence were committed in the postmenstrual week.[19]

Lest anyone suggest that women's rights should some way be restricted because of their periodic tendency to hostility, let me point out that from mouse to man, with very few exceptions, the male is the more aggressive sex. Recent statistics show that the homicide rate is five times as great for the male and that the armed-robbery rate is about twenty times as great.

As Broom and Selznick said, "Compared with females, males have a greater excess of crimes in all nations, all communities within nations, all age groups, all periods of history for which we have statistics, and for all types of crime except those related to the female sex, such as abortion."[20]

There appears to be good clinical evidence that a limited number of individuals show an irritable aggression reaction when their blood chemistry is altered by a sudden drop in blood sugar. This is the state of hypoglycemia. At least one controlled study supports the clinical findings. Dr. Ralph Bolton spent considerable time with a very hostile tribe of Peruvian Indians, called the Qolla. He hypothesized that the exceptionally high level of social conflict and hostility in the society could be explained in part by the tendency to hypoglycemia among the community residents.[21]

Peer ratings of aggressiveness (which had an acceptable reliability) were studied in relationship to blood-sugar levels as determined by a 4-hour glucose-tolerance test. The aggression ratings were not known to the individuals who read the glucose levels. A chi-square analysis of the data showed a statistically significant relationship between aggression and the change in blood-glucose levels during the test. In view of all the other possible causes of aggressive behavior, this is a remarkable finding and indicates that the relationship must be a powerful one.

Allergies

Another change in the blood chemistry that can result in irritability and hostile tendencies is that produced by certain allergens in some particularly susceptible people. The term "allergic tension-fatigue syndrome" was introduced in 1954 to describe the allergic behavior pattern.[22] It is important to note that behavior disturbances are only one of many possible allergic reactions and that all individuals with allergies do not show a behavioral alteration.

A classification of allergic reactions in the nervous system includes the following:

> *Emotional immaturity reactions.* Included under this heading are temper tantrums, screaming episodes, whining, impatience, and excitability. Patients of this type are inclined to be erratic, impulsive, quarrelsome, and irresponsible. Many admit to having childish compulsions.
>
> *Antisocial behavior.* These patients are inclined to be uncooperative,

pugnacious, sulky, and perhaps cruel. Most have learned enough self-control to avoid serious abberations of behavior.[23]

It is difficult to determine how extensive a problem allergic aggression is. There are relatively few studies comparing aggressive tendencies in allergic individuals with control subjects. And since it is clear that all allergic individuals do not have nervous system involvement, such studies would not be particularly meaningful. Although there are a large number of case studies in the literature showing that individuals with allergic tension-fatigue syndrome lose that symptomatology under allergy management, the only reasonable way to determine whether the syndrome is an allergic one is to eliminate the allergen from the environment until the symptoms abate and then reproduce the symptoms by reintroducing the allergen into the environment, the so-called challenge technique. Crook, et al., reported on fifty patients who had five signs and symptoms of allergy: fatigue, irritability and other mental and emotional symptoms, pallor, circles under the eyes, and nasal congestion. The majority of the patients in this study had their symptoms relieved and reproduced by the challenge technique. The fifty patients reviewed in this research were seen in the group pediatric practice during a four-year period. The authors concluded that allergy as a systemic or generalized illness is much more common than is usually recognized by most allergy textbooks.[24]

Allergens that can produce the allergic tension-fatigue syndrome are highly varied. It can be produced by pollens;[25] a variety of inhalants;[26] drugs;[27] and many foods, of which milk, chocolate, cola, corn, and eggs are the most common.[28] The sensitivity of the individual varies idiosyncratically and according to the type of allergen. One patient showed such exquisite sensitivity to onions that she could tell when they were being cooked not by the odor but by her sudden and intense nervousness and irritability.[29]

The basic physiological cause of the irritable allergic reaction is not yet clear. Perhaps the most reasonable hypothesis is suggested by Gottlieb, who considers the possibility that the symptoms are due to allergically caused circumscribed angiodema (noninflammatory swelling) of the brain.[30] There is some evidence that such localized edema occurs in the brain as a result of allergies just as localized edema occurs in the skin. Both types of edema are reversible. As with the skin, there is evidence that the edema may be localized in different parts of the brain. Thus the number and kinds of symptoms will be a function of the particular location of the resultant pressure in the brain. If the angioedema occurs in any one of several portions of the brain through which the neural system for irritable aggression courses, the pressure of the swelling may sensitize or activate those neural systems with the resultant feeling of hostility and/or aggressive behavior.

Aggression Control

It is probably true that most of the time for most crimes, the most relevant variables are social, sociological, and cultural. In the broad meaning of the term, they are the result of *learned reactions*. They come from changes in the brain that occur in the cortex and are the result of experience. Thus there can be no doubt that some of the most important methods for the control of criminal and antisocial behavior involve retraining, reeducation, and social changes. That is, the external environment is manipulated in some way to alter the individual's behavior or his potential for socially unacceptable behavior. However, if this model has any validity, it should be possible to change certain kinds of aggressive behavior by influencing the internal milieu, by producing changes in the individual's physiology.

I should emphasize at this point that what is possible is certainly not necessarily desirable. I shall discuss what is possible and later will consider some of the implications of those possibilities.

Brain Lesions

If there are neural systems that are active during and responsible for aggressive behavior, it should be possible to reduce or eliminate aggressive tendencies by interrupting or interfering with those neural systems. There is now abundant evidence that such a procedure is possible. As might be suspected when dealing with neural systems rather than neural centers, there are a number of different brain areas that may be lesioned to delimit aggressive tendencies.

One can take the wild cat, Lynx rufus, which will attack with the slightest provocation, and make it tame by burning out a very small part of the brain called the *amygdala*. After the operation, it will never be violent again.[31]

The same operation can be performed on the wild Norway rat, one of the few animals that will attack without apparent provocation. If a bilateral amygdalectomy is performed on this animal, as soon as it comes out of the anesthetic, it will become docile. In fact, a technician could pick it up and carry it around in his lab coat pocket.[32]

Just as there are wild cats and wild monkeys, there are wild people; individuals who have so much spontaneous activity in the neural systems that underlies aggressive behavior that they are a constant threat to themselves and to those around them. These are individuals who are confined to the back wards of mental hospitals under either constant sedation or constant restraint. The homicidal hostility of these people can also be reduced if appropriate brain lesions are made to interrupt the functioning of the systems for irascibility.

There are a number of surgeons now who have done essentially the same operations on humans as just described for the cat and the rat—that is, a complete or partial bilateral amygdalectomy. The Japanese investigator Narabayashi and his colleagues, for example, indicate that they get 85 percent success in the reduction of violent behavior after a bilateral amygdalectomy.[33] Dr. Heimburger in Indiana claims that he gets 92 percent increase in docility in these extremely violent patients through the same operation. Not only was it possible to put those individuals in the open wards, that is, take them out of isolation, but two of his patients have been released into society and are making at least a reasonable adjustment.[34]

There can be no doubt that a number of different brain lesions can reduce the tendency of an individual to both feel and express hostility. That fact is of considerable theoretical significance. It confirms many of the findings on animals and substantiates predictions from the model described before. However, as a practical therapy for the control of aggressive behavior, it leaves much to be desired. There are very few individuals for whom such a drastic approach would be indicated. The most serious problem with the use of lesions for the control of aggression is that the operation is not reversible. Once the lesion is made, nothing can be done to restore the individual to the preoperative state. When the operation is not successful, and it sometimes is not, the patient is brain damaged to no avail. It therefore appears clear that surgery should be a last-resort therapy and should be used only after all other types of control, both psychological and physiological, have been tried. There is evidence that in some of the hospitals around the world in which aggression-control operations are performed, relatively little care is taken to ensure that brain surgery is indeed the last-resort therapy that it should be.

Brain Stimulation

The control of aggressive behavior can also be achieved by the activation of those neural systems that send inhibitory fibers to the aggression systems. Jose Delgado has repeatedly shown that vicious rhesus monkeys can be tamed by the stimulation of aggression suppressor areas.

To eliminate the need for restraint and the necessity for connecting wires to the head, a technique was developed by which the brain of the subject could be stimulated by remote, radio control. The monkey wore a small stimulating device on its back that was connected by leads under the skin to the electrodes that were implanted in various locations in the brain. The leads were connected through a very small switching relay that could be closed by an impulse from a miniature radio receiver that was bolted to the animal's skull. The radio receiver could than be activated by a transmitter that was some distance away. With this system it was possible to study the monkeys while permitting them to roam free in the caged area.[35]

In one experiment the subject was the aggressive boss monkey that dominated the rest of the colony with his threatening behavior and overt attacks. A radio-controlled electrode was implanted in the monkey's caudate nucleus. When the radio transmitter was activated, the boss monkey received stimulation in the caudate nucleus with the result that his spontaneous aggressive tendencies were blocked. His territoriality diminished, and the other monkeys in the colony reacted to him differently. They made fewer submissive gestures and showed less fear of the boss. When the caudate nucleus was being stimulated, it was possible for the experimenter to enter the cage and catch the monkey with his bare hands.

During one phase of the experiment just described, the button for the transmitter was placed inside the cage near the feeding tray and thus made available to all of the monkeys in the colony. One small monkey learned to stand next to the button and watch the boss monkey. Every time the boss would start to threaten and become aggressive, the little monkey would push the button and calm him down. I'll leave it to the reader to decide what the political implications of this experiment are. I must say that it's the first experimental evidence I know of, of Saint Matthew's prediction that the meek shall indeed inherit the earth.

Humans also have neural systems in the brain that, when activated, function to block ongoing aggressive behavior. Dr. Heath from Tulane has reported on a patient who had an electrode implanted in an area of the brain called the *septum*. When this extremely hostile patient was brought into the room raging, threatening, swearing, and struggling, if his electrode was connected and the septal region was stimulated (without his knowledge, of course), he immediately relaxed, became docile, and assumed a positive attitude. Further, he was unable to account for the sudden change in his behavior. When the stimulating electrode is in the septal area, the patient may tell a dirty joke or reveal plans to seduce the waitress down at the corner bar. There are other suppressor areas, however, that do not activate sexually toned responses.

It would be possible to run the wire from that electrode down the back of this patient's neck to a battery pack that he could wear on his belt. You can then give him an "antihostility button," and whenever he began to feel very mean, he could press the button, calm himself down, and bring himself back into the civilized world.

The technology has already been developed. Heath developed it as a therapeutic device for an individual with narcolepsy.[36] Narcolepsy, as you probably know, is a disorder in which the individual falls asleep at inappropriate times. I have had many students afflicted with this disorder. This particular patient suggested that his narcolepsy was very troublesome because it interfered with his profession. He was a night club entertainer and would sometimes fall asleep in the middle of his act. Dr. Heath implanted an electrode in the arousal system of his brain, and a wire was then brought down to a transistorized stimulation unit, and the patient was given an "on" button. Whenever he started to drift off to sleep, the patient could press his on button and turn himself back on. He had a type of narcolepsy in which he sometimes fell asleep before he could get to the button. His friends soon learned, however, that when he did that, they could reach over and press his on button to bring him back into the conversation.

I pointed out that Delgado had his monkey hooked up to a radio. There is no reason why exactly the same technique could not be used on humans. At least four people reported in the literature have been under radio control of one sort or another.[37] An electrode could be placed in a suppressor area of the brain just as Delgado did with the boss monkey. It could be brought out to a radio bolted to the subject's head. His brain could then be activated by a transmitter, and the patient could then move as widely as the area that the transmitter reached.

There are of course some problems with this approach. Since the radio has to be bolted to the skull, it means that the bolts have to go through the scalp. This is a constant possible source of irritation and a source of infection. There are also psychological problems. People report that they feel conspicuous with radios on their heads.

Even those problems are being solved by the recent developments in microminiaturization in electronics. It is now possible to take the radio, the power to operate it, and a radio transmitter that will send out brain waves and put them all into a unit that is about the size and the shape of a half-dollar. The electrode can be put in place and attached to this unit, which can be implanted under the skin anywhere. As soon as the patient's hair grows back, he looks like anyone else. In fact, it is technologically possible right now that the next person you meet on the street will be under radio control and you would not know it unless he parted his hair wrong that morning.

The suppression of aggression by electrical stimulation is, I think, of considerable theoretical importance. We know that humans possess these neural suppressor systems, and we are gradually learning many of the characteristics of suppression mechanisms. However, like brain lesions, this is not yet a reasonable nor useful therapeutic technique.

The surgical risk of mortality through electrode implants is even lower than that of stereotaxic brain lesions and can be considered negligible. There are, however, other serious side-effects that merit a great deal more research before electrical stimulation of the brains of humans can be considered risk free. Although there are no data on humans, it has been shown in mice, rats, cats, and monkeys that repeated, brief, subthreshold stimulations of the amygdala result in a progressive lowering of the seizure threshold and ultimately in behavioral convulsions. This increase in seizure potential resulting from brain stimulation has been referred to as the *kindling effect*. Goddard, who has studied this phenomenon is some detail, concludes that the kindling effect is a relatively permanent transynaptic change resulting from the stimulation. It is not due to tissue damage or scar formation.[38]

It may someday be possible to circumvent the kindling effect. Until then, however, any procedure that involves repeated electrical stimulation of the human brain places the patient at risk.

Hormones

Our physiological model of aggressive behavior indicates that the neurological systems for aggressive behavior are sensitized by chemical factors in the blood stream. These are primarily but not exclusively hormones. An understanding of the endocrinology and blood-chemistry influences on aggression should ultimately lead to a rational therapy for certain kinds of hostility in humans. The woman, for example, who suffers from periodic hyperirritability every month has a physician who either isn't aware of the problem or doesn't keep up with the literature. There are a variety of therapeutic measures now that can be taken to alleviate that problem.

There are also people who show a kind of aggressive behavior known as *sex-related aggression*. These are the violent individuals for whom the object of aggression is the same as the object for sexual behavior. These are the men who commit the brutal sexual murders.

Aggressive behavior that is directly associated with sexual behavior, either heterosexual or homosexual, can sometimes be controlled by reducing or blocking the androgens in the blood stream. The simplest and most obvious method of accomplishing this is through the operation of castration. There is now considerable evidence that this operative procedure is effective in reducing the level of sexual arousal regardless of its direction. This is a drastic therapy, and there are obvious problems with it: It is permanent and irreversible. There are also a variety of physical and psychological side-effects. However, it has been offered to sex criminals as an alternative to prison in some countries.[39]

More recently some investigators have attempted to block the effects of the male hormone by giving estrogenic or progesteronic hormones or antiandrogenic drugs. Although a great deal more work needs to be done and the problems of side-effects must be considered, these techniques do show promise.[40]

Drugs

The activity of the neural systems responsible for aggressive behavior and feelings of hostility can also be reduced by the use of drugs. Although there is currently no drug that is a completely specific antihostility agent, there are available a significant number of preparations that do reduce aggressive tendencies as one component of their action. However, the problem of predicting which drug will be effective in the inhibition of hostility in a given individual is a difficult problem. Aggressive behavior has many causes and can result from a variety of neural and endocrine dysfunctions. There are not as yet good diagnostic tests that permit a rational pharmacotherapeutic approach to hostility control. However, in spite of this lack of a perfect predictability in the matching of a specific drug to a particular patient, there are now a large number of substances that are useful in the management of aggression. It is already possible to reduce or eliminate much of the irrational, nonadaptive hostility found in psychotic, neurotic, and ostensibly normal individuals.

It is not possible to review here the extensive literature on the pharmacological control of aggression. However, it should be indicated that most of the major tranquilizers such as chlorpromazine appear to have an antihostility effect over and above their sedative action. This also appears to be true of many of the minor tranquilizers including librium and valium. There are many other pharmaceutical agents that have a taming effect, but none of them works on all patients, and some may even exacerbate the hostile tendencies in some patients. Until more precise diagnostic procedures are available, the simple dictum for treatment will remain: If the first drug on the list does not work, try the next one.

Limitations of Physiological Control

The control techniques just discussed are powerful, but their limitations should be clearly understood. These methods would be ineffective in controlling the aggressive actions of a "trigger man for Murder Incorporated" or those of a bomber pilot over North Vietnam. Both are engaged in instrumental aggression, and neither may have any feeling of hostility toward his victims. When his radar indicates that it is time to press his bomb-release button, the pilot may do so without the slightest feeling of antagonism. His bombs may destroy the homes and lives of hundreds of people. He has behaved as he has been trained to behave, and emotional responses may not be involved at all. The "trigger man for Murder Incorporated" kills because he is financially rewarded for killing. He may not know his victim and may feel no animosity toward him whatsoever.

These individuals have engaged in learned behavior. As of now, there is no physiological manipulation that can selectively affect learned responses. Further, with the current state of the art, no such method is likely to be found in the near future. It is not even clear where to start looking for that type of method. That kind of control must await major, and as yet quite unpredictable breakthroughs.

The distinction between instrumental aggression and aggressive behavior containing an affective component has important implications for the abuse potential of the physiological control of aggression. The use of physiological controls may in fact be counterproductive for an individual who wishes to control the rebellious tendencies of a particular population. One reaction to oppression, political or otherwise, is to become angry and as a result of that anger, to evolve a plan that may involve aggressive behavior, to alleviate the oppression. Another reaction to oppression is to recognize it as such, intellectually, and to come to the conclusion that the oppression must be eliminated. A plan, which may involve aggressive behavior, is then worked out. Antihostility drugs in the water supply or other physiological measures will affect only the anger; they will have no influence on the intellectual processes involved in the aggressive plans. In fact, if the anger is controlled, the plans may be more effective because they will not involve the impulsive quality that often results from the urgency of anger. Further, because the emotional component will not function as a distractor, the intellectual processes may function more efficiently.

In 1971 Kenneth B. Clark started a monumental controversy when he suggested that the necessary resources in terms of scientific personnel and research facilities be mobilized "to reduce human anxieties, tension, hostilities, violence, cruelty, and destructive power irrationalities of man which are the basis of wars."[42] He further suggested that world leaders accept and use the first form of psychotechnological biochemical intervention that would reduce or block the possibility they would use their power destructively. He implied that the adequate use of the new physiological technology of hostility control could eliminate destructive wars. Since, as this chapter has shown, a great deal is now known about hostility control and the potential for further developments in those types of controls is great, it is important to attempt to relate these developments to Clark's proposals.

If one assumes that modern wars result from the impulsive behavior of world leaders who are acting in anger, Clark's proposal would be a reasonable one, and adequate antiaggression therapy for world leaders would, in fact, significantly reduce the possibilities of armed conflict. Further, given the current status of our understanding, it is highly likely that a concentrated research program could develop pharmaceutical agents that, either singly or in combination, could eliminate feelings of anger and hostility and the irrational decisions based on those feelings. A number of drugs are available now, but considerable research is needed to establish the types of aggressive behavior affected, and more needs to be known about possible side-effects. When these drugs are perfected, as they certainly will be, and we know with some assurance that there are minimal risks of such effects as paradoxical reactions, I agree with Kenneth Clark that they should be taken by those who hold positions of political power. The world can ill afford the luxury of world leaders who are subject to fits of anger that may result in impulsive and irrational aggressive behavior.

However, the unfortunate fact is that although the psychotechnical revolution may ultimately reduce feelings of anger and their resultant behavior, it is not likely to eliminate destructive war. Much, if not most, of the aggression involved in war in instrumental. That is, it is directed at achieving certain gains—the acquisition of territory, the settlement of disputed boundaries, the expansion of a sphere of influence, or the economic exploitation of another country. Those motives may have essentially no emotional component, and anger may play no role. Once again, it should be emphasized that no known physiological manipulation can selectively influence particular learned behaviors. The psychotechnological revolution is not even close to being able to influence those kinds of behavior; thus war based primarily on nonemotional motivations will not be curtailed by physiological manipulations.

Some Final Implications

It can be seen from the preceding discussion that an understanding of the physiology of aggressive behavior provides some new insights into the complex problem of aggression and introduces a somewhat different view of man. This view reintroduces the importance of physiological mechanisms as a contributor to the determination of behavior. Environmental conditions and learning are powerful factors that influence behavior, but they clearly operate on a soma that may enhance or reduce their effects. There are wide individual differences in physiology among men. These differences are at times powerful determinants of behavior.

Humans have always recognized that behavior can be changed by altering an individual's environment or his experience. It must now be recognized that behavior can be changed, sometimes drastically, by altering his internal milieu. That conclusion is now inescapable. The implications of this view of humans are profound and will change history. Our understanding of the psychological mechanisms underlying behavior is in its infancy. However, as knowledge increases, powerful new forces for influencing man's destiny will be available. The increase in our knowledge of atomic forces moved man into a new era. The increase in our understanding of the physiology of behavior will move us into another, and the effects will be even more profound.

Notes

1. This chapter is based in part on and is an extension of the author's earlier works. A more detailed presentation of some of the concepts may be found in the following two sources: K.E. Moyer, *The Psychobiology of Aggression* (New York: Harper and Row, 1976), and K.E. Moyer, *The Physiology of Hostility* (Chicago: Markham Press, 1971).

2. K.E. Moyer, "Kinds of Aggression and Their Physiological Basis," *Communications in Behavior Biology* 2 (1968): 65–87.

3. M.E. Egger and J.P. Flynn, "Effect of Electrical Stimulation of theAmygdala on Hypothalamically Elicited Attack Behavior in Cats," *Journal of Neurophysiology* 26 (1963): 705–720.

4. B.W. Robinson, M. Alexander, and G. Browne, "Dominance Reversal Resulting from Aggressive Responses Evoked by Brain Telestimulation," *Physiology and Behavior* 4 (1969): 749–752.

5. H.E. King, "Psychological Effects of Excitation in the Limbic System," in *Electrical Stimulation of the Brain,* ed. D.E. Sheer (Austin: University of Texas Press, 1961), pp. 477–486.

6. C.W. Sem-Jacobsen, *Depth-electrographic Stimulation of the Human Brain and Behavior* (Springfield, Ill.: Thomas, 1968), R.G. Heath, et al., *Studies in Schizophrenia* (Cambridge, Mass.: Harvard University Press, 1954), pp. 83–84.

7. W.H. Sweet, F. Ervin, and V.H. Mark, "The relationship of Violent Behavior to Focal Cerebral Disease," in *Aggressive Behavior,* eds. S. Garattini and E. B. Sigg (New York: Wiley, 1969), pp. 336–352.

8. C.E. Lyght, ed., *The Merck Manual of Diagnosis and Therapy* (West Point, Pa.: Merck, 1966).

9. H. Gastaut, "Interpretation of the Symptoms of 'Psychomotor' Epilepsy in Relation to Physiologic Data on Rhinencephalic Function," *Epilepsia* 3 (1954): 84–88.

10. M.A. Falconer, D. Hill, A. Meyer, and J.L. Wilson, "Clinical, Radiological, and EEG Correlations with Pathological Changes in Temporal Lobe Epilepsy and Their Significance in Surgical Treatment," in *Temporal Lobe Epilepsy,* eds. M. Baldwin and P. Bailey (Springfield, Ill.: Thomas, 1958), pp. 396–410.

11. R.S. Schwab, W.H. Sweet, V.H. Mark, R.N. Kjellberg, and F.R. Ervin, "Treatment of Intractable Temporal Lobe Epilepsy by Stereotactic Amygdala Lesions," *Transactions of the American Neurological Association* 90 (1965): 12–19.

12. A.E. Walker and D. Blumer, "Long Term Effects of Temporal Lobe Lesions on Sexual Behavior and Aggressivity." Paper presented at the Houston Neurological Symposium on Neural Bases of Violence and Aggression, Houston, Tex., 9–11 March 1972.

13. H. Bernstein and K.E. Moyer, "Aggressive Behavior in the Rat: Effect of Isolation and Olfactory Bulb Lesions," *Brain Research* 20 (1970): 75–84.

14. M.D. Wheatley, "The Hypothalamus and Affective Behavior in Cats," *Archives of Neurology and Psychiatry* 52 (1944): 296–316.

15. R.J. Bandler and K.E. Moyer, "Animals Spontaneously Attacked by Rats," *Communications in Behavioral Biology* 5 (1970): 177–182.

16. K. Lagerspetz, "Studies on the Aggressive Behavior of Mice," *Annales Academiae Scientiarum Fennicae,* Series B, 131 (1964): 1–131.

17. E.A. Beeman, "The Effect of Male Hormone on Aggressive Behavior in Mice," *Physiological Zoology* 20 (1947): 373–405.

18. K. Dalton, "Menstruation and Acute Psychiatric Illness," *British Medical Journal* 1 (1959): 148–149; K. Dalton, "Schoolgirls; Misbehavior and Menstruation," *British Medical Journal* 2 (1960): 1647–1649; K. Dalton, "Menstruation and Crime," *British Medical Journal* 3 (1961): 1752–1753; K. Dalton, *The Premenstrual Syndrome* (Springfield, Ill.: Thomas, 1964).

19. J.H. Morton, H. Addition, R.G. Addison, L. Hunt, and J.J. Sullivan, "A Clinical Study of Premenstrual Tension," *American Journal of Obstetrics and Gynecology* 65 (1953): 1182–1191.

20. L. Broom, and P. Selznick, *Sociology: A Text with Adapted Readings* (New York: Harper & Row, 1957).

21. R. Bolton, "Aggression and Hypoglycemia among the Qolla: A Study in Psychobiological Anthropology," *Ethnology* 12 (1973): 227–257.

22. F. Speer, "The Allergic Tension-Fatigue Syndrome," *Pediatric Clinic of North America* 1 (1954): 1029–1037.

23. M.B. Campbell, "Allergy and Behavior: Neurologic and Psychic Syndromes," in *Allergy of the Nervous System,* ed. F. Speer, (Springfield, Ill.: Thomas, 1970), pp. 28–46.

24. W.G. Crook, W.W. Harrison, S.E. Crawford, and B.S. Emerson, "Systemic Manifestations Due to Allergy: Report to Fifty Patients and a Review of the Literature on the Subject," *Pediatrics* 27 (1961): 790–799.

25. I.S. Kahn, "Pollen Toxemia in Children," *Journal of the American Medical Association* 88 (1927): 241–242.

26. B.C. Eisenberg, "Etiology: Inhalants," in *Allergy of the Nervous System,* ed. F. Speer (Springfield, Ill.: Thomas, 1970), pp. 143–197, T.G. Randolph, *Human Ecology and Susceptibility to the Chemical Environment* (Springfield, Ill.: Thomas, 1962).

27. P.M. Gottlieb, "Allergic Neuropathies and Demyelinative Disease," in *Allergy of the Nervous System,* ed. F. Speer (Springfield, Ill.:

Thomas, 1970), pp. 79–121; N. Schaffer, "Personality Changes Induced in Children by the Use of Certain Antihistaminic Drugs," *Annals of Allergy* 11 (1953): 317–318.

28. F. Speer, "Etiology: Foods," in *Allergy of the Nervous System,* ed. F. Speer (Springfield, Ill.: Thomas, 1970), pp. 198–209. Crook, et al., supra, n. 24.

29. C. Frederichs and H. Goodman, *Low Blood Sugar and You* (New York: Constellation International, 1969).

30. Gottlieb, *supra,* n. 27.

31. L. Schreiner and A. Kling, "Behavioral Changes Following Rhinencephalic Injury in Cat," *Journal of Neurophysiology* 16 (1953): 643–658.

32. J.W. Woods, "'Taming' of the Wild Norway Rat by Rhinencephalic Lesions," *Nature* 178 (1956): 869.

33. H. Narabayashi, T. Nagao, Y. Saito, M. Yoshido, and M. Nagahata, "Stereotaxic Amygdalotomy for Behavior Disorders," *Archives of Neurology* 9 (1963): 1–16.

34. R.F. Heimburger, C.C. Whitlock, and J.E. Kalsbeck, "Sterotaxic Amygdalotomy for Epilepsy With Aggressive Behavior," *Journal of the American Medical Association* 198 (1966): 165–169.

35. J.M.R. Delgado, "Cerebral Heterostimulation in a Monkey Colony," *Science* 141 (1963): 161–163.

36. R.G. Heath, et al., *Studies in Schizophrenia* (Cambridge, Mass.: Harvard University Press, 1954), pp. 83–84.

37. J.M.R. Delgado, V. Mark, W. Sweet, F. Ervin, G. Weiss, G. Bach-Y-Rita, and R. Hagiwara, "Intracerebral Radio Stimulation and Recording in Completely Free Patients," *Journal of Nervous and Mental Diseases* 147 (1968): pp. 329–340.

38. G.V. Goddard, "Long Term Alteration Following Amygdaloid Stimulation," in *The Neurobiology of the Amygdala,* ed. B. Eleftheriou (New York: Plenum, 1972), pp. 581–596.

39. J. Bremer, *Asexualization* (New York: Macmillan, 1959).

40. T.L. Chatz, "Management of Male Adolescent Sex Offenders," *International Journal of Offender Therapy* 2 (1972): 109–115.

41. K.E. Moyer, *supra,* n. 1, 1976.

42. K.B. Clark, "The Pathos of Power: A Psychological Perspective," *American Psychologist* 26 (1971): 1047–1057.

Commentary

Cleon H. Foust and
D. Robert Webster

Stanton Samenow remarked that the causes of crime are complex and at present not identifiable by medicine, biology, sociology, or psychiatry. These disciplines are all in their infancy in the search for causes. At the moment we can identify only relationships with crime. For example, Samuel Yochelson abandoned the search for causes at an early point and began identifying thinking patterns and the relationships to criminal activity. He and Samenow identified fifty-two patterns of thought consistent in every criminal regardless of the specific crimes committed.

Other investigators have identified physiological, dietary, allergical, and other relationships. These hint at genetic bases, but the fact remains even though there is a relationship such as aggression to hypoglycemia, not all people with hypoglycemia become aggressive. So the combined physiological base and learned response produce as yet unsolved complexities.

In a longitudinal study of what makes a criminal, one wonders whether Stanton Samenow considers his work as parallel with, tangential to, or at a much later stage than that of Moyer. In any event he expressed great admiration for Moyer's work.

George Beto commented that perhaps the title *Criminal Personality* of the Yochelson and Samenow three-volume work was misleading because many who commit no criminal acts have the prescribed personality traits—manipulation and deviousness—but not to the same degree. Turning to Dr. Moyer, he suggested that the difference may be a matter of learning.

Dr. Moyer agreed that regardless of his threshold to aggressive behavior, an individual can be taught to respond with some control or vice versa. But a learned response can be altered only with further learning—learned habits cannot be altered by drugs, electrotherapy, or surgery. Medicine may facilitate the process; for example, antihostility drugs may reduce anger and enable one to apply new, learned responses, but it is still a matter of learning.

In a discussion session, Dr. Moyer added, "In my own field, of course, there is a great need for research. In particular, there is a need for the kind of research that can be done in a laboratory, but such research must be integrated so that the very large number of findings that we have can be made intelligible. Currently nobody knows what all those findings mean."

4 The Implications of Deterrence and Incapacitation Research for Policy Evaluation

Philip J. Cook

The North Carolina State Police implemented a well-publicized crackdown on speeding over Labor Day weekend, 1977. Patrol cars were out in full force on the interstate highways, and the advance publicity had indicated that the 55-mile-per-hour speed limit was to be taken literally. I had occasion to drive several hundred miles that weekend and can testify that cars in the right-hand lanes were indeed driving 55, with hardly anyone daring to use the passing lanes. Conformity was so complete that weekend that the number of speeding citations issued was actually *below* average. The result that weekend was to save a number of travelers from injury or death. Needless to say, with the crackdown long since ended, drivers are now taking their usual liberties with the speed limit, with the consequent loss of some of the potential benefits of the law.

The deterrent effect of the threat of punishment has been observed, and occasionally carefully documented, in a wide variety of contexts and types of offenses. While it cannot be proved, I believe it reasonable to assert that the bulk of the criminal justice system's influence on crime rates results from the deterrence mechanism, by which the threat of punishment serves as an incentive to potential criminals to conform with the law.[1]

The potential crime-preventive effects of punishment are of course not limited to deterrence. A few types of criminal offenses are commonly punished with jail and prison terms, which have the effect of incapacitating convicts—physically preventing them from committing crimes (except within the confines of the prison) for the duration of their sentence. There is also a possibility that punishment will reform the convict or at least provide him with attractive legitimate alternatives to crime as a result of participation in rehabilitation programs.[2] Since rehabilitation is treated elsewhere in this book, this chapter focuses for the most part on the deterrence and incapacitation mechanisms.

What a Policymaker Should Know about Deterrence

The *raison d'etre* of the criminal justice system is to reduce crime. The major policy instrument available to the criminal justice system is punishment, that is, the ability to threaten criminals with unpleasant consequences for their acts and to actually impose these unpleasant consequences on some fraction of the criminals. Other branches of government also influence crime rates through a variety of policy instruments ranging from street lighting to the public elementary school curriculum. But for criminal justice system authorities, the key questions center on punishment. The most common punishment in criminal cases is a fine, but the proper use of the more severe punishments—incarceration and execution—has rightfully been the most important concern of scholars, legislators, and criminal justice system authorities. These severe sanctions are very costly both in terms of the inmate's suffering and in the high cost to taxpayers of expanding prison capacity and maintaining inmates. Since the benefit from using this costly disposition is crime reduction, it is clearly important in evaluating possible changes in the current system to have at least an approximate idea of the magnitude of this benefit. How *much* could crime rates be reduced by the construction of a new $5-million prison that would house one hundred inmates at an annual operating cost of $1 million? Even more important is the question of how best to allocate prison capacity among convicts: What sentencing policy would have the greatest impact on the amount and seriousness of crime? Should prison be reserved for warehousing a relatively few hardcore criminals for long periods, or should prison be allocated in smaller doses to a larger fraction of convicts? And finally, what, if anything, is to be gained by the reinstitution of capital punishment?

These and other questions require the best available information on the preventive effects of punishment, but unfortunately the best information is not nearly adequate to making truly well-informed decisions. In general terms, the state of the art can be characterized by three propositions:

1. The threat of punishment deters a wide variety of crimes, and the size of the deterrent effect tends to increase with the perceived certainty of punishment. Predicting the actual magnitude of the deterrence effect generated by a specific policy change (for example, a change in sentencing laws) is not possible with any reasonable degree of accuracy.

2. Estimates of crime-reduction effects due to incapacitation are somewhat easier to come by (though still quite rough). Available estimates suggest that rather large increases in the size of the prison population will be necessary in order to achieve a modest reduction in crime through the incapacitation effect alone.

3. There is widespread agreement (though little empirical evidence) that an increase in the likelihood of imprisonment has a greater deterrent effect than an increase of similar magnitude in the average length of a prison term. If true, then there appears to be a conflict between a punishment policy designed to maximize the incapacitation effect of available prison capacity and a policy designed to maximize the deterrence effect.

A brief review of the evidence in support of these conclusions is presented here, together with recommendations about how more detailed and useful information can be acquired in the future. More important than the empirical results is the theoretical view of crime and criminals that helps explain the deterrence effect and that provides some guidance to policymakers. The policy-relevant implications that follow from this theory are developed in the final section.

Deterrence

Theory

The preventive effects of punishment can be classified as either "general" or "special." The special effect of a punishment refers to its effect on the amount of crime committed by the particular convict who is punished; the general effects are those restraining influences that operate through the threat of punishment rather than through its direct effects on those convicts who are subjected to it. Rehabilitation and incapacitation are special effects, whereas deterrence is a general effect: Potential criminals are deterred by the threat of punishment, which threat is made believable by the actual imposition of punishment on some of those who were not deterred.

During the last decade economists have been primarily responsible for developing the theory of deterrence. It is not surprise that this recent development in the economics literature harks back to Jeremy Bentham:

> [T]he profit of the crime is the force which urges a man to delinquency: the pain of the punishment is the force employed to restrain him from it. If the first of these forces be the greater the crime will be committed; if the second, the crime will not be committed.[3]

The threat of punishment is in effect a government-imposed tax on criminal activity; the higher this tax, the fewer the criminal opportunities that will be deemed worthwhile by potential criminals.

There are of course several complications that have to be taken into account. First, the "tax" is imposed with some probability less than one, and its magnitude (the severity of sentence) is also highly uncertain in practice. Thus the decision whether to commit a crime is analogous to a decision whether to gamble, play the stock market, and so on; it depends on the individual's perception of the risks and the degree to which he is averse to taking risks. Second, information on the true magnitude of the "tax" (that is, the actual probability and severity of punishment for a particular crime) is communicated in a very haphazard fashion. Perceptions of this threat may differ widely among potential criminals and may be only loosely related to the true threat level. It may be important in some circumstances then to maintain a distinction between perceived and actual threat levels in developing the implications of the theory (though this has not been done).[4] Third, the severity of a given punishment (for example, one year in prison) will be measured differently by people with differing tastes and circumstances; the person with a high standard of living and a good reputation has much more to lose from incurring this sentence than does a reprobate. Fourth, for crimes that require a substantial amount of time to plan and execute, the opportunity cost of a person's time (legitimate wage rate) will influence his perception of profitability.

For these four reasons then a given criminal opportunity will look more profitable to some than to others, even if we abstract from interpersonal differences in moral outlook. But for all rational potential criminals, it will be true that any of the following changes should have a deterrent effect: an increase in the perceived probability or severity of punishment, and increase in the effort required to commit a crime, a reduction in the payoff to crime, or an improvement in legitimate economic opportunities.[5]

These qualitative implications follow from a theoretical analysis of rational behavior under uncertainty that has also been applied to a number of other economic choices. The approach assumes then that in its essential aspects the crime choice is not unique and that there is no need to presuppose a distinctive set of motivations in analyzing criminal behavior. Even deviant crimes of sex and violence and noninstrumental crimes (illicit drug use) are readily analyzed within this framework, though the notion of how to define the payoff to such crimes becomes a bit murky. The implications of the theory with respect to deterrence are not changed but are of course restricted to that segment of the population that derives enjoyment from such activities.[6]

One interesting application of the theory is to the old question of whether changes in the certainty of punishment can be expected to have a greater effect than changes in the severity of punishment. First, the question has been restated more precisely: Is the elasticity of the crime rate with respect to a change in the proability of punishment greater than the elasticity with respect to a change in the severity of punishment?[7] For example, would a 20-percent increase in the probability of being imprisoned for committing a burglary (an increase from, say, a probability of .05 to .06) cause a greater reduction in the burglary rate than a 20-percent increase in the average length of the prison term (an increase, say, from ten months to twelve months)? The answer that follows from the theory in one important circumstance is clearly no. If the typical severity of punishment for a particular crime is insufficient to make that crime unprofitable and the punishment were to be applied with certainty, then changes in the actual probability will not influence the amount of that crime. Increases in severity, on the other hand, may have an effect. This point is salient to those large urban jurisdictions that are following the practice of giving probation to convicted robbers and burglars who lack a felony record ("the first one is free").

In cases where severity is sufficiently great, on the other hand, the theoretical answer conforms with the conventional wisdom in this matter. If potential criminals "discount" the future, then the threat of a two-year prison sentence with probability .10 will be a less effective deterrent than the threat of a one-year sentence with probability .20; the elasticity of crime with respect to probability will be less than the elasticity with respect to severity.[8]

The economist's work on the general deterrence mechanism has been useful in developing the implications of a long-neglected notion in criminology literature, that criminals can be usefully viewed as rational decision makers intent on furthering their personal welfare in an environment that provides crime opportunities coupled with sanction threats. This view can be caricatured and made to seem absurd by conjuring up an image of the criminal as a sophisticated planner and decision analyst who researches each rape or robbery thoroughly before making his move. There is no doubt that many criminals are impulsive and poorly informed about the possible consequences of their acts, just as many other people may *conform* to the law out of unthinking habit. The "rational criminal" is nevertheless a useful theoretical abstraction for understanding and predicting criminal behavior so long as there is some degree of calculation on the part of some proportion of the potentially criminal population.

There is a missing link in deterrence theory that is potentially of considerable importance to criminal justice policymakers: By what mechanism or mechanisms do changes in the actual probability and severity of punishment get communicated to the relevant public? Clearance rates, needless to say, are not common knowledge, and court proceedings go largely unnoticed by the public. In some cases an increase in the threat level may be signaled by advance publicity and/or an increase in visible police presence, but such cases are relatively rare. I believe that most information regarding the likelihood and severity of punishment is communicated (rather unsystematically) by personal observation and word of mouth. When the neighborhood dope dealer gets arrested, the subsequent disposition of his case will be known to his acquaintances and interpreted as evidence on what might happen to them if they are arrested. If he ends up with "hard time," then a greater threat is conveyed to his acquaintances than if he is referred to a drug-rehabilitation program by the court. The hypothesis then is that each individual case has an important influence on the perceptions of a small group of people for whom the case is salient, while going unnoticed by most everyone else. If the fraction of arrests for dealing (to continue the example) that result in prison terms increases from 10 to 15 percent, then a correspondingly larger number of "observers"—friends and acquaintances—will be left with the impression that dealing is taken seriously by the courts. This informal threat-communication mechanism provides a plausible explanation for why even a small increase in criminal justice effectiveness may have some deterrent effect.

The simple deterrence mechanism just discussed is not the only general preventive effect of punishment. Other general preventive mechanisms have been widely discussed in the literature: Zimring and Hawkins assert, for example, that the threat of punishment can be a teacher of right and wrong, a stimulant to habitual law-abiding conduct, a mechanism for building respect for the law, and a rationale for conformity.[9] It is important to note the potential conflicts between the predictions that follow from consideration of these mechanisms and the implications of the simple deterrence form.

Lags in the Effect

While the simple deterrence theory presumes that changes in the threat level will have their full impact on crime rates the moment these changes are perceived the potential criminals,[10] effects that operate through other mechanisms may not have their full impact for some years. It has often been asserted, for example, that law-abiding behavior is habitual for many people, and the force of habit precludes them from taking advantage of profitable criminal opportunities even if they are virtually risk free. If an effective criminal justice system is one stimulant to individuals initially acquiring this habit, then the possibility arises that an era of mild and infrequently applied criminal sanctions may produce a whole generation of people who fail to see any rational reason to acquire the habit of law-abiding behavior. The ramifications of this failure could be reflected in the crime rate for years, even if a subsequent increase in the effectiveness of the system were achieved. Similarly, if criminal law and the effectiveness with which it is enforced shape the framework for the moral education of youth, then a reduction in the effectiveness of law enforcement may contribute to the production of an amoral, crime-prone generation: "It would be difficult to teach honesty, nonviolence, and similar positive values in a society where these rules were openly and commonly broken without punishment."[11] In both the mechanisms of habit formation and moral education then, an initial failure in deterrence produces long-term consequences for the crime rate.

One implication of these hypothesized lags in the general preventive effect of law enforcement is that the full magnitude of a change in the threat level cannot be assessed by observing its apparent short-term influence on the appropriate crime rate. Indeed, the virtual impossibility of measuring directly the full, long-run effect suggests once again the importance of a priori reasoning and indirect evidence. The notion that "crime breeds crime"—especially if the crime is uncompensated by punishment—is a powerful one and should be given more serious attention by scholars.

The Importance of Severity in Punishment

The legislated (and actual) severity of penalty for a particular offense may influence the public's feeling for the seriousness or moral repugnance of this offense. The famous quote from Stephan expresses the point well:

> Some men, probably, abstain from murder because they fear that, if they committed murder, they would be hung. Hundreds of thousands abstain from it because they regard it with horror. One great reason why they regard it with horror is, that murderers are hung with the hearty approbation of all reasonable men.[12]

Murderers are no longer hung; in fact, the median time served in prison by those convicted of homicide before their release on parole is less than five years.[13] Andenaes notes that "in the long run, such a reduction in penalty might also reduce the inhibitions against committing murder in situations where murder seems a tempting escape from a situation of emotional conflict."[14]

The issue for our purposes is whether considering the moralizing influence of a severe penalty might change the conclusions concerning the relative magnitudes of the responsiveness of crime to changes in the probability and severity of punishment that follow from an analysis of simple deterrence. In the long run, for those crimes in which "moral inhibition" plays an important role, maintaining high severity may be more important than a high probability of punishment.

Other Characteristics of the Law-Enforcement Process

I have argued that the moralizing influence of law enforcement may influence the public's attitudes toward illegal activities and hence the propensity to engage in such activity. A related but logically distinct mechanism by which law-enforcement activities may inhibit crime is through the influence of these activities on the public's respect for the law as such. If the process by which laws are made and enforced is generally viewed as legitimate and just, then many will obey the law simply out of a sense of obligation to honor its authority. The economist's term for this is "honesty preference," which will "bias" people's decision in favor of law-abiding behavior.[15] Behaviorally, this preference would mean that an individual would abstain from illegal behavior unless such behavior was perceived as sufficiently profitable (net of the threat of punishment and other considerations) to overcome the individual's preference for doing things legally.

The importance of honesty preference in inhibiting criminality is well expressed by Andenaes:

> A certain degree of respect for the formal law is probably essential for the smooth functioning of society. Where it is lacking, law enforcement agencies play a role similar to that of an occupying army in foreign territory, a comparison which has been made often enough with regard to the law enforcement agencies in the ghettos of American cities. Experience shows that an occupying army may be able to create a high degree of order and compliance if it is prepared to use sufficiently harsh terror methods. But such a reign of terror is fundamentally different from the system we are used to in democratic societies.[16]

The arguable importance of respect for the law adds a new dimension to the relationship between law-enforcement efforts and the degree of compliance with the law: Respect is influenced by the manner in which the law is enforced. If enforcement efforts are viewed as corrupt, arbitrary, or (worse) biased, unresponsive to the needs of the community, and liable to error,[17] then disrespect for the law and the prohibitions the system enforces is likely to be a natural consequence.[18]

The implication of this argument is that the general preventive effects of law-enforcement efforts are not transmitted through the probability and severity of punishment alone but also by the public's perception of the quality of the process that produces these threats.[19]

The arguments concerning the qualitative effects of these mechanisms are persuasive to the extent that they are consistent with one's beliefs concerning human nature, the socialization process, and so on. Unfortunately, there is little direct evidence on the quantitative importance of these mechanisms. Most of the available studies, summarized in the next sections, have focused on the simple deterrence mechanism.

Evidence from Natural Experiments

A wide range of criminal activity is subject to the influence of legal threats.[20] The most clear-cut evidence comes from "natural experiments"—sudden, large changes in the likelihood and severity of punishment. Andenaes has reported a number of such instances, including police strikes and anecdotes from World War II. For example, in 1944 the Nazis arrested the entire Copenhagen police force and provided no replacement for maintaining civil order. The result was an increase in the rates of theft crimes by a factor of about ten. The outburst of looting in some areas of New York City during the recent blackout is also a fairly clear-cut example of the importance of maintaining a credible legal threat to potential criminals. Two recent instances of sudden, large *increases* in police manning have been carefully studied and provide further support for the deterrence effect of a visible change in the threat of punishment. First, an evaluation of the introduction in 1965 of saturation policing of New York subways during the evening and nighttime hours found immediate and substantial drops in the subway felony rates during those hours.[21] Apparently this effect persisted at least through 1973, when the hourly felony rate was three times as high during the daytime as it was during the nighttime saturation period; in 1964, felony rates were about the same over the course of the day.[22] Second, a study of the effects of a 40-percent increase in police assigned to the twentieth precinct in 1966 estimated that the outdoor felony rate was reduced 36 percent below what it would otherwise have been during the experimental period.[23] (As expected, the estimated effect on indoor felony rates was much less, only 5 percent.)

The results of the famous Kansas City Preventive Patrol Experiment conducted from 1972–1973 might seem to be counterevidence to the claim that police can deter crime. The experiment consisted of dividing a contiguous fifteen-beat area up into two experimental regions and a control region—preventive patrol was increased substantially in one experimental area, and eliminated in the other. The well-known result that the experimental changes had little or no effect on crime rates cannot be interpreted as a failure in the deterrence process because these changes in preventive patrol activity had no effect on the actual threat level—neither police response time to citizen calls nor the arrest rate differed among the three groups of beats.[24] (In both the twentieth precinct case and the case of saturation police manning of the New York subways, arrest rates increased substantially.)

While few people would have trouble accepting the proposition that large and clearly visible changes in the threat of punishment will influence the incidence of robbery, burglary, and the like, evidence of a strong deterrence effect operating for more exotic types of crime may come as a greater surprise. Yet persuasive evidence is available for draft evasion, airline hijacking, drunken driving, and—perhaps the greatest surprise of all—Prohibition. Each of these is discussed briefly below.

Blumstein and Nagin's recent study of draft evasion during the Vietnam era found that evasion rates were quite responsive to conviction rates. Jurisdictions that took these cases relatively seriously were apparently successful in gaining a higher level of conformity. While draft resistance was an act of strong moral commitment for some, there were apparently many others whose decision was marginal, being subject to change depending on the likelihood of imprisonment.

The virtually complete effectiveness of antihijacking measures instituted in 1973 is taken for granted now, but it serves as an interesting object lesson nonetheless. The number of hijackings dropped from twenty-seven in 1972 to exactly one in 1973, and there have been only ten more from 1974–1976.[25] (All these hijackers were apprehended or killed.) That this crime proved to be deterrable (albeit at high cost) is surprising, given that hijackers are surely a rather desperate group of people.

Ross reports that some experts expressed considerable skepticism during the Parliamentary debates over the British Road Safety Act of 1967.[26] This act established a scientific definition of drunken driving—driving with blood alcohol content in excess of 0.08 percent—in order to overcome the difficulties in obtaining drunken driving convictions under the earlier, vaguer legal standard. The objective of the act was to persuade drivers to stop driving after drinking in order to reduce serious highway accidents. The experts' doubts stemmed from their belief that a large fraction of such accidents involved alcoholics rather than social drinkers and that alcoholics would be very difficult to deter by an increase in the likelihood of punishment (in this case, a mandatory one-year license suspension). Nevertheless, the road fatality rate for October 1967 (the first month the act was in force) was 25 percent below the September rate. Ross presents utterly convincing documentation for his claims that this initial drop was the result of the deterrence effect engendered by the massive publicity effort that attended enactment. Unfortunately, the public's initial illusion that a high fraction of drunk drivers would be caught and convicted under the new law proved to be false, primarily because the police failed to be sufficiently aggressive about enforcing it. The illusion of effective enforcement could not be long sustained in the face of contrary evidence, and Ross reports that the initial deterrent effect had been lost by 1970. In an interesting footnote to this history, Ross recently reported that the deterrence effect was temporarily regained in Cheshire several years ago as a result of a well-publicized order by the chief constable that breathalyzer tests be administered to every driver involved in an accident or traffic violation.[27]

The story of Prohibition is particularly fascinating because of the widespread misimpression that it failed, that "you can't legislate morality." In fact, social historians agree that the early phase of the "Great Experiment" was a smashing success. Burnham reports:

> The decreases from about 1915 to 1920–22 in arrests for drunkenness, in hospitalization for alcoholism, and in the incidence of other diseases, such as cirrhosis of the liver, specifically related to drinking was remarkable. The low point of these indexes came in 1918–1921, and then they climbed again until the late 1920's.[28]

The significance of this pattern in their indexes of alcohol abuse is that Prohibition did not come suddenly with the passage of the Volstead Act in 1919 but was effectively in force several years earlier due to state and local prohibition ordinances that began to be enacted in large numbers starting in 1907. The apparent increase in alcohol consumption during the 1920s has been attributed to the increasing failure on the part of both Congress and many state legislatures to appropriate the funds to finance effective enforcement. Interpreting the initial success of widespread prohibition requires some care. It is not known how much of the reduction in consumption was the result of its direct deterrent effect on the demand for alcohol and how much was due to supply effects: increased price, reduced availability, and uncertain quality. Supply effects on consumption are not properly classified as a "deterrence" effect, in the sense of being a response to the threat of legal punishment. Nevertheless, both the initial success and subsequent failure (due to lack of enforcement) of the Great Experiment are at least compatible with the predictions of the deterrence notion.

Evidence from Correlational Studies

Research on deterrence during the last decade has not been limited to theoretical developments and evaluations of natural experiments. Indeed, there has been a considerable boom in econometric studies relating various sanction measures to crime-commission rates, based for the most part on cross-section data for states, cities, of even precincts within a city. The basic ideas underlying these analyses are straightforward: For a variety of reasons, some jurisdictions are more successful in apprehending and convicting, say, robbers than other jurisdictions. These differences in criminal justice system effectiveness are assumed to be measured with reasonable accuracy by an indicator such as the fraction of robberies that result in conviction and incarceration. Jurisdictions also differ with respect to the average severity of punishment, commonly measured as the average prison term given to convicted criminals. A number of studies using a variety of data sets and crime types have found a negative interjurisdiction correlation between the probability of punishment (as defined above) and crime rates.[29] In some cases, a negative correlation between severity of punishment and crime is also reported. These results are interpreted as evidence that crime rates are indeed responsive to differences in sanction levels. This basic approach has been refined to a considerable degree as this literature has developed: Recent studies control for a number of socioeconomic differences among jurisdictions and also attempt to take account of the fact that crime rates can influence sanction levels as well as vice versa.[30] The results of these studies are estimates of magnitudes that criminal justice planners would love to know. For example, Ehrlich estimated (on the basis of 1960 cross-section data on states) the reduction in the rate of each index crime that would result from specified increase in the average prison sentence given to convicts, and also estimated the crime-rate reductions which would result from an increase in the probability of incarceration.[31] Such information would obviously be relevant to a variety of state criminal justice system planning decisions.

Evaluating this type of correlational study of the relationship between sanction levels and crime was the principal activity of the National Academy of Science's Panel on Research on Deterrent and Incapacitative Effects. The panel's report concluded that these studies were subject to a number of methodological problems, some of them quite serious, and that the published estimates were not to be trusted. "The major challenge for future research is to estimate the magnitude of the effects of different sanctions on various crime types, an issue on which none of the evidence available thus far provides very useful guidance."[32]

Thus the policymaker is left with the problem of taking into account the possible deterrence effects of proposed policy changes without much guidance as to their importance. About all that can be said with confidence is that it would be unwise to disband the police and close the prisons; contrarily, with sufficient effort and budget the criminal justice system could deter a large fraction of drunk driving, subway robberies, and so on. But while the deterrence literature does not provide specific answers to criminal justice policy problems, the deterrence effects of any important policy change should be considered in evaluating the change. A case in point is the recent majority opinion in *Gregg* v. *Georgia,* which noted the inconclusiveness of statistical studies of the deterrent effect of the death penalty, but then asserted:

> We may . . . assume safely that there are murderers, such as those who act in passion, for whom the threat of death has little or no deterrent effect. But for many others, the death penalty undoubtedly is a significant deterrent. There are carefully contemplated murders, such as murder for hire, where the possible penalty of death may well enter into the cold calculus that precedes the decision to act. And there are some categories of murder, such as murder by a life prisoner, where other sanctions may not be adequate.[33]

Incapacitation

Punishment in the form of a prison term serves to incapacitate the inmate as well as provide a warning to potential criminals. That crime rates are reduced by the incapacitation effect of prisons is readily understood and not subject to serious question for most crime types. Deriving estimates of the magnitude of the incapacitation effect is subject to both conceptual and statistical difficulties but is nevertheless more straightforward than estimating deterrence effects. Estimation of these incapacitation magnitudes is a useful exercise because they serve as lower bounds for the *total* preventive effect (including deterrence) of a particular use of imprisonment. It may be possible to justify adoption of a career criminal program, for example, on the basis of the projected incapacitation effects alone, in which case the problem of estimating deterrence effects of the program becomes less important if they are assumed to operate in the same direction. However, most studies of the incapacitation effect have concluded that it is weak. Indeed, if incapacitation were the only preventive effect of prison, then we might be better off to close the prisons entirely or perhaps reserve them for a select few convicts.

The incapacitation effect derived from the incarceration of any one convict can be defined as the crimes he would have committed during his prison term if he had remained free during this period. Several recent studies have attempted to measure what could be called prospective incapacitation effects:[34] the crimes that would have been avoided if some individual or group of individuals who were in fact free had been incarcerated for a specified period. The operational problem in this case is "simply" to measure the number of crimes actually committed by the group in question during the specified period. The only data usually available for this purpose are from arrest records, which of course bear a somewhat shaky relationship to the true crime rate of the group. Greenberg, for example, found that 3–4 percent of arrests for index crimes in California involved people who had been released from prison during the preceding year. He concluded that if one year had been added to every prison sentence in California, the index crime rate would have been reduced by about 3–4 percent through the incapacitation mechanism alone.

A recent cohort study of violent crime defendants in the District of Columbia Superior Court finds a similarly weak prospective incapacitation effect, even from greatly increased use of prison.[35] In practice, only a rather small fraction (about 13 percent) of the 4,000 male violent crime defendants arrested in 1973 were convicted and sent to prison.[36] Yet this cohort accounted for only 12 percent of arrests for violent crime in D.C. during 1974. The implication is that even if *all* the 1973 defendants had somehow been incarcerated during 1974, violent crime rates would have fallen only about 12 percent through incapacitation. (It should be noted that theft crime rates would have fallen also since people arrested for violent crimes are prone to switching among different types of crime.) Some subgroups within this 1973 cohort had much higher than average rearrest rates for violent crime—for example, youthful robbery defendants with prior violence arrest records—and the prospective incapacitation effect appears correspondingly larger for such groups. But the impression remains that even extremely large increases in prison populations would have relatively little effect on crime rates. Cohen estimates that in most states the total prison population would have to increase 10 percent or more to accomplish a 1 percent reduction, through incapacitation, in the rate of index crimes.[37]

Several recent studies have attempted to estimate the total incapacitation effect of the *current* use of prison, what might be called the "status quo incapacitation effect." Unlike the prospective incapacitation studies previously cited, the status quo effect studies must provide an estimate of the hypothetical crime rate of criminals who were in fact incarcerated during some period of time, under the assumption that they had been free during that period. The usual method, not entirely convincing in practice, is to infer this hypothetical crime rate from the observed crime rate of a group that was not incarcerated and that is thought to be comparable in other respects to the incarcerated group of interest. Clarke, for example, studied criminal activity by the 381 juveniles in Wolfgang's Philadelphia cohort (about 10,000 boys born in 1945 who lived in Philadelphia while teenagers) who were incarcerated at least once. Clarke calculates crime rates per "free year" by age and race for this group. By assuming that these crime rates can be applied to measuring the number of crimes averted by any particular spell of incarceration, Clarke derives an estimate of the proportion of serious crimes prevented by the use of training schools during this period. Cohen's refinement of this study yields an estimate that if the training schools had been closed, the number of index arrests would have increased 15–30 percent due to the elimination of the incapacitation effect.

The assumption that incapacitation is the *only* effect of imprisonment is crucial to each of these results. If the threat of prison deters crimes, then the postulated effects of greater or less use of prison would of course be larger, possibly much larger.[38] Indeed, if the deterrence mechanism is effective, it is not even clear how to *define* the incapacitation effect. A simple example serves to illustrate the problem. Assume that under current practice in arresting and sentencing criminals, each criminal commits five crimes per year of freedom. Assume further that if the prisons were closed (and no institutional alternative were created) that each criminal, now relieved of the threat of a prison term, would commit twenty crimes per year. What then is the "total incapacitation effect" of the current use of prison? Should we multiply the current prison population by five or by twenty or by some number in between? Recent studies, by assuming away deterrent effects, use current crime rates (five per year, in the example) as the basis for estimating the incapacitation effect. This procedure is appropriate if the objective is simply to estimate lower bound on the preventive effect of prison. What seems unwarranted is to conclude from incapacitation estimates that prison has only a small impact on crime. The total preventive effect of prison may be a large multiple of the incapacitation effect.

Conclusions on Policy and Policy Evaluation

In my view the most useful effect of the resurgence of interest in the deterrence mechanism during the last decade has been to restore the Benthamite notion of the rational criminal to modern criminology. The idea of the criminal as a rational calculator of costs and benefits is a useful abstraction in several ways. First, it suggests that people who engage in criminal activity are not necessarily that different from the rest of us and in particular are capable of assessing the consequences of their acts and making decisions that are in rough accord with their self-interest. This characterization does not apply to all criminals all the time, but it appears to have wide applicability. Second, it offers useful guidance to criminal justice system planners and others who are concerned with reducing crime. Generally speaking, the implication of viewing criminals as rational is that crime rates can be reduced by increasing the certainty and severity of legal penalties for criminals and by reducing the benefits of crime. Contrarily, it is *not* necessary to reeducate or "cure" criminals, or to restructure society, in order to reduce crime, and that is good news given well-founded doubts about our ability to perform these tasks.

Unfortunately, substantial increases in the certainty and severity of punishment are probably available only at high cost. The use of prison is particularly costly, both in terms of the financial burden on taxpayers and the costs of all kinds suffered by the incarcerated convict. More successful enforcement of the drunk driving laws, with the resulting reduction in the highway fatality rate, may require the police to give breathalyzer tests more frequently than is currently the practice, at some cost to drivers (some of whom will be innocent) who are thus inconvenienced. An extreme case is provided by antihijacking measures; it has been estimated that current airport security measures cost about $6 million for every hijacking that is thereby prevented.[39] There is a real question here of how much crime reduction we can afford or really want. For any particular proposed crime-reduction strategy, the question is whether the magnitude of the expected crime-reduction benefits justifies the costs of implementing the program. Many people feel strongly, for example, that the social costs (broadly construed) of capital punishment are so great that we should abolish its use, even if it can be shown to be a strong deterrent to some potential murderers.[40]

The financial and human costs of incarceration as a means of punishing convicted offenders pose a real dilemma for the criminal justice system policymakers and, ultimately, for the public. This dilemma is resolved in widely differing ways in different jurisdictions and over time; we are much more prone to incarcerate convicts now than in 1973, as reflected in the rapid growth of prison populations in recent years. Even now, however, it is true that only a fraction of the adults convicted of serious crimes are sentenced to jail or prison, and a much smaller fraction of serious juvenile offenders are incarcerated. The first one or two convictions are often essentially "free," with the result that there is little deterrent to people *starting* a career in crime (except possibly the threat of the stigma of conviction). One partial solution to this dilemma would be to institutionalize the use of punishments other than incarceration that would be less costly and more appropriate for serious juvenile offenders or adult first offenders. If most such offenders lack the financial means to pay a fine, the punishment may have to be in terms of mandatory, closely supervised jobs on public projects at an appropriate rate of pay from which the fine would be deducted. I believe that this type of alternative deserves careful consideration by judges and sentencing commissions.

The same theoretical viewpoint that suggests that punishment deters crime also suggests that reducing the benefits to criminal activity will also reduce crime. For example, the large increase in the price of sugar several years ago greatly curtailed moonshining. The proposal to stop cigarette smuggling by equalizing tax rates across states would surely be successful. Arson in decaying neighborhoods could be brought under control by insuring that claims were settled at less than the true market value of burned structures. A well-focused police policy of disrupting fencing activities might take some of the profit out of burglary.[41] These and similar ideas derive their credibility from the view of criminal activity for pecuniary gain as similar in fundamental respects to licit economic activity.

Program Evaluation

The view of criminals as rational and hence potentially responsive to changes in the legal consequences of criminal activity has implications for program evaluation as well as policy design. A crucial consideration in program evaluation is that the deterrence mechanism may produce unintended consequences of programs that are designed with quite different objectives in mind. Consider, for example, the proper evaluation framework for a pretrial-diversion program initiated with the hope of rehabilitating defendants and saving on court processing and costs of correctional supervision. An attractive model for such a program is Vera's Supported Work Experiment, which employed a large number of ex-addicts in public jobs paying good wages and offering a chance to gain valuable work experience in a low pressure environment. A careful evaluation found that the program was successful in reducing criminal activity among participants and concluded on the basis of this and other economic considerations that the program was extremely worthwhile.[42] Note that this evaluation focused on the effects of the program on the participants, which seems appropriate given the nature of the program. If a program such as this were adapted as a dispositional alternative to be used in lieu of probation or as a basis for pretrial diversion, however, the appropriate evaluation framework would have to be expanded to include the possible antideterrent effects of the program. The contingency established by such a diversion program can by phrased as follows: "If you commit a crime and are caught, then you will be placed in a job which is more lucrative and has a better future than would otherwise be available to you." This program would quite literally reward crime and do so with the official approval and support of the state. While it might be successful in reducing criminal activity by participants, the overall crime level might nevertheless be increased by generating an antideterrent effect on the friends and acquaintances of the participants. (Note that the difficulty here is *not* in encouraging defendants or probationers to find jobs and work but rather in giving them special access to good jobs that are not open to nonoffenders.)

The example is hypothetical and may have no actual counterpart in diversion programs currently in effect. But the point concerning the appropriate evaluation framework for a rehabilitation program remains valid. The overall impact of the program on crime rates should be considered, not just the apparent impact on program participants.

This possible conflict between rehabilitation and deterrence has been widely noted. Less apparent is the possible conflict between incapacitation and deterrence. A deterrence-oriented strategy in prosecution and sentencing would have as an objective the maximization of the proportion of defendants who were convicted and punished. Given scarce resources available for prosecution and incarceration, a consequence of such a program would be that the average prison sentences would have to be rather short. If we accept the hypothesis that criminals are more responsive to changes in the likelihood of punishment than to changes in the severity of punishment, however, it makes sense from a deterrence viewpoint to use available resources in this fashion. A strategy designed to maximize the *incapacitation* effect of punishment would look quite different, however. Prosecution and correctional resources would be devoted to identifying those defendants who were most criminally active (as indicated, say, by their prior arrest record, age, and nature of most recent crime), gaining felony convictions for these defendants, and locking them up for a long time. This is precisely the strategy employed in career criminal programs. An appropriate evaluation framework for a career criminal program should then consider any loss in general deterrence that may result from concentrating criminal justice system resources on a relatively few defendants as well as measuring possible gains in incapacitation from this policy.

While it is important to consider deterrent (and antideterrent) effects in evaluating programs, the fact is that the *magnitude* of these effects will be difficult to project on the basis of the empirical deterrence research currently available. Furthermore, for ordinary program innovations that are modest in scope and impact, it will be difficult or impossible to assess the program's net effect on crime even after several years of experience with it. Crime rates are influenced by many factors, and it is exceedingly difficult to assess the influence of any one program unless it is very large and visible such as the British Road Safety Act. I would put forward three recommendations related to these observations:

1. In deciding on whether to adopt a program innovation that may have a deterrent effect, this effect should be guesstimated by thinking carefully about the effect of the program on potential criminals' perceptions of the certainty and severity of punishment and then projecting the deterrent effect of these changes under reasonable assumptions concerning the responsiveness of crime to sanction threat levels. The incapacitation effects can also be projected, and usually with greater precision.

2. In assessing the impact of a program innovation after the fact, it may be much easier to measure the effect on performance measures of the system other than on the crime rate itself. A great deal can often be learned from these performance measures. For example, the fact that intensive preventive patrol in Kansas City neither reduced response time nor increased the arrest rate is very useful information, which would have justified the cost of the experiment even if no information on crime rates had come out of it. The apparent fact that the arrest rate for drunk driving did not increase under the British Road Safety Act foretold and explained the eventual failure of this act and was again very useful information in itself.

3. On relatively rare occasions when a state or local jurisdiction decides to experiment with a really major change in policy—a change in the legal drinking age or a major speeding crackdown or a 50-percent increase in the size of the police force—then there is a good opportunity to do a complete evaluation. Such an evaluation, if done properly, can contribute to the growing fund of knowledge on the preventive effects of punishment and may also serve to demonstrate whether the change was worthwhile.

My overall conclusion? Simply that we are a very long way from replacing common sense with hard scientific findings in predicting the effects of criminal justice system policies. It has been shown conclusively that the threat of punishment is an inhibitor to criminal behavior in a wide variety of circumstances. But that general proposition stops far short of the detailed information useful for decisions about each of the specific programs that constitute criminal justice system policy. And it should not be forgotten that even if we had that information, there would remain some very hard value judgments. There is no good substitute for wisdom.[43]

Notes

1. The long-run effects of CJS activities on socialization, attitudes, and habits may be more important in some sense then short-term deterrence effects, but it is hard to imagine how one would measure such effects. The discussion in this chapter elaborates on the nature of these effects.

2. Philip J. Cook, "The Correctional Carrot: Better Jobs for Parolees," *Policy Analysis* 9 (1)(1975): 11-54. Ann Witte, "Work Release in North Carolina: A Program that Works?," *Law and Contemporary Problems,* 41 (1)(1977).

3. Quoted in Franklin Zimring, and Gordon Hawkins, *The Legal Threat in Crime Control* (Chicago: University of Chicago Press, 1973), p. 75.

4. One possibly important mechanism by which an individual's perceptions of the threat level may be modified is by actually being subjected to a criminal sanction. Actually experiencing a prison sentence may increase the criminal's perception of the severity of this punishment and persuade him that "crime does not pay." It is my impression that it is this possibility of a punishment-induced change in perception of the legal threat to crime that distinguishes the term "special deterrence" from reformation or rehabilitation. It is difficult to distinguish between these mechanisms empirically.

5. The results are not so clear-cut if we ask what effect these changes have on the rate at which people will commit crimes.

6. This segment may be larger than we would like to admit. See Johannes Andenaes, *Punishment and Deterrence* (Ann Arbor: The University of Michigan Press, 1974), p. 20, where he observes "that rape ... is a crime not alien to the normal human personality, can be verified in times of war and occupation. In an occupation army where discipline in this matter is lax, the incidence of rape is commonly high."

7. Michael Block and Robert Lind, "An Economic Analysis of Crimes Punishable by Imprisonment," *Journal of Legal Studies* 4 (1975): 479-492. They observe that "elasticity" is a measure of the responsiveness of one variable to changes in another: In particular, the "elasticity of crime with respect to the severity of punishment" is defined as the percentage change in the crime rate that would result if the severity of punishment were increased by 1 percent.

8. Ibid., p. 489. The authors argue, using the same assumptions, that increasing the variability of sentences reduces the deterrent effect of a given average length of sentence—an argument for determinant sentencing.

9. Jack Gibbs, *Crime, Punishment and Deterrence* (New York: Elsevier, 1975). At p. 68, he uses the terms "habituation," "normative validation," and "enculturation."

10. It should be noted that additional lags may occur if the supply of criminal opportunities is slow to respond to initial changes in the crime rate caused by the change in the threat level. For example, homeowners may respond only slowly to a reduction in the burglary rate. Eventually, they would be expected to reduce their expenditures on self-protection, thus increasing the quality of burglary opportunities, but it is doubtful that this response would occur as quickly as the initial deterrence effect. If these suppositions are correct, then the initial drop in the burglary rate due to the increase in sanction threat will be followed by a partial remission as burglars find that opportunities have become more attractive.

11. J. Andenaes, supra, n.g., p. 124. An interesting bit of evidence is that Reiss and Rhodes, in their study of juvenile delinquency in Nashville, found that the delinquency rate of upper-class boys was heavily influenced by the delinquency rate of the neighborhood in which they lived. Albert Reiss and Albert Rhodes, "The Distribution of Juvenile Delinquency in the Social Class Structure," *Am. Soc. Rev.* 26 (1961): 720.

12. James F. Stephan, *A General View of the Criminal Law of England* (London and Cambridge: Macmillan, 1863).

13. D. Gottfredson, M. Neithercutt, and V. O'Leary, *Four Thousand Lifetimes: A Study of Time Served and Parole Outcomes* (Davis, Calif.: National Council on Crime and Delinquency, Research Center, 1973). It was recently reported that 20 percent of those convicted of homicide in New York City were freed on probation. An additional 59 percent of those convicted of homicides received prison sentences that would make them eligible for parole in three years or less. *New York Times,* 27 January 1975, p. 1, col. 3.

14. J. Andenaes, supra, n.g., p. 59. The "reduction in penalty" that he is hypothesizing in this paragraph is a reduction to "three or four years imprisonment."

15. Heineke Block, supra, n. 7, p. 314. One would suppose that the stigma of being convicted of a crime in a community that generally had respect for the law would be greater than in a community where such respect was lacking, and that community-wide respect for the law would thereby increase the deterrence value of criminal sanctions.

16. J. Andenaes, supra, n.g., 6, p. 316.

17. The simple deterrence effort of sanctions is also weakened to the extent that potential criminals believe that the criminal justice system is prone to punish innocent people. In an extreme case, if the probability of being punished were perceived as unrelated to guilt or innocence, the law would have no deterrent effect.

18. For evidence see Nehemiah, Friedland, John Thibaut, and Laurens Walker, "Some Determinants of the Violation of Rules," *J. Applied Soc. Psych.* 3 (1973): 103. The authors conducted a laboratory experiment to measure the effect on rule violations of the probability and severity of sanc-

tions and the "fairness" of the surveillance methods. Surveillance methods that were perceived as unfair generated a higher rate of rule violations than fair surveillance methods, *ceteris paribus.*

19. Note the error in John Harris, "On the Economics of Law and Order," *Journal of Political Economy* 78 (1970): 165. He assumes that legal safeguards for criminal suspects will increase the supply of criminal offenses, other factors (including the probability and severity of punishment) being equal. The argument should be that such safeguards, if they are viewed as enhancing the legitimacy of the process, will reduce crime if they do not reduce the probability and severity of punishment.

20. Franklin Zimring, "Policy Experiments in General Deterrence, 1970–1975," in *Deterrence and Incapacitation: Estimating the Effects of Criminal Sanctions on Crime Rates,* eds. Alfred Blumstein, Jacquelin Cohen, and Daniel Nagin (Washington, D.C.: National Academy of Sciences, 1978), pp. 140–186. Zimring provides an extremely useful summary of natural experiments in crime prevention taken from recent years, including several cases in which the expected deterrent effect apparently did not emerge.

21. J. Chaiken, Michael Lawless, and Keith Stevenson, "The Impact of Police Activity on Subway Crime," *Urban Analysis* 3 (1974).

22. *New York Times,* 10 October 1973, p. 49, col. 7.

23. S. Press, *Some Effects of an Increase in Policing Manpower in the 20th Precinct of New York City* (New York: Rand Corporation, 1971).

24. G. Kelling, T. Pate, D. Dieckman, and C. Brown, *The Kansas City Preventive Patrol Experiment: A Summary Report* (Washington, D.C.: Police Foundation, 1974).

25. William Landes, "An Economic Study of U.S. Aircraft Hijacking, 1960–1976," *The Journal of Law and Economics* 21 (1978): 336–360.

26. H. Lawrence Ross, "Law, Science, and Accidents: The British Road Safety Act of 1967," *Journal of Legal Studies* 2 (1973): 1–78.

27. H. Lawrence Ross, "Deterrence Regained: The Cheshire Constabulary's 'Breathalyzer Blitz,'" *Journal of Legal Studies* 6 (1977): 241–249.

28. Ross, supra, n. 26, p. 60.

29. Daniel Nagin, "General Deterrence: A Review of the Literature," in Blumstein, et al., supra, n. 20, pp. 95–139. He provides a good summary of the results of those studies.

30. This latter difficulty is called the "identification problem" by econometricians and is perhaps the most serious source of doubt about these studies. See F. Fisher and D. Nagin, "On the Feasibility of Identifying the Crime Function in a Simultaneous Model of Crime Rates and Sanction Levels," in Blumstein, et al., supra, n. 20, pp. 361–399.

31. I. Ehrlich, "Participation in Illegitimate Activities: A Theoretical and Empirical Investigation," *Journal of Political Economy* 81 (1973).

32. Blumstein, et al., supra, n. 20, p. 7. An extensive critique of the

same literature with a similar conclusion is in Philip J. Cook, "Punishment and Crime: A Critique of Current Findings Concerning the Preventive Effects of Punishment," *Law & Contemporary Problems* 41 (1) (1977): 164–204.

33. 428 U.S. 153, 185–186 (1976).

34. Jacqueline Cohen, "The Incapacitative Effect of Imprisonment: A Critical Review of the Literature," in Blumstein, et al., supra, n. 20, pp. 187–243. She provides an extremely useful review and reanalysis of these studies and presents some original results. See also D. Greenberg, "The Incapacitative Effect of Punishment: Some Estimates," *Law and Society Review* 9 (4) (1975): 541–580, and R. Shinnar and S. Shinnar, "The Effect of the Criminal Justice System on the Control of Crime: A Quantitative Approach," *Law and Society Review* 9 (4) (1975): 581–611.

35. Philip J. Cook and Daniel Nagin, *Does the Weapon Matter? An Evaluation of a Weapons Emphasis Policy in the Prosecution of Violent Offenders* (Washington, D.C.: Institute for Law and Social Research, 1978).

36. The 13-percent figure is calculated from 1974 data on the disposition of violent crime arrests. The likelihood of incarceration given arrest ranged from 34 percent for murder to 5 percent for assault, with robbery and rape both at about 20 percent.

37. Her method of deriving these estimates is complex and will not be explained here. States differ widely on this dimension according to the fraction of the criminal population that is already incarcerated. A 10-percent increase in Mississippi's prison population has a much larger proportional effect on crime than a comparable increase in Massachusetts.

38. It should be pointed out that there is also the possibility of a "replacement effect" that works in the other direction. In crimes such as prostitution, drug dealing, and fencing, the incapacitation effect of locking up some criminals may be undercut by the entry of new criminals to take their places. See Cook, supra, n. 32, pp. 169–172, for a fuller discussion of this issue.

39. The estimate is in W. Landes's article.

40. The scientific debate over whether capital punishment has a marginal deterrent effect continues to rage. The major proponent has been Issac Ehrlich, who set off the current debate with his 1975 article. See the review and critique of some of this literature in Lawrence Klein, Brian Forst, and Filatov, "The Deterrent Effect of Capital Punishment: An Assessment of the Estimates," in Blumstein, et al., supra, n. 20.

41. See the interesting analysis in G. Robert Blakey and Michael Goldsmith, "Criminal Redistribution of Stolen Property: The Need for Law Reform," *Michigan Law Review* 74 (1976): 336.

42. Lee Friedman, "An Interim Evaluation of the Supported Work Experiment," *Policy Analysis* 3 (2) (1977): 147–170.

43. Sections of this article first appeared in the author's "Punishment and Crime: A Critique of Current Findings Concerning the Preventive Effects of Punishment," *Law & Contemporary Problems* 41 (1) (1977): 164–204.

Commentary

Ezzat Fattah

The central thesis of Professor Cook's paper is that "deterrence works" and "the threat of punishment does deter a wide variety of crimes." Hence by increasing actual and perceived certainty and severity of punishment, crime can be substantially reduced. Legislators and policymakers would therefore be well advised to make deterrence the primary goal of criminal justice policy. Professor Cook's dismissal of rehabilitation as a failure and his contention that deterrence is the most sensible strategy of crime prevention are in line with the position of many economists who recently have discovered the field of criminology and have enriched the existing literature on deterrence. Professor Cook's stand is also convergent with the current popular ideology of crime control that discredits rehabilitation and stresses the efficacy of criminal sanctions.

Since the state of our knowledge at present does not warrant a categorical acceptance or rejection of the deterrence doctrine, policymakers would be, in my view, on shaky ground if they based their strategy for crime control on the unproven assumption that criminal sanctions are the best available means to deter criminal behavior and to reduce recidivism.

Professor Cook's strong advocacy of deterrence is based on a set of dubious assumptions, and this paper will address three major ones: (1) Criminals are rational decision makers and careful calculators of the costs and benefits of criminal activities; (2) crime is a freely chosen activity; and (3) crime can be prevented if the expected net gain from criminal activities is reduced.

First, it is postulated that criminals are rational decision makers who carefully calculate the costs and benefits of their illegal behavior. They are deterred by the threat of punishment and encouraged by the prospect of differential illegitimate rewards. In Professor Cook's words,

> criminals can be usefully viewed as rational decision makers intent on furthering their personal welfare in an environment that provides crime opportunities coupled with sanction threats.[1]

This is a rephrasing of Ehrlich's claim that offenders, as a group, respond to opportunities (costs and gains) available to them in legitimate and criminal activities in much the same way that those engaged in strictly legitimate activities as a group do.[2]

The suggestion that criminals are rational decision makers is not new. It was made by Beccaria and Bentham when they defended deterrence as the goal of a utilitarian system of punishment. It would of course be preposterous to argue that all criminals are irrational or abnormal in some way. Yet the common-sensical view of man as a rational, hedonistic being endowed with free will is nothing more than a philosophical abstraction that bears no great resemblance to the majority of criminals. The classical view that sees man as a reasonable, sensible being who reflects before he acts, who ponders the consequences of his behavior, and who carefully weighs the potential advantages of his crime against the pain and suffering awaiting him if he is caught is certainly atypical. If man is the rational being behavioral economists suggest he is, why is it necessary to force car drivers to fasten their seat belts by means of criminal legislation? Many criminals are adventure seekers who commit crimes (for the excitement or to feel superior to the law-enforcement machinery. Others are attracted to criminal activities by feelings of guilt and a subconscious desire to be punished. Those who in varying ways are "abnormal" are not governed in their actions by rational considerations of loss or gain.

Economists contend that an effective system of punishment is one that would make criminal activities unprofitable and irrational. But the notions of profitability and rationality are linked to, and dependent upon, the nature and strength of the individual's motives. Since motivations vary considerably in type and intensity, the profitability and rationality of any behavior are both subjective and relative, which poses a formidable obstacle in the way of implementing an economic model of deterrence. On the one hand, it is impossible to institute a punishment that would make a certain behavior appear irrational to all those who may contemplate engaging in that behavior. On the other hand, punishment, mild or severe, is unnecessary to deter those who are not motivated to commit the crime while swift, harsh penalties are unlikely to deter those with a strong urge to do it. That rationality is relative can be easily demonstrated if we examine the criminal offense of rape. Forcible rape is punished by life imprisonment in some states and by death in others. If criminals were rational in the same way those who judge them are, this punishment would certainly be sufficient to eliminate the crime of rape. Judged from our own perspective, the prospect of death or life imprisonment, no matter how improbable or remote it may be, is undoubtedly enough to offset the prospect of a sexual pleasure that lasts only a few minutes. Yet many people are not deterred by the threat, and rape continues to be committed. What punishment then would make this behavior irrational and unappealing to the potential rapist?

Becker's model that served as the starting point for economic studies of deterrence assumed that criminals are motivated by the expected net gain from the use of available resources in criminal activity compared with the expected net gain from the use of the same resources in legitimate activity.[3] When the expected gain from crime is higher than the gain from legitimate activity, individuals can be expected to engage in criminal activity. Economists therefore suggest that an effective crime-prevention policy would increase the cost of crime to those who engage in it, reducing the expected net gain and consequently the amount of crime engaged in. The problem is, the pay-off to any crime is very subjective, and there is no way of objectively measuring it. Since there is no way of objectively assessing the pay-off to a certain crime, how can it be possible to come up with a socially acceptable punishment that is unpleasant enough to offset it? Even when the net gain from the crime is strictly monetary, the subjective value of the same amount varies greatly from person to person. So varies the unpleasantness of the punishment. The same fine does not mean the same financial loss to people of different wealth. Prison for one person can be a highly traumatic experience, while for another it may mean food and shelter. Even death is not regarded by every human being as an undesired or unpleasant occurrence. The matter is complicated further by the fact that what really counts is not the objective probability of punishment but rather the subjective judgment of the risk of being detected, arrested, and convicted. As Zimring puts it:

> Subjective judgments about personal chances of being caught, rather than the cold mathematics of crime, will determine how an individual responds to the threat of consequences—and the relationship between such judgments and objective probabilities is imperfect... . People may underestimate or overestimate the probability that they will be caught because of incomplete information about impunity rates for a particular crime. In addition, factors other than objective probability, such as personal feelings of optimism or pessimism, or propaganda about the chances of apprehension, may play an important role in personal judgments about the element of risk in a specific crime.[4]

Individuals vary considerably in their estimates of the risks of detection, apprehension, and conviction. And yet an economic model of deterrence requires that these subjective estimates be raised to, and maintained at, a level consistent with deterrence. Despite empirical evidence to the contrary, Professor Cook assumes that individuals in the population at risk perceive the salient aspects of existing sanctions more or less accurately. Available studies show that the public, in general, knows very little about either severity or certainty of sanctions. Among the most cited studies is the one undertaken in California in the late sixties at the request of the Assembly Committee on Criminal Procedure.[5] The study found Californians to be extremely ignorant of penalties for crime: Of 11 possible items, the mean score was only 2.6 correct answers. Most people underestimated the severity of current penalties. Because of widespread ignorance of actual sanctions, changes in the severity of sanctions are not likely to have an effect unless they are adequately communicated to the public. It also means that public beliefs about sanctions may in fact be more important than what the sanctions actually are.

Rational calculations of gain and loss that economists deem to be essential if punishment is to act as a deterrent are hindered further by the time factor. As Honderich points out,

> [I]t is a truism that people do not choose between possible courses of action in a prudential way if the possible consequences of one course are distant in time and the consequences of the other immediate. A penalty is a distant possibility; the gain from an offence is usually immediate.[6]

Hell is a terrifying but remote prospect. No doubt, it is this remoteness that makes the threat of hell rather ineffective in deterring people from sin.

Second, another doubtful assumption underlying Professor Cook's arguments is that of "freedom of choice."[7] Cook sees crime as a freely chosen activity and believes that the crime choice in its essential aspects is not unique. In this he concurs with most economists who view criminal behavior as a purposeful, instrumental, and profit-oriented activity. Many crimes are no doubt instrumental and profit oriented, but not all crimes are motivated by the pursuit of pleasure or gain. Crimes against the person are preponderantly expressive, and certain property offenses are committed for motives other than pure financial gain. Vandalism and nonfraudulent arson are two good examples. Professor Cooks argues, however, that "even deviant crimes of sex and violence and noninstrumental crimes such as illicit drug use can be readily analyzed within a framework of economic choices." What about those crimes that are impulsive or compulsive in nature? Could they also be analyzed according to the principles of "economic opportunities" and "freedom of choice"? Could it be said that a rational, reflective decision is made in such cases or that the offender has carefully weighed the risk involved against the actual or potential pay-off? What about those crimes that are committed in the heat of anger, passion, or as a spontaneous response to a sudden arousal or provocation? The behavioral sciences have cast a serious doubt on the assumption of "freedom of choice," which is basic to the doctrine of moral responsibility and that of deterrence. Without subscribing to a totally deterministic view of human behavior, we have to admit that many crimes are produced by endogenous impulses and/or exogenous forces that are not entirely within the control of the offender. One need not be a behavioral scientist to realize that man is not always capable of choosing or controlling his own behavior. The simplistic unnuanced view that man is able to control his behavior in all circumstances overlooks the fact that such ability varies from one person to the other, from one situation to the other, and according to the nature and type of behavior. While the majority of people may be able to control their behavior under normal circumstances, it is doubtful that they will be able to exercise adequate or equal control when under the influence of alcohol, drugs, sexual stimulation, or provocation. All these conditions, and many others as well, pose serious limitations to the effectiveness of deterrence. They mean that if deterrence does work, it is likely to affect only the rational, thoughtful, premeditated behavior of normal people under normal circumstances. The problem is, very few normal people will commit serious, premeditated crimes under normal circumstances! Von Hentig, an early critic of deterrence, has pointed out that usual methods of deterrence proceed from the assumption that (a) men know in every case what is harmful to them; (b) men are in every case frightened by danger; and (c) men realize in every case the correct steps to avoid peril.[8] All these suppositions, writes Von Hentig, assume the behavior of the average man under average conditions of life. In many cases they do not come true, and the exceptions to the rule extend from the psychological or normal stages of nondeterrability to the pathological stages of fearlessness.

Third, Professor Cook suggests that crime rates can be brought down by reducing the benefits of criminal activities through an increase in the certainty and severity of penal sanctions. He argues that the threat of punishment is in effect a government-imposed tax on criminal activity; the higher this tax, the fewer the criminal opportunities that will be deemed worthwhile by potential criminals. It follows that if the punishment is sufficiently severe and the risk of conviction reasonably high, criminals will abandon their illegal activities and switch to legitimate and more profitable ones. The problem is, for most criminals, in particular, professional criminals, it is not possible to switch to any other activity since neither normal job opportunities nor other legal alternatives are available to them. Add to this that raising the penalties substantially for certain crimes may result in some criminals switching to more serious ones. If the punishment for breaking and entering is raised to the same level as that for armed robbery and assuming an equal or similar level of certainty, some professional burglars may turn to bank holdups.

In many countries the penalties for drug trafficking were substantially raised in the hope that drug traffickers would abandon their trade. Despite an accompanying increase in the level of enforcement, the results have been rather disappointing. The higher risk led to a sharp increase in the price of drugs on the illicit market, which made the business more attractive. Not only did the traffickers persist in their trade but the prospects of high profits attracted new elements to the market. Even a seemingly rational activity such as drug trafficking may be enhanced rather than curbed through the institution of higher penalties. One can give countless examples to show that the optimism of many potential offenders is such that no level of objective certainty or severity may be able to overcome it. Many criminals, especially professional criminals, instead of being deterred by the threat of punishment consider it a professional risk in the way a physician considers the risk of contamination, a miner the risk of an accident, or an aviator the risk of a plane crash. No matter how certain the punishment may be, it is still a remote risk. Quite often, an increased level of certainty and severity, instead of deterring, will simply develop a greater sense of caution in the criminal. Rather than refraining from acting, he will try to find better ways and more ingenious methods of evading detection and avoiding punishment. Furthermore, the drive toward the threatened behavior may be so strong and the motivation so powerful that the individual may be willing to risk the consequences regardless of how certain or severe they may be. This is particularly true in the case of compulsive behavior and may partly explain why heavier penalties or stricter law enforcement are not very effective in deterring such behavior.

Moreover, a criminal sanction can be neutralized through a process of rationalization in which the probability of incurring that sanction, its negative aspects, and its harmful consequences are minimized. Man is not a rational being, he is a rationalizing creature. The rationalism that economists ascribe to most criminals and that supposedly will restrain them from violating the law when the illegal behavior is unprofitable may in fact operate the other way round making the behavior appear profitable when actually it is not. In either case, the motivation and the urge to commit the crime rather than the severity or certainty of punishment are the determinant forces behind the decision.

Research on deterrence—in particular, the choice of data, the selection of method, the interpretation of the findings—requires a sound theoretical framework and valid theoretical assumptions. If the framework is unsound or if the assumptions underlying the research are invalid, then the least that can be said about the conclusions is that they are questionable. How else can we explain Hahn's conclusion that

> by using Ehrlich's techniques in a more appropriate manner, one can just as easily derive findings that do not support the hypothesis that executions deter murder, but instead support the hypothesis that increased use of the death penalty *increases* the murder rate, perhaps by providing a brutalizing example for the rest of society.[7]

The growing interest among economists in the study of crime, punishment, and deterrence is certainly to be welcomed. Econometric studies might in the future prove helpful in testing a sophisticated deterrence theory. But it is too early to hail the findings of available studies as providing strong evidence that an increase in the threat of punishment (both certainty and severity) can significantly reduce the amount of crime. Not only are there enormous methodological and data problems to overcome but there is also a great need for a refined theoretical framework. Econometric studies of deterrence have used sophisticated statistical techniques, but they are still based on simplistic notions of human behavior or uncritical assumptions about hedonism and rationalism, and abstract and ideal conceptions of the average man.

Central to all economic models of crime is the belief that the threat of punishment, actual or perceived, is influential (or can be made influential) in the decision whether or not to commit the crime, whether or not to engage in illegitimate activity. This belief is based on common-sense assumptions and conventional wisdom, not on solid empirical evidence or hard scientific facts. Students of criminal behavior know too well that many crimes are prevented or committed independently of the penalties prescribed for them. In economists' discussions of deterrence, it is often overlooked that punishment is not the only operative mechanism of social control but that it acts in conjunction with other social processes and jointly with several other mechanism of inner restraint and social control. In some cases, punishment is not even necessary to curb the incidence of a socially undesirable behavior. For example, I doubt that one can find significant difference in the incidence of incest between culturally similar societies, some of which have criminalized incest, while the others have left it a noncriminalized social taboo.

Economists and criminologists seem to agree that for punishment to be an effective deterrent, its certainty has to reach a minimum level. In many cases, however, it might be infeasible, impractical, or too costly to bring the certainty level of a specific punishment to the point necessary for achieving a reasonable degree of deterrence. We can probably eliminate speeding and many other traffic violations by placing police at every mile of our roads. But this is practically infeasible. The relevant question to the issue of deterrence is not whether deterrence is theoretically possible but whether it is practically feasible and whether it can work effectively within reasonable, economical, and practically attainable levels of certainty and severity. No one denies that punishment deters *some* people, in *some* situations, *some* of the time, from *some* crimes. But this is not the point. The point is whether an increase in the actual (or perceived) probability of punishment and above all whether an increase in the actual (or perceived) severity would, as economists claim, lead to a substantial reduction in crime, provided the opportunities for crime remain unchanged.

Behavioral psychologists have shown through laboratory experiments that punishment administered under certain conditions can be an effective technique to suppress and control behavior. However, laboratory conditions necessary for the effectiveness of punishment, in particular, the contingency between response and punishment, are very different from conditions under which criminal punishments are currently administered by the legal system. Moreover, laboratory studies show that the ideal punishment situation (that is, a situation in which the misbehavior is invariably detected and reliably evokes appropriate and immediate punishment) is probably one that can never be achieved in actual life. We know therefore that punishment deters. We need no proof that it does. What we need to know is who is deterred from what, by what, under what conditions? We need no evidence that deterrence works in *some* circumstances, but we need to find ways to make it work in *most* circumstances. We need not argue about the principle of deterrence but about the complexities of deterrence, not why it works, but why in many cases it does not work. We need to find ways to overcome the limitations of deterrence and to make it effective, practical, economical, and humane.

Professor Cook buttresses his arguments about deterrence by citing evidence from natural experiments and from correlational studies of deterrence. But a careful look at the results of the experiments and the findings of the studies shows that they lend themselves to interpretations other than the one providing support for the deterrence hypothesis.

If the efficacy of deterrence is highly dependent on the probability of punishment, then such efficacy will vary widely with changes in certainty brought about by variations in law enforcement: Strict enforcement of the law will enhance deterrence while lax application of the law will weaken it. Proponents of deterrence are always quick to refer to waves of crime taking place in situations of police immobilization and in periods of police strike as well as to reduced crime rates resulting from experiments of stricter law enforcement, as a proof of deterrence. But the matter is not that simple because those same situations, aside from producing changes in the level of certainty of punishment, do create other conditions conducive or aversive to the commission of certain crimes. Police immobilization such as the Danish experiment and police strikes are invariably accompanied by improved chances of criminal–goal attainment. Police crackdowns and stricter law enforcement, on the other hand, always result in fewer criminal opportunities and reduce the criminal's chances of successfully completing his crime. To my knowledge, no study has treated those conditions as distinct from that of increased or reduced certainty or has attempted to separately assess their impact on crime rates. In fact, researchers seem to confuse the fear of punishment with the fear of failure and to treat them as if they were one and the same. Yet a subtle distinction has to be made between the two. If a potential criminal refrains from committing a crime be it a burglary, theft, robbery, or rape because he has doubts about the possibility of achieving his goal, because of lack of the right opportunity, or because the target has been hardened through an antitheft device, an armed guard, or a watchful dog, this can hardly be ascribed to the success of deterrence or used as evidence that the threat of punishment is effective. When at the sight of an armed guard ready to foil his plans and make it impossible for him to obtain the money he wants, a potential robber turns away from the bank he intended to hold up, it cannot be said that the crime was prevented by the threat of punishment. The looting that takes place in a city during a blackout or during a police strike cannot be solely attributed to a reduced level of certainty of punishment since at the same time the number of available opportunities is increased and so are the criminals' chances of achieving their goals. The higher incidence of arson during strikes by firemen is not due to any changes in the certainty or severity of punishment. On the other hand, the decrease in certain crimes during experiments of saturation policing cannot be attributed only to a heightened fear of arrest and punishment. Part of the decrease is no doubt a result of growing skepticism among many potential criminals as to the feasibility of attaining their goal. There are even serious doubts that crime rates go down at all as a result of saturation policing since the observed decrease may simply be a matter of geographical displacement. It is no surprise that the police currently prefer prevention programs aimed not at raising the level of enforcement but at hardening the targets. Programs such as "operation identification" are meant to dissuade potential criminals from stealing marked property not by increasing the probabilities of arrest but by making it more difficult for them to dispose of the stolen property.

Some proponents of deterrence confuse the effect of physical deterrents with that of legal deterrents. Professor Cook cites "the virtually complete effectiveness of antihijacking measures instituted in 1973" to prove that this particular crime is deterrable. He forgets that airport security measures, which effectively curbed the incidence of skyjacking, were not aimed at increasing the certainty of punishment but to make it more difficult for potential hijackers to seize the planes. It is a good illustration of cases in which physical deterrents may succeed where legal deterrents have failed.

Experiments to deter drunken driving through legal sanctions, the most famous of which is the British Road Safety Act of 1967, have not been very successful in the long run. The reductions in crashes, injuries, and lives lost produced by the legislation are usually short lived, and the immediate effect of the legislation gradually vanishes once the initial shock wears off. If the deterrent effect of punitive sanctions is as effective as its proponents claim it to be, why is it then that it does not have long-lasting or everlasting effects? The challenge to researchers is to find out why the initial success is reducing the undesirable behavior is always temporary even when enforcement and publicity are maintained at high levels.

In 1973 Robertson, Rich, and Ross used the interrupted time series to study the effect on fatalities in Chicago of the highly publicized use of seven-day jail sentences as a countermeasure against driving while intoxicated during the winter and spring of 1971.[10] Arrests and processing of cases were also examined. The authors concluded that the change in motor-vehicle fatalities that occurred during the Chicago crackdown on drivers convicted of driving while intoxicated was only a chance variation from the fatality rate over the preceding five years. They also concluded that if the publicity received by the crackdown was effective in reaching those who subsequently were involved in fatal crashes, then the punitive threat of seven-day jail sentences did not deter them from getting into crashes. This finding led the authors to suggest that a strictly punitive approach to persons convicted of driving while intoxicated and persons involved in crashes after excessive drinking is not likely to be successful in deterring many of these persons from repeat performances.

L.H. Ross reports that the widespread belief that tougher laws against drunken driving in Sweden and Norway have been effective deterrents is not supported by available evidence.[11] Analysis of the arguments in favor of the deterrent hypothesis showed them to be weak and unconvincing. Ross then applied interrupted time-series analysis to series of motor-vehicle casualty data from the two countries. According to the deterrence hypothesis, casualty data would be expected to show changes corresponding to the initiation of the legal reforms in question. The expectations were not fulfilled and the data failed to support the deterrence hypothesis.

The story of Prohibition is probably the worst example that can be cited in support of the deterrence proposition. It is well known that the experiment was a dismal failure and that compliance with Prohibition laws, in particular, to the dispositions pertaining to the possession and consumption of alcohol, was very low. The unavailability of alcoholic beverages on the licit market resulted in much higher prices, which in turn made alcohol unaffordable to a large number of people and forced others to cut down on the quantities they imbided. The beneficial effects, namely, the decrease in arrests for drunkenness, in hospitalization for alcoholism, in cirrhosis of the liver were in all likelihood the result of a forced decrease in consumption and not of a widespread compliance with the law out of fear of punishment.

In support of his arguments about deterrence, Professor Cook also quotes evidence from correlational studies, in particular, econometric studies that related various sanction measures to crime-commission rates. On the one hand, he seems to be of the opinion that those studies provide some "evidence that crime rates are indeed responsive to differences in sanction levels." On the other hand, he seems to agree with the conclusion of the Panel of the National Academy of Science that "those studies were subject to a number of methodological problems, some of them quite serious, and that the published estimates were not to be trusted."

Professor Cook's position vis-a-vis incapacitation seems to be one of healthy skepticism. He has doubts that a criminal policy based on incapacitation would substantially reduce rates, and he justifiably believes that "even extremely large increases in prison population would have relatively little effect on crime rates." He points to the astronomical costs of an effective strategy of incapacitation in terms of money and human suffering. More important still is the real danger that incapacitation may be counterproductive. We have some empirical evidence showing that, other things being equal, those sent to prison will recidivate more often than those given conventional, noninstitutional sentences. For various reasons, incarceration may have the effect of raising postrelease criminal activity of the offender to a much higher level than it would normally have been had he not been incarcerated. A higher postrelease recidivism rate may therefore offset or counterbalance any reduction in crime produced by the incapacitation effect of incarceration.

Professor Cook's position regarding rehabilitation is more problematic. Surely the grave doubts that still exist concerning the deterrent efficacy of punitive sanctions are in no way less serious than those that currently surround the efficacy of rehabilitation. Yet Professor Cook is willing to accept the former and to reject the latter as the ultimate goal of criminal justice.

To summarize, it can be safely concluded that the available evidence does not warrant an affirmative conclusion regarding deterrence; neither does it warrant a categorical rejection of the deterrence doctrine. Statements to the effect that "punishment deters," that "reducing the benefits to criminal activity will reduce crime," or that "increasing certainty and severity of punishment will enhance its deterrent effect" are axiomatic. Declarations such as "it has been shown conclusively that the threat of punishment is an inhibitor to criminal behavior in a wide variety of circumstances" can hardly be of any help to legislators or policymakers. Economists can greatly contribute to existing knowledge about deterrence and can greatly help policymakers if they tell us, for instance, how severity and certainty of punishment can be reconciled. Empirical evidence points to an inverse relationship between the two variables with increased severity inevitably leading to reduced certainty. They should tell us whether reducing the benefits of certain activities does in fact decrease the total volume of crime or whether it simply results in technical displacement with criminals switching from less profitable criminal activities to more profitable illegitimate ones.

Conflicting views and contradictory research findings on deterrence do indicate that there is a great need for a sophisticated theory of deterrence, a theory capable of explaining the differential reactions to the threat of sanctions, and the variations in the effectiveness of punishment from one offense to the other and from one situation to the other. Because in all probability, deterrence is irrelevant to the bulk of the population, to the mass of people who have interjected the moral norms of society and who do not commit crimes not because of the threat of sanctions but because their self-concepts, their moral and religious convictions, will not permit them to do so. As Toby said, it is the socialization process that keeps most people from committing crimes, not the police.[12]

The notion that every crime can be deterred by the right punishment and that every individual can be deterred from any crime if severity and certainty of punishment are maintained at an optimal level is simply fallacious, and even more so in our system of justice where this optimal level can never be attained. We had better accept the fact that some people will not commit the crime regardless of how mild or uncertain the punishment may be. Others will commit the crime regardless of how severe and certain the punishment is. A third group (the marginal group, as Hawkins calls it) might be deterred if severity and certainty are adjusted to the right level.[13]

The problem is that this optimal level varies infinitely depending on the individual, the offense, and the situation and that it is totally impossible to translate it into a legislation of general applicability. Since a separate deterrence model for every offense is obviously infeasible, the task of legislators is not easy. Legislators and policymakers are faced with a dilemma: Should they opt for a policy of harsher penalties and lengthy prison sentences despite the financial and human costs involved in the hope of deterring some individuals who otherwise might not be deterred, or should they opt for milder, less costly penalties at the risk of failing to deter some individuals who otherwise would have been deterred? Economists seem to lean toward the former strategy; criminologists should advise policymakers to opt for the latter.

Notes

1. P.J. Cook, "The Implications of Deterrence and Incapacitation Research for Policy and Policy Evaluation," paper prepared for presentation at the Criminality Colloquium organized by the Indiana Lawyers Commission, Indianapolis, September 1978. See chapter 4.
2. I. Ehrlich, "The Deterrent Effect of Criminal Law Enforcement," *Journal of Legal Studies* 1 (2) (1972): 259–276.
3. G.S. Becker, "Crime and Punishment: An Economic Approach," *Journal of Political Economy* 76 (1968): 169–217.
4. E.F. Zimring, *Perspectives on Deterrence* (Washington, D.C.: U.S. Government Printing Office, Center for Studies on Crime and Delinquency, National Institute of Mental Health, 1971).
5. California Assembly Office of Research, *Deterrent Effects of Criminal Sanctions*, Sacramento, Progress Report of the Assembly Committee on Criminal Procedure, 1968.
6. T. Honderich, *Punishment: The Supposed Justifications* (Middlesex: Penquin Books, 1971), p. 56.
7. P.J. Cook, supra, n. 1.
8. H. von Hentig, "The Limits of Deterrence," *The Journal of Criminal Law and Criminology* (1938): 551–561.

9. R.G. Hann, *Deterrence and the Death Penalty: A Critical Review of the Economic Literature* (Ottawa: Ministry of the Solicitor General of Canada, 1977), p. 3.

10. L.S. Robertson, R.F. Rich, and H.L. Ross, "Jail Sentences for Driving While Intoxicated in Chicago: A Judicial Policy that Failed," *Law and Society Review* 8 (1973): 55–59.

11. H.L. Ross, "Scandinavian Myth: The Effectiveness of Drinking and Driving Legislation in Sweden and Norway," *Journal of Legal Studies* 4 (1976): 285–310.

12. J. Toby, "Is Punishment Necessary? *Journal of Criminal Law, Criminology and Police Science* 55 (1964): 332–337.

13. G. Hawkins, "Deterrence: The Problematic Postulate," *Australian and New Zealand Journal of Criminology* 2 (1969): 132–148.

Part II
Criminal Process

5 The Police: An Important Substantive Policy-Making Agency of Government

Frank Remington

Over the past twenty years, the importance of discretionary decisions made by American police has been increasingly recognized. Before that time there was a widespread uncritical acceptance of the myth that police are ministerial officers whose job it is to fully enforce the law.[1] The reality that police do in fact make important discretionary decisions was initially documented in detail in the important American Bar Foundation Survey of the Administration of Criminal Justice in the United States,[2] particularly in the book *Arrest* by LaFave[3] and in Goldstein's provocative article,[4] which was stimulated by the initial drafts of the Bar Foundation reports. In the past decade or so recognition of the importance of police discretion has become increasingly common.

For a time it seemed that this increased recognition of the importance of police discretion would lead to the development and implementation of written law-enforcement policies relating to the substantive responsibilities of the police, particularly local police agencies.

The American Bar Association (ABA) and the International Association of Chiefs of Police approved *Standards Relating to the Urban Police Function,* which recommends:

> Police discretion can best be structured and controlled through the process of administrative rule-making by police agencies. Police administrators should, therefore, give the highest priority to the formulation of administrative rules governing the exercise of discretion, particularly in the areas of selective enforcement....[5]

By "selective enforcement" was meant the extent to which police would or would not invoke a criminal statute such as battery in responding to a social problem such as intrafamily violence.

In the introduction to the ABA police function volume, Chief Justice Burger is quoted as saying:

> It is often overlooked that no public officials in the entire range of modern government are given such wide discretion on matters dealing with the daily lives of citizens as are police officers. ... [W]e must recognize that we need not choose between no guidelines at all and perfect guidelines. There must be some guidance by way of basic concepts that will assist the officer in these circumstances.

> Basically, as I suggested, it is a matter of common sense and sound judgment, and yet we know that one man's common sense may be another man's mistake. Hence this need for carefully devised basic standards to guide the exercise of this discretion . . . .[6]

It seems apparent that by "common sense and sound judgment," the Chief Justice was referring to the manner in which police respond to important social problems that they confront, problems such as intrafamily violence.

More recently the administrative law section of the ABA adopted the following resolution:

> American police are typically confronted with a wide range of conduct which calls for exercise of police discretion, including decisions as to whether or not to act on a problem at all, whether to rely on the criminal justice system or on some alternative such as a mental health system or a detoxification program, and whether to act against all or only some violators.
>
> We recommend:
>
> 1. That top officers in each department should generally lay down the main lines of policy through rules.
>
> 2. That the rules should be open to the public unless some special reason requires concealment of a particular rule.
>
> 3. That the rules should in general be formulated with the assistance of qualified professional staffs, except that departments may copy and adapt rules formulated by other departments or by study groups.
>
> 4. That in absence of special reason for not doing so, each department should ordinarily prepare proposed rules on the basis of staff studies, publish them, invite written comments from any member of the public, revise on the basis of the comments, and then publish the final rules.
>
> 5. That rules should govern policy, but that each rule should leave room for whatever individualizing by a particular officer may be needed.
>
> 6. That a patrolman should not have discretion about overall enforcement policy but should have discretion to do the needed individualizing in applying the policy embodied in the rules to the facts and circumstances of each particular case.[7]

Again it seems evident that the administrative law section has in mind substantive policy making; that is, policies with respect to how police respond to problems they confront, including the extent to which a criminal statute will or will not be enforced under certain circumstances.

Some police departments and some national groups have tried to develop policies to guide and control the exercise of law-enforcement discretion.[8] However, almost all the efforts to date limit their attention to means or methods rather than substantive law-enforcement objectives.[9] The policies that have been developed deal frequently with the issue of the use of deadly force and somewhat less frequently with issues such as the stopping and questioning of suspects, the search of vehicles, and the use of identification procedures.[10] Almost no effort has been made to develop substantive policies such as a departmental policy with respect to the police response to instances of intrafamily violence (or juvenile vandalism or shoplifting or residential burglary or other substantive responsibility of police).[11]

Illustrative is a recent project in which the Boston Police Department prepared guidelines for Boston police officers.[12] The objectives included investigative procedures such as search, arrest, and identification procedures and substantive programs, particularly the department's response to the narcotics problem. The guidelines for investigative procedures have been prepared and published. The guidelines on the narcotics program were never prepared.

There are exceptions to this general picture, although they are rare. One current exception is the Madison, Wisconsin, Police Department, which has just formed four teams to deal with the problems of juvenile alcohol abuse, business crimes, traffic law enforcement, and sexual assault.[13] The objective of each team includes the development of a written policy with respect to the police response to the particular problem dealt with.

The prevalent failure to develop written policies with respect to substantive objectives is explainable in large part because there are lingering doubts, on the part particularly of lawyers, as to whether substantive policy making by police is lawful, desirable, or of practical significance.[14]

All agree that police do in fact often decide whether certain criminal laws are to be enforced at all or, if enforced, the extent to which they are to be enforced.[15] Most agree that it would be preferable for the legislature to decide all the important substantive policy issues, leaving to police only the task of applying the legislation to the particular facts.[16] This would be consistent with a basic commitment of our society that ours is a government of law, not of individuals. But there is also agreement that legislatures have neither the inclination nor the capacity to decide all the important policy issues, and that therefore the necessity will remain for police to exercise an important policy judgment in deciding what laws to enforce under what circumstances.[17]

There is disagreement as to whether it is desirable for police to deal openly with substantive law-enforcement issues by a process of administrative policy making. There is support for doing so from the ABA Standards Relating to the Urban Police Function, the ABA administrative law section of the Association, and many who have written on the subject.[18] There is, however, dissent from some writers[19] and from some practitioners such as many district attorneys who argue that it is undesirable as a matter of policy for police to make general policy decisions about which laws are to be enforced and to what degree.[20]

There is even greater disagreement as to whether it is legally proper for police to engage in substantive policy making, the way economic regulatory agencies do. In a recent thorough and thoughtful article, Allen argues that it is not lawful for police to adopt substantive enforcement policies by means of a process of administrative rule making.[21] Davis, on the other hand, argues persuasively that it is lawful for police to make substantive enforcement policies by means of rule making.[22]

The Circumstances in which Police May Adopt Substantive Enforcement Policies

Although it is now widely recognized that police commonly exercise discretion in the enforcement of the substantive criminal law, there remains no clear answer to the question of whether the exercise of that discretion can legally be guided or controlled by the adoption of substantive enforcement policies on a department-wide basis. There has been widespread content with the myth of full enforcement—the assumption that police ought not to decide substantive enforcement issues. For legislatures, courts, and the community generally, the myth of full enforcement is consistent with the principle that ours is a government of law and not individuals. For the police administrator it avoids the very difficult questions that would have to be dealt with in the development of substantive enforcement policies; and for the individual police officer, it allows him to in fact exercise discretion when necessary but not be accountable to departmental policy in doing so.

Discontent with the myth of full enforcement appears, however, to be increasing. Minority communities have long been aware of the importance of police discretion and, during the 1960s, expressed a great deal of frustration over their inability to find out what policies were being followed and over the inability to discuss the propriety of those policies.[23] More recently the women's rights movement has focused attention on the fact that police do not fully enforce the battery statute in intrafamily violence cases, even when the evidence and resources are adequate.[24] Unlike the minority community, women have the political power to have their voices heard and their views taken into account.

The question of whether police administrators can deal openly with substantive law-enforcement issues seems likely to be raised with increasing frequency.[25] Thoughtful police administrators are beginning to realize that the myth of full enforcement is an impediment to careful reevaluation and improvement in the quality of police programs.[26] The question of whether the police administrator can lawfully develop and enforce substantive law-enforcement policies is important and deserves an answer.

Legislative Expectations of the Proper Function of Police

It has been commonly assumed that legislatures intend that police should enforce all criminal statutes whenever available evidence and available resources make it feasible to do so. This position is effectively stated in a recent article by Allen. He bases his conclusion in large part on so-called full-enforcement legislation, which he says "consistently purports to deny police the discretion not to invoke the criminal law."[27]

The difficulty is that legislatures have not acted as if they really expected or desired full enforcement. Legislatively enacted criminal statutes can be classified in at least three groups.

First, statutes such as the common gambling statute are drafted to cover a great deal more conduct than the legislature intends to be subject to enforcement. When legislators are told that a proposed statute would make criminal a wide variety of conduct such as flipping for a cup of coffee or playing bridge for a hundredth of a cent a point, the usual legislative response is that one can assume that police will use common sense.[28] In fact, the legislative purpose seems clearly to be to give broad authority to police to deal with serious forms of gambling, primarily commercial gambling. A law-enforcement policy that provided for enforcement only in cases of commercial gambling would be consistent with the legislative purpose. A policy (whether formal or informal) of fully enforcing the gambling law would in fact be contrary to the legislative purpose and in this sense unlawful. Thus when striking or otherwise disgruntled police officers fully enforce statutes of this type (traffic laws, for example), they are in a real sense perverting the legislative purpose.

A second category of statutes are those as to which there is a clear legislative purpose to have full and uniform enforcement. This seems evidently true with respect to very serious crimes such as murder, armed robbery, or rape. But it is also true with respect to less serious offenses such as those requiring that taverns close at a prescribed hour, reflecting a legislative purpose to have a state-wide, uniform closing hour rather than a situation in which the closing time is locally decided.[29] The failure of police to enforce these statutes when evidence and resources are adequate would be clearly contrary to the legislative purpose.

There is a third category of statutes in which the legislative purpose is unclear. This is unfortunately a characteristic of a substantial percentage of criminal statutes. For example, it is not evident that a legislature intends that the common battery statute be enforced in every case of minor bodily contact without consent, even though the language of the statute is broad enough to cover this kind of bodily contact.[30] In fact, a legislative desire for full enforcement may not be evident even in the case of a more serious injury such as occurs frequently in cases of intrafamily violence. Although it may be perfectly clear that the conduct of a husband violated the criminal battery statute, the legislature may have also provided for emergency detention or civil commitment for those whose alcoholism or mental illness is manifested by recent dangerous overt acts or may have provided shelter facilities for the wife and children. Legislatures are obviously aware that they have created alternative responses to a wide variety of conduct, some of which has already been defined as criminal. It is possible, for example, that a legislature intends that the authority to detain a mentally ill person on an emergency basis is to be used only where the conduct of the person is not in violation of a criminal statute. Much more likely is a legislative purpose to allow emergency detention of the mentally ill as an alternative to an arrest for disorderly conduct, battery, or other offense that may have been committed.

Although legislative alternatives are frequently provided, the legislature seldom indicates which alternative should be used in a given situation. Whether the legislature has deliberately left the choice to the police is unclear. What is clear, however, it that an uncritical assumption that there must be full enforcement of all criminal statutes would not serve the legislative objective.

The only conclusion that seems clearly supportable is that legislatures have on occasion wanted their proscriptions to be fully enforced; on other occasions have wanted police to use common sense in deciding whether to enforce the statute; and on most occasions have given no very clear indication of what, if anything, was intended at the time of the enactment of a particular criminal statute. As a consequence, it is not surprising that there exist widely differing perceptions of what police are expected to do. For example, the administrative law section of the ABA asserts:

> American police are typically confronted with a wide range of conduct which calls for exercise of police discretion, including decisions as to whether or not to act on a problem at all, whether to rely on the criminal justice system or on some alternative such as a mental health system or a detoxification program, and whether to act against all or only some violators.[31]

Allen, on the other hand, says that the police function is:

> [To] enforce prohibitions articulated by the legislature. We do not say to the police: "Here is the problem. Deal with it." We say: "Here is a detailed code. Enforce it." ... The purpose of the police ... is not regulation of deviant behavior; it is enforcement of legislative proscriptions.[32]

In fact, neither position accurately reflects the legislative purpose on all occasions. No legislature has acted with that degree of consistency.

There are, in fact, situations in which the enactment of a criminal statute is a mandate to enforce the statute whenever it is possible to do so. This assumption is valid with respect to the traditional serious crimes such as murder, robbery, and rape. As to these offenses, Allen is undoubtedly right in asserting, "We do not say to the police: 'Here is a problem. Deal with it.' We say: 'Here is a detailed code. Enforce it.'"

In other situations the legislature has enacted statutes with no expectation of full enforcement; in fact, with the expectation that the criminal statute would be used only when to do so constitutes an effective response to the social problem being dealt with. This appears obvious with respect to broadly worded statutes such as disorderly conduct and also, though somewhat less clearly, with respect to statutes such as the battery statute. As to these offenses, the administrative law section is right in urging that police confront problems that require police to make choices, including a choice as to whether to enforce a particular criminal statute such as the disorderly conduct or the battery statute.

Judicial Reactions to Substantive Policy Making by Police

Because police administrators have not developed substantive enforcement policies, courts have not been required to confront the issue of the legal authority of the police administrator to do so.

There are obvious doctrinal problems that confront the proponent of police policy making. These are thoroughly discussed in the recent article by Allen.[33] In addition to the obstacle presented by common full-enforcement statutes, substantive policy making by police would, Allen argues, constitute an unconstitutional delegation of legislative authority to an administrative agency and would violate the constitutional requirement of separation of powers.[34] The doctrinal difficulties lead Allen to conclude that police cannot legally adopt substantive enforcement policies where such policies provide for nonenforcement of a criminal statute unless the nonenforcement results from lack of evidence or lack of sufficient enforcement resources.

It is possible to rationalize a program of police policy making in a way that avoids the difficult doctrinal issues. Experienced police administrators have commonly explained policies of nonenforcement on the basis of lack of adequate evidence or adequate law-enforcement resources. Courts have accepted this as an appropriate rationale:

> Furthermore, the amount of protection afforded by any individual police department is necessarily determined by the resources available to it. The

> determination of how these resources can most effectively be used is a legislative-executive decision.[35]

Although in reality unavailability of evidence and unavailability of resources are important, neither explain a great deal of prevalent police practice such as the failure of police to enforce the gambling statute against minor types of social gambling or the choice by a police officer of a referral of a husband to a mental-health facility or the wife to a shelter facility rather than making an arrest for a battery to the wife. The explanation of the nonenforcement against some common forms of social gambling is that no one, including the legislature, wants enforcement. The explanation of the use of alternatives to arrest in the case of the battery to a wife may be less clear, but in some situations the use of an alternative to arrest results in a more effective response to intrafamily violence than would an unthinking enforcement of the battery statute.

The problem is more than a semantic one. If the reason for nonenforcement against social gambling is lack of resources, then it follows that it is appropriate to enforce whenever resources are available. And, if the reason for using a shelter facility rather than an arrest in an intrafamily violence case is lack of evidene or resources, it follows that arrests should be made when evidence and resources are available. To make enforcement against social gambling in a given situation dependent on whether resources are adequate to make an arrest seems a clearly inappropriate basis for making the decision. And although adequacy of evidence and adequacy of resources are important considerations in deciding whether to arrest, to refer to a mental-health agency, or to take the wife to a shelter facility, those decisions ought also to involve careful consideration of which of the alternatives is the most effective response to the particular instance of intrafamily violence.

Recent indications are that courts do recognize that it is a gross oversimplification to assume that the function of police is to fully enforce the law except where insufficient evidence or resources prevent them from doing so. For example, the New York Court of Appeals recently said:

> The role of the police in our society is a multifaceted one. On the one hand the police are mandated to enforce the law ... . On the other hand, and more important, we must recognize the multiplicity and complexity of tasks assumed by the police. As public servants, the police perform the lion's share of services expected of local government. Among other functions, the police in a democratic society are charged with the protection of constitutional rights, the maintenance of order, the control of pedestrian and vehicular traffic, the mediation of domestic and other noncriminal conflicts and supplying emergency help and assistance ... .

Recognition that police do more than "enforce the law" inevitably leads to the conclusion that police often must choose whether to enforce the criminal statute or to utilize an alternative response. The court of appeals for the state of Washington has said that police

> Engage in the resolution of conflict such as that which occurs so frequently between husband and wife . . . without reliance upon criminal assault or disorderly conduct statutes. These . . . reflect our views on the discretionary nature of the police function as it pertains to use of the criminal process in handling domestic controversies.[37]

A New York court dealing also with the problem of intrafamily violence has said:

> Plaintiffs do not seek to abolish the traditional discretionary powers of the police; they merely seek to compel the police to exercise their discretion in each "particular situation" and not to automatically decline to make an arrest solely because the assaulter and his victim are married to each other.... .
>
> This court has the power to compel the police department defendants to perform the duty imposed upon them by law to exercise their discretion, and to exercise it in a reasonable, non-arbitrary manner.[38]

Had the New York court thought it proper, it could easily have said that the duty of police is to enforce the appropriate assault or battery statute whenever there is sufficient evidence to make an arrest. Instead the court assumed it appropriate for police to be given a choice between arrest and other alternatives, but subject to the requirement that the choice be made in "a reasonable, non-arbitrary manner."

It would probably be possible for a legislature to draft a spousal battery statute that specifically provided for situations in which an arrest of the offending spouse should be made. It would have to specify the seriousness of the injury to avoid *de minimus* situations and also to specify when alternatives such as emergency mental commitment or shelter facilities should be relied on rather than making an arrest. Instead of a fairly short, generally worded battery statute, there would be a long specifically worded provision providing when an arrest should be made. The problem lies in the difficulty of the legislature's doing this. Whatever the desirability, the history to date has been that legislatures are incapable of dealing with all social problems with the degree of care and specificity that would make possible a ministerial application of the statute to the variety of factual situations that arise.

Courts have insisted on some degree of legislative specificity to minimize the risk of arbitrary implementation. This was of obvious concern in *Papachristou*:

> Where, as here, there are no standards governing the exercise of discretion granted by the ordinance, the scheme permits and encourages an arbitrary and discriminatory enforcement of the law.[39]

If opportunity for arbitrary enforcement were limited to ambiguous statutes, the solution would be to be more precise in the specification of the conduct that comes within the statutory prohibition. The difficulty is that room for arbitrary enforcement equally exists in statutes that are clear but whose broad scope is such that it covers a wide range of conduct from the more to the less serious and, in consequence, is likely not always to be equally enforced. Reference to this was made by the U.S. Supreme Court in a footnote in *Spence* v. *Washington*, which involved a broad but unambiguous flag–misuse statute. In a footnote to the *per curiam* opinion:

> Statutes of such sweep suggest problems of selective enforcement. We are, however, unable to agree with appellant's void–for–vagueness argument... . The law in Washington, simply put, is that *nothing* may be affixed ... on a United States flag... . Thus, if selective enforcement has occurred, it has been a result of prosecutorial discretion, not the language of the statute.[40]

Certainly, broadly worded statutes such as the gambling or battery statutes do more than "suggest problems of selective enforcement." In fact, they are, perhaps with rare exceptions, selectively enforced. What ought the court's response be to the issue thus created? There are alternatives, as follow.

The legislatures could be required to revise all broadly defined statutes so that their scope is precisely limited to situations in which the legislature does in fact want full enforcement. The chance that this will be done is at best remote.

Or courts could hold all broadly worded statutes unconstitutional, at least whenever there is reason to believe that the broad statute is selectively enforced. This has been done when the broad statute creates a threat to constitutionally protected rights. In his opinion in *Gregory* v. *City of Chicago,* Justice Black said:

> [W]e have been careful to point out that the Constitution does not bar enactment of laws regulating conduct, even though connected with speech, press, assembly and petition, if such laws specifically bar only conduct deemed obnoxious and are carefully and narrowly aimed at the forbidden conduct.[41]

Despite cases like *Gregory* that urge that statutes be "carefully and narrowly aimed at the forbidden conduct," it seems unlikely that courts will go so far as to declare unconstitutional all statutes whose scope is so broad as to result in selective enforcement.

A third alternative is that courts could adopt a principle making broad statutes invalid unless such selective enforcement as occurs is a result of lack of enforcement resources. This would maintain the principle of legislative preeminence and at the same time acknowledge the reality of less than full enforcement. It would, however, result either in the giving of untrue explanations for selective enforcement or in a great number of statutes' such as gambling and battery being declared invalid because they are not enforced for reasons other than the lack of adequate enforcement resources.

A fourth alternative would be for courts to sustain selectively enforced, broadly worded statutes provided: (a) The broadly worded statute does not cover constitutionally protected conduct such as that involved in the *Gregory* case; (b) there is an indication that the legislature intended selective enforcement and gave sufficient indication of the basis upon which the selective-enforcement decisions should be made (for example, the gambling statute enforced to prevent commercial gambling); and (c) there are in existence police enforcement policies that are consistent with the legislative purpose and that adequately guide and control the decisions of the individual officer.

This fourth alternative has the advantage of safeguarding constitutional rights, maintaining the preeminence of the legislature in the determination of basic substantive criminal law policy, and being realistic with respect to current day-to-day law enforcement; and it should encourage the open adoption of sensible and, it is hoped, effective enforcement policies. For example, a police department could adopt a policy of enforcement against commercial gambling and perhaps against specified types of social gambling. The explanation for the policy should make explicit that the policy is consistent with the apparent purpose that the legislature had when the gambling statute was enacted in the particular jurisdiction.

There is some judicial support, although not a great deal, for this approach. In *United States* v *Shreveport Grain Co.,*[42] a case involving an indictment for misbranding certain articles of food, the Supreme Court said:

> The contention that the act contravenes the provisions of the Constitution with respect to the separation of the governmental powers is without merit. That the legislative power of Congress cannot be delegated is, of course, clear. But Congress may declare its will, and after fixing a primary standard, devolve upon administrative officers the "power to fill up the details" by prescribing administrative rules and regulations. That the authority conferred by the act now under review in this respect does not transcend the power of Congress is not open to reasonable dispute. The effect of the provision assailed is to define an offense, but with directions to those charged with the administration of the act to make supplementary rules and regulations allowing reasonable variations, tolerances and exemptions, which, because of their variety and need of detailed statement, it was impracticable for Congress to prescribe. The effect of the proviso is evident and legitimate, namely, to prevent the embarrassment and hardship which might result from a too literal and minute enforcement of the act, without at the same time offending against its purposes. The proviso does not delegate legislative power but confers administrative functions entirely valid within principles established by numerous decisions of this court... .[43]

It would seem appropriate for a police policy to exempt certain forms of social gambling from enforcement, explaining the action as making "supplementary rules and regulations allowing reasonable variations, tolerances and exemptions, which, because of their variety and need of detailed statement, it was impracticable for" the legislature to prescribe; and do so "to prevent the embarrassment and hardship which might result from a too literal and minute enforcement of the act, without at the same time offending against its purposes."

In addition, for example, a police department could adopt a policy of referring husbands to a legislative authorized mental-health process, under circumstances prescribed in the policy, rather than making an arrest for a violation of the battery statute even though there is sufficient evidence of battery and even though the mental-health referral may require more police time and resources than would be required to make an arrest for battery. The explanation for the policy should indicate that the policy is consistent with the apparent legislative purpose reflected in the enactment of a criminal battery statute and an emergency mental-health statute, both of which are applicable to the conduct of the husband in some intrafamily violence cases. There is some judicial authority that arguably supports this position. In *Cox* v. *Louisiana*[44] the Supreme Court said:

> It is apparent that demonstrators, such as those involved here, would justifiably tend to rely on this administrative interpretation of how "near" the courthouse a particular demonstration might take place. Louisiana's statutory policy of preserving order around the courthouse would counsel encouragement of just such reliance. This administrative discretion to construe the term "near" concerns a limited control of the streets and other areas in the immediate vicinity of the courthouse and is the type of narrow discretion which this Court has recognized as the proper role of responsible officials in making determinations concerning the time, place, duration, and manner of demonstrations... . It is not the type of unbridled discretion which would allow an official to pick and choose among expressions of view the ones he will permit to use the streets and other public facilities... . Nor does this limited administrative regulation of traffic which the Court has consistently recognized as necessary and permissible, constitute a waiver of law which is beyond the power of the police. Obviously telling demonstrators how far from the courthouse steps is "near" the courthouse for purposes of a permissible peaceful demonstration is a far cry from allowing one to commit, for example, murder, or robbery.[45]

The same reasoning ought to justify police in deciding in an intrafamily violence case, for example, whether the circumstances make it appropriate to make a mental-health referral because the husband's conduct and history seem to indicate mental illness and overt conduct indicative of danger to others; to take the wife and children to a shelter facility when to do so will afford greater protection to the wife and children than would an arrest and early release on bail; or to make an arrest in the view that the circumstances justify the use of the criminal justice process.

Traditionally, choices such as those involved in the enforcement of the gambling or battery statutes have been made on an ad hoc basis by individual officers. The ad hoc decisions, in fact, have often been clearly inconsistent with the legislative purpose. For example, when legislatures provided that drunks should be taken to detoxification facilities instead of being arrested, some officers continued to make arrests not for public drunkenness but for disorderly conduct. To deal with this, the Madison, Wisconsin, Police Department adopted a department-wide policy that provided in part:

> It is important to recognize that some of the behavior necessary to objectively evidence incapacitation by alcohol might also conceivably be used to substantiate a disorderly conduct charge. In order to insure that the authority granted law enforcement officers in Wisconsin under s.51.45 Wisconsin Statutes is applied in a manner consistent with the intent of the Alcohol and Intoxication Treatment Act and with the objectives of the Department, the officer in charge of the station will be held affirmatively responsible to carefully review the circumstances of any arrest for disorderly conduct of an "intoxicated person" or a person who appears as if he might be "incapacitated by alcohol" to preclude the processing of an individual through the criminal justice system when that person's behavior might more appropriately be dealt with in the medical care system.[45]

The obvious and apparently correct assumption underlying the Madison policy is that the legislature intended the detoxification alternative to be used by police even when the conduct of the drunk was in violation of a criminal statute such as the disorderly conduct statute.

Should there be dissatisfaction with the administrative interpretation of the legislative purpose in providing police with alternative responses, there are ways of expressing legislative disapproval. Legislative supervision would inevitably be more effective with respect to department-wide written policies than with respect to the largely invisible ad hoc decision of an individual police officer.[47]

Even opponents of substantive rule making by police would appear not to disagree entirely with the conclusion just reached. For example, Allen says that substantive policy making is appropriate where the criminal statute is designed to "facilitate the *regulation* rather than the *prohibition* of certain activities,"[48] and he also urges that "our legislatures should begin to consider explicitly providing the police with a set of flexible responses to certain illegal conduct.[49] The difference of opinion is thus probably one of degree, and recognizing this is a major advance, in my judgment. The question is not then *whether* police policy making is proper but rather *when* police policy making is proper. The debate as to "when," which has unfortunately not as yet taken place, could make a very substantial contribution. For example, I would urge that common gambling statutes are in fact designed to "regulate" rather than "prohibit" gambling and would also urge that legislatures have provided the police with "flexible responses" (for example, arrest, referral to mental-health facility, or the use of a shelter facility) to the important problem of intrafamily violence. But I may be wrong, and it would be helpful if there were a more thorough study of such legislative history as does exist with respect to a particular statute such as the gambling or battery statute,[50] and it would be of even greater help if the legislative purpose, often implicit, were in the future made explicit by legislatures.

The Practical Significance of Substantive Policy Making by Police

Professionals are typically preoccupied with methods, thus the teacher, with class size; the prison warden, with security procedures; the police, with departmental organization, personnel recruitment and training, the function of middle management, team policing, one- or two-man cars, and the like.[51] Unlike the professional, however, the consumer is much more interested in results: Is there good education? Do prisons accomplish their purpose? Is police service effective? But traditionally the consumer of police service has been silent, politically powerless; or when questioning has been told something to the effect that police only enforce the law. Happily that situation may be changing. The women's movement constitutes an informed, articulate and politically powerful voice increasingly concerned over issues such as intrafamily violence and its victims. The demand is for an effective response to the problem. There is little interest in departmental organization, one- or two-man squad cars, team policing or other administrative matters, except as they contribute to an effective police response.

Obviously, the consumer of police services has an interest in the police response being as effective as is possible. But it is unrealistic to expect improvement if police are saddled with the myth of full enforcement; required to make ad hoc responses to important social problems; and required to give often untruthful reasons (for example, lack of evidence or of resources) in explanation of such decisions as are made. So long as this situation prevails, police will continue to lack the ability, the resources, the knowledge, or the assistance necessary to improve the quality of their services, and the consumer of those services will suffer the consequences.

There are practical reasons why lawyers should be increasingly interested in the issue of administrative policy making by police. An equal-protection issue might arise where there is less than full enforcement, a possibility that is increased if there is a failure to carefully consider the enforcement policy to ensure that the classification is not an arbitrary or otherwise impermissible one. The relative lack of equal-protection litigation in the past probably reflects the lawyers' unawareness of the issue because of the uncritical acceptance of the myth of full enforcement and because of the cost of bringing a successful denial of equal-protection defense to an often fairly minor criminal charge.[52] The increase in publicly funded defender agencies will probably eliminate the economic barrier to the raising of the equal-protection issue.

Recent developments in Fourth Amendment litigation also signal the increased importance of understanding the reason for a stop or an arrest that is accompanied by a frisk or other search of the person. In *United States* v. *Robinson*[53] and *Gustafson* v. *Florida,*[54] the Supreme Court held that a search of the person is valid if made incidental to a valid "custodial arrest." In a concurring opinion in *Gustafson,* Justice Stewart said:

> [A] persuasive claim might have been made in this case that the custodial arrest of the petitioner for a minor traffic offense violated his rights under the Fourth and Fourteenth Amendments. But no such claim has been made.[55]

Apparently Justice Stewart was not raising the issue of whether there was sufficient evidence to arrest for the minor traffic offense but rather whether that offense was normally subject to enforcement and, if so, whether the enforcement was by means of a custodial arrest. A similar question can be raised with respect to custodial arrests for gambling, disorderly conduct, battery, and a wide variety of so-called minor offenses. Illustrative is the recent case of *State* v. *Hoven,*[56] in which the court held a search incident to a traffic arrest invalid, saying in part:

> The Supreme Court has held that to be reasonable a search must either be conducted pursuant to a valid search warrant or fit into one of the exceptions to the warrant requirement that it has defined... . *A pretext arrest* to permit an otherwise unauthorized search is not one of these exceptions.[57] (Emphasis added)

How can one tell whether an arrest for a minor offense is a "pretext arrest?" The sensible answer would seem to be when a custodial arrest is not usually made as a matter of departmental policy absent a desire to search the person arrested. Defense counsel, in making a motion to suppress, should inquire whether a custodial arrest is usually made, as a matter of departmental policy, absent a desire to search. If the officer answers that the decision as to whether to arrest is left to the individual officer, this ought not be adequate to persuade the court that it was not a "pretext arrest'' unless the officer can also relate what his individual policy is with respect to the enforcement of the particular statute. From the prosecutor's point of view, it would be better for the officer to be able to testify as to what the policy of the department is with respect to making a custodial arrest for violation of the particular criminal statute involved. If the law develops this way, as I believe it will, it will become of practical importance for counsel to know what departmental policy is with respect to the making of custodial arrests, and this fact should serve as an inducement to prosecuting attorneys to encourage police to develop departmental enforcement policies at least with respect to the making of custodial arrests in situations where a search may be made as an incident to that arrest.[58]

An increasing number of cases are directly challenging practices of police departments.[59] Although courts have taken a traditional and inadequate approach to the substantive issues involve,[60] the fact of increased litigation tends to focus attention on the importance of police policies and practices.

There are other practical reasons to support substantive policy making by police. In police labor disputes, it has been increasingly common for the police union to threaten full enforcement as a pressure on administration and the community to settle the labor dispute. The myth of full enforcement has given this tactic the appearance of propriety and has left members of the community defenseless against clearly inappropriate enforcement practices. Adequate development of substantive enforcement policies would afford a basis for identifying inappropriate enforcement practices whether engaged in to justify an otherwise illegal search or to exert pressure on the community to make concessions during a police labor dispute.

Policy Mehods That Minimize Objections to Police Policy Making

In the development of substantive policies, police should use procedures that minimize, insofar as possible, legitimate concerns about the propriety of police policy making. There are several ways of doing this.

First, an effort should be made to determine what the legislature intended. Apparently, full enforcement is legislatively desired with respect to serious crimes such as murder, robbery, and rape. With respect to these statutes, the only issue is as to means, that is, how to bring about effective full enforcement. But, with respect to other statutes such as gambling, there is adequate legislative history to demonstrate that full enforcement against minor forms of social gambling was not legislatively intended. With respect to this type of statute, the need is for the development of a substantive enforcement policy that will best achieve the legislative purpose; which will, for example, effectively deal with commercial gambling. Finally, in some situations legislatures have provided alternatives as in the case of the public drunk or intrafamily violence. Here again the need is for the development of a substantive enforcement policy that will best achieve the legislative objective, the most effective treatment of the drunk; the greatest safety for the victim of intrafamily violence. The policy will vary from locality to locality depending, for example, on whether there is an adequate detoxification facility, a shelter home for battered wives, or an emergency mental-health response capability.

Second, policies should be developed in cooperation with the prosecuting attorney of the local jurisdiction. The legality of prosecutor discretion, although not free from controversy, has been more traditionally recognized as appropriate. And the active involvement of the prosecutor, particularly in rural areas, is one effective way of substantive policy making where the individual police agencies are small and do not have the resources necessary to engage in a process of substantive policy making. Involving the prosecutor may also allay some of the fears of prosecutors who see a process of police policy making as a threat to the role of the prosecutor as the principal law-enforcement officer for the jurisdiction. The rural prosecutor tends to be at least as well informed as local police agencies with respect to a wide range of enforcement issues. The urban prosecutor, on the other hand, has often concentrated attention on the trial of serious crimes and has left to the police the response to a wide variety of social problems such as intrafamily violence.

Third, substantive policies should also be worked out in cooperation with other local policymakers. For example, in some states, the local legislative body has "home-rule" authority that gives to that local legislative body opportunity to modify state-wide legislation to meet the needs of the locality. In this situation it might be possible, for example, for the local legislative body to provide for alternative responses to important substantive problems such as intrafamily violence.

Conclusion

An important contribution was made a couple of decades ago by discussions focusing on the existence and importance of police discretion. Important contribution has also been made during the past decade by the debate over whether it is desirable and legally proper for police to develop substantive enforcement policies to guide and control such discretion as exists. With the benefit of the past, we ought now to move the discussion to a higher level of sophistication. In fact, there are situations in which legislatures do intend for there to be full enforcement. It is important that these be carefully identified and that efforts be made to develop effective ways of enforcing those statutes. It is also the fact that there are situations in which legislatures have intended to leave choice to enforcement agencies. Because the police are the first-line enforcement agency, it is therefore appropriate for them to exercise leadership in the development of substantive enforcement policies that will be both consistent with the legislative purpose and effective in responding to the social problems such as intrafamily violence whose complexity is such as to call for responses more flexible and more effective than an unthinking application of a criminal statute.

Notes

1. There were a few exceptions such as J. Hall, "The Police and Law in a Democratic Society," *Ind. L. J.* 28 (1953): 133.

2. The American Bar Foundations's study was of criminal justice administration including police practices. It was conducted during the mid-1950s in the states of Kansas, Michigan, and Wisconsin.

3. W. LaFave, *Arrest* (Boston: Little, Brown, 1965).

4. J. Goldstein, "Police Discretion Not to Invoke the Criminal Process: Low Visibility Decisions in the Administration of Criminal Justice," *Yale L.J.* 69 (1960): 543.

5. American Bar Association Project on Standards for Criminal Justice, *Standards Relating to the Urban Police Function* (Washington, D.C., § 4.3, 1973.)

6. Ibid, p. 2.

7. The resolution was adopted by the Administrative Law Section and was forwarded to the Criminal Law Section for comments and with the hope that the Criminal Law Section would also approve the resolution. To date there has been no response from the Criminal Law Section.

8. These are cited and discussed in H. Goldstein, *Policing a Free Society* (New York: Ballinger, 1977), p. 117.

9. The distinction between means or methods and substantive objectives is difficult for some people. Lawyers are familiar with the substantive-procedural distinction although the line may at times be difficult to draw. Whether given conduct constitutes first-degree murder under the law of the state is clearly a substantive question. Whether police can search the home of the suspect for the murder weapon is a procedural issue. Lay people have apparently had less occasion to make this kind of distinction, which might also be defined as one of "substantive goals" rahter than "procedural means." As a consequence, police administrators often assert that they have adopted substantive policies pointing to increasingly common police policies relating to searching persons or places, conducting identification procedures, and the like.

10. There is greater support for administrative rule making with respect to means or methods such as search of vehicles than there is with respect to substantive objectives such as how to respond to intrafamily violence. See, for example, Comment, "Judicially Required Rulemaking as Fourth Amendment Policy: An Applied Analysis of the Supervisory Power of Federal Courts," *Nw. U. L. Rev.* 72 (1977): 595.

11. This is often phrased as whether police can properly engage in a process of selective enforcement. So stating the issue tends to distort the question because it seems to suggest a deliberate police decision to act contrary to the mandate of the legislature.

12. Boston Police, *Criminal Investigative Procedures, Search Warrants, Motor Vehicle Searches, Searches Incident to Arrest, Stop and Frisk, Arrest, Eyewitness Identification,* 1978. The Boston project is discussed in S. Krantz, *Policymaking to Structure Discretion: The Boston Experience* (Boston: Boston University School of Law, Center for Criminal Justice, October 1978.) This report also contains a most helpful review of the literature on police discretion and policy making and an analysis of why the substantive narcotics policy-making effort did not succeed.

13. *Madison* [Wisconsin], *Police Department Newsletter* 6(5) (7 September 1978).

14. This is undoubtedly a principal reason why the Criminal Law Section of the ABA has not adopted the substantive policy-making recommendation of the ABA Administrative Law Section.

15. This is conceded by Professor Ronald Allen who opposes substantive rule making by police.

16. This is the position of Professor Kenneth Culp Davis, a proponent of substantive rule making by police. For purposes of this chapter, it is appropriate to assume the desirability of total legislative preeminence in determining what conduct is to be made criminal and for that conduct always to be subject to enforcement. In fact, legislative preeminence may be no more desirable in the criminal law field than it would be in the field of economic regulation.

17. F. Remington and Victor Rosenblum, "The Criminal Law and the Legislative Process," *U. Ill. L. F.* (1960): 481.

18. See for example, the President's Commission on Law Enforcement and Administration of Justice, *Task Force Report: The Police* (Washington, D.C.: U.S. Government Printing Office, 1967), ch. 2, pp. 21–23.

19. The most thorough and able presentation against substantive policy making by police is found in Ronald Allen, "The Police and Substantive Rulemaking: Reconciling Principle and Expediency," *U. Pa. L. Rev.* 125 (1976): 62; R. Allen, "The Police and Substantive Rulemaking: A Brief Rejoinder," *U. Pa. L. Rev.* 125 (1977): 1172.

20. The tradition in this country has been to recognize the prosecuting attorney as the chief law-enforcement officer in the jurisdiction. To an

extent this is in fact the case, particularly in rural areas where the prosecutor is as knowledgeable as police about community problems and is able to fashion an appropriate enforcement response to those problems. In urban areas, however, the prosecutor is less involved and less informed about many community problems like, for example, intrafamily violence. This is particularly true when the alternatives to the criminal justice system are commonly utilized. In these situations, the police, not the prosecutor, are best able to develop an appropriate overall response to the problem including but not limited to the use of the criminal justice system. The need is for a cooperative approach with each agency contributing according to the nature of the issue and the knowledge and involvement of the agency.

21. See Allen, supra, n. 19, 1976.

22. K. Davis, *Police Discretion* (Minneapolis: West Publishing, 1975); K. Davis, "Police Rulemaking on Selective Enforcement: A Reply," *U. Pa. L. Rev.* 125 (1977): 1167.

23. See Report of the National Advisory Commission on Civil Disorders (Washington, D.C.: U.S. Government Printing Office, 1967), pp. 164–165.

24. The House of Delegates of the American Bar Association, at its 1978 summer meeting, adopted a resolution that would require police to state reasons if an arrest is not made. See *A. B. A. J.* 61 (1978): 1343; *Criminal Justice* 6 (Summer 1978): 3.

25. See discussion infra at n. 26.

26. See Goldstein, supra, no. 8, ch. 5. It is significant that the International Association of Chiefs of Police endorsed the ABA Standards on the Urban Police Function and gave particularly strong support to the concept that police policy making is primarily an administrator's responsibility.

27. Allen, supra, n. 19, 1976.

28. The use of the gambling statute as an illustration is common. See, for example, Remington and Rosenblum, supra, n. 17.

29. During the academic year 1970–1971, which I spent at the Minnesota Law School, the Minnesota League of Municipalities asked whether a local law-enforcement officer has discretion to decide not to enforce a state statute requiring a license to serve "setups" and allow customers to bring their own liquor. The small town restaurant could not economically spend the cost of the license. My reaction was that a licensing statute is the type of law that is either fully enforced or the pressure of competition would make any enforcement difficult. Although there was no explicit legislative history, I would be confident that the Minnesota legislature did in fact intend full enforcement.

30. A Wisconsin Legislative Council Committee on Domestic Violence has just proposed a threats statute that will make it a crime to threaten

injury by the use of any device or instrument. In a meeting police officers pointed to the extremely broad wording resulting in the fact that an arrest could be made in every marital dispute to which police respond. The answer by the senior legislative attorney was that police have to recognize the political reality, the political support for a broad provision, and would be expected to exercise "common sense" in the enforcement of the statute. The suggestion that the legislature should furnish criteria was met with the response that to do so was not politically realistic.

31. See n. 7 supra.

32. Allen, supra, n. 19, 1976, at 97–98.

33. Ibid.

34. Allen, supra, n. 19, 1976, at 86–109.

35. *Walters* v. *Hampton,* 14 Wash. App. 548, 543 P.2d 648, 651 (1975).

36. *People* v *deBour,* 40 N.Y. 2d 210, 352 N.E.2d 562, 568 (1976).

37. See n. 35, supra.

38. *Bruno* v. *Codd,* 90 Misc. 2d 1047, 396 N.Y.S.2d 974 (1977).

39. *Papachristo* v. *City of Jacksonville,* 405 U.S. 156, 170 (1972).

40. *Spence* v. *Washington,* 418 U.S. 405, 414 n. 9 (1974).

41. 394 U.S. 111, 118 (1969).

42. 287 U.S. 77 (1932).

43. 287 U.S. at 85.

44. 379 U.S. 559 (1965).

45. 379 U.S. at 568–569.

46. Madison [Wisconsin] Police Department, *Manual of Policy, Regulations and Procedures, Policy 4–1600 Alcoholism and Intoxication, Policy 4–1605 Other Charges,* 17 August, 1976.

47. Accomplishing effective legislative oversight would be difficult. It is presently difficult with respect to administrative rules commonly adopted by state economic regulatory agencies. Clearly there is presently no effective legislative oversight of ad hoc decisions made by individual police officers. Department-wide administrative policies are more likely to be known and to be subject to challenge if they conflict with legislative purpose.

48. Allen, supra, n. 19, 1976, at 92–93, n. 138. The difficulty is in knowing what is "regulation" and what is "prohibition."

49. Allen, supra, n. 19, 1977, at 1180. The difficulty is in knowing when the legislature has provided a set of "flexible" responses.

50. Scholarship has been lacking with respect to the legislative purpose in the enactment of criminal statutes. The issue is not confined to statutes enacted so long ago that legislative history is unavailable.

51. I have been for several years a member of the board of directors of the Police Foundation, funded originally by a grant of $30 million from the Ford Foundation. I originally thought that the foundation would give

priority to the improvement of the quality of police service by research designed to increase existing knowledge about how to deal with a variety of social problems defined by legislatures as involving criminal conduct. It is a fair generalization, however, that the Police Foundation has been almost totally preoccupied with "means" rather than with the acquisition of knowledge to improve substantive objectives of policing.

52. See, for example, *People* v. *Harris,* 182 Cal. App. 2d Supp. 837, 5 Cal. Rptr. 852 (1960); F. Remington, D. Newman, E. Kimball, M. Melli, and H. Goldstein, *Criminal Justice Administration* (Indianapolis: Bobbs-Merrill, 1969), pp. 311–326.

53. 414 U.S. 218, (1973).

54. 414 U.S. 260, (1973).

55. 414 U.S. at 266–267.

56. ——— Minn. ———, 269 N.W.2d 849, 23 CrL 2464 (July 21, 1978).

57. 23 CrL at 2465.

58. The issue is being litigated with decreased frequency not to the making of an arrest but the analogous issue of an investigative stop of the person or of a vehicle See., for example, *Keziah* v. *Bostic,* 452 F. Supp. 912 (W.D.N.C. 1978), holding improper random vehicle stops for a license check.

59. See, for example, *San Jose Peace Officer's Assn.* v. *City of San Jose,* 144 Cal. Rptr. 638 (1978), no duty to bargain over firearms policy because the formulating of this kind of policy is a managerial responsibility.

60. Such challenges as have occurred to substantive programs of the police have been rejected on the somewhat surprising ground that the managers of police departments were not shown to have any knowledge or involvement in the practices that were challenged. See *Rizzo* v. *Goode,* 423 U.S. 362 (1976).

Commentary

Patrick Murphy

The police have discretion and always will. Therefore the great need is to improve and upgrade the police. There are many problems in upgrading or attempting to upgrade the police. Eleven years after the President's Crime Commission and five years after the National Advisory Commission standards and goals, very little progress has been made.

It is frustrating to have to report in 1978 that we are not making much progress, and in some quarters we are moving backward. In the state of Florida, the sheriffs' association went on the record in opposition to a bill that would require that a person be a high school graduate to become a sheriff in the future. That fact will give you some idea of the state of our thinking within the police world about the importance or value or wisdom of upgrading and moving in the direction of professionalism.

In addition, the police are badly fragmented. Although crime is very heavily concentrated in large cities, there are more than 17,000 police departments in the United States. Of the 17,000 police departments, approximately 200 deal with most of the crime and employ the vast majority of police officers. But the small departments have great power within our professional association. It is not a professional association; it is a social organization. But the small town chiefs of police, because they bear that title whether they have two or five or fifteen officers, have a great negative influence in impeding movement toward police professionalism.

Professor Remington made a reference to arrest productivity. One of our difficulties in attempting to do research in arrest productivity is to find a definition of "arrest." Very few police departments know what an arrest really means in their department. Eleven years after the beginning of our Law Enforcement Assistance Administration Program, the states have not bitten the bullet regarding crime. State governments rather consistently have avoided accepting more responsibility for creating standards for the police for developing the records and information systems I referred to. We cannot develop a reasonably effective police service in the United States without the support and influence of the states. Beyond that, the state must play a much more significant role in servicing the police and in supporting the research that is badly needed for influencing education and training. The FBI, for example, has over the years developed a fingerprint file, to which the National Crime Information Center's laboratories have contributed. In addition, there is cooperation among jurisdictions in narcotics, organized crime, and interstate crimes, especially interstate auto thefts and bank robberies. However, neither the states nor the federal government have done nearly enough, and until the states do more in establishing standards and upgrading the police, we will continue to make very little progress. The strongest opposition to the states' taking on that essential responsibility comes from within the police world itself.

Written policies can limit but never eliminate discretion at any level of policing in my opinion. By definition, a good police officer (sergeant, lieutenant, captain, or chief) is one with good judgment in exercising his or her broad and powerful discretion at all levels. Many complaints about discrimination on the part of the police in providing services exist. The police do not respond, for example, to calls for assistance in family fights, lost children, minor illnesses, or accidents in the home. In many cities these complaints are an everyday occurrence. In certain parts of the city, the charge is often made that the police are discriminatory on how these services are provided. And, of course, there are the complaints about the police's being discriminatory in how they enforce the law.

It is my view that in the use of force, the enforcement of ordinances and regulations, a very difficult problem is presented. Consider as an example how the police deal with the prostitution problem. It is very obvious to a knowledgeable police chief that there are certain parts of his city in which a prostitute should never be found soliciting on the street corner. Someone might have his job for that. On the other hand, there may be parts of the city where prostitution is not condoned by the police necessarily, but where they simply cannot enforce the law in all cases, and so there are prostitutes soliciting on those streets. People live on those streets, and they are very offended that their children see this going on just as people are very offended about drugs being sold on their street or their children watching gambling. Strict enforcement of all laws at all times is probably an unreachable goal.

The police chief in the first instance exercises his discretion in a number of ways in determining what work his department will do. For example, in police departments across the United States, there is an enormous variation in the number of officers assigned to juvenile work. The problem is further complicated by the fact that in some departments juvenile work is done by the officers in a patrol division. In other departments it is done by the officers in a detective division. In still other departments it is a separate division. If we go one step further and look at what these patrol divisions do, how they function, or how the decisions to make an arrest are made, again we will see enormous variations. One reason for these conditions is that knowledge is not communicated very well in this insular world.

Looking at the differences, it becomes very clear that the chief does exercise enormous discretion. Will he assign 5 or 20 percent of his force to traffic? Although in some communities the mayor or city council may influence those decisions and although there is entirely too much political interference in police departments, it is often surprising to observe how freely the chief may make these decisions in shifting people from one function to another without any oversight from any part of municipal government.

Excellently written policies would be only one step. Additionally, and probably as necessary, would be good management in seeing to it that these written policies are meaningful. Police departments are among the worst examples of bureaucracy. As a result, it is very difficult to make police officers conform to policies no matter how well they are articulated.

This discretion, which I believe will always be exercised at several levels in any police department, is a subject worthy of much more attention than it has been given. As Professor Remington has pointed out, it certainly is worthy of a great deal of research.

Commentary

Roger Parks

Professor Remington does us a great service by recognizing the great discretion exercised by police officers on the streets. In our current system police discretion is controlled by a number of mechanisms. The first is certainly legislative enactment; second, judicial and prosecutorial oversight within the context of those legislative enactments, certainly by departmental policy, peer pressure from other officers on the street, and citizen request in a particular situation.

Nevertheless, I see some potential problems with administrative rule making. First of all, will administrators jump in where legislators have feared to tread? Consider the gambling statute. Will the police chief in Indianapolis be willing to enunciate a public policy that on-street gambling will be allowed in Adam, Baker, and Charlie sectors? Similarly, will he go public with a policy and administrative rules that prostitution will be allowed on Illinois Street? Will he, in the face of demands by women's groups, clarify the policy on battery arrests and family disturbances; that is, for example, police officers will arrest husbands in situations where wives have broken bones or exhibit some bleeding but not in other situations? I think that poses a major problem for administrative rule making. Second, as I read the process of formal administrative rule making, open public discussion of the proposed rules is an essential element. I wonder if open public discussion can develop consensus on these kinds of issues. The third point has to do with the impracticality of rules' covering all or even a substantial portion of varying circumstances.

The product of the administrative rule-making process will take one of two forms: either generalities that officers will certainly recognize as such or extremely detailed rule books that will be ignored.

Given these concerns I have about the proposals for administrative rule making, I still see substantial benefits in the debate over the propriety of rule making in that it opens the closet door, and it makes the exercise of discretion a legitimate subject of public discussion. Most importantly, it allows and indeed calls for research to focus on alternative police responses to common situations. It goes beyond simplistic statements that police enforce only the law.

Commentary

Cleon H. Foust and
D. Robert Webster

"Police discretion" invariably provokes comment as it did in this case. Without identifying the sources, the general thrust of comment on the police function was as follows:

Since police serve as the front-line selectors of the grist for the system, police management should be aware of system capacity in order to avoid an overload. It is generally agreed that the system works badly when overloaded. Inevitably attention to overload raises the issue of police discretion. While considering the problems of poor arrests (one facet of discretion), one needs to understand that sometimes it is necessary (for puposes of safety) to arrest even though the arresting officer is aware prosecution is unlikely.

And it is true that prosecutorial discretion can serve as a safety valve when overload threatens, but ideally the use of prosecutorial discretion for that purpose could be avoided by police-prosecutor coordination.

Police discretion is a necessary and inevitable ingredient in the system. For example, Pat Murphy pointed out that the appropriate mediator for a family dispute is the policeman who is called. If he doesn't, the judge will be forced to mediate it. But two observations should be made about police discretion: (1) We need to know more about police performance, that is, how the discretion is exercised, and (2) standards, guidelines, controls, or whatever one prefers to call them need to be administratively imposed to bring the exercise of discretion out into the open and to provide general direction in its front-line use.

In short, discretion is exercised all across the system as adjustments become necessary. The concern was expressed, however, that to the extent determinate sentencing deprives a judge of his "adjustment" capacity in sentencing, then those "adjustments" are made at an earlier level by police and prosecutor.

6 Symbolic Justice: The Trial of Criminal Cases

Nicholas Kittrie

The Function of Court Trial

In 1967 the President's Commission on Law Enforcement and Aministration of Justice noted, "The courts are the pivot on which the criminal justice system turns."[1] The observation was a gross exaggeration then. It is doubly inaccurate now. The criminal courts in America are not in the mainstream of criminal justice and are not central to the gross operations of the system of crime and punishment. At best the courts offer an opportunity for the stylized enactment of selected performances, which alternate between morality plays and modern versions of trial by ordeal. These dramatic enactments affect a relatively small segment of the criminal justice population. But much like theater and cinema, they are observed directly or through mass-media reporting by large segments of the population, and consequently they affect the public consciousness. It is in this function that the courts stand out for their role as symbols of justice.

That the population processed by the courts is but a small sample of criminal justice reality should have been fully realized by the president's crime commission. The 1965 figures developed for the commission regarding adults suspected of index crimes, reflect the flow as shown in table 6–1.

In sum, observed later by the National Advisory Commission on Standards and Goals, only about 8 percent of those apprehended as suspects were processed fully through the formal steps of criminal prosecution or trial. There is an inadequate knowledge as to what happened to the other 92 percent.[2]

Table 6–1
Adults Suspected of Index Crimes (1965)

Apprehended	*Not Charged or Lesser Charge*	*Formally Charged*	*Went to Trial*	*Convicted*
467,000	290,000	177,000	38,000	30,000

Source: President's Commission on Law Enforcement and Administration of Justice, *The Challenge of Crime in a Free Society* (Washington, D.C.: U.S. Government Printing Office, 1967), pp. 262–263.

More recent statistics in the 1976 Uniform Crime Reports tell an even more fragmentary story. The outgoing decade's well-financed, national campaign for better reporting and more effective controls of crime resulted in more vigorous activity but little change in the sampling function of the criminal justice process. With regard to index crimes (murder, robbery, burglary, aggravated assault, rape, larceny, and motor-vehicle theft), the 1976 figures are shown in table 6–2.

The 1976 developments meant that, overall, arrests were effectuated in 20.5 percent of all reported crime cases, that in only some 9.2 percent of all reported criminal cases was an offender prosecuted, and that only in a mere 5.96 percent of all reported crimes was a conviction secured as charged. A breakdown of the particular offenses within the index crime group tells the story even more poignantly as shown in table 6–3.

The judicial process, it is evident, continues to screen only a relatively small fragment of those who encounter the criminal system. Major portions of the offender population are either never detected (30 percent of all the burglary offenses go without clearance) or are never prosecuted (31 percent of those arrested for rape are not tried) or if prosecuted, are either convicted of lesser offenses (which is what happens to 14 percent of those tried for murder) or are fully acquitted (the acquittal rate for those tried for rape being 49 percent).

It is therefore clear that while large numbers of the criminal justice population are affected by police practices and come in direct contact with both the prosecution and defense functions, their exposure to the trial process is relatively limited. For them the police and, to a lesser degree, prosecution are central, while the functioning of the criminal trial have more limited bearing. Yet it is this very trial process that appears to carry great symbolic weight for the general populace.

Granted that the trial directly affects a small sample of those involved in the criminal process, the impact of this on the goals of the system requires some initial scrutiny. There is currently a major debate underway in American between the therapeutic nihilists ("no treatment works") who

Table 6–2
Index Crimes (1976)

Crimes Reported	*Apprehended*	*Prosecuted*	*Guilty as Charged*	*Lesser Conviction*	*Acquitted or Charge Dismissed*
11,304,770	2,317,811	1,046,407	673,983	86,179	287,655

Source: Clarence Kelley, *Uniform Crime Reports 1976* (Washington, D.C.: U.S. Government Printing Office, 1976.)

Table 6–3
Index Crimes Grouped by Offenses

Offense	*Crimes Reported*	*Apprehended (Number and Percent of Reported Crimes)*	*Prosecuted*	*Guilty (Number and Percent of Prosecuted Adults)*	*Lesser Conviction*	*Acquitted or Dismissed*
Murder	18,870	14,836 (79)	10,113	4,854 (48)	1,416	3,843
Robbery	420,210	113,457 (27)	56,365	31,565 (56)	4,509	20,291
Burglary	3,089,800	525,266 (17)	202,962	119,748 (59)	22,326	60,889
Larceny	6,270,800	1,181,452 (19)	547,949	400,003 (73)	27,397	120,549
Motor-vehicle theft	957,600	134,064 (14)	35,233	18,673 (53)	5,990	11,979
Aggravated assaults	490,850	309,236 (63)	177,501	92,301 (52)	23,075	62,125
Rape	56,730	29,500 (52)	16,284	6,839 (42)	1,466	7,979

Source: Clarence Kelley, *Uniform Crime Reports 1976* (Washington, D.C.: U.S. Government Printing Office, 1976).

seek deterrence and those who believe that "just desert" and deterrence must be second to rehabilitative objectives and programs. For the most part, the country is composed of the uncommitted who maintain serious doubts whether either treatment or deterrence alone can be counted to do the job of crime control. Yet even if either were fully proved to be effective, the limited sample of those finally processed by the system would negate an effective outcome.

Certainly neither incapacitation nor deterrence can be counted on much if there is a chance of only nearly one in twenty that the offender will be given his "just desert." When nineteen offenders out of twenty do not earn their just desert, criminality remains a low-risk business. Crime certainly has greater appeal than many other small businesses that require greater education or capital. Criminality, in fact, does pay. Neither can rehabilitation promise much if only one out of some twenty offenders is exposed to treatment. Even if all those incarcerated and treated were to be reformed, what about the nineteen who have not been "saved"? With less than full certainty regarding the real effectiveness of either "punishment" or "rehabilitation," the present debate on the choice between them appears to be primarily academic. It promises little, other than intellectual or philosophical satisfaction, for the reformation of the system of crime and justice in America. The sample of those who encounter the trial system remains too small to believe that the *choice* of dispositions is likely to have a major effect on future criminal conduct.

The Pretrial Process: For More Fairness and Less Delay

The criminal trial is a heavily documented American institution: in literature, the films, television, and in factual reportage. At the criminal trial, the status of the accused (affected by the conflicting claims of the state versus the defense) is adjudicated. "Adjudication ... is the Anglo-American formula par excellence for conflict resolution, and the criminal trial is a major demonstration of that process. At adjudication the judge—an impartial, solemn umpire representing the sovereign authority—is vested with the power to decide the matter in dispute. The decision-making process for reaching the judgment is adversary in character, permitting each party to put forth its best factual and conceptual-legal positions. Adjudication, thus viewed, is both a product and beneficiary of a conflict between parties—much as capitalism is expected to benefit (the people and the system) by free economic competition. Modern adjudication is the child of the Age of Reason: the conflict is resolved by intellectual (and scientific) debate and persuasion, unlike earlier resort to trial and judgment by witchcraft, magic, fire or ordeal."[3]

It has been observed that the goal of the adjudicatory process is to convince the umpire, by rational means, of one's factual superiority and that a given disposition of the case is more in conformity with public policy, as embodied in law, than the disposition urged by the opposing party. The hallmarks of adjudication in Anglo-American law are reliance on intellectual persuasion, the regulated conflict of parties, a highly visible, duly constitutional procedure, and the independence of the umpire, modified by the popular input of the jury.

The conflict resolution of the Anglo-American trial was designed to take place in open court. The trial was not viewed as a cooperative venture, it was intended to be adversary. The rules of evidence were developed to insist on the adversary posture, with each party advancing its most defensible yet extreme positions. Much as fierce individualistic economic competition was to produce better and cheaper products for all to share in, fierce adversity in court was to produce the truth. Just like combinations in restraint of trade were viewed as negating economic competition, the competition for truth was not to be modified by less stringent adversity. Consequently, the rules of evidence (See Wigmore's earlier editions) failed to permit pretrial discovery that in any way would interfere with each party's conduct of its own trial strategy. To this day the equivalent of the reporter's "scoop"—the "surprise" witness, document, or demonstrative evidence—loom as dramatic highlights of the trial process.

It was the growth of constitutional protectionism in criminal procedure and the influx of cases requiring alternative handling that modified the traditional trial format. The pretrial process was developed as a significant stage in criminal cases mostly in the second half of this century. In the first place, there was an increasing resort to pretrial motions as a means of protecting the accused against illegally obtained evidence. With the growth of the suppression doctrine, constitutional issues of arrest and search were being taken up prior to the actual trial stage as a means of a more effective criminal defense strategy.

Increasingly, also, pretrial exchange of information and consultation were being advanced as a means for planning diversion programs. The recognition that dismissal or informal dispositions would be desirable in the case of marginal offenders who require treatment or diversion to other community programs increased resort to pretrial efforts involving counsel and at times the court.

In 1967 the president's crime commission advocated a general increase in pretrial discovery as a guarantee of fairer trials. Taking notice of a growing change in the characteristics of the American trial process, the commission stated:

> Over the past generation broad discovery, by examination of witnesses and evidence, has become commonplace in civil cases, but its utilization in

> criminal cases has been slowed by fears that pre-trial disclosure of the Government's case would lead to perjury and threats to witnesses, and that undue disclosure of confidential criminal files would impede ongoing investigations. The defendant's privilege against testifying forecloses the full mutuality of discovery by both sides that exists in civil cases and could place an unfair additional burden on the prosecution.[4]

The president's commission sensed the trend of the following years when it expressed its general support for the "expansion of pre-trial discovery and dispositions in criminal cases to ensure the fairness and accuracy of trial and pre-trial dispositions."[5] Advocated also was expanded mutual discovery, by both defense and prosecution, within constitutional limits. In return for the prosecution's release of information concerning its witnesses and their statements (including statements by the accused to the police or grand jury, medical, scientific, and expert witness reports and details of tangible evidence)—the defendant was expected to behave likewise. With the expansion of pretrial discovery, the defendant is required in many jurisdictions to disclose in advance whether he will assert particular defenses such as insanity or an alibi, what witnesses he will call, and what physical evidence he will present.

The shift from the "close to one's chest" trial adversity of the past to the new cooperative search of "fairness" is well underway. But not only constitutional protection and the search for fairness account for this departure from the traditional trial and rules of evidence. In part, the pretrial process was accepted as a tool for more efficient and effective adjudication. By having time-consuming conflicts of evidence resolved separately and earlier, it was expected that the formal and central trial process would be simplified and expedited.

The outcome is not yet clear and certain. Pretrial, in many instances, has become minitrial with its own time-consuming schedules. For some counsel, the fierce adversary process is now repeated in several separate arenas. The beneficial effects of discovery and other pretrial measures on the main trial have not been fully measured or documented. The American trial process has been dramatically modified. In many ways it now resembles the accusatory process of the European law system more than ever before. But to some of those who sought to simplify the American trial, the present system seems to have substituted, if biblical illusion is to be allowed, many "stations of the cross" for the original single station.

The Plea-bargaining System: Greater Justice or its Miscarriage?

"The question of guilt or innocence is not contested in the overwhelming majority of criminal cases," reported the president's crime commission in

1967. "A recent estimate is that guilty pleas account for 90 percent of all convictions, and perhaps as high as 95 percent of misdemeanor convictions."[6] The statistics were accurate; but the assertion regarding the failure to contest guilt was misleading.

The guilty plea, which in frequency has replaced the trial process, is no manifestation of the defendant's urge to confess. Instead, it is the result of an elaborate system based on prosecutional overcharging, defense denials of any wrongdoing and subsequent bazaar-like negotiations whereby the accused pleads guilty to some related or lesser offense in return for the prosecution's agreement to a lenient sentence. In reality, the defendant strikes a bargain in lieu of taking chances with an uncertain court outcome. The prosecution, likewise, may have legitimate reasons for bargaining with the defendant. These may relate to the strength of the state's case and the time, expense, and uncertainty of a contested jury trial. "Furthermore," notes Delmar Karlen, "in light of the general severity of American penal statutes, the bargaining plea is a useful device for insuring that the defendant will be punished while avoiding an unduly harsh penalty."[7]

Offenders do not necessarily view plea bargaining as a benevolent experience. The New York State Special Commission on Attica reported: "What makes inmates most cynical about their preprison experience is the plea-bargaining system... . Even though an inmate may receive the benefit of a shorter sentence, the plea-bargaining system is characterized by deception and hypocrisy which divorce the inmate from the reality of the crime...almost 90 percent of the inmates surveyed had been solicited to enter a plea bargain. Most were bitter, believing that they did not receive effective legal representation or that the judge did not keep the state's promise... ".[8] To the extent that a declaration of guilt is intended to serve a cathartic function for both society and offender, this is not accomplished when a plea bargain is struck. The plea bargaining process may serve to further reinforce the offender's sense of injustice and self-righteousness and his resistance to "rehabilitation." Frequently the suspicion that defense counsel opted for a speedy outcome and fee, instead of an uncertain trial, is not totally without justification.

Criticism of plea bargaining comes also from other directions. For it is suspected that the frequent result of the practice is that defendants are not dealt with as severely as might otherwise be the case, thus reducing the deterrent impact of the law. The prosecuting attorney is thus viewed as the culprit, for failing to fully enforce the requirements of the law. Most observers have therefore concluded that although pragmatic and time-saving, the practice is unseemly and ethically questionable.

In its 1973 report, the National Advisory Commission on Standards and Goals recommended that as soon as possible, but in no event later than 1978, "negotiations between prosecutors and defendants—either personally or through their attorneys—concerning concessions to be made in return for guilty pleas should be prohibited.''[9] In this total condemnation of plea bargaining, the commission reached a conclusion contrary to the 1967 president's crime commission and the ABA's Standards for Criminal Justice. Both the crime commission and the ABA found much to criticize in the plea-bargaining practice and pointed out the potentials for abuse inherent in the discretion permitted the prosecution. Yet the conclusion favored the implementation of reform that would ''render plea negotiation not only acceptable but valuable.''[10] Among the suggested reform there is a class for full judicial review of the terms of all plea agreements, for a careful formulation of uniform administrative standards and criteria to be used by the prosecutorial staff in all plea negotiation, for the defendant's right to representation by counsel during negotiation, for the prohibition of certain prosecutorial threats and inducements, and for disregarding the defendant's plea entry in determining sentence.

The debate on plea bargaining is far from concluded. Some self-described pragmatists assert that the overburdened American justice system is no longer capable of coping with the influx of cases requiring full-dress judicial handling. They claim that even a fragmentary reduction in guilty pleas and a consequent doubling of cases that require trial would pose an unbearable burden for the system. Some supporters view plea bargaining as a fully acceptable and respectable conclusion of prosecution. ''Both the shame of compromise and the righteous demand for full retribution must fade. Instead, attention should be focused, without apology, on assuring legal regularity in the process. Too, the quasi-religious view of the plea as a blind and penitent confession must yield to the pragmatic ideals of an informed and voluntary choice of mutually advantageous terms between adversaries. Judgment by plea, properly supervised, is no inferior brand of justice to judgment by verdict.[11]

Others view the continuation of plea bargaining as inimical to the very concept of ordered justice and an independent judiciary. They believe that a citizen's right to his ''day in court'' means precisely that and not less. The delegation of judicial fact finding and guilt to an administrative officer—the prosecutor—is described as contrary to constitutional propriety. It is basic to the position of these ''traditionalists'' that consideration of time, cost, and efficiency cannot be allowed to water down the requirements of proper legality. The conclusion reached is that the modification proposed for plea bargaining cannot remake it into an acceptable process and, on the other hand, that it is not unrealistic to expect that adequate resources can and will be furnished to allow the adjudicatory system to meet its full-fledged obligations.

While the debate continues, the evidence at hand shows no movement toward the abolition or the radical reform of plea bargaining. The supporters continue to argue pragmatic considerations. Yet the basic flaws in the practice are of such dimensions as to challenge fundamentally the moral and ethical foundations of the system. Without a sense of popular and professional respect and confidence in the basic operations, no system of justice can survive.

The Trial: Time, Staging, and Actors

It was long assumed that a speedy trial is the right of and in the interest of the defendant. But for the modern accused who, unlike past defendants, is not subjected to confinement, the trial might be an unwelcome event. Possibly the strongest claim for speedy trials is derived therefore from community interest. Delays adversely affect the availability and recollection of witnesses, and since the burden of proof rests on the prosecution, passage of time is likely to dilute its case. If the community's sense of justice is to be assuaged by the judicial process, one requires action while the memory of the crime still prevails. Neither is the impact of either punishment or rehabilitation, imposed on the defendant, likely to be most effective when the passage of time has turned the initial crime into a remote and forgotten occurrence.

The complaint often heard about American criminal trials is that they are long in coming and lengthy in making. The National Advisory Commission on Standards and Goals pointed out that it is not uncommon for ten to twelve months to elapse between the apprehension of an alleged offender and his trial.[12] Time is consumed by grand jury indictments, preliminary hearings, ineffective scheduling procedures, and unreasonable continuances. Neither is delay in the actual trial process unusual. The commission cited a recent trial in which four months were consumed in selecting a jury. More frequent, though less dramatic, delays result from conflicting scheduling, routine court adjournments, counsel's response to unexpected evidence, introduction of irrelevant evidence and evidentiary challenges, preparation of jury instructions, and so on.

In great part, the delay in bringing a case to trial is attributable to the overcommitments and the lack of a sense of urgency on the part of the defense and at times also on the part of prosecuting counsel. The scheduling machinery of the courts has not effectively coped with counsels' inefficiency or delaying tactics. The delay in actual trial, on the other hand, is primarily a consequence of the traditional role definitions for prosecuting and defense counsel and their interaction with the judicial officer. It has been suggested that more speedy and effective trials can be brought about by improvements in judicial administration and by a streamlining of the court procedure.

The president's crime commission in 1967 produced a model timetable for the processing of criminal cases.[13] (See figure 6–1) It focused special attention on seven points in the process: (1) arrest; (2) first judicial appear-

Figure 6–1. Model Timetable for Felony Cases, Projected by the President's Commission on Law Enforcement and Administration of Justice. Taken from the Commission's *Task Force Report: The Courts,* 1967, pp. 86–87.

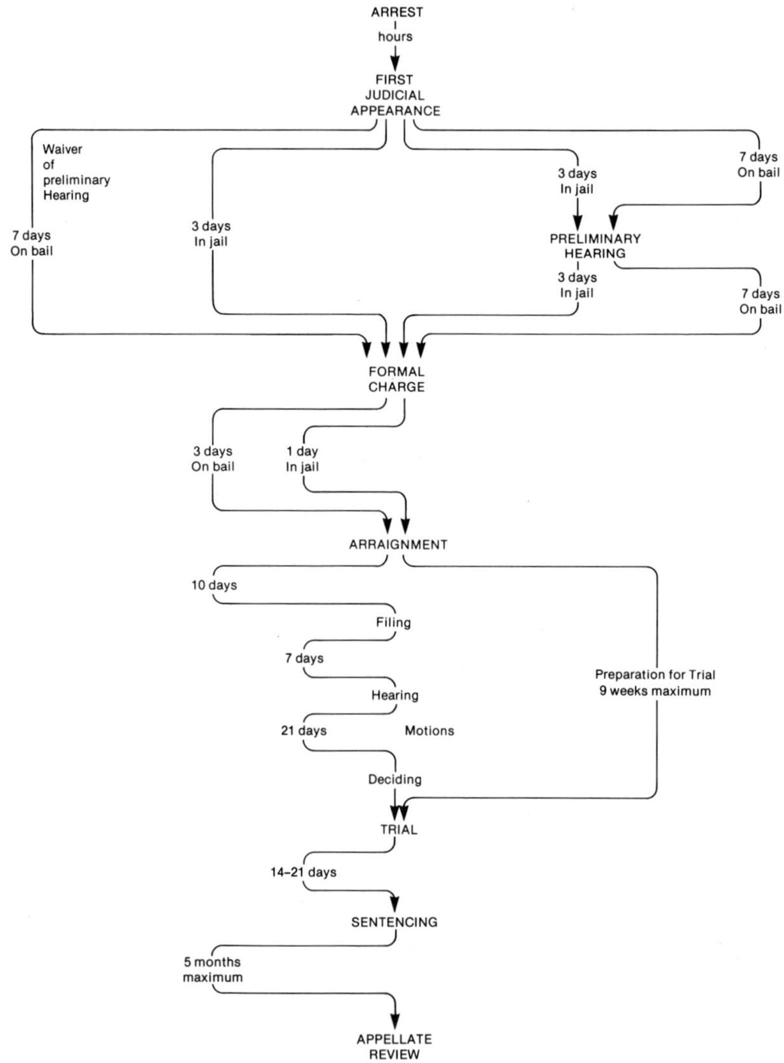

Arrest to First Judicial Appearance: Many States and the Federal courts require appearance "without necessary delay." Depending on the circumstances, a few hours—or less—may be regarded as "unnecessary delay." Compliance with this standard may require extension of court operating hours and the continual availability of a magistrate.

First Judicial Appearance to Arraignment: Standards here are complicated because: (a) a shorter period is appropriate for defendants in jail than for those released; (b) preliminary

ance (presentment or preliminary hearing); formal charge (indictment or filing of information); (4) pretrial motions; (5) trial; (6) sentencing; and (7) appellate review.

The timetable projected a tight schedule. The time from arrest to the first judicial appearance was not to exceed twenty-four hours. After the filing of the information by the prosecutor, no more than seven days were to elapse before the defendant was taken to arraignment. In case the grand jury returned an indictment, its filing should be no later than fifteen days after the first judicial appearance, and the accused should be granted arraignment and should be heard within one week of filing. Judges were expected to decide pretrial motions within three weeks of hearing. Barring exceptional circumstances, trial should follow within nine weeks of arraignment. Again, absent exceptional circumstances, sentencing should follow within fourteen to twenty-one days of conviction. The conclusion of appellate review was to occur not later than five months from the time of sentence. The total time from arrest to conclusion of appeal thus would not exceed nine months.[14]

The 1973 National Advisory Commission on Standards and Goals repeated the quest for a model timetable.[15] (See figure 6-2) It projected a total of fourteen days between arrest and preliminary hearing, fifteen days from the hearing to the filing of pretrial motions, eight days for the resolution of the motions, two days for the pretrial conference, thus requiring a total of sixty days from arrest to felony trial.[16]

It is possible for trials to be conducted within such specified times. Whether it is likely for such firm schedules, requiring coordination of judges, juries, prosecutors, defense counsel, witnesses and experts, to be established and implemented is less certain. The greatest difficulty rests in the fact that for each of the parties the given case is merely one of many, each fitting in a complicated and diverse schedule.

---

hearings are waived in many cases, and the formality and usefulness of the hearing varies; (c) formal charge in some cases is by grand jury indictment, while in others by prosecutor's information—usually the right to indictment can be waived by the defendant; and (d) in many jurisdictions proceedings through preliminary hearing in felony cases are in one court while grand jury charge and subsequent proceedings are in another. While in all cases these steps should take no more than 17 days, in most cases it should be possible to accomplish them in substantially less time.

Arraignment to Trial: Many of the increasing number of motions require the judge to hear and decide factual issues. Discovery orders may require time for the assembling and screening of documents. The recommended standard would allow slightly more than 5 weeks for these steps and would allow a total of 9 weeks between arraignment and trial. Where complicated motions are not involved, the period before trial should be shortened.

Trial to Sentence: During this period a presentence investigation should be completed.

Sentence to Appellate Review: This standard is based on the time periods of the proposed Uniform Rules of Federal Appellate Procedure. Many jurisdictions would have to change existing practices concerning printing and preparation of records to meet this standard.

Figure 6–2. Model Timetable for Felony Cases to Achieve Trial Within Sixty Days, Projected by the National Advisory Commission on Criminal Justice. Taken from their "Standards and Goals Reports," in *Courts,* 1973:XX–XXI.

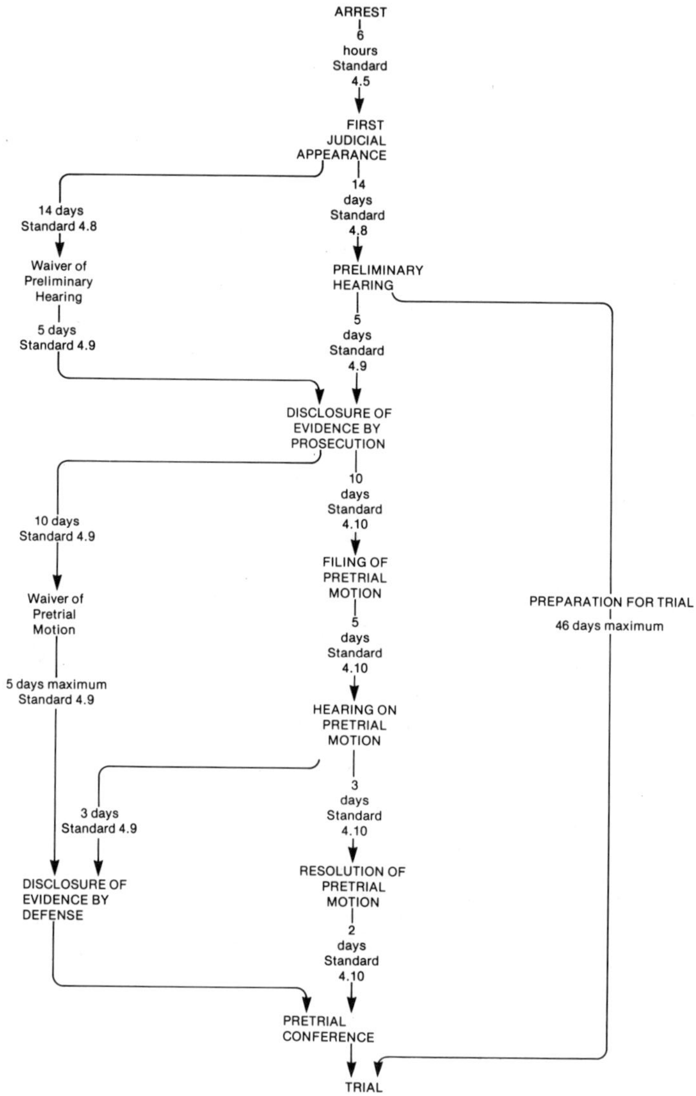

In some felony cases, the commission recommends that a summons or citation be issued in lieu of arrest. In such instances, there would be no first judicial appearance, and the commission calls for a preliminary hearing within fourteen days of the issuance of citation or summons. In felony cases in which there is a grand jury indictment, the commission recommends that no

Reducing the time requirement from arrest to trial is the first step toward a more timely, efficient, and effective trial schedule. Little affected, under the proposals, will be the trial process itself, that is, the procedure for the selection of jurors, the submission of evidence, the examination of witnesses, the legal arguments and instructions, the production of the verdict, and the sentencing. Many trial experts view the American process as overly technical and cumbersome. It has been observed that the net effect of American practices, as compared to the English, "is to shift ultimate power from the trial (judge) to the jury and appellate court, and to denigrate the position of defense counsel, while exalting the role of prosecutors and the accused himself.[17] Critics point to the English and European practices as more satisfactory models. Particular criticism is directed against abusive American practices in jury selection, evidentiary objections, witness examinations, in the right to opening and closing statements.

Some reforms have been advocated. It has been suggested that expedited trial proceedings "require that as much as possible be known before trial about the issues and admissible evidence. Moreover, defendants aware of the strength of the prosecution case against them seem more willing to plead guilty than those who believe there may be a chance to defeat the government at trial. Consequently, all proposals for modernized criminal procedure include quite broad provisions for discovery."[18] It has also been pointed out that under the English practice there is no *voir dire* examination during which prospective jurors can be questioned by counsel in an effort to determine not only their fitness but also their sociopsychological inclinations. Stricter control of the practice and placing the examination in the hands of the judge himself have been recommended as protection against abuse. The delay produced by counsels' incessant and vociferous arguments in court regarding admissibility of evidence are rare and consume no time in the English courts. It has been suggested that defense counsel in the United States, traditionally deprived of pretrial discovery and so being ignorant of the prosecution's evidence, tend to object out of a sheer fear of the unknown. Another fact is that English barristers frequently agree between themselves before trial as to what evidence is and is not admissible.[19] For the reduction of delaying practices at trial, some have suggested greater resort to pre-trial discovery, dropping the American rule that error cannot be considered on appeal unless objected to at the trial court level, and also a more effective delegation to judges of the function of preparing and delivering jury instructions.

In great part, the suggestions for a more effective trial process require reliance on learned judges who are to be central and dominant figures in the

---

preliminary hearing be held. The time limits and steps shown as following the preliminary hearing become applicable upon apprehension of the indicted individual or upon service of a summons following the indictment.

courtroom, as well as greater cooperation and professional courtesy between counsel. The smaller and more select English bar makes these practices easier. The less professional American judiciary makes some of these developments difficult.

Diversion, Alternatives, and the Future

It was submitted at the beginning of this chapter that the number of criminal cases reaching the trial stage was too minute a portion of the criminal scene to have an impact on either deterrence or rehabilitative goals. The segments that followed explored existing criminal justice procedures that further affect or diminish the effectiveness of the trial process. Among these, we considered pretrial discovery, court congestion and delay, plea bargaining, and time-consuming trials.

Even if the pretrial and trial processes were to be streamlined, it is doubtful that the courts could cope with a substantially larger number of trial cases than are now handled. If plea bargaining were to be abolished or drastically curtailed or formalized, the reform again would place an added burden on the trial court. Concluding that the trial system has reached its optimum capacity and capability, the majority of judicial experts and reformers have been seeking solutions in other quarters.

"One reason for the present saturation of the criminal courts throughout the country is the long-standing assumption that the criminal law is the most effective cure for most of society's ill," writes George.[20] That assumption is no longer current. So much disillusionment has set in about the criminal process that total "decriminalization" has become a major movement everywhere. A different technique for "purging the criminal justice system of bootless prosecutions" is "screening," a systematic *termination* of prosecutions in "deserving," less serious situations, or "diversion," a referral of selected cases, otherwise criminal, from the courts to other social agencies that can better handle them.

The diversion movement has sought to leave the mainstream of criminal trials unaffected, while reducing its load through a siphoning off to other agencies. A yet broader move toward different alternatives to conventional adjudication has also been underway.[21] Alternatives to conventional adjudication can assume a variety of forms. A major segment of these alternatives is designed to change criminal offenses into administrative violations, particularly in such areas as traffic, housing, or other regulatory infractions, thereby permitting administrative dispositions in lieu of the conventional criminal process. The institution of various arbitration tribunals and informal community courts is also part of the alternatives approach.

The growing flock of diversions and alternatives has been looked on as a major tool for the reform and restructuring of the trial process. But a comprehensive study of this movement, recently concluded, points to some shortcomings and limitations:[22]

1. Recently instituted alternatives to conventional adjudication (with the exception of a few programs such as those decriminalizing public intoxication) affect only a small portion of all cases that require disposition, while the conventional system of justice continues to be little affected.

2. The primary impact of alternatives is on lower criminal or misdemeanor courts. The alternatives movement has provided a long overdue infusion of new programs, procedures, and personnel into these courts. In many jurisdictions, the climate of justice in the lower courts has been improved.

3. Alternatives to conventional adjudication are usually designed to deal with minor and nonviolent crime and cannot be expected to have a noticeable direct impact on major street crime.

4. While alternatives to adjudication encroach on the traditional concept of the offender's "day in court," they equally deprive society of the symbolic value of an official finding of offender accountability. The loss of both symbols in serous criminal cases can critically affect the functioning of criminal justice.

5. Many alternatives, especially pretrial diversion programs, have tended to become substitutes for decriminalization; they have thus exerted a conservative influence on criminal justice by reducing pressure for legislative decriminalization.

6. There has been a decline in popular participation in the adjudicatory process due to the reduced role of the grand and petit jury as well as a diminishing use of lay justices of the peace. This trend should be reversed, and new forms of popular participation should be encouraged.

7. The pragmatic and symbolic values of conventional adjudications have been constantly eroded by procedural complexity and delay, excessive plea bargaining, and the small sample of all serious criminal offenders standing full trial. The community's "sense of justice" requires greater reliance on traditional adjudication for serious offenses.

8. Informal and inexpensive alternatives to adjudication have their place and require encouragement in intrafamily, school, work, and neighborhood disputes, where mediation and other possibilities of popular conflict resolution are likely.

9. Lesser infractions of the law—in the areas of vehicular, housing, and other regulatory requirements—should be increasingly handled through administrative adjudications.

10. Minor infractions of law, especially in the areas of private morals and so called victimless or complaintless offenses, can be handled more

appropriately and inexpensively through legislative decriminalization than through referral to more costly adjudicatory alternatives.

Some concluding comments are in order. Criminal labeling is counter-productive and should be avoided whenever possible. A criminal justice process that relies on a small sample of enforcement is ineffective and requires a curtailment of scope. A substantial reduction in criminality, and therefore in subsequent enforcement and trials can be produced through decriminalization. Minor offenses can be better handled through administrative rather than penal measures and institutions. Regarding the core of criminal offenses (which pose serious threats to life, limb, or property), formality and visibility should not be sacrificed. A greater commitment to the principle of "legality" prevailing on the Continent, contrasted with the American principle of "opportunity," would require substantially more funding and a tightening up of the trial process. But in this wealthiest of nations, we cannot subscribe to the argument that crime control and justice are too expensive.

Notes

1. President's Commission on Law Enforcement and Administration of Justice, Task Force Report: *The Courts* (Washington, D.C.: U.S. Government Printing Office, 1967).
2. Task Force Report, supra, n. 1.
3. Nicholas N. Kittrie, et al., *The New Justice: Alternatives to Conventional Criminal Adjudication* (Washington D.C.: NILECJ, U.S. Department of Justice, 1977), p. viii.
4. President's Commission, supra, n. 2, pp. 138–139.
5. Ibid.
6. Task Force Report, supra, n. 1.
7. Delmar Karlen, *Anglo American Criminal Justice* (New York: Oxford University Press, 1967), p. 177.
8. *Attica: The Official Report of the New York State Special Commission on Attica* (New York: Bantam Books, 1972), pp. 30–31.
9. American Bar Association, *National Advisory Commission on Criminal Justice Standards and Goals* (Washington, D.C.: U.S. Government Printing Office, 1973), std. 3.1, p. 46.
10. Ibid., p. 49.
11. Reprinted with permission from a symposium entitled Criminal Process in the Seventies, *Law and Contemporary Problems,* vol. 41, No. 1, at p. 130 (Winter 1977), published by the Duke University School of Law, Durham, North Carolina. Copyright 1977 by Duke University.
12. Standards and Goals, supra, n. 12.

13. Task Force Report, supra, n. 1., pp. 84–87.

14. Ibid.

15. Standards and Goals, supra, n. 12.

16. Ibid.

17. Karlen, supra, n. 10, p. 177.

18. Reprinted with permission from the symposium entitled Criminal Process in the Seventies. *Law and Contemporary Problems,* at pp. 90, 94 (Winter 1977) published by the Duke University School of Law, Durham, North Carolina. Copyright 1977 by Duke University.

19. Karlen, supra, n. 10, p. 186.

20. George, supra, n. 21, p. 90.

21. Kittrie, et al., supra, n. 6.

22. Ibid., pp. xi–xii.

Commentary

Terrence McCarthy

I disagree with Dean Kittrie's premise that the criminal trial is relatively unimportant to our criminal justice system. I have never been impressed by criminal justice statistics, and I think most of us in the field understand why. In any event, I think we could all agree that few cases are tried. Nevertheless, trials and how they are conducted are important to certain people. They are certainly important to the defendant. They are important to the prosecutor, to the judges, and to myself as a defense attorney. I do not deny, and I do not understate, the importance of other agencies in the criminal justice system, but I respectfully suggest that if one is to consider criminal law as a whole, it must be concerned with cases that are tried and how those cases are tried.

This is not to say, of course, that the trial procedures cannot and indeed should not be reviewed from time to time, and in fact, they are. I cite to you probably the most significant contribution to criminal justice in the last hundred years. It is *The American Bar Association's Standards on Criminal Justice.* The standards are exellent models. I cite to you also, the work of the various procedural rule committees of the states and the federal government. They constantly reevaluate the criminal trial. One other preliminary comment if you will: The criminal trial, contrary to popular tradition, is not totally adversary in nature. For example, take the *Brady*[1] decision, which says, in effect, if the prosecution has evidence favorable to a defendant, it must be revealed to him. That is not totally adversary. Conversely, defense attorneys are not always in a truly adversary position. As a matter of fact, defense attorneys do not have an obligation to produce the truth. Obviously, one cannot support falsehoods, but let me tell you that I have no obligation to support the truth. For example, I might in a given case tell a particular client that I do not want him to take the stand. I want him to assert the Fifth Amendment, or his right not to take the stand, in a criminal case. Certainly, that is not supportive of the truth. Again I might move to suppress evidence in a case notwithstanding that evidence is supportive of the truth. I also believe in reciprocal discovery up to a point—the point at which it interferes with the constitutional protections of the defendant.

The second pretrial procedure that Dean Kittrie mentioned is the raising of constitutional issues by motions to suppress. Rather than hindering the entire system of criminal justice, motions to suppress assist it. If I file a motion to suppress before trial and I lose, the possibility is strong that I may end up pleading the defendant guilty, thereby relieving the system of a trial. Or the possibility is present that I may appeal solely on that record, again precluding the necessity of a trial. And if I happen to win that motion to suppress, of course we have eliminated the trial from the system.

As for plea bargaining, I agree that there has been much abuse in the past, but I disagree with the idea that not too much has been done recently in the area of plea bargaining. The last few years have seen much improvement. The ABA standards on guilty pleas are an example. Second, plea bargaining has been recognized and received judicial approbation from no less an authority than the Chief Justice. However, I agree that we must eliminate the hypocrisy in plea bargaining. We must involve the defendant, place everything on the record, and encourage prosecutors not to overcharge. Although it happens, plea bargaining should not be the result of a weak case by the prosecutor, nor should it be the result of an understaffed prosecutor's office. If that is the basis of plea bargaining, then the major fault lies in the fiscal support of the office. Finally, the ABA standards should be adopted, and judges should be taken out of plea bargaining.

I am a bit concerned with the suggestions that I read in Dean Kittrie's paper that we streamline and expedite the court proceedings. This is a refrain I hear constantly. It is suggested that experts view our process as overly technical and cumbersome. What would be eliminated or changed? The three things mentioned leave me aghast. Evidentiary objections? Witness examinations? Opening statements and closing arguments? These are essential to our system of trial, and they work.

In summary, look to the ABA standards, and one will find proper trial procedures. Many states have adopted the Federal Rules of Criminal Procedure, and more recently several states have adopted the Federal Rules of Evidence. I think they are generally excellent.

Finally, concern should be shown for the professional status of judges, prosecutors, the defense bar, and particularly the public defenders' offices.

Note

1. 373 U.S. 83 (1963).

Commentary

Earl J. Silbert

When we talk about crime, we tend so often to divide up the institutions of the criminal justice system. We talk about police, prosecutors, courts, corrections, and perhaps parole boards and probation officers. What we never really look at is how we are going to respond as a society to the unitary problem of crime. It is not just a matter of a defense attorney's determination whether there is a good motion to suppress or a speedy trial claim nor the police decision whether to arrest or the prosecutor's to present the case in court. The problem of crime cuts across society in so many different ways that a broad look at the criminal justice process mandates change. Can one look at the statistics of reported crimes, observe that only a few cases ultimately are brought to trial, and still say a trial represents nothing more than a morality play? I think not. I do not disagree with the statistics; they are basically accurate. I do disagree with the interpretation of the statistics. Certainly there are not many trials, and there are some trials that do appear to take on the significance of a morality play. But to draw significance from a Watergate trial or from a Charles Manson trial is to miss entirely what is happening. The significant trial is of the person who chokes a woman as she is walking home carrying grocery bags or a trial in which no one is present except for a defense attorney, the judge, the prosecutor, and the witnesses.

And what does the paucity of trials mean? Does that mean that something is wrong with the process? No. It reflects what is going on if the police and prosecutors are working together.

How does one go about doing something about the crime problem? If there are one thousand reported robberies, does that mean there are one thousand alleged robbers? Actually, the chances are that there are one hundred robbers or fifty robbers who committed them. So the fact that you perhaps catch only a robber on one good solid charge hardly means that you have got one robber out of a thousand. The question is, after proper determination that an offender is a repeater, what do we do with him? The real objective is for prosecutors and police to focus their resources on the repeater. If necessary, bring them to trial, of course, but also bring all the appropriate information to the sentencing judge, defense attorney, and probation officer so that a meaningful sentence can be imposed.

The criminal justice system is a complex process. What we have to do in responding to the problem of crime is to develop an ability to deal with crime in a meaningful and individualized manner. It is necessary to have within the police department, persons with special competence. Prosecutors must be able to work with investigators and compel the production of documents and testimony. Rules must be properly developed. While there are many ABA standards with which I disagree, they certainly are a first-rate starting point.

So far as discovery is concerned, my comments are brief. I share with others the view that if there is to be discovery, it must be mutual. Discovery should be full and complete with the important exception, of course, of the Fifth Amendment right of the defendant. But in the development of pretrial procedures, and particularly when dealing with common-law crimes as one is in the state court process, there has to be a triple focus. The focus cannot be as it often is on the accused alone or the state alone.

A third element is the victims and witnesses of the crime. I never hear their concerns or problems analyzed whenever I hear a discussion of pretrial procedures. It is assumed that they can come to police line-ups, to the grand jury, and to multiple interviews with police and prosecutors. That is both unrealistic and unfair. There have been studies indicating (particularly in the area of common law and street crime, robbery, burglary, rape, murders) that however sophisticated and skillful the police may be, the solution depends on citizen and witness cooperation. If the process we developed, pretrial and trial, is so burdensome on them that they fail to cooperate, the process cannot succeed.

Finally, we are in need of a coordinated system. Currently we have a system that lacks essential coordination, that is totally fragmented, and yet somehow we are expected to solve the problem of crime as though crime is singular, as though it is confined to an isolated jurisdiction. That is a pipe dream, and as long as we do nothing about the pipe dream, we are going to be sitting in places like this trying to solve the problem of crime and making very little progress.

7 The New Indiana Sentencing Code: Is It Indeterminate Sentencing?

Andrew von Hirsch

This decade has witnessed a striking shift of opinion about sentencing reform. Whereas an earlier generation of reformers stressed flexibility and discretion, the emphasis is now on consistency and limits on discretion. As the old rehabilitative ideology loses its influences, there is renewed interest in such once–alien notions as "just deserts." Indeterminacy of sentence has come under attack, and determinate sentencing is coming into vogue.[1]

The new Indiana sentencing code[2] is often spoken of as an embodiment of these new ideas.[3] Certainly, the code seems at first glance to have many of the newly fashionable features. It sets forth standards for sentencing basing the amount of punishment chiefly on the gravity of the crime. The *presumptive sentence* device is used: The code sets forth a definite amount of punishment for each of seven gradations of gravity, with variations permitted on account of specified aggravating and mitigating circumstances. The convicted offender supposedly learns the duration of his stay in prison when the judge passes sentence; he need no longer await the decision of a parole board many months, or possibly years, later.

As one of those who have been urging these new ideas of reform,[4] however, I would like to examine the Indiana statute more closely. Are the code's provisions really consistent with the notions of consistency and justice that underlie the reformers' proposals? Does the new statute try to achieve the substance of reform, or does it merely use the form?

To do this, I shall try in the first part of this paper to summarize what the new reformers' aims have been. Then I shall consider the Indiana law to see whether and to what degree it furthers those aims.

In so doing, I shall be looking at the statute on its face. Having not studied how the Indiana law works in practice, I am not in a position to describe the statute's actual impact on sentencing decisions. I shall be asking the question a legislative analyst might ask: If the statute were implemented more or less as it is written, would it help achieve the fairness and predictability that reformers have been seeking?

I am writing this from a definite theoretical perspective, the perspective embodied in the literature on determinate sentencing that has appeared since the early 1970s. I am asking whether *these* purposes are furthered by the Indiana law. Possibly, this perspective is a mistaken one, and the path of reform should lie elsewhere. But I shall not deal with that larger question here.

The Reformers' Aims

The reformers' aims are neatly summarized in the title of one of their reports, *Fair and Certain Punishment.*[5] In seeking fairness and greater certainty, they have stressed two major themes: *predictability* and *commensurability*. The caprice of present sentencing practice should be replaced by predictable punishments and regulated by standards, and penalties should better reflect the degree of blameworthiness of the criminal conduct.

The new literature on determinate sentencing stresses the disparities that have attended wide-open sentencing and parole discretion. Punishments, it is said, must be brought under the rule of law.[6]

Enhancing predictability, according to this literature, involves two steps. First, standards or guidelines should be adopted that specify how much punishment offenders are to receive for various kinds of criminal conduct. Second, when an offender is sentenced to prison, he should be informed early of his expected length of stay. Traditional sentencing practice was seen as indeterminate in two senses: in having no general standards to control individual sentencers' discretion and in making the imprisoned offender suffer the needless anxiety of waiting before learning how long he may expect to remain confined. Determinate sentences then are sentences that both (1) operate under standards, and (2) inform prisoners early of their length of stay in prison.

The literature suggests some variety in the manner of drafting the standards. Some writers urge that there be specific amounts of punishment prescribed as the presumptive sentences for various crimes.[7] Others would prescribe suggested ranges of penalties instead.[8] Some would devise an intricate code of penalties, with major crimes broken down into numerous subcategories, each with their prescribed punishments.[9] Others would have a simpler and more flexible system, consisting of a limited number of gradations of penalties, and more discretion residually allowed to individual decision makers.[10] There also are variants on *who* should set the standards. Some reformers have urged that the legislature itself write the sentencing standards.[11] California has adopted this approach in its new sentencing code.[12] Others suggest that there be a specialized rule-making body, a sentencing commission, to perform this task.[13] Minnesota has recently established such a body.[14] Still another proposal has been to use the parole board as the vehicle for determinacy, and Oregon has opted for this method. Under legislation adopted there in 1977, the state parole board is required to write standards for duration of confinement. Those standards must look chiefly to the gravity of the offense; the board is also required to inform the individual prisoner of his expected release date shortly after he enters prison.[15] (Which of these standard-setting agencies are to be preferred is something I have discussed in a recent study.)[16]

Behind this variety, however, there is a definite theme: There should be standards that regulate the amounts of punishment offenders should receive and that guide and limit individual sentencers' discretion. And those limits on discretion should work both upward and downward. It is not merely that judges and parole agencies should be prevented from imposing lenient penalties for serious crimes (as proponents of mandatory minimum sentences have also urged), but that there be equally effective limits on the imposition of severe punishments. Consistency is the aim, not toughness.

The dominant sentencing ideology of earlier decades focused on rehabilitation and prediction. The sentence supposedly would promote the offender's return to a law-abiding existence. If he could not be cured, he was to be isolated. Experts would determine which offenders were dangerous and confine them so long as they remained so. The offender's past criminal conduct was seen as significant only to the extent it helped predict future behavior.

The new literature criticizes this ordering of priorities as fundamentally unfair, as punishing people for what they *will* do, instead of for what they have done. Commensurability is thus given new emphasis.[17] Punishment, it is said, ascribes blame: It is thus a requirement of justice that the amount of punishment (and hence of implicit blame) should comport with the degree of blameworthiness of the criminal conduct. Only grave offenses merit severe penalties. Nonserious crimes deserve nonsevere punishments. Sentences must be commensurate in their severity with the seriousness of the criminal conduct.[18]

Among those who have stressed the importance of commensurability, there are some differences. In *Doing Justice,* I argued that desert considerations should define the amount of punishment an individual offender should receive. Variations in punishment would be permissible only to the extent they reflected variations in the gravity of the criminal conduct.[19] Norval Morris has argued that desert should be a limiting principle instead. It should set upper and lower bounds on the permissible quantum of punishment, within which the penalty might vary on other (for example, deterrent or incapcitative) grounds.[20]

Behind such diversities are important areas of agreement. The seriousness of the criminal conduct is now seen as a vitally important criterion for deciding penalties—much more so than it was under the traditional rehabilitative ideology. More important still is the emphasis on maintaining a reasonable proportion between the amount of the penalty and the gravity of the conduct. Severe penalties are seen as justified only where the conduct is heinous enough to merit that much condemnation. Inflating punishments to the point where they cease to comport with the blameworthiness of the conduct—even if this were effective as a crime-control technique—is ruled out as unjust.

How effective will such a scheme be in reducing crime? Some writers on determinacy—including Norval Morris and myself[21]—have doubted that there will be any great crime-reduction payoff from this (or any other) change in sentencing methods. Others such as James Q. Wilson have expressed more optimism. In a determinate-sentencing system, any one convicted of sufficiently serious criminal conduct would face time in prison; he could no longer escape with probation because that would supposedly rehabilitate him better. This could enhance deterrence, Wilson argues, by increasing the likelihood that commission of a serious crime would result in substantial punishment; it could also have incapacitative benefits since persons convicted of such crimes would be taken out of circulation for a period of time.[22] (Whether these benefits materialize remains to be seen. Determinacy can ensure only that those *convicted* of serious crimes get a substantial penalty: there remains the uncertainty about being caught and convicted. Hopes for increased deterrence and incapacitation could be disappointed if too many of those who commit serious felonies are not caught or are able to bargain charges down sufficiently.)[23]

But the pursuit of such crime-control aims must, in any event, be constrained by the moral limits of commensurability. One is an attempt in the first instance to create a fairer system. Wilson himself makes this clear in an illuminating passage from a 1977 article:

> Were I given the task of designing penal sanctions, I would begin as a retributivist—i.e., as one who sees the first task to be that of justice. I would try to propose penalties that seemed morally suitable for crimes and circumstances of various kinds. [Others] and I might disagree about some of these penalties, though I am willing to guess that, locked in a room for a day or so, we would find that we disagree on relatively few. But in justifying that schedule of penalties, based in the first instance on a concept of "just deserts," I would try to estimate the gains to society that might result from the deterrent or incapacitative effects of those penalties. Such facts and estimates would help society decide whether it agreed with those penalties and whether it was prepared much or little to see them institutionalized.[24]

The goal then is not to simply pursue whatever works. Rather, it is to try to create a reasonably just system—that is, to seek effectiveness within limitations of justice.

Does the Indiana Statute Promote Those Aims?

Now let us turn to the Indiana statute. In doing so, we should be realistic in our expectations. No actual statute or regulation, adopted in a welter of conflicting pressures and constituencies, can neatly reflect a theoretical blueprint. When pursuing the practical business of change, reformers have no choice but to accommodate their aims to political and institutional realities. Half a loaf—perhaps with some not-so-palatable morsels—may be the best one can achieve. What we must ask therefore is whether the Indiana law furthers *on balance* the aims of which we have been speaking.

The statute creates the appearance of definiteness. Each class of felony has its presumptive sentence, and judges must consult a statutory list of aggravating and mitigating circumstances if they wish to vary from these penalties. Behind this appearance, however, lies a different reality, huge discretion still vested in judges and correctional officials. That discretion comes from two major sources in the law.

Discretion to Aggravate and Mitigate

The amount of deviation permitted for aggravating and mitigating circumstances is enormous, as shown in table 7-1. Thus rape committed while armed with a weapon, a Class A felony, carries a thirty-year presumptive sentence, but this can be raised to fifty or reduced to twenty years, a thirty-year spread! Armed robbery, a Classs B felony, starts with ten years, but then the judge can add another ten or subtract four—so that the effective range is six to twenty years. A common unarmed burglary is a Class C felony for which the presumptive sentence is five years, but the judge can go up to eight years or down to two years.[25]

The width of these ranges gives great significance to the statutory aggravating and mitigating factors. Yet some of these factors are extraordinarily vague, and they also reintroduce rehabilitation and prediction as major determinants of the amount of sentence. The armed robber with the ten-year presumptive sentence can find his amount doubled if the judge

Table 7-1
Sentencing Deviations Based on Aggravating and Mitigating Circumstances (*Years*)

Class Offense	*Presumptive Prison Term*	*Enhancement for Aggravation*	*Reduction for Mitigation*
Murder	40[a]	1-20	1-10
Class A felony	30	1-20	1-10
Class B felony	10	1-10	1-4
Class C felony	5	1-3	1-3
Class D felony	2	1-2	NA
Class A	up to 1	NA	NA

Source: Ind. Code, § 35, arts. 43, 44, and 50.

[a]Or death.

determines that he is "in need of correctional or rehabilitative treatment that can best be provided by his commitment to a penal facility." Or else he can find the sentence reduced by 40 percent, if the judge decides that "the character and attitudes of the person indicate that he is unlikely to commit another crime."[26]

Discretion on "Good Time"

When a convict is sentenced to prison under the new law, he is initially entitled to a credit for good behavior of 50 percent off his sentence—one day of reduction for each day served. He loses this right, however, if found by a corrections department disciplinary committee to have violated any of the department's rules. This credit-time is not vested. The statute states that "a person can be deprived of any part of the credit time he has earned if he violates a rule or regulation of the department."[27] Some of the departmental rules, for which such large amounts of credit-time may potentially be lost, proscribe such vaguely worded conduct as "failing to work as instructed by a supervisor" and "disturbing the peace and quiet, or orderly running of the institution or other area where the inmate is located."[28] This places enormous discretion over time actually served in the corrections department. And it widens the effective ranges still further. Our convicted armed robber, if he gets the most mitigated sentence from the judge and then is allowed to keep his credit-time, will actually serve three years, wheras another armed robber who gets the most aggravated sentence and has his credits taken away could actually serve twenty years.

The credit-time provisions also reintroduce another species of uncertainty, that of making it difficult for the prisoner to foretell when he will leave prison. Any disciplinary infraction, committed at any time, can effectively double the length of his stay. There are no vesting provisions such as the new California statute has;[29] nor are there any requirements that an independent agency must find the infractions to be "serious," as Oregon requires.[30] Only a prisoner with remarkable self-control could feel confident that he could, during a stay of several years in prison, avoid all rule violations altogether. Once a supposed violation had occurred, it would lie in the corrections department's discretion whether to bring it up to the department-wide disciplinary committee that can take away credit-time. As with unreformed parole, the prisoner cannot really be certain of the length of his stay until he actually leaves. (True, he may be able to get impressions about which kinds of cases lead in practice to denial of credit-time and which do not; but this would not be dissimilar to a prisoner's efforts to glean a parole board's releasing policies under the traditional indeterminate sentence. Guessing what a disciplinary committee might do is a far cry from being *prima facie* entitled to release at a specified time.

Severity

A still more disturbing feature of the new law is the great severity of its penalties. The figures mentioned already should suggest this: presumptive penalties (after deducting credit-time) of five years' actual confinement for a first offense of armed robbery; three years for a first burglary committed without a weapon, and so forth. A recent study by Todd Clear and his associates makes this still more apparent.[31] Clear took a sample of first-time felony offenders admitted to the Indiana Department of Corrections during the first half of 1976 and estimated how much time they would serve under the old Indiana sentencing system and under the new code. The results are shown in table 7-2. The comparable amounts of imprisonment that such first offenders would receive under Oregon's new guidelines[32] are shown in table 7-3.

Table 7-2
Estimate on Time Served—Previous Indiana Sentencing Provisions versus New Indiana Sentencing Provisions

Offense	*Time Served Old Law (Years)*	*Time Served New Code (Years)*	*Percent Increase or Decrease*
Rape	5.2	11.0	+112
Armed robbery	3.8	4.9	+ 29
Unarmed robbery	4.2	4.7	+ 12
Burglary	1.8	3.8	+111
Theft	2.2	1.2	− 45

Adapted from Todd R. Clear, John D. Hewitt, and Robert M. Regoli, "Discussion and the Determinate Sentence: Its Distribution, Control, and Effect on Time Served, *Crime and Delinquency* 24, 1978, p. 42. Reprinted with permission.

Table 7-3
Estimates on Time Served—Oregon Sentencing Guidelines versus New Indiana Sentencing Code

Offense	*Time Served Oregon Guidelines (Years)*	*Time Served Indiana Code (Years)*	*Percent Excess Indiana Over Oregon*
Rape	4-5	11.0	+144
Armed robbery	2-2.5	4.9	+122
Unarmed robbery	1.3-1.8	4.7	+213
Burglary	1.3-1.8	3.8	+153
Theft	0.5-0.8	1.2	+ 50

Are Indiana's penalty levels justifiable? Remember, I am not asking whether there might be any possible rationale to support them (Conceivably, one might wish to argue for them on a theory that concerned exclusively deterrence and incapacitation and that did not consider commensurability at all, although even this is debatable.) My question is a narrower one: Can such penalties be defended as commensurate or deserved?

Here one must also bear in mind that questions of commensurateness—how much punishment is deserved for different categories of offenses—is a matter of judgment, about which reasonable people may differ. Oregon's guidelines, which I have used in the preceding comparison, represent only one jurisdiction's judgment, made under a statute that expressly calls for "punishment which is commensurate with the seriousness of the prisoner's criminal conduct."[33]

Yet the penalties under the Indiana statute are so high as to render them suspect. Is nearly four years' *actual* confinement a proportionate penalty for a first offense of burglary? Is four and a half years deserved for a first offense of unarmed robbery? To conclude affirmatively would call for heroic assumptions, either about the great heinousness of felonies commonly considered to be in the intermediate range of gravity, or else about the great mildness of the prison sanction as it is experienced in Indiana prisons.

The direction of change is also worrisome. Under a rationale stressing commensurateness, long confinements—being as severe as the are—would have to be reserved for the worst offenses. One would expect an allocation of penalties that would *reduce* confinements for the lesser felonies and reserve any increases for the most violent crimes. Yet the next largest percentage increase shown in Clear's table, 111 percent, is for the most frequently occurring felony and certainly not one of the worst: burglary.

Clear's figures, moreover, represent only averages in time served. They conceal the possibility of still more draconian penalties in individual cases. Whereas the average time for a first offense of armed robbery would be 4.9 years, an individual judge can impose much more, up to an effective duration of confinement (even after deducting credit-time) of ten years. And that may be imposed even if the robbery, in the particular circumstances, were not an abnormally heinous one since the judge can, as we saw, increase the sentence for rehabilitative ends.

Will this mean that felons who commit burglaries and robberies will actually serve these long terms in Indiana? Not necessarily since the statute leaves so much leeway for plea bargainers to reduce the charges.[34] These crimes may, in practice, be bargained down to common thefts, which carry more modest penalties. But if Indiana's punishments are commensurate only to the extent that the formal penalty scheme is disregarded, this scarcely speaks for the justice of the formal scheme.

A recurring theme in the determinate-sentencing literature, which the drafters of the Indiana code seem to have ignored, is that penalties tend to become less certain as they are made more severe.[35] The higher the penalties prescribed in the formal standards, the greater becomes the incentive to bypass them through informal accommodation. The pressures to reach such accommodations become well-nigh irresistible, to the extent that the formal penalties exceed the actual resources of the system.

There is now considerable debate about whether formal standards can ever effectively constrain penal practice. Critics of determinate sentencing such as Albert Alschuler[36] suggest that such standards tend merely to shift discretion from the more visible stages of the process (sentencing and parole) to the less visible stages (especially prosecutorial decision making). Proponents of determinacy such as James Q. Wilson[37] argue that standards *are* capable of influencing actual dispositions, provided that the prescribed penalties are perceived as reasonable by most participants in the process. Which view is closer to the truth remains to be determined by examining the impact of standards in jurisdiction (for example, Oregon and California)[38] which have opted for determinacy.

Any chances of success will, however, diminish as penalties are escalated. I have not conducted an empirical study of the effects of the Indiana system, and others' research is yet to be published. But I venture to predict that penalties as harsh as these—nearly four years' imprisonment for burglary and nearly five for robbery—will serve mainly to penalize those rash, few defendants who refuse to accept the plea bargains offered them. As the system is forced to rely increasingly on informal accommodation, any hoped-for predictability will be lost. And the actual penalties will be the product of law visibility, discretionary choices by individual actors in the system.

How Can the Statute Be Improved?

There are some changes that might improve specific aspects of the law. If credit-time were vested—a proposal I understand is being considered—some of the uncertainties now associated with disciplinary infractions might be reduced.

But any fundamental improvement in the statute would necessitate reducing its penalties to fairer and more realistic levels. Merely narrowing the penalty ranges will not help, and may make things still worse. If one keeps the presumptive penalty for robbery at its present high level, halving the permissible range for aggravation and mitigation would effectively increase the severity of the formal sanction, and thus further increase the incentives to avoid that sanction through plea bargains. Severity and certainty, as I said, are linked: Success will not be achieved in making the penalties more predictable unless they are made less severe.

This raises the question of which agency should set the sentencing standards. Indiana chose the legislature as the body to write the norms. Legislatures are under strong political pressures to keep escalating sanctions, as the Indiana experience exemplifies. Perhaps we should consider shifting toward a system that delegates the standard—setting task to a specialized rule-making body—one that has more time to write and review the standards and that is somewhat better insulated from political pressures.[39] Minnesota and Oregon have different variants of such a system,[40] and they are worth examining.

Any final evaluation of Indiana's sentencing code must await empirical studies of its effects in practice. However, the way the code has been drafted, particularly, its combination of wide ranges and great severity, will seriously diminish, I think, its chances for success as a determinate-sentencing system.

Notes

1. The literature advocating determinacy of sentence includes: American Friends Service Committee, *Struggle for Justice* (New York: Hill and Wang, 1971); Marvin E. Frankel, *Criminal Sentences* (New York: Hill and Wang, 1972); Norval Morris, *The Future of Imprisonment* (Chicago: University of Chicago Press, 1974); James Q. Wilson, *Thinking About Crime* (New York: Basic Books, 1975); Kay M. Harris, "Disquisition on the Need for A New Model of Criminal Sanctioning Systems," 77 *West Virginia Law Review* 77 (1975): 263; David Fogel, *We Are the Living Proof ... The Justice Model of Corrections* (Cincinnati: Anderson, 1975); Ernest van den Haag, *Punishing Criminals* (New York: Basic Books, 1975); Andrew von Hirsch, *Doing Justice: The Choice of Punishments* (New York: Hill and Wang, 1971); Twentieth Century Fund, Task Force on Criminal Sentencing, *Fair and Certain Punishment* (New York: McGraw-Hill, 1976).

2. Ind. Code, § 35-1-1 et seq., which was mainly added by P.L. 148 of the 1976 session laws.

3. See, for example, Stephen P. Lagoy, Frederick A. Hussey, and John H. Kramer, "A Comparative Assessment of Determinate Sentencing in Four Pioneer States," *Crime and Delinquency* 24 (1979): 385.

4. von Hirsch, *Doing Justice,* supra, n. 1.

5. Twentieth Century Fund, Task Force on Criminal Sentencing, supra, n. 1.

6. Supra, n. 1.

7. von Hirsch, *Doing Justice,* supra, n. 1, ch. 12; Twentieth Century Fund, Task Force on Criminal Sentencing, supra, n. 1.

8. Morris, supra, n. 1, ch. 3; see also, Don M. Gottfredson, Leslie T. Wilkins, and Peter B. Hoffman, *Guidelines for Parole and Sentencing* (Lexington, Mass.: Lexington Books, D.C. Heath, 1978).

9. Twentieth Century Fund, Task Force on Criminal Sentencing, supra, n. 1.

10. von Hirsch, *Doing Justice,* supra, n. 1, chs. 12 and 16.

11. Fogel, supra, n. 1; Twentieth Century Fund, Task Force on Criminal Sentencing, supra, n. 1, p. 123.

12. Cal. Stats. 1976, ch. 1139, as amended by Cal. Stats. 1977, ch. 165, and by Cal. Stats. 1978, chs. 579 and 582. For a description of the California system, see, April Kestell Cassou and Brian Taugher, "Determinate Sentencing in California: The New Numbers Game," *Pacific Law Journal* 9 (1978): 1.

13. Frankel, supra, n. 1, ch. 9.

14. Minn. Stats. 1978, ch. 723. The Minnesota sentencing commission has recently been established and is required to formulate its guidelines for sentencing by 1 May 1980.

15. Ore. Stats. 1977, ch. 372.

16. Andrew von Hirsch and Kathleen J. Hanrahan, *The Question of Parole: Retention, Reform or Abolition?* (Cambridge, Mass.: Ballinger, 1979), ch. 9. The conclusions of this study are summarized also in a monograph: Andrew von Hirsch and Kathleen J. Hanrahan, *Abolish Parole?* (Washington, D.C.: National Institute of Law Enforcement and Criminal Justice, Criminal Justice Perspectives, 1978), pp. 29–38.

17. John Kleinig, *Punishment and Desert* (The Hague: Martinus Nijhoff, 1973); Morris, supra, n. 1, ch. 3; Harris, supra, n. 1; Twentieth Century Fund, Task Force on Criminal Sentencing, supra, n. 1.; von Hirsch, *Doing Justice,* supra, n. 1.

18. The rationale for commensurability is set forth in more detail in Kleinig, supra, n. 17, and in von Hirsch, *Doing Justice,* supra, n. 1, ch. 8.

19. von Hirsch, *Doing Justice,* supra, n. 1, chs. 8 and 12.

20. Norval Morris, "Punishment, Desert and Rehabilitation," lecture reprinted in *Hearings on S 1437 Before the Subcomm. on Criminal Laws and Procedures of the Senate Comm. on the Judiciary,* 95th Cong., 1st Sess. p. XIII (1977), p. 9321.

21. See, for example, Morris's and my comments at the Congressional Research Service workshop on Federal Criminal Justice Legislation held on 1 December 1976. The proceedings of the workshop were published in 95th Cong., 1st Sess., Subcomm. on crime of the Comm. on the Judiciary of the U.S. House of Representatives, *New Directions for Federal Involvement in Crime Control,* Committee Print No. 2, April 1977, pp. 45–61.

22. Wilson, supra, n. 1, chs. 8 and 10.

23. See, for example, Andrew von Hirsch, "Giving Criminals Their

Just Deserts," *Civil Liberties Review,* April/May 1976, pp. 23, 27. For a recent (rather pessimistic) assessment of our present ability to estimate the magnitude of deterrent and incapacitative effects, see, National Academy of Sciences, Panel on Research on Deterrent and Incapacitative Effects, Report in Alfred Blumstein, Jaqueline Cohen, and Daniel Nagin, eds., *Deterrence and Incapacitation: Estimating the Effects of Criminal Sanctions on Crime Rates* (Washington, D.C.: National Academy of Sciences, 1978).

24. James Q. Wilson, "Thinking About 'Thinking About Crime,'" *Society,* vol. 14, no. 3, 1977, pp. 10, 20. Reprinted by permission. © 1977, by Transaction, Inc.

25. Ind. Code, § 35, arts. 43, 44, and 50.

26. Ind. Code § 35–41–4–7 (Supp. 1978).

27. Ind. Code § 35–50–6–5 (Supp. 1978).

28. Id.

29. Under California's vesting provisions, an inmate may not lose more than ninety days' worth of credit–time during the eight months during which the misbehavior took place. Cal. Penal Code §2932, and Cassou and Taugher, supra, n. 12, pp. 77–84.

30. Under the new Oregon statute, the parole board must notify the offender with six months of his commitment when his release date will be. That date may subsequently be postponed on account of disciplinary violations only if the parole board, after a hearing, finds "that the prisoner engaged in serious misconduct during his confinement." The statute specifies further that the parole board "shall adopt rules defining serious misconduct and specifying periods of postponement for such misconduct." Oregon Revised Statutes §144.125.

31. Todd R. Clear, John D. Hewitt, and Robert M. Regoli, "Discretion and the Determinate Sentence: Its Distribution, Control and Effect on Time Served," *Crime and Delinquency* 24 (1978): 428.

32. Oregon Administrative Rules §§ 254–30–030 thru 254–30–032. The Oregon parole board's rules makes the duration of confinement depend on (1) the seriousness of the current offense and (2) a "criminal history/risk assessment" score. The calculations in table 7–3 assume that the offender has had no prior convictions and is between ages of nineteen and twenty-five. If the offender had a prior record of convictions, the duration of confinement would be longer under the Oregon rules.

33. Oregon Revised Statutes §§144.780. The full statutory language calls on the parole board to write its standards for duration of confinement in such a manner as to achieve these objectives: "(a) Punishment which is commensurate with the seriousness of the prisoner's criminal conduct; and (b) To the extent not inconsistent with paragraph (a) ... the deterrence of criminal conduct ... and the protection of the public from further crimes by the defendant."

34. Clear, et al., supra, n. 31.

35. Andrew von Hirsch, "The Aims of Imprisonment," *Current History,* July/August 1976, pp. 1, 5; Twentieth Century Fund, Task Force on Criminal Sentencing, supra, n. 1, pp. 31–34; Wilson, supra, n. 1, p. 179.

36. See, Albert W. Alschuler, "Sentencing Reform and Prosecutorial Power: A Critique of Recent Proposals for 'Fixed' and 'Presumptive' Sentencing," *University of Pennsylvania Law Review* 126 (1978): 550.

37. James Q. Wilson, "The Political Feasibility of Punishment," in *Justice and Punishment,* eds. J.B. Cederblom and William L. Blizek (Cambridge, Mass.: Ballinger, 1977), pp. 107, 115–116.

38. Sheldon Messinger, Richard Sparks, and the present author are now heading an LEAA-funded research project to evaluate the effects of the Oregon and California systems. Project on Strategies for Determinate Sentencing, NILECJ Grant No. 78-NI-AX-0082.

39. See, for example, von Hirsch and Hanrahan, *The Question of Parole,* supra, n. 16, ch. 9.

40. Notes 14 and 15, supra.

8 Punitive Sentences

Ernest van den Haag

Deterrence is the sole purpose of threats of punishment and even of punishment itself. (I shall deal separately with incapacitation.) Therefore, in prescribing sentences, there is no need to consider separately either desert or rehabilitation. Sentences can be determinate and legislatively prescribed since the deterrent effect is independent of the personality of the offender and of individual circumstances. At present several contradictory criteria—for example, desert, rehabilitation, and deterrence—must be compounded by judges and parole boards. This produces chaotic inconsistencies, many of which can be avoided when deterrence (apart from incapacitation) is recognized as the exclusive purpose of sentencing. Philosophical problems connected with retribution and/or rehabilitation can be avoided as well.

The Deterrent Purpose of Legal Threats

The criminal law tries to influence future conduct by threatening to punish persons who do what it prohibits. Deterrence is the sole purpose of threatening punishment.[1]

Would-be offenders see the threats of the criminal law as dangers. Most people, including most would-be offenders, most of the time, respond to dangers, be they natural or legal, by adapting their behavior so as to minimize risks. Otherwise, the survival of the human race would be hard to explain. Hence all systems of punishment rest on the justified belief that, *ceteris paribus,* more severe or frequent punishment, greater danger, deters more. Yet no legal threat, however great the danger it produces, can deter everybody. Responsiveness varies. A few people are altogether unresponsive to danger. Many more are not deterred because the dangers produced by legal threats are not great enough to deter them. Such people might respond to more severe threats or to threats more likely to be carried out. Accordingly, to reduce the crime rate, the severity of threatened punishment can be increased, and it can be carried out more frequently. But even an unlimited increase of severity and frequency of punishment cannot eliminate all offenses since historically no Western system of criminal justice has been able to catch and convict more than a small proportion of all those threatened.[2,3,4] However, we need not make it as hard to catch and convict them as we do, via judicial interpretations of the Constitution that have led to the creation and extension of the exclusionary rule and to some absurd probable-cause decisions.[5]

Threat Size, Frequency of Punishment, Justice, and Deterrence

Increases in the severity of threats and in the frequency with which they are carried out usually are limited by considerations of justice, which impose restrictions of two kinds. First, rules instituted to protect nonoffenders and to restrain law enforcers protect many offenders from apprehension and conviction because insufficient evidence becomes available and admissible under these rules.[6] Legal threats are not carried out often enough to deter those offenders who might respond if threats of punishment were more frequently carried out.

Second, although the only purpose of threatening punishment is to deter offenses, an attempt is made as well to "do justice": to proportion the size of each threatened punishment to the perceived gravity of the offense and to other threats that are so proportioned. However, the threat size required to deter successfully from an offense does not depend on its gravity but on its attractiveness to prospective offenders. Whenever the attractiveness of the offense exceeds its perceived gravity, threats, the size of which is proportioned to the gravity of the offense, are unlikely to deter those who might respond only to more severe threats, proportioned to its attractiveness.

A word on the notion of gravity may not be amiss. It roughly equals the malevolently intended harm done. Gravity is an uneasy compound of disparate ingredients since the degree of wrongful intention or of any culpability may be independent of the harm done and the two are not commensurable. However, this compound often coincides with the perceived need for deterrence from the offense, although that need depends exclusively on the harm the offense might do. It is because both depend heavily on harm done that gravity and the need for deterrence often coincide. Thus both the gravity of and the need to deter from pickpocketing or from parking violations are thought to be minor. The size of the threat is small and hardly deterrent since it does not offset the attractiveness of the offense. The threat against murder is severe because the offense is considered grave and the need to deter great enough to maximize the threat size.

When the two criteria that determine the size of legal threats yield different sizes, the severity required by the need for deterrence from the offense may exceed the severity required by the gravity of it. In Adam Smith's example of the sentry who is executed for falling asleep, the gravity of the offense is perceived as minor, the need to deter from it as major.[7] The need to deter prevails, which leads to a harshness Smith laments as necessary but unjust. Often, however, when deterrence requires harshness and gravity does not, gravity prevails as criterion, and we threaten but mild punishment. Our mild threats against drunken drivers who do harm—for that matter against any drunks who do harm—may be just, considering the lack of malevolent intent, but they certainly do not satisfy the need for deterrence. Nor do our threats against juvenile offenders. Justice to potential offenders here—proportioned to their culpability—often involves injustice to potential victims, many of whom might be spared by more deterrent threats.

From Threats to Punishment: Is Retribution Implied?

Whatever its additional purposes, punishment carries out legal threats that have failed to deter. Punishment thus seems necessarily retributive since, unlike a threat, punishment refers to past offenses. Courts ascertain who has incurred guilt in the past and punish them accordingly. Even the most ardent rehabilitationists and deterrence theorists usually concede that a just distribution of punishments, a distribution according to guilt, can be explained only by resorting to the concepts of retribution and desert.[8]

I have been inclined to this view myself. But I have now concluded that the concept of retribution according to what is deserved by guilt is not needed to explain or justify the distribution of punishments or even the size of threats. Specifically, retributionist theories are not needed to tell us (a) why we threaten; (b) why we punish; (c) why we punish only the guilty; (d) why we threaten or punish them to the degree to which we do. According to Occam's razor (*essentia non sunt multiplicanda praeter necessitatem:* Concepts should not be multiplied beyond need), retributionist theories are not needed within any legal (as distinguished from moral) discourse. The social need for deterrence alone can be shown to justify and to limit the size of penalties and their distribution exclusively to the guilty.

We threaten to punish only because we want to deter. And we do punish only because we must carry out our threats. For if we did not carry out legal threats, they would not remain credible and would become ineffective as deterrents as they lose credibility. The deterrent purpose of legal threats—their only purpose—would be defeated. Further, if not carried out, legal threats also would deceive the law-abiding public at large, which relied on the promise that lawbreakers will be punished.[9]

If punishment is not retribution for guilt, why not punish the innocent? The reason is simple: It would not be deterrent to threaten or punish those who are not believed to have violated the law. Punishing the innocent may be as deterrent as punishing the guilty, only if the innocent are believed guilty. But that belief would be hard to produce unless we do our best to single out the guilty for punishment. ("Our best" depends on the state of the art. It may involve witch doctors, if that is the best we can do, or lawyers and courts, if that is. But it must be believed to be the best we can do.) Thus if we want to deter them, we must threaten those who might incur guilt, and, as threatened, punish those and only those who have.

Since the deterrent effect is produced by perceived and not necessarily by actual guilt, it can be argued that it would be deterrent to punish suspects believed to be guility, as long as only authorities such as courts know them to be innocent. It is the moral (retributionist) objection that causes revulsion at this thought: Punishment is morally justified only when deserved by a blameworthy act committed by the person punished. Yet this moral argument—whatever its merits—is not needed. The deterrence criterion also requires and permits the punishment only of actually guilty persons. Anyone known by the authorities to be innocent, and punished as guilty, can in the long run become known to have been innocent. And it can become known that the authorities allowed him to be punished even though his innocence was known to them. Indeed, there is a very high risk that this will become known. If it does, it would undermine the deterrent effectiveness of distributing punishment only to the guilty as well as confidence in the distributing authorities.[10] Hence from a purely deterrent viewpoint, there is sufficient reason, apart from morality, not to punish anybody who can be known to have been innocent. There is no need to resort to retributive arguments. Moreover, the price of the virtues or retributionism—simplicity and intuitive appeal—is high. First, since they bear no relation to social needs, criteria of desert tend to be abandoned wherever the punishment deserved and the punishment needed for deterrent purposes clash. Second, appearances nothwithstanding, retributionism cannot tell us what size of penalties is just.[11] Finally, to say that a penalty is deserved by the gravity of an offense is to express a feeling, more or less widely shared, rather than to give a reason. In contrast, deterrence is, in principle and in fact, a measurable quantity. It prescribes sentences determined by expected and measurable social effects.

Sometimes it is argued that the deterrence argument could permit altogether different objects of punishment—for example, we could threaten to punish the children or wives of the guilty. But there would be no deterrent advantage in such an injustice. Guilt would still have to be ascertained and a direct threat against the guilty would be more deterrent.

Just Desert, Gravity, and Threat Size

Together with the need for deterrence from it, the gravity of the offense determines the size of threats and of actual punishments. The gravity of an offense depends on the moral or material harm it does and on the culpability of the offender.[12] The harm, it is thought, gives rise to the need for deterrence, while malevolent intent, culpability in any form, usually is thought to codetermine the size of the punishment deserved. Thus threats proportioned according to the gravity of offenses are thought to be proportioned according to desert. However, it is quite possible to derive the wish to allow culpability to codetermine the size of threats and punishments exclusively from their deterrent function and to dispense with the notion of desert and of retributive justice here too.

Offenders are the more guilty the more the courts find they wrongfully intended to do the harm they did. Culpability is a measure of guilt. *Ceteris paribus,* threats are the more deterrent the more specifically they are directed to and carried out against those guilty of breaking the law. Thus if the harm the offense did is held constant, it will be most deterrent to threaten and punish most severely the offenders whose culpability is greatest since only those culpably intending to commit offenses can be deterred by the threats that punishment makes effective. Therefore, a deterrent threat must take account not just of the harmfulness of the offense but also of the degree of culpability of the offender. Justice must be done for the sake of being deterrent as much as for the sake of being just.

Unfortunately, whether one wishes to maximize deterrence or justice according to desert, the difficulties of compounding culpability and harmfulness remain. And the deterrence criterion, based on harm and culpability, still may lead to ineffective threat sizes whenever the attractiveness of the offense is great and the harm it does is not. In such cases the wrongful intent does not weigh heavily because of the comparative harmfulness of the offense. On the other hand, threat sizes above those justified by culpability are likely whenever the need for deterrence is thought overwhelmingly great because of the harm done. In such cases the fact that there was little or no wrongful intent is disregarded because of the harmfulness of the offense. This may offend our sense of justice. Indeed, strict liability does. It is acceptable, nevertheless, because the deterrent threat can be effective in some types of offenses even without a showing of individual culpability, although, almost by definition, the punishment inflicted is undeserved.

Intuition and the Rule of Just Desert

It seems contrary to our intuition to deny a role to retribution and desert in the theory of punishment. These concepts are indeed essential to moral theories that help explain why the community does or should prohibit certain actions as wrong. Moral theories also help explain the amount of harm done by prohibited actions and therefore the intensity of the need to deter from them. Further, moral theories influence the rules of evidence and procedure, which protect individual rights, for example, privacy, and set limits to punishment threats, for example by prohibiting punitive torture. But the belief that moral concepts such as desert and retribution must play a role in the theory of punishment itself is mistaken. It rests on an insufficient distinction between moral theories and theories of punishment.[13] Indeed, if one takes as a datum whatever the law prohibits as harmful, concepts such as desert are not needed in the theories of punishment that explain who is threatened and punished, why, and how much. Threats and punishments, their sizes, and their distribution can be explained entirely by the need to deter without resort to retribution. What about rehabilitation and incapacitation?

Punishment and the Future

If the act for which a reward was promised has been done, the promised reward must be given, regardless of how the person to whom the promise was made is likely to behave in the future. His future conduct is relevant only to future promises and rewards. Analogously, a threatened punishment must be carried out independently of the future conduct of the person against whom it was threatened. His future conduct is relevant only to future threats and punishments. Punishment then *need not* rest on anything but past threats; and it *cannot* rest on the desire for rehabilitation or incapacitation, both of which refer to future conduct. To be sure, both may coincide with punishment. But they also may be separately produced, and punishment need not produce either. However useful a role punishment plays in rehabilitating or incapacitating, neither is logically related to the essential function of punishment: to *deter* from crime.

Since punitive sentences carry out legal threats made beforehand, they must be determined by the threat made against the offenses committed and not by conjectures about the future behavior of the offender. However, postoffenses (and additional objective factors) may predict the likelihood of future offenses. If that likelihood is great enough, threats and sentences may include provisions for nonpunitive incapacitation for the sake of social defense.

Rehabilitation

Although rehabilitation is incidental to punishment, punishment usually is essential to rehabilitation. Without punishment, rehabilitation is unlikely to take place, for it is the experience of punishment and the threat of future punishments that suggest to offenders that their criminal conduct is self-defeating; punishment gives them the main motive for rehabilitation. In the absence of such a motive, rehabilitation cannot be helped by any program of treatment.[14] Punishment and the threat of punishment often are not sufficient, but they are necessary for rehabilitation. On the other hand, rehabilitation is neither necessary nor sufficient to stop a punishment inflicted to carry out a threat against an offense committed in the past.

Incapacitation

Confinement is not essential to punishment, which may consist of a fine. Nor is punishment essential to confinement, which may be imposed for nonpunitive reasons on the insane, or on those suffering from infectious diseases or on those held for trial. Punishment is not a necessary reason for incapacitation then, although it is a sufficient one. And incapacitation is felt to be punitive because it is involuntary. Still incapacitation need not be punitive in function.

Whereas punishment is threatened to deter, and imposed because threatened, incapacitation may be imposed for reasons that have nothing to do with deterrence. If we knew, by revelation, that a person will throw a bomb harming the community, we certainly would incapacitate him for as long as we knew him to be willing and capable of throwing the bomb, regardless of whether his intent is criminal or his mind deranged. By incapacitating him, we do not intend to punish him—he has done nothing as yet justifying punishment. We cannot punish anyone for what he has not done.[15] We can incapacitate him, however, to avoid harm to us. Incapacitation then is a measure of preemptive social defense, quite independent of punishment.

Now, in practice, certainty about what anyone will do is hard to come by. However, we have statistical probabilities that may vary from offender to offender and that can be calculated. They tell us that those convicted of a second offense, particularly if they are young, are much more likely to commit other offenses than those who are not, and those convicted of a third offense are still more likely to continue criminal conduct. It is also statistically likely that those convicted of second and third offenses have already committed many more offenses of which they were not convicted.[16]

There is no reason why the punishment threatened for the second offense should not exceed that threatened for the first. The community may wish to deter not only from specific offenses but also from continued offending. And, quite apart from punishment, the community may also rely on offenses combined with other relevant factors for statistical prediction of the likelihood of further offenses. Where such likelihood is found to be considerable and to significantly exceed the average likelihood of offenses by nonoffenders, the offender likely to commit further offenses of sufficient harmfulness should be incapacitated for as long as that likelihood remains high. This may lead to postpunishment incapacitation of some young recidivists up to the age of forty. Some older recidivists may be incapacitated up to the age of fifty if our data relating age and past offenses to continued recidivism are correct.[17]

There are two major arguments against postpunitive incapacitation on the basis of categorical (statistical) prediction.[18] First, by imposing such incapacitation, we punish for what will or might be done, not for what has been done. This argument either fails to distinguish between incapacitation and punishment, despite the conceptual difference or more often relies on the fact that from the viewpoint of the person incapacitated, the actually felt difference between punitive incapacitation and preventive incapacitation may be so small as to be invisible. He will feel punished because he is deprived of liberty by the decision of a social authority. This point must be granted, even if the preventively confined person is allowed to live in more pleasant conditions than the punitively confined.

However, to the legal threat of punishment we may add for second or third offenders a legal threat of incapacitation beyond the punishment. Our motive may well be preventive. Yet as far as the offender is concerned, the added nonpunitive incapacitation is part of what was threatened, part, if he so conceives it, of the punishment threatened. He is incapacitated for what he has done, for committing a second or third offense. Unlike the insane, he is as able to avoid the threatened incapacitation as he is to avoid the threatened punishment that precedes it, by avoiding the second offense. He volunteers for the risk of both punishment and postpunitive incapacitation and cannot complain if that which he risked happens.[19]

Second, the more cogent argument against postpunishment incapacitation rests on our limited ability to predict. We can statistically predict that some offenders are more likely to offend again than others, depending on the category into which they fall. But our probabilities are no more than that. If not incapacitated, many of those statistically likely to commit additional offenses, perhaps a majority, may never actually do so; at least they may never be convicted of other crimes. Statistical predictions can be improved, but it is unlikely that they will ever approach certainty. A considerable number of persons might be incapacitated who if free would not have done any harm. They volunteered for that risk by committing the offenses they did commit.

There is a social and moral cost when persons are incapacitated who need not be and who have served the punishment required by their offenses. Against that social cost we must weigh the social gain produced by incapacitating the offenders most likely to commit further crimes. The outcome of the calculation is hardly in doubt even if all third offenders were permanently incapacitated—which would go far beyond what is suggested by appropriate calculations of the likelihood of recidivism since few people over forty engage in violent or physically demanding crimes.

In war, we shoot at enemy soldiers who individually may not be guilty of anything, not even of being hostile to our country or cause. Yet we can defend our country and prevent harm to it only by shooting enemy soldiers who otherwise might shoot us. Social defense against internal enemies admittedly is different from social defense against external enemies. For one thing, less is at stake for the country as a whole. But there are similarities as well. In both cases we must defend the community against harm by incapacitating both actual and potential enemies. Those who have enlisted in the criminal army are personally more guilty than those who serve in the enemy army. Criminals are volunteers. They usually serve no cause but their own advancement whereas enemy soldiers usually are draftees who do not serve to advance their personal fortunes. But both criminals and enemy soldiers must be incapacitated as long as we have reason to believe that they will harm us if free to do so. Postpunitive incapacitation is among the risks second offenders volunteer for. It is less of a risk and more easily avoidable than the risk the draftee runs. I can see no reason why repeated offenders should not be threatened with that risk.

Let me draw attention now to some further consequences of the deterrence approach to sentencing.

Juveniles

Juveniles who have committed acts defined as crimes when committed by adults should be tried and sentenced by the same courts adults are tried by and under the same laws. If counsel for the defense wishes to plead diminished capacity for *mens rea,* or any other legal excuse or mitigating circumstance, he can do so. But the law or the court should not assume a priori that the age of juveniles is a mitigating circumstance, let along a legal excuse.[20] There is no evidence to indicate that juveniles, owing to their age, are unaware of the gravity of their offenses or are unlikely to be deterred by threats.

Juveniles cannot be deterred, or for that matter, rehabilitated, by promising them immunity from serious punishment, as we have done hitherto. And they are not less, and often more, socially dangerous than older offenders.[21]

Determinate Sentences, Parole, and Probation

There never was a justification for having sentences second-guessed by nonjudicial personnel. Parole boards know nothing the sentencing judge could not know, except for some superficial information about the offender's conduct in prison. Such conduct is not relevant to the punishment to which he has been sentenced in view of his offense; and conduct in prison does not predict future conduct outside prison (which also is irrelevant to his punishment). Hence parole should be abolished. It rests on considerations that, apart from being materially wrong, are irrelevant under the deterrence criterion. Some credit for good conduct in prison, granted at the discretion of prison authorities may help prison discipline and may be useful as long as it does not significantly modify sentences. It should be available to all prisoners who have not violated prison rules according to an established point system; but the maximum credit given should not exceed 10 percent of the sentence—else indeterminacy is reintroduced.

If parole is abolished, long sentences threatened and given in view of the likelihood of parole should be reduced; legal threats should be modified accordingly. Threats and sentences should be altogether determinate, leaving judges little discretion. To be deterrent, sentences must be predictable, and the relevant prediction refers to the time that actually must be served. "Little discretion" may mean reducing or increasing the legally threatened sentence by 10 percent. If a judge wishes to go beyond this discretionary variation because of circumstances he deems exceptional, he may increase or decrease the prescribed sentence by up to 30 percent, but his sentence must automatically be reviewed by an appeals court, empowered to let it stand or bring it back to the sentence threatened for the offense.[22] When neither seems satisfactory, the appeals court may ask the lower court to reconsider the sentence. Unless the discretionary limits are exceeded, sentences should not be appealable. Discretion given judges does not adopt the sentence to the personality of the criminal, as was hoped, but to that of the judge. Neither adaptation serves the purposes of criminal justice, and both lead to sentences being perceived as arbitrary and capricious. Hence discretion should be narrowly limited.

Probation and suspended sentences should be available only to first offenders and only for comparatively minor offenses. If judges grant probation otherwise, the sentence must automatically be reviewed by a higher court empowered to reject probation.

Prison Space and Prison Treatment

It is often argued that the sentencing criteria suggested would intolerably increase the shortage of prison space. Undoubtedly, the increasing severity of sentences, which is already occurring, requires more prison space than is now available. Enactment of some of the reforms proposed here may require still more. How much additional prison space is permanently required is not easy to say. If more severe and frequent prison sentences are given, a higher proportion of offenders will be in prison. But if these sentences deter, fewer offenses will be committed.[23] Thus the total number of offenders will decrease, and the actual prison population may not increase much in the end.

Yet at least temporarily, more prisons will have to be built. Sometimes it is argued that doing so will be too costly. It is cheaper to build prisons than to tolerate a higher crime rate, although taxpayers rather than crime victims may have to bear the cost. At any rate, the cost of imprisonment is far higher than it need be for three reasons, quite apart from waste and corruption.

First, fairly costly attempts are made to provide rehabilitative services and various amenities for the prisoners that have never been shown to contribute to any of the purposes of punishment (including rehabilitation). Television is not required as part of humane treatment or of rehabilitation; nor is tennis or conjugal sex.[24] A prisoner is intentionally severed from his normal environment and from amenities. There is no reason to provide either at government expense. If the amenities of which the prisoner is deprived or his normal environment had been helpful in producing lawful behavior in the first place, he probably would not be in prison. Nor is there any reason to believe that television viewing, tennis playing, sex, or newspaper reading will lead to rehabilitation.

Second, prisoners are not given productive work, and they are not allowed to earn enough to pay for their keep. Most legal experts are in favor, as I am, of normal wages and work opportunities for prisoners. I also favor incentive pay. Even nonmonetary work incentives such as shortening of sentences according to work performed are not altogether inconsistent with deterrent punishment if kept within narrow limits. (Appropriate deductions from pay, for example, for room and board and for court-ordered compensation of parties harmed, would have to be made.) I will not dwell on this matter. The obstacles come from labor unions and business, and the problem is political. But it must be noted that prisons are costly only because we insist on making them costly. Else they could be self-supporting, and, if prisoners become taxpayers, they could increase government revenue. Lawful work at normal wages within prisons may even be rehabilitative. It is one "treatment" that has never been tried.

Third, the most costly part of imprisonment consists of the measures taken to prevent escape. These measures also raise prison-building costs. However, many inmates are neither violent nor prone to escape. They may have surrendered voluntarily and may prefer to serve their time rather than add to it by escaping and living as fugitives. Accordingly we should create small prisons with supervision but with no more security provided than in a factory. Roll calls will be needed but no actual measures to prevent flight.

In doubtful cases prisoners working in these prisons may provide bail, forfeited if they escape. In other cases this may be unnecessary. If only actual security risks, violent, or escape-prone prisoners (a category that may include all young offenders sentenced to long terms) are kept in high-security prisons, imprisonment will become much cheaper than it is now.

Those who most lament prison crowding and wax eloquently about the inhumane conditions it creates are often the very persons who did their best, for ideological reasons, to prevent the building of additional prisons. They helped create the conditions that they now use to insist that offenders should not be confined as often or as long as is needed to protect the community. Most of them persist in opposing the building of prisons, and I have found it impossible to rehabilitate them.

Conclusion

Deterrence is the only criterion needed to justify threats of punishment and the infliction of punishment. Deterrence also justifies and determines the length of sentences and their distribution. Both deterrence and retribution require the distribution of punishment to the guilty for independent reasons; but neither rehabilitation nor retribution are needed as justification or as sentencing criterion. In specifiable cases, postpunitive incapacitation is justifiable as a measure of (nonpunitive) social defense.

Notes

1. *General deterrence*—the attempt to restrain people from unlawful acts by threatening to punish them—is distinguished from *special deterrence*—the expected restraining effect of actual punishment on offenders. General deterrence refers to the effect of potential punishment on potential offenders, on the public at large, whereas special deterrence refers to the effects of actual punishment (for example, confinement) on the future conduct of actual offenders. This distinction is useful. However, special deterrence is indistinguishable from rehabilitation. When successful, the effect of either is future lawful conduct of the offender, and when unsuccessful, recidivism. (The ingredients of rehabilitation and of special deterrence differ but vaguely. Similar disincentives and incentives are involved with the latter stressed in rehabilitation.) Since the detectable effects of rehabilitation coincide with those of special deterrence, one of the two terms is redundant. Hence "special deterrence," so often confused with general deterrence, can be dropped and replaced by "rehabilitation" without loss to anyone but writers who like to make distinctions where there are none. In the

rest of this chapter, nonrecidivism of released offenders is referred to as *rehabilitation*.

2. Japan has lower (and declining) crime rates and far higher apprehension and conviction rates than any Western country. Japan not only has fewer criminals per capita than any Western country, it also has far fewer lawyers. I cannot say whether there is a causal connection behind this statistical association, or behind the fact that the United States has greatly increased its production of lawyers and of criminals.

3. Police may arrest offenders even when the evidence is insufficient for a lawful arrest, for example, when probable cause it not demonstrable. And police may make arrests when the admissible evidence is obviously insufficient for conviction. Police officers tend to be credited and promoted according to arrests made, not according to convictions obtained. However, because such arrests lead nowhere, prosecutors usually release the suspects before arraignment; if not, they are released on arraignment. One may refer to the released persons as apprehended but not convicted or as not apprehended. A similar semantic decision must be made about offenders released or not even arrested because the police officer to whom the complaint was made anticipates witnesses and victims to be too fearful or unwilling to testify or to be likely to lose their resolution after a series of adjournments or after threats by the suspect's friends.

4. In a well-organized system, the chances of repeat offenders being caught and convicted are comparatively high since they become known to law-enforcement agencies and multiply their risks. But habitual offenders usually are not deterred, and perhaps not deterrable, by available threats. However, actual punishment can prevent additional offenses of recidivists by incapacitating them.

5. See Ernest van den Haag, "The Growth of the Imperial Judiciary," *Policy Review,* Spring 1978, pp. 62–63 [discussing *U.S.* v. *Montgomery,* 561 F.2d 875 (1977)].

6. These rules range from the requirement of jury unanimity to the exclusionary rule and the probable-cause rule.

7. Herbert W. Schneider, ed., *Adam Smith's Moral and Political Philosophy* (New York: Harper Torchbooks, 1970), pp. 129–130.

8. This explains why rehabilitationists regard punishment according to guilt with misgivings. They would prefer a medical model, which makes guilt and justice irrelevant, substituting social and individual "needs for treatment" and "curing" crime like "curing" hepatitis. For a discussion of the justice and medical models, see my *Punishing Criminals: Concerning a Very Old and Painful Question* (New York: Basic Books, 1975), pp. 117–123.

9. The legal threat is an obligation not to the person threatened who is merely the object of the threat but to those who relied on it, that is, to law-

abiding citizens. Because of the threat, they did not act as they might have otherwise: (1) They did not protect themselves from harm caused by crime (at least not to the degree they would have in the absence of the legal threat of punishment); nor did they directly exact vengeance or compensation from those who caused it; (2) they did refrain from unlawful actions, which they might have undertaken but for the threats of the law. Unless threats are carried out, the law abiding are placed at an unwarranted disadvantage.

10. The gospels present a remarkable case in point, and the Dreyfus case shook the French Republic.

11. See my *Punishing Criminals,* pp. 171–175.

12. Harm often is morally evaluated. The relative gravity of rape and burglary is rated morally. This moral evaluation determines the felt need for deterrence, which determines the threat size independently of desert.

13. Moral theories are theories of right and wrong, good and bad, and so on. Theories of punishment deal with *social devices* to control what moral theory tells us to control. Punishment and the threat of punishment are more or less effective *means* of social control, means used to accomplish the (moral) ends incorporated in the law.

14. So far no treatment program has been shown anywhere to regularly and significantly increase the rate of rehabilitation (defined as nonrecidivism) of those treated over what it is with nontreated control groups. (See, for example, R. Lipton, R. Martinson, and J. Wilkes, *The Effectiveness of Correctional Treatment* (New York: Praeger, 1975).

15. Here the deterrent and the retributive conclusions coincide, though the arguments differ. However, incapacitation is independent of either argument.

16. Marvin E. Wolfgang, "Crime in a Birth Cohort," *Proceedings of the American Philosophical Society* 117 (5) (1973): 404–411.

17. Ibid.

18. I deliberately exclude clinical psychiatrist prediction, which has been shown to be unreliable and capricious.

19. The length of postpunishment confinement depends on other factors besides the offense, such as age. This poses no difficulty. Either the threat is varied according to the age of the offender, or it is so formulated as to make the length of postpunishment confinement dependent generally on the statistical likelihood of recidivism.

20. Prisons for various age groups may be separated.

21. Children below the age of ten should be dealt with by parents and legal guardians, regardless of offenses. The likelihood of full understanding of the wrongfulness of their offenses is small. Hence there is little point in legal proceedings. (Parents and guardians should be civilly liable for harm done by children.) If parents or legal guardians abdicate responsibility, whether because of their disabilities or because of offenses or misbehavior

by the children in their care, the children should be dealt with exclusively by social agencies other than courts. (This solution might also be used for juveniles between ten and seventeen if they are not convicted of offenses but merely rejected at home.) Preferably they should be adopted or have foster parents or, as a last resort, be kept in nonpunitive boarding schools or institutions. Institutionalized children should be released as soon as it is safe to do so.

22. Thus if the law prescribes a sentence of ten years, the court, within its discretion, may impose a sentence of anywhere between nine and eleven years without review of the sentence. If the court, explaining the exceptional circumstances that lead to its decision, increases the sentence up to thirteen years or decreases it to seven years, an automatic review follows.

23. The lengthier and more frequent incapacitation of habitual offenders will add to that effect.

24. The absence of sexual gratification, although unpopular, has never been shown to be harmful, romantic psychologists notwithstanding.

9 Crime Victims: An Agenda for the 1980s

Eric Younger

The Discovered Victim

It seems characteristic of our society—perhaps of democratic societies in general—that once we discover a social problem we have ignored, we discover it with a vengeance.

One need not think very hard to come up with examples of concerns, unheard of a decade ago, that have captured the public consciousness. How many nonbiologists had heard of ecology before 1970? A few short years ago the people we now call Native Americans were "Indians" and their squalid existence on reservations and skid rows bothered few opinion leaders. From obscure diseases to pet overpopulation, to being sure the earth's ozone layer wins the battle with our deodorant, our capacity for doing combat is dramatic.

While much of it is indeed *mortal* combat, none of these examples being imaginary, our zeal goes through highly patterned stages: After the ignoring or "occasional voice in the wilderness" phase comes the expose or banner-headline period (the Snail Darter, receiving more volume inches than Montgomery at El Alamein). Next comes legislative tokenism, judicial avant-gardism,[1] and finally, perhaps, long-range progress.

Concern for crime victims fits this model well. Prior to the mid-1960s, individual, familial, or community concern might well be felt for a victim, and national outrage was even available to a publicized few such as the Lindberghs, but there was little comprehension that each victim was merely an example, who varied largely in degree of tragedy from his or her fellows. Scholarly or popular literary attention to the victim per se was virtually nonexistent,[2] and while England, some of the Commonwealth nations,[3] and California[4] developed compensation statutes in the mid-1960s, the vast majority of victims suffered in silence.

It cannot be said with any confidence what made crime victims, as such, visible. Some suggest that a greater interest in law and order, spurred by former President Nixon's stress on the issue in the 1968 campaign, is the factor. Others point to a swing of the pendulum away from the Supreme Court's protection of criminal suspects. Still others, emphasizing the championship of the victim cause by liberals such as the late Senator Hubert Humphrey suggest humanitarian motives.

All may be correct. But what can be said with confidence is that victims have arrived as an identifiable constituency in the headlines. Books,[5] articles,[6] and even national organizations[7] have proliferated, and all the television networks have done segments on victims.[8]

Now we are in the period of legislative tokenism. While nearly half the states[9] have passed compensation statutes, many include embarrassing welfare-style requirements such as applicant poverty,[10] and some states' funds are in trouble.[11] The U.S. Congress, in a bipartisan effort to encourage state-compensation laws through financial subvention, proposes to limit the federal share to 25 percent of awards, hardly a dramatic inducement for the poorer states.[12]

The problem of crime victims is that society can easily be made to feel sympathy for any deprived group so long as the prerogatives and well-being of other key groups are not materially threatened. One example is the superimposition on the work force of new people, often possessing neither the trade-union-honored seniority nor the public sector's civil service, exam-measured merit, in the name of affirmative action. There, we can focus on one easily identifiable group that had struggled for a beneficial position (that is, those with seniority or test-demonstrated merit) seeing its position seriously threatened by some newly visible interest. Progress for the "new" group, which is quickly launched in a period of governmental and journalistic support—including the full American panoply of federal grants, commissions, and committees—all of a sudden reaches the "wait just a damned minute" point, just as did one Alan Bakke, on seeing his place in professional school filled by an alledgedly less-qualified, minority-group member.[13]

But there's nothing very revealing in all of this. What does it have to do with crime victims and a potential impasse in the improvement of their lot?

The answer is abundantly simple: All success achieved by victims to date has been delivered with no damages to criminal defendants and/or the defense bar.

Criminals as such have of course a very modest lobby. Few local pimps gain prominence in the chamber of commerce, and drug rings' sponsorship of little-league teams has remained rare. But the accused, a group that, it is hoped, overlaps with the guilty by more than a chance proportion, has attained statutory and especially judicial protection beyond the comprehension of our constitutional forebearers.

In much the same fashion as attends the new recognition of victim problems, dramatic attention and relief was brought to the criminal suspect by the Warren Court[14] and the society that produced it. Spokesmen as worthy as the attorney general of the United States assured us that we were all to blame for crime and that racial and economic injustice was at the root of our seemingly epidemic crime problem.[15]

Consider the *nature* of the progress to date in the victim area. In addition to throwing money and academic and journalistic concern at the problem, politicians have endorsed "Forgotten Victims' Weeks"[16] at the state and national level, affording opportunities to make speeches about what a bad thing it is to be a victim. Judges are not far behind, announcing that victim restitution will become a part of all probation conditions, clearly a dramatic benefit for the one victim in a thousand with a compensable financial loss combined with an apprehended and solvent attacker. Police agencies form victim-assistance units and offer roll-call training to officers to improve sensitivity. None of these things is bad.

But note that not one has any direct tendency to reduce victimization or crime itself. To the contrary, each such measure tends to make the symptoms of victimization more bearable and, like aspirin or stronger drugs, presents the danger of keeping our minds too well off the disease and its potential cures.

If I sound concerned at the threat of an impasse in improvements in victims' conditions, I am. We have done the easy, the painless. We have walked as far as possible without stepping on toes. Permit me to describe an agenda of three major problem areas, each much in need of redress, in which we've just begun.

The Victim in the System: From "Evidence" to "Person"

With much of what is possible to achieve through cosmetic programs already achieved, where do we go from here? If those of us who favor *real* improvement in the lot of victims expect continued unanimity of support and act on such expectations, the answer is probably "nowhere."

Studies of victim and witness complaints about the criminal justice system are interesting in the uniformity with which certain issues arise,[17] regardless of methodology, population sampled, or part of the country.

You cannot imagine, for example, what it is like to come out of a movie house in the middle of the night in Cambridge, Massachusetts, to find your car stolen and then calling the police from a phone booth only to be told that auto-theft reports must be made *at the station* and that, "Sorry, no transportation can be provided." Almost the perfect "Catch 22"—if you had a car to get to the police station, you would not need to report it stolen.

From this modest example to the sometimes reported[18] asking a rape victim if she experienced an orgasm, the police need to improve their service orientation vis a vis victims; and while tending to matters as mundane as transportation to court may be both philosophically and economically difficult, such measures may be needed and will probably marginally increase at least the reporting of crime and perhaps even general cooperation with officers.

Of the various institutions, the police are already clearly the best in dealing with victims. Prosecutors may well be the worst, though the judiciary can never be counted out in any contest of paucity of response to victim needs.

There is a substantial split in prosecutorial and judicial feeling on just what the role of the victim should be. As is true, whenever well-fenced terrain is in danger of being violated, emotions run deep as is exemplified by the reactions of many DA's and judges to a proposal known as "victim allocution," that is, asking the *victim as well as the defendant* if he has anything to say before sentence is pronounced. This sort of proposal is not earth shattering, but what is remarkable is the number of judges and prosecutors who ought to know better speaking of such a practice as "letting laymen decide what the sentence should be." Obviously, whether the practice is good or bad, it is absurd to equate the right to be heard on an issue to the right to decide it.

While prosecutors seem very wary of allowing any direct participation in the trial process to victims, preferring the more comfortable "victim as evidence" posture, to their credit, they have not formally tended to oppose suggestions or professional standards imposing a duty to keep the victim informed of the progress of a case, presently an almost uniformly unmet need and a very serious one.[19]

Conditions confronting victims and witnesses brave enough to "get involved" are simply indecent in most places. As good as our physical plants tend to be in Southern California, the specter of a victim waiting within an arm's length of the defendant or his family in the hallway or courtroom is commonplace. Child care, convenient free parking, and on-call status programs are real luxuries in most urban areas.

The literature finds only "fear of reprisal" (28 percent) leading "attitude" by officials (20 percent), speed (20 percent), and facilities (12 percent), among witness complaints.[20]

A dramatic problem, from the author's personal experience, is the near impossibility of finding out anything about the progress of a case once it is in the judicial system, even assuming the victim determines, Merlin-like, whether an arrest has been made in his case. More than idle curiosity is at stake: Potential retaliation ("Is the accused in custody or on bail?"), personal planning ("Can I go on vacation in July, or will the trial be then?"), and economic need ("When will they release my TV?") are all involved.

A quiet revolution in moral and professional performance is going to have to come upon those of us who judge, prosecute, and police, if progress, in human terms, is to come to victims.

The Domestic Victim: Up from Invisibility

Obviously, the type of crime that has the greatest emotional impact on all of us in terms of fears for our own well-being is what is generally known as "stranger to stranger street crime." A look behind the annual FBI statistics and political speeches on the subject of crime tells us, however, that a very high proportion of it does not occur between strangers or on the street. Armchair crime statisticians have long known that the substantial majority of homicides flow from the actions of friends (perhaps more properly, "former friends) and relatives. But until very recently, little attention was given to the tremendous proposition of other crimes (overwhelmingly non-reported) that occur in a domestic setting. These crimes are impossible to measure effectively because of the underreporting and the nondifferentiation between various types of assaults (domestic versus otherwise) in the statistics that do exist.[21] Suffice for the present purpose to say that the volume of domestic assaults is very high.

But the unique problem with domestic assaults is not their volume; it is society's ambivalence in dealing with them. Until relatively recently in our history, it was legally acceptable for a husband to beat his wife, and while statutes have changed our legal posture, certainly the number of nonfatal assaults by husbands against wives (or vice versa) that are formally prosecuted is significant compared even to the reported incidents.[22]

Much is owned to the women's movement, particularly to its leaders in the organized bar,[23] for forcing this issue—or perhaps, more accurately, this conceptual framework within which many issues arise—on the still largely male-controlled justice system. While the author does not confess to some of the more strident allegations, that is, that the situation is some sort of male chauvinist plot to keep women in their places or that women are twice as safe on the street as at home,[24] there can be little question that police, prosecutors, and courts have tended to view assaults within the home at least less formalistically, if not less seriously, than those occurring outside it.

A lot of energy has been put into trying to enunciate proper policy postures in this area, and it's a good trick. Some representatives of the women's movement, for instance, have sought to have domestic assaults prosecuted and sentenced as if there were no relationship between the parties. Whether or not this is politique, it seems conceptually defective in that the relationship between the perpetrator and the victim is the kind of factor that a judge or prosecutor quite properly takes into account in determining whether to prosecute or how to sentence. Most obviously, there may be provocation factors present in any close relationship, domestic or otherwise, that are nonexistent in stranger-to-stranger situations.

More important, however, for the purposes of *this* discussion, are some of the consequences of the change in the enforcement and prosecution practice that the women's movement seems to be seeking. Those of us in social strata in which violent crime is relatively rare fail to comprehend the frequency with which assailant and victim not only know each other but exist in close proximity. This factor cannot help but be amplified if more formal sanctions are sought against wife and child beaters. The net result will be a demand for new sorts of victim services, temporary shelters for victimized spouses and children.

Urgent philosophical issues, not the least of which is the extent to which the criminal process should be permitted or encouraged to intrude in domestic relationships, must be addressed, and it seems highly likely that the next decade will see a good deal of change in this area.

The Intimidated Victim: Trial by Terror

While writing this paper, I handled felony preliminary hearings involving a shooting incident at a gas station. When the prosecutor asked the victim about earlier threats from the defendant, the former testified he had heard none. Ten minutes later, under cross-examination, he inadvertently referred to the threats, and a police officer later testified persuasively to the victim's earlier assertions about them.

I know that the defendant was a gang member, and at the conclusion of the hearing, I learned that the district attorney had failed to file previous cases against him because of witnesses' refusals to testify. Then I saw his "rap sheet," indicating two murders (as a juvenile); by age twenty-one, he has committed every known violent felony.

The bailiff interviewed the victim in the hallway and was told that the defendant (out on bail) and his brother had paid him a visit two days earlier, threatening to "break an arm and a leg" and "cut off his daughter's ear," should he testify.

And I sat there watching the defendant and a friend try rather visibly to terrify the witnesses, I thought to myself, "This is crazy. Here I am writing about victims' rights, and intimidation is going on right now in my courtroom, and my legal authority to do anything about it is precisely zero!"

What I did, based on the information I had, was increase the man's bail so that he personally would be remanded to custody. Under present California law, the protection of victims and witnesses prior to trial is *not* a legal basis for increasing bail. While I had some additional lawful rationale for my actions, to the extent that I cheated, I can be comforted only by the fact that every judge has done so under similar circumstances.

There is for the most obvious of reasons no meaningful data on intimidation, but it is rampant. More than a quarter of witness complaints relate to fear of reprisals and the felony/misdemeanor classification of the underlying case is irrelevant.[25]

To make matters worse, laws on the subject are a patchwork of weak, confused, and illogical relics of the distant past. Seven states appear to have no witness-intimidation statute at all![26] Many consider bribery more serious than physical coercion. A number treat threats arising from misdemeanor cases as misdemeanors and those in felony cases as felonies, regardless of the nature of the conduct itself.[27] The Indiana statute, in making intimidation in a broad range of circumstances a felony, is better than most.[28]

Those of us who make our living in the system must come to grips with the reality that we have all *encouraged* intimidation. The victim who fails to show up in court, for example, brings us a shorter working day. We dismiss the case with "if he doesn't care enough about his car to testify against the guy who stole it, why should we?" The very real possibility is that he cared plenty about his car but even more about his skin.

In addition to this bureaucratic preference for the intimidated victim, as opposed to the troublemaker who actually comes to court, myths in the minds of the public and even the justice system professionals charged with dealing with victim problems are cumbersome. We are used to thinking of Jimmy Cagney's on some late, late show saying, "If you go to the law, I'll get you later!" This type of intimidation, to be sure, occurs but is not nearly as pervasive as more subtle forms of intimidation—the anonymous phone call or fleeting gesture in the courtroom.

If there were even an area in which consciousness raising would be desirable, it is here. Many opinion leaders, in the comfortable and relatively safe world of suburbia, fail to comprehend that resort to the formal criminal justice system is almost unheard of for victims in certain cultural settings. Perhaps this gets beyond intimidation and into actual taboos in the anthropological sense, but suffice to say that a young woman victim in a Latin barrio will receive dramatic and usually successful pressures from sources as astonishing to the nonresident as her own family.

Intimidation must be drastically reduced if a system advertising "justice" as a product is going to afford any to crime victims. The laws against witness intimidation are so rarely enforced as to be virtually worthless. Prosecutors point, doubtless with accuracy, to the difficulty of "making a case" in an intimidation situation, and even those who would prefer to try harder indicate that courts frequently give concurrent sentences for the intimidator who is also convicted of the substantive offense (prosecution for which is generally the subject of the intimidation).

We, as a society, need to take an across-the-board look at the intimidation issue, shoring up our statutes to eliminate, for example, concurrent sentences. Enforcement, investigation, and prosecution of intimidation, particularly offensive as it goes to the ability of the justice system itself to function, must be enhanced.

What Now?

Victims have found a voice. Their problems, while certainly not new, have at least been discovered. There is at least a presentation in the Indiana Colloquium on the subject, which there would not have been in years past. There are committees, organizations, lobbies.

Now those of us committed to being victim advocates must press the advantage. Judges, prosecutors, and the police must change practices; it must become professionally "right"—professionally demanded—to deal humanely with victims.

The terror of the battered wife whose assailant and breadwinner are the same man and the intimidation that so totally cuts off access to justice is made painful to legal practitioners.

But a word of caution is in order here. At this writing, California has just passed the well-known Jarvis-Gann Initiative, Proposition 13, the impact of which may well be to cut back dramatically on the money available to local governments for victim services and everything else. While Washington has been asked to foot some of the bill, particularly with respect to compensation programs,[29] it is unrealistic to expect massive amounts of federal money in this area. With the bleak economic picture in mind, private groups must be encouraged to enter the victim-service field, as is already occurring on an important scale.

Envision, if you will, the potential for private groups long on desire to help but short on cash, setting up systems to find out information about the progress of cases from the police and prosecutors. Such groups, merely by learning the jargon of the criminal justice industry, can do tremendous work in informing victims whether an arrest has been made, whether the suspect is on bail or in custody, and so forth. Such groups can assist in cutting the red tape of the return of stolen property, help "broker" continuances or other scheduling issues through the prosecutor's offices and the courts, and, perhaps most importantly, can provide relief from fears of intimidation through hot lines and other devices that are highly beneficial to the substantial proportion of cases in which the immediate physical presence of a law-enforcement officer is not required to reasonably protect a victim or witness from harm.

Government, including the courts, must improve its work. But in the best American tradition, citizens helping other citizens, will spell the difference between victory and continuing defeat for crime victims.

Notes

1. Macklin Fleming, *The Price of Perfect Justice* (New York: Basic, 1974).

2. Richard Knudten, "Crime Victim Compensation: Laws and Programs," Center for Criminal Justice and Social Policy, Milwaukee, Marquette University Press, 1975, p. 3.

3. Ibid.

4. Cal. Govt. Code §§13959 et seq.

5. For example, Frank Carrington, *The Victims* (New Rochelle, N.Y.: Arlington House, 1975).

6. For example, George Nicholson, ed., *Forgotten Victims: An Advocate's Anthology,* California District Attorneys Association, Sacramento, 1977.

7. For example, National Organization of Victims Assistance; National District Attorneys Association Commission on Victim Witness Assistance.

8. An excellent example, CBS's "Sixty Minutes" segment on Victims (Horvath, producer 5 December 1976), was shown by the ABA's Committee on Victims at the Chicago Annual meeting of the association in August 1977.

9. Anonymous, "Help for Victims and Witnesses," Lexington, Ky., National District Attorney's Association, 1976; a handful of states have passed statutes since the survey therein.

10. Kannensohn, J., "A Report on State Crime Compensation Programs," Council of State Governments, 1975, p. 8.

11. For example, New Jersey, as indicated in the Statement of Attorney General Hyland, Hearings, 94th Cong., House Judiciary Comm., Ser. no. 39 (1975–76), p. 287.

12. At this writing, S. 551 (Humphrey) has passed the Senate and awaits Conference Committee action with a virtually identical House bill. Indications are that the president will sign the final bill.

13. *Bakke* v. *Bd. of Regents of Univ. Calif.,* 98 S. Ct. 2733, 57 L. Ed. 2d. 750 (1978).

14. For example, *Mapp* v. *Ohio,* 367 U.S. 643 (1961); *Gideon* v. *Wainwright,* 372 U.S. 335 (1963); *Escobedo* v. *Illinois,* 378 U.S. 478 (1964); *Miranda* v. *Arizona,* 384 U.S. 436 (1966).

15. Ramsey Clark, *Crime in America* (New York: Simon and Schuster, 1970).

16. The endorsements in the beginning of *Forgotten Victims,* supra, n. 6, are continued, ad nauseum, at p. 223.

17. Frank Cannavale, et al., eds., *Witness Cooperation* (Washington,

D.C.: The Institute for Law and Social Research, 1976). This is a very thorough and interesting study, filled with hundreds of footnotes and bibliographic references to others.

18. Bacon, mod., American Bar Association, 1977 Annual Meeting program, August 8, "Rape: Rhetoric and Reality in the Criminal Justice System," American Bar Association, Section of Criminal Justice.

19. E. Younger, American Bar Association, Section of Criminal Justice, *Report of the Committee on Victims Advocating Amendments to the Standards Relating to Criminal Justice,* 12 April 1977.

20. Cannavale, supra, n. 17, at 57. "Witness pay" is also listed as a complaint but probably relates mostly to nonvictim witnesses.

21. Nordenbrook, S., American Bar Association, Section of Criminal Justice, *Report of the Committee on Women and Criminal Justice on Domestic Violence,* 16 December 1977, p. 3.

22. Ibid.

23. Chairpersons Bacon (see n. 18, supra) and Nordenbrook (see n. 21, supra) of the ABA's Committee on Women in Criminal Justice are excellent examples.

24. Address by Gloria Steinem, Nordenbrook, n. 21, supra, at p. 4, n. 9.

25. Cannavale, n. 17, supra, at 55.

26. "Help for Victims and Witnesses," n. 9, supra, at 70.

27. Ibid.

28. Ind. Code § *35-44-314* (1977 supp.); n. 9, supra, p. 70.

29. N. 12, supra.

Commentary

Edith Flynn

We examine the trial process from the defense and prosecution point of view, but what about the victim? It should be clear by now that our system of criminal justice is neither perfect nor is it the best in all respects. Particularly is this true when we consider the plight of many victims of crime.

We know from existing research that it is very important for the success of any court case to increase the speed within which a particular offense is reported to the police. The longer a victim waits, the less likely the case will ever be resolved or the offender ever apprehended. We also know from the highly innovative and successful Prosecutor's Management Information System (PROMIS) that the cooperation among citizens, victims, witnesses, and the various components of the criminal justice system is essential to the successful resolution of criminal cases. If we examine victim–assistance programs, we find some notable attempts to ease the burden of crime. The Vera Institute of Justice in New York has recently begun a victim–assistance program and thus continues to break ground in the improvement of criminal justice practice in the nation.

Looking at restitution for victims, we find a curious historical phenomenon. When criminal justice practice first evolved in this country, restitution was usually made directly to the victim. We are all aware of the gradual erosion of this process and the fact that fines levied for crimes now go directly to the county or state. Why should moneys go into federal, state, and county coffers and not to the individual who has been hurt? I really see no other reason than the fact that government is getting bigger and bigger and that its need for financing resembles nothing short of the proverbial bottomless pit. Available research on restitution tells us that courts often fail to inform the victims of court–ordered compensatory measures imposed on their behalf. Further, victim perception of fairness in court–ordered compensation is at least in part a function of the court's access to reliable information on the culpability of the offender for the damage sustained by the victim. The desirability of a contract between victims and offenders is seen by some researchers as a necessary condition if court–ordered compensation awards are to be viewed as fair by the victim. But I am fully aware that the institution of such a process would present yet another burden to the courts that are already drowning in administrative matters. Thus the reform envisioned here cannot be obtained without added resources.

While the idea of restitution has considerable public acceptance, the utility of these programs is at least questionable to some degree. Compensation often places a greater burden on the disadvantaged offender than it assists most victims of property offenses. Further, restitution programs may simply lead to more stealing in order to pay off specific judgments. It also appears as if restitution programs work best when applied to homogeneous social systems and may well be inapplicable to social structures characterized by economic inequality, as is the case in the United States. In short, restitution programs should be viewed with caution since they may give the appearance of homogeneity in society while doing very little to affect the conditions that promote crime and discord in the first place.

Finally, there are some questions about restitution that have yet to be answered by further research. When and to what degree should compensation by the offender be partial rather than sufficient to cover the victim's loss? To what degree should compensation occur in the form of service rather than money? This last area may well be one on which we should concentrate because it is easier to design innovative sentencing programs in relation to service rather than money. Still other questions in need of answers deal with the issue of whether it is feasible for an incarcerated offender to be required by the court to provide even partial compensation to the victim? How can such an offender pay when his prison income amounts to $1 a day? At what point does a restitution program become self-defeating, if not oppressive, and counterproductive to rehabilitation?

Let me turn to a brief examination of the relationships among the victim, the witness, and the criminal justice system. As previously mentioned, cooperation between all these actors is of utmost importance if the fate of victims and witnesses is to be improved. Too often the victim and the witness are ignored, abused, or exploited. There is much that could be done to improve the situation. If we look at the problem of urban disturbances and the victimization of our minority communities, it is important to note that the conventional approaches tend to focus on microscopic issues by examining primarily the victim/offender relationships. Such orientations lose sight of the fact that there are many cases of "pure victimization" perpetrated collectively on social groups, which happen to be, in most instances, members of minorities. It becomes self-evident at this point that the traditional focus on this microlevel only helps maintain the status quo in society and thus effectively prevents any serious examination of socioeconomic conditions or intergroup conflict. We all know about the social inequalities existing in our society, but there is a prevailing tendency in the criminal justice system to support (and thereby maintain) the social and political status quo. This is something to be considered in our dealings with victims, offenders, and programs designed to alleviate the burden of crime.

In the law-enforcement area, relationships between victims and the police are improving. Programs have been developed to assist victims of rape, a crime that is significantly increasing in the United States, including special police units trained to understand better the victims in their plight, and in the collection of evidence.

In the courts the "victim as witness" in an adversary process poses many problems for the prosecutor as well as for the defense. From the prosecutor's point of view, the victim is often seen as a respectable citizen and creditable witness. In fact, it is the job of the prosecutor to create and sustain this ideal image of the witness throughout the public examination process. The defense, in contrast, tries to discredit the victim with vigor. Too often the victim and/or the witness pays an inordinate price in humiliation and embarrassment under these circumstances.

As far as the sentencing process is concerned, it is worth noting that victims have long been denied a formal role in this facet of jurisprudence. The opinions, interests, and wishes of victims are rarely taken into account at time of sentencing. To remedy this situation, we need to develop the means on the basis of which the victim's role in the sentencing process could be formally recognized. But such a development would probably require changes in substantive and procedural law, the implications and costs of which should be assessed beforehand.

Judge Younger has discussed the problem of the battered spouse. To this I would like to add yet another issue, the abused child. Battered and sexually abused children are also a long-neglected topic. Research indicates that there appears to be a real increase in this type of crime. There is also evidence that violence in the home occurs predominantly among members of the lower socioeconomic classes. In view of the growing seriousness of the problem and the many physiological and psychological consequences for the victims, I would recommend that solutions to these problems be found outside the purview of the criminal justice system—to the degree that this may be possible. Clearly, support and assistance programs would be preferable to prosecution because condemnatory approaches often exacerbate the domestic situation and may lead to more punishment inflicted on the victim. But there is also a practical reason for the social-welfare approach recommended here. The criminal justice system is hardly equipped to cope with its present caseload let along the additiona of child-abuse problems despite their seriousness.

The final category of victims I would like to discuss are the elderly. While research concerning the relative incidence of crimes against the elderly provides us with mixed results, there is sufficient information available to point to the special vulnerability of elderly people to predation. Older persons, often neglected and lonely, are easy targets for robbery, muggings, assaults, arson, vandalism, intimidation, quackery, and other forms of exploitation. There is also sufficient evidence indicating that the elderly are the victims of much fear and isolation. Since we seem to be able to deal with only one or two social problems at a time, it is unlikely that the elderly will be discovered as victims in the immediate future. I know of no existing consistent or concerted efforts to assist the elderly. However, significant changes in the age structure of our population will make it quite likely that the coming decade will bring substantial change.

In conclusion, any consideration of the functioning of the criminal justice system would be painfully deficient if it did not expand its focus to include the victim of crime and the injuries and losses sustained by victims because of crime or call for adequate mechanisms of compensation and restitution. As we become increasingly cognizant of the plight and needs of the victims of crime, it is equally important to recognize that victims are also too often the victims of the criminal justice system as well. While defendants' rights are protected from invidious discrimination and acts that violate their fundamental rights as guaranteed by the Constitution, there are no counterbalancing charters protecting the rights of victims. If any jurisdiction wishes to improve its criminal justice system, it cannot omit the consideration of the victim's right to restitution and compensation, or the pursuit of fair and humane treatment of victims by the criminal justice system.

Part III
Disposition

10 A Proposal for Jail Reform

Ronald L. Goldfarb

The reality is that correctional reform must be sold to the public on grounds of public safety and economics. The surprise is that, generally, this can be done.

Jail reform is an exemplary case. The American public will never endorse and support jail reform on the basis of inspirational churchly preachings about humanitarianism or even in response to hortatory judicial pronouncements of constitutional principles. The public will support reform when it can be shown that people get a better "bang for their tax buck" by changing the pretrial justice system, or if it could be made clear that reform measures will lessen their chances of getting a bigger bang on their heads returning home some dark night.

For this reason, much of the reformist activity of the last decade has caused little fundamental change. Reformers in and out of courts thought they had begun an era of change; but their opponents outwaited and ultimately outsmarted them. Observers saw activity; but it proved to be an illusion of reform. Poor people still are detained before trial if they cannot afford bail; dangerous defendants with serious criminal records are released because they can afford bail. Jails are overcrowded and disgusting. They are filled with sick people, drunks, addicts, kids, along with the dregs of society. Society continues to react only to riots and emergencies, and the usual response is to build new buildings.

Criminal justice planners need a new strategy. They could take a page from either the neoconservative tax reformers who are managing to cut social-service and welfare programs or from liberal, sunset law proponents who are demanding accounts by public officials before public programs are refunded.

Most people in American jails do not need to be detained at all. Those necessarily detained should be detained in different places. The rest of the prototypical jail population needs other kinds of community programs or other kinds of institutional help.

Planners must resist the reformer's natural inclination to try to improve jails instead of replacing them. Real reform will not come from bringing medical facilities into jails, by sending guards to sociology courses, by bringing the community and its facilities into jails: That route leads only to the corruption of those programs. The answer is to send jailed people to the community facilities, to bring Mohammed out to the mountain, if you will, not the other way around.

Jails should be used only to do what they are designed to do—to detain dangerous people. The community can then use or develop proper alternative institutions and programs for clients who need other services. To eventuate a whole new concept of jail design and use it necessary.

Those cases that would require a new pretrial detention institution include: (1) the pretrial detainee who may not otherwise show up for trial or who is too dangerous to be released; (2) the offender whose problem is one of health or welfare, not the need for punishment; offenders who need to be held briefly, only in order to be examined and quickly channeled to other, appropriate, specialized institutions; and (3) convicted offenders who require some local correctional institution to house them when they are being reintegrated into the community or diverted out of the formal criminal justice system.

Ideally, jails as we have known them should be eliminated. They should be replaced by a network of metropolitan (in the big cities) and regional (in rural areas) detention centers. These facilities would have three separate wings to carry out three specific services. No convicted offender would serve sentences in these proposed detention centers. Instead, correctional authorities would have to service convicted defendants in prisons or in community correctional programs.

The housekeeping functions presently performed in jails by convicts would have to be absorbed by staff. Alternatives would have to be found for short-term misdemeanants who presently are housed in jails. These alternatives exist: Public and community-based programs could be used regularly for this class of usually petty offender (youthful misconduct, vice, drunk charges).

The detention centers of the future would house those defendants in pretrial status who present clear and demonstrable threats of flight before trial or whose personal dangerousness warrants limited pretrial detention. They also would serve as short-term reception, diagnostic, classification, and referral institutions for those who have been arrested but could be serviced better in other institutions, particularly youngsters, alcoholics, addicts, and physically and mentally sick people. Third, these centers could be used as dormitories to house convicted convicts who are placed in community programs without residential facilities halfway-in and halfway-out defendants, defendants on work-release and furlough status, and defendants who participate in restitution programs. These individuals would not be detained for correction. They simply would be provided a dormitory service.

These future detention centers should be administered not by the police but by the local human resources department or its counterpart agency.

with several distinct functions and roles, they would have to be divided into three separate wings. One wing would be for detention only. A second wing would be to provide diagnosis to inmates and refer them to appropriate outside programs or institutions, only housing defendants short term in the course of their treatment or diagnosis. The third wing would be a dormitory, providing only augmented social services to assist transition back to a completely free status.

A deputy would supervise each of the three component parts of the center. A court official would run the pretrial facility. A medical official would supervise the diagnostic and referral wing. A social-welfare or correctional department official would direct the third wing for people in the community housed under correctional supervision. Each state human resources department should have the statutory obligation to set strict standards for the operation and maintenance of these detention centers and to inspect them regularly to assure the standards are met.

Wing 1: Pretrial Detention to Prevent Flight or Crime

The first wing, for detention, would house dangerous adult and juvenile defendants for limited times before trial under special conditions and under court order. While far too many people end up in jail because they cannot afford bail, too many people who present clear and present dangers of hurting others are able to avoid detention because of the vagaries of the money bail system. To a great degree, we have ended up with a paradox of injustice: Many of the wrong people are in jail while many of the wrong people are on the street. Freedom that is against the public interest should not be bought, nor should imprisonment result simply from one's disadvantaged economic status.

The only way to perfect the pretrial system is to abolish money bail completely and to devise an open and careful scheme for determining pretrial release and detention. A new pretrial system should include a clear judicial procedure that would strike a reasonable balance between proper demands for detaining the few defendants who are dangerous and assuring the freedom of the many defendants who are not. Some defendants may require some supervision short of jail. Some people should be detained to protect others. Detention should not result from the fact that a defendant cannot afford a bail bond; it should arise only when defendants are demonstrably dangerous.

In an earlier book, *Ransom,* I suggested that the American bail bond system be scrapped, that a fair pretrial detention system be developed and that these goals be carried out in a new pretrial proceeding, which I detailed there and which I will summarize and expand on here.[1]

This new pretiral procedure would govern the status of all criminal defendants from the time of arrest until trial. The pretrial procedure would take place in two steps: the first, a judicially sanctioned release procedure, would cover the great majority of cases; the second, a pretrial detention hearing, would affect, I should guess, about 10 percent of the criminal cases.

Step 1 would include two classes of situations: one, the majority of cases when the judicial process is called into play and supervised release is ordered; the other, when a summons would suffice, and the judicial pretrial process could be avoided or significantly limited. There would never be more than the briefest and most perfunctory incarceration prior to trial under a step 1 proceeding. There could be pretrial imprisonment only after a step 2 proceeding, which would deal only with this issue, instituted only in prescribed situations, and carried out in carefully prescribed situations, in a procedurally circumscribed manner and administered in a special facility. When appropriate officials decide to initiate the criminal process against a person whom they believe or suspect committed a crime, they would proceed under step 1 in one of two ways.

If the crime is not a serious one (a petty offense, some misdemeanors), the first approach would be followed. Instead of arrest or at the time of arrest (but without taking a person physically into custody), or a very few hours thereafter (if there had been an arrest, booking, perhaps some brief incarceration demanded by the particular exigencies of the case), the defendant would be summoned by a delegated police official to appear in court at a later date for trial. If refused the summons in one of these situations, a defendant could demand to be brought before a court that, except for some extraordinary reason, would release him and order him to appear for arraignment or trial.

This phase of step 1 would include both the true police summons (instead of an arrest) and police ROR (that is, summons soon after arrest and a limited background investigation). The defendant would have to agree to appear in court as a condition of his release. Administrative officials of the court in charge of overseeing the pretrial release system would be responsible (in conjunction with the police) for record keeping, trial notification, and general control of this group of defendants during the time they are free in pretrial status.

If the crime is a serious one (aggravated misdemeanors or felonies), the accused would immediately be brought under the control of the courts (under similar time requirements, usually within forty-eight hours, as now exist in general practice regarding mandatory appearance before a judicial officer for arraignment). Depending on the nature of the crime, the background of the defendant, and any other meaningful circumstances of the case, the court then would either order the defendant to appear for later arraginment or trial and release him or place him under the control of a designated official for investigation and then release him under the supervision of that court officer, whichever seem appropriate.

Under either phase of step 1, both unnecessary imprisonment and improper release based on the absence or presence of money bail would be eliminated, and with it would disappear the role of the bondsman in the administration of justice. Where a summons is issued, there is no imprisonment.

In other cases, at the first meeting with a defendant, the judge would order appropriate controls short of imprisonment to assure the defendant's presence at trial. This might be a simple order by the court to be there; or it might be an order when to appear with an assignment to and the assumption by some third party of the responsibility to insure his presence. If appropriate (and it would be in most cases), the court would make an assignment to some administrative court official to investigate the defendant's background and supervise the defendant and assure his appearance at trial. This function could be assigned to any court official, even one who dealt solely with this task. The responsible official could fulfill his duty to assure the defendant's presence at trial by any program short of imprisonment.

The supervisory officer for the court could draw on the techniques of any sensible program to administer defendants' releases. He or she might require a defendant to report periodically; or to turn over a driver's license or passport; or to deposit a bank book, even a sum of money if it were an appropriate control and as long as release was not dependant solely on the ability to make a financial deposit and detention did not result from inability to afford the sum. Only a letter or a phone call to keep in contact would be necessary in some cases. In others, third-party parole could be used. Under this concept, the assistance of an organization, employer, counsel, a relative, or a member of the clergy is enlisted to supervise the defendant prior to trial.

The point is that the court official, with the opportunity to satisfy himself that the defendant is not dangerous can be released, as would be the case most of the time, should not be limited in the variety of methods by which he or she could administer this step 1 release proceeding.

Flight would present a problem for the court and police, but experienced law-enforcement officials have pointed out that fugitives from justice are relatively rare. There is no reason to believe that the bail bond system would have prevented or terminated even these escapes. To this low figure of fugitives must be added the impressive record of the FBI in capturing even this small percentage of people. The police investigative agencies are quite adept at this function. Of the few defendants who become fugitives, even fewer get away. Natural deterrents like lack of money to hide indefinitely, the inevitable personal ties to one's home, people, and community, and the omnipresent paper world of records we are all tied to combine to minimize the problem of flight.

Where there is a real and obvious danger of flight, detention under step 2 could be considered.

The courts have both punitive and administrative powers to deal with the inevitable but unusual cases when a defendant does not appear for trial. They also have the contempt power to punish swiftly and violation of their orders to appear for trial. Fleeing from a trial could be made a crime in those places where it is not already. Proof of flight may be offered at trial as evidence of a defendant's consciousness of guilt. If a defendant is not dangerous and he escapes, it is not a serious problem anyway.

Charging fees for bonds or imprisoning the nonrisk defendants, as is now done, is an unsatisfactory way to deal with these relatively few cases. The present system imprisons the mass of defendants to protect against the potential few who might flee or do harm. The proposed system would free the mass of defendants who deserve freedom and provide a special machinery to deal differently with the exceptions.

Defendants then would be released prior to trial: (a) in petty offenses and minor misdemeanor cases after only a summons to appear, or a brief arrest and then a summons by a police official who would administer the bookkeeping needed to record and administer the event, or (b) in more serious cases, after being brought swiftly before a court and either simply ordered to appear and after some investigation placed under third-party control or official supervision.

This procedure should cover 80–90 percent of all criminal cases, and it would assure the release of most defendants under a rational scheme. It would take no more time or administrative effort than present procedures, possibly less.

Step 2 would cope with the relatively small, special, and very important class of cases for which compelling reasons exist to warrant detention until trial. Under step 2 an effort would be made to balance the safety of society with the rights of accused individuals and to secure a proper relationship between public control and personal freedom.

To occur after arrest at the arraingment, such a procedure must take into account the need to prevent unnecessary and predictable crimes, especially crimes of violence, whenever possible; and the importance of maintaining the working philosophy about crime that no man should lose his liberty without due process of law, that accusation is not conviction, that until conviction a man is presumed innocent, and the burden is on the government to prove otherwise.

A statute should list the cases where the step 2 proceeding would be permitted. This law should include crimes of extreme violence; pathological crimes; subversion cases where violence, sabotage, or treason were involved; and cases where recidivism or obstruction of justice is anticipated. Defendants who would not cooperate with the court official in charge of release also could be included here. In no other case would a step 2 pretrial detention be permitted.

To warrant this invocation of commitment, the government should be required to make a very strong showing of the existence of these special conditions. The defendant must have the fullest and fastest opportunity, with counsel, to oppose the government by presenting arguments in his defense. Careful procedures whould have to be developed to satisfy the touchy constitutional questions about self-incrimination and the right to counsel that arise here.

Only if the court should decide after a speedy, full, and fair hearing to order special commitment would the defendant be incarcerated. Even in this case, every step should be taken to make this a special kind of detention. No imprisonment is pleasant, and calling it something else does not make it any better. As Blackstone said:

> This imprisonment, is only for safe custody, and not for punishment; therefore, in this dubious interval between the commitment and trial, a prisoner ought to be used with the utmost humanity, and neither be loaded with needless fetters nor subjected to other hardships than such as are absolutely requisite for the purpose of confinement only;...[2]

Admittedly, there is a chance that this procedure would be declared unconstitutional because no matter how circumscribed and how restrained, it sanctions imprisonment without the traditional trial and all its concomitant protections. In the context of today's punitive jails, this argument is persuasive. A new kind of detention institution probably would be required to save even the most carefully designed pretrial detention procedures form constitutional challenge.

A pragmatic argument must be accepted to support this admittedly precipitous procedure: It is that since we frequently practice preventive detention under the present bail system and since it has never been considered unconstitutional, step 2, which provides a much more clear and more direct procedure surrounded with more careful safeguards, perhaps should not be considered unconstitutional either.

How carefully step 2 was implemented would be an important factor in assaying whether it was a reasonable and fair procedure. If used, it must be done carefully. The basic point is that step 2 proceeding would result in far less improper official conduct and less pretrial incarceration than under the present bail system, and it would better protect both society and defendants.

There would be less chance for judges to abuse their powers—their reasons and the basis for them would appear on an appealable record. Detention would be less punitive than it is under existing procedures. The individual's trial would be expedited. His period of incarceration would be made as tolerable as possible. He could receive medical and other special services if they were warranted.

If this two-step procedure were adopted, the jails would be emptied of the many poor defendants who are neither dangerous nor likely to flee, and yet are the majority of most jail populations. The money saved by eliminating them from the jail system could be used to administer the judicial system to supervise this part of the pretrial process.

A great deal must be done to make this incarceration less personally destructive than is the case during pretrial detention. A special facility or wing of the future pretrial detention facility (separated from any convicted prisoners) should be used. It should be made as physically pleasant as possible. No cells nor cages nor crude crammed dormitories would be permitted.

A prisoner's family should be allowed to visit at any reasonable time. The defendant should be able to work at controlled employment to earn some reasonable income during this time before trial. He should be assisted to find employment if he is acquitted. All social and medical services that would be helpful to him or his family ought to be provided. Where the crime charged or the background of the defendant indicates a special problem, voluntary treatment could begin immediately. Particularly in the cases of the uncontrollable recidivist criminal, or the pathological or insane criminal, step 2 could convert to a more permanent medical supervision if appropriate.[3]

This pretrial incarceration should not be counted as an arrest record if the defendant is acquitted. Trial dates should be expedited by giving calendar preferences to these cases. The time of pretrial detention should be reduced from any subsequent sentence after the trial. The defendant should be released at the time of trial, and the fact of his incarceration should not be brought to the jury's attention.

If these changes in effect make the facility a sort of short-term hotel for the containment of involuntarily registered and closely supervised clients, then that reality can be faced. A jail is not a prison, and there is no good reason why it should look or operate like one. Even though it would have an incidental, similar function—detention—the similarities must end there. The pretrial detention facility and the correctional facility used after conviction are fundamentally different institutions with different basic purposes. This wing of the detention center of the future would reflect those differences in every way: architecturally, administratively, and programmatically.

Wing 2: Intake, Classification, and Referral

The second wing of the jail of the future would be completely segregated from the others. With a medical staff and orientation, it would serve a diagnostic and referral function for sick defendants and those with special problems.

The two-step pretrial arraignment procedure advocated for adults also would apply to children. Only the patently dangerous young offender—never the noncriminal, uniquely juvenile offender—would be detained in the juvenile section of wing 1 described earlier.

The juvenile court and the administrators of early entry parts of the system would determine and supervise appropriate community controls of youngsters involved in the system. Detention could result only in the special circumstances described earlier regarding dangerous defendants, and then under careful, special procedures.

Young Offenders and Juveniles in Trouble

In the juvenile system, however, the release practices are more difficult to design than those for the adult system. Unlike the case of most adult detention, some form of pretrial residential care for juveniles often is necessary. In many instances, a youngster first comes to the attention of the juvenile court because of problems in his normal home environment. Depending on the nature of the trouble at home, such a crisis may prompt the child to commit a peculiarly juvenile offense, or it may stimulate a parent or guardian to file a "PINS" petition against the child. Under these circumstances, it would be unrealistic to release children in trouble to await court action at home. While generally the artificially maintained duality that now exists between the adult "criminal justice system" and the counterpart "juvenile justice system" is a false and pernicious one, in the case of pretrial services, the needs of adults and young people differ significantly in this one regard.

A variety of pretrial, nondetention alternatives to America's atrocious "child jails" exist. These alternatives are not, in the traditional sense, forms of juvenile detention. But proposed systems for group homes, foster homes, and even so-called home detention do involve significant restrictions on a youngster's freedom. Because they require that new temporary residential arrangements be made for children, or that existing arrangements be modified significantly, these alternatives to pretrial custody are very sensitive and peculiarly demanding.

With children, unlike adults, it cannot be assumed that the pretrial placement that most closely approximates an individual's prearrest status is the most desirable placement. Before a realistic pretrial placement is made for any child in trouble, some inquiry into the child's background and family situation is required. In addition to providing the basis for such a temporary placement, an early investigation into a child's background may provide valuable clues to the causes of his or her predicament—the scars of parental child abuse, the signs of a crippling but correctable learning problem, or the symptoms of a lingering physical illness.

As it is presently constituted, the juvenile justice system is particularly ill-suited to making necessary inquiries concerning children in trouble. The juvenile court intake officer has time and skill enough to make only an uninformed and largely intuitive choice between detention and release. From this point forward, all discretion lies with the juvenile detention system's own staff. Unfortunately, thorough testing and competent evaluation of children in trouble is a rarity.

The diagnostic wing of the detention center of the future, through its one-stop referral center for troubled adult arrestees, could have a key role to play in a rational, humane system of juvenile detention. In the past, social reformers have insisted on a clear separation between the adult and juvenile justice systems. All too often, the result has been that children in trouble inhabited "the worst of both worlds." Conventional thinking in the area of juvenile detention takes the desirability of complete segregation of adult and juvenile detainees as an absolute tenet. All too often, the result is that young people inhabit institutions even viler than those reserved for adults and receive services that are unresponsive to their needs.

As the detention center of the future replaces the present network of jails, many of the traditional arguments against jointly housing adult detainees and children in trouble might disappear. Considerations of efficiency suggest that when a jurisdiction invests in a centralized diagnostic wing of a detention center for adults and staffs that center with professional medical personnel, social workers, and counselors, the same center also should provide threshold diagnostic services for children. Anticipating this function for the diagnostic wing of the new detention center, from the outset its designers should provide for a specialized children's section with separate living, dining, and recreation areas, but with access to common medical facilities and to the offices of professional staff members whose skills can benefit adults and children alike.

A large group of children in trouble would not become residents of the diagnostic wing or the detention wing. This group would include the youngsters whose "crimes" are minor and whose family ties strong; they would be released to their parents by a police officer immediately after arrest. Rather than taking such children into custody, the arresting officer would merely leave a notice of violation, returnable at a set hearing date, with the parents.

This group of children would include those with responsible families who could not be located immediately by an arresting officer but could later be traced by the juvenile intake staff of the detention center. For them the diagnostic wing would provide merely a neutral place to wait until a family member appeared to take custody.

For many other children, however, an immediate and unconditional release could do more harm than good. The existing juvenile detention system, which gives little or no attention to threshold evaluation, does these children a disservice. Some youngsters are released back to the very conditions that precipitated the crisis leading to their arrest. Others are confined under equally unsatisfactory conditions for long periods. A few are referred to alternative noncustodial residential facilities or specially supervised programs; but such referrals are unusual, the result of good fortune.

By instituting procedures under which children who could not be released immediately and unconditionally, would be held in diagnostic custody for a very brief period (surely not to exceed forty-eight hours), the juvenile justice system could rationalize its detention decisions. During this brief stay in the children's diagnostic section, each child could be evaluated individually and adequately. Public and private pretrial service agencies, which would maintain liaision offices at the diagnostic wing, could be consulted, as could referral agencies specializing in service brokering between the child and the community. Urgent medical needs could be treated and less urgent ones identified.

There is a present debate in reform circles over the right of any system to force unwilling, unconvicted kids into programs, however sensible and benign they may be. Coercive treatment, even testing, of unconvicted youngsters should be reserved to extraordinary situations. The social services of wing 2 would be available for pretrial juvenile defendants on a voluntary basis, however, and those facilities could be used pending disposition of their cases and thereafter.

Those children who are dangerous and require secure detention could be isolated in the detention wing and referred to the juvenile court for an immediate hearing analogous to the step 2 hearing in the adult pretrial procedure outlined above. At the end of forty-eight hours, every arrested child should have been brought before the court or released into the care or under supervision of a designated pretrial service program after receiving a notice of the next scheduled hearing date in his case.

The use of the diagnostic wing of the the new detention center as a screening center for children in trouble could not itself solve the problems of juvenile detention. Each community also would have to provide an adequate range of alternative pretrial housing and supervision programs for young people. The savings that would accrue from an end to wholesale juvenile detention could be expected to contribute toward financing this alternative-care network. The Youth Service Bureau model, which has met with notable success in the few jurisdictions where it has been tested, suggest that an umbrella organization operating outside the juvenile justice system could assist children.

The child's brief stay in the diagnostic wing of the new detention center might fill another need as well. All experts agree that the implementation of diversion is the key to reform in juvenile justice. The best way to protect children from abuse in juvenile courts, reform schools, or training homes is to see that as few children as possible ever come into contact with these institutions. At the diagnostic wing, an important diversion program could be administered. During the forty-eight-hour evaluation period, the child and the state could agree to a diversion "contract." In appropriate cases, if the child then met its terms whether by attending school, by participating in a specified program, making restitution, or merely by staying out of further trouble, charges might be dismissed.

Today as many as 50 percent of all charges lodged against children are "adjusted," but the very informality of this haphazard diversion procedure casts doubt on its effectiveness. Ad hoc adjustments relieve pressure on the system, but they may do little or no good for the child. By formalizing early exit procedures within the juvenile justice system and by providing the diagnostic wing of the new detention center as a meeting ground for all persons concerned in the decision to divert, the architects of criminal justice reform could extend the benefits of true diversion to young people.

Sick Defendants

The physically or mentally sick defendant poses a perfect example of the kind of person who could be serviced by the second wing of the detention center.

Providing every prisoner who is detained with high-quality diagnostic services and with any required preventive or corrective medical care should be a major priority of any detention system. The general scrutiny of all arrestees to discern public health problems and suggest candidates for related, nonpenal institutions and programs should be the other major function of this medical wing.

To provide such services and care, this wing of the detention center must have new equipment and larger medical budgets, nurses or medical paraprofessionals, meaningful amount of physician's time, and the space and materials medical employees need to work.

Furthermore, new strategies of cooperation with other public and private institutions must be devised. At best, a large urban detention center cannot provide all the services its mixed population of sick inmates may require. A jail infirmary cannot become a complete substitute for a hospital, and specialist doctors will not be available to serve as full-time jail staff members. Before the health of the inmate population can be improved substantially, walls of isolation between the jail and the community must come down.

Affiliation agreements between local detention administrators and nearby public health facilities (particularly teaching hospitals) would be one direct and efficient means of improving the delivery of health care to detained inmates. Under such an agreement, medical teams would be available for duty inside, and hospital beds would be available for inmates outside the detention center. The gulf between the limited care to which inmates now have access and the complete care to which all free patients at least can aspire would narrow or close. Such reform would be expensive, and it would require that both the jailing system and the health-care establishment abandon their traditional habits of insularity.

A properly staffed, well-equipped, and fully affiliated jail medical unit could provide a wide range of low-intensity services to a large number of detained people. It can assure that no inmate's medical problem goes unrecognized and undiagnosed. It can provide post-release referrals to community treatment services. In many instances it can initiate the delivery of simple, urgent health-care services during detention.

The detention center of the future should be treating the limited inmate population in its diagnostic wing at the same time as it checks and diagnoses all other arrestees who are not required to be detained. Many miscellaneous prisoners, for whose health today's jail is responsible, would not be detained in the first instance under fair and rational pretrial-realease procedures along the lines of those recommended earlier. Other "problem prisoners" in today's jail, including the drunkenness offender, the addict, and the police "mental-health pickup," could be taken to specialized hospitallike facilities immediately. Incarcerating them need not be a function of the detention center of the future. Instead, many defendants could be examined and released while the medical staff and resources of the center concentrated on delivering high-intensity services to the relatively small and coherent population in detention.

Under the pretrial-release procedures proposed, a defendant's dangerousness or risk of flight would be the only justifications for his pretrial detention. The defendants detained under such procedures would have their share of medical problems. As is the case with most jail inmates today, many prisoners received at such a detention facility would be men or women who have had little or no prior professional medical attention. Diagnostic and treatment resources could be concentrated on giving these prisoners the aid they need and want.

This medical wing then would provide a short battery of tests and a basic physical examination of all arrested defendants during the brief time between their arrest and arraignment. The only exceptions would be those defendants whose crimes were so minimal, dangerousness so unlikely, and condition apparently normal that an early decision to release has been made by the police or juvenile authorities. Perhaps this group too should be required to submit at some date before their trial or other disposition of their case to this brief public health examination. Clearly, they should be given the option of submitting to this examination and any course of treatment that is recommended. The recommendation of the staff of this wing would be available to assist the court in determining release conditions under the proposed step 1 proceeding.

Second, for all those defendants who are detained under step 2, submission to diagnosis and recommended referral to appropriate outside programs should be required, at least where there is a relation between the offense charged and the condition diagnosed. This would lead to alternate treatment programs and diversion in many cases if the court adopted the medical wing's recommendations. If there is no relation between the offense and the condition diagnosed, I would recommend that any subsequent referrals be only on a voluntary basis.

In some cases this useful social service could be strictly a public health function, tangential to the criminal justice system. In other cases, it could lead to major alternative correctional programs such as with the cases of alcoholics and addicts.

The fashionable term "diversion" embraces a variety of programs. Some of these programs supply complete alternatives to criminal prosecution, others provide participants with an opportunity to defer and possibly avoid prosecution, still others merely provide special services outside the criminal justice system for defendants awaiting trial.

All diversion programs have one thing in common: before any accused offender can be removed from the criminal justice system and introduced to useful social and medical services, his personal problems first must be recognized and analyzed. No present functionary or institution of the criminal justice system is required or prepared to fulfill this professional diagnostic responsibility—at least of all the present jail and its staff. Routine jail-intake procedures now overlook even the grossest physical, psychological, and social handicaps. They are completely inadequate to discover the subtler, often equally crippling, personal problems of people in trouble.

The diagnostic wings of the detention centers of the future should concentrate any professional skills that exist in the present criminal justice system and would add and coordinate new professional capabilities the pretrial system badly needs. As a one-stop center for social service and medical examination and referral, it would replace the haphazard aggregation of part-time physicians, probation officers, court social workers, and volunteers who now inadequately share this responsibility.

The medial wing of the proposed new multipurpose detention facility would provide for hospital wards, secure individual rooms and dormitories, interview areas, physician's offices, medical laboratories, as well as office space for representatives of community programs that accept referrals.

The diagnostic wing would not dispense long-term treatment. Only when an inmate was in need of immediate help would its personnel provide short-term, crisis-intervention medical services. No inmate would be held there beyond the brief period (usually days and rarely more than weeks) required to assess his problems and to complete a referral. Not every person diverted through the diagnostic wing would be a complete volunteer, but its diversion procedures would be designed to encourage the client's participation in the referral process.

The class of people who would be served by this diagnostic wing would be the people who are most seriously misserved by present-day jails: the men, women, and children whose offenses are identical with or directly caused by their afflictions.

The diversion of alcoholics and addicts concerns a large and special class of arrestees worth individual attention. The gradual reform of law enforcement regarding alcoholics could provide the eventual decriminalization of the offense of public intoxication. Even where the offense remains on the statute books, there is an increasing interest in noncriminal alternatives for handling the public drunk.

Decriminalization will not end the problem drinker's involvement with the criminal justice system. Intoxicated men and women will continue to be arrested for a variety of alcohol-related criminal offenses, ranging from simple disorderly conduct to manslaughter in the course of drunken driving. Police will continue to bear primary responsibility for removing helpless and vulnerable drunks from the streets.

Of all the emerging alternatives for dealing with alcoholic petty offenders and simple drunks, the medical detoxification unit or "sobering-up station" is the most promising. Short-term care for acute intoxication and alcoholic withdrawal is simple, inexpensive, and effective. For some problem drinkers, detoxification proves to be the first step on the long, difficult road to abstinence, sobriety, and future avoidance of the criminal justice system.

Experiments in a number of American cities have demonstrated that the usefulness of specialized detoxification units has two significant, practical limitations. The first is the police officer's common reluctance to bring even seriously intoxicated men and women to the local "Detox." Often this reluctance is the result of the unit's inconvenient location, the time-consuming paperwork involved in admitting a drunk to the unit, or the officer's dislike for non-law-enforcement duties.

The second is the detoxification unit's typical separation from medical and social aftercare systems that could provide continuing support for its short-term patients. By definition, a detoxification unit is a limited-purpose facility, set up to deliver a few days of high-quality sobering-up service at low costs. Referral help, where it is provided at all, generally amounts to an administrative afterthought.

Both these limitations could be offset or eliminated by making the detoxification unit a part of the new detention center's diagnostic and referral section. As a centrally located, professionally administered, and law-enforcement oriented facility, the new center could offer an alcoholic-detoxification program that tradition-minded police officers could accept.

The "alcoholic ward" of the detention center of the future—a humane and scientific version of the notorious "drunk tanks" to today's jail—would receive a variety of patients. In addition to simple, public drunks (picked up for their own protection, at their own request, or after violation of a minor public intoxication ordinance), the ward also could house severely intoxicated drunken drivers, disorderly persons, and even arrestees charged with serious alcohol-related offenses. Unlike the chronically overcrowded specialized detoxification units, which often must limit the care they provide to two or three days of medication and bed rest, the new center should be programmed and staffed to provide the five to seven days of care that experts agree is required for thorough detoxification.

With its complete medical-social diagnostic staffing, the new center could provide drunks with services beyond the capability of any specialized detoxification unit. During the sobering-up period, the patient would have the opportunity to undergo a full physical examination and a battery of psychological tests. For the Skid Row drunk, this sort of evaluation can be especially useful. Often his intoxification masks serious physical and psychological handicaps that have never been diagnosed or treated. Evaluation and diagnosis would enable the professional staff of the new diagnostic center to design individualized aftercare plans for alcoholic-detoxification programs, making use of all available community resources. Medium-term residential alcoholic-treatment centers, AA groups, halfway houses, sheltered workshops, out-patient mental-health facilities, even family units from which the drunk presently is estranged, all could be resources to which the center might refer appropriate cases.

On completing detoxification, most patients from the new center's alcohol ward could be discharged outright. In jurisdictions where public drunkenness is fully decriminalized, there would never be any criminal charges against them. Their stay in the alcohol ward would have been voluntary from the outset. In other jurisdictions, successful detoxification could be made a condition for the later automatic quashing of a summons or notice of violation issued at the time of drunkenness arrest.

Where the condition of a simple drunk indicated it was necessary and apt (and where local statutes permitted), physicians could initiate proceedings leading to short- or medium-term civil commitment to a public alcoholic-treatment center or mental hospital. Those patients who were charged with minor alcohol-related offenses (other than simple drunkenness itself) would be eligible for immediate pretrial release under the step 1 release procedure already described. Only a tiny minority (repeaters or those charged with manslaughter, perhaps) might be subject to a later step 2 pretrial-detention hearing and possible detention.

Before leaving the alcohol ward, each detoxified patient would have the opportunity to discuss and plan his future program with a specialist counselor, to question or modify the planned program, and ultimately to accept or reject it. In some cases, this conference would be the first step in a true scheme of diversion. Acceptance of participation in aftercare referrals might be wholly voluntary, flowing from the confidence created by a positive detoxification experience. On whatever terms the aftercare referral is made, however, the personnel of the new center would assume responsibility for completing the connection with the facility or agency to which the patient is referred. Counselors would be available to accompany each patient from the alcohol ward to the next way station, and to help him avoid relapse.

Building alcoholic-detoxification services into the detention centers of the future would assure the institutionalization of the tentative measures that some communities have taken to assist indigent problem drinkers. Incorporation of an alcohol ward into the diagnostic wing of the new detention center would amount to the necessary recognition that alcohol is America's favorite intoxicant, and problem drinking is an inevitable and major problem. If the excesses of America's underprivileged problem drinkers must remain a law-enforcement or police problem, at least the poor drinkers will be provided the humane and scientific treatment that their affliction deserves and their wealthier counterparts usually get.

Alcohol, the public drunk, and the alcohol-related offense will be widespread social problems in any foreseeable American society. The same is not necessarily true of narcotics, narcotics addiction, and drug-related crime. The heroin epidemic, urgent as it is today, may be on its way toward being checked, reversed, and controlled by a combination of law-enforcement and public health strategies. For the moment, however, narcotic drug use is a unique public problem: an easily contracted social disease that has criminal activity as one of its most prominent symptoms. Any modern detention facility must be designed, staffed, and programmed to identify and assist arrested narcotics addicts.

For trained professional or paraprofessional staff, the diagnosis of narcotics addiction presents no substantial problems. A routine of physical examinations, coupled with interviews and urinalysis testing, will miss few active narcotics users. Every new jail should be designed to perform this identification function quickly and accurately in a nonpenal, medical setting. When properly performed, addict identification of arrestees can be completed within only a few hours.

Under the pretrial-release procedure of step 1 outlined above, many accused offenders (those not apparent addicts) would be released immediately after arrest, without any formal preliminaries other than the issuance of a police summons. These accused offenders would not be subject to screening for drug use, and the addicts among them would go undetected and untreated—at least temporarily. To this extent, the jail of the future would not perform the complete task of identifying every addict who comes into contact with the criminal justice system unless all arrestees were required to submit to testing, even if released prior to their trials.

The diagnostic personnel of the medical wing of the detention center could identify addicts charged with serious offenses, addicts whose condition had aroused the concern of police officials or judicial officers supervising prerelease proceedings, and addicts who regardless of the nature of their alleged offenses requested medical help at the time of arrest. As the criminal justice system operates today, the number of addicts in the last category would be minimal. The risks of identifying oneself as a narcotics user to an arresting officer are serious despite the possible personal benefits from self-identification. In a system where diagnostic centers earn a reputation for providing high-quality care on a nonstigmatic, nonpunitive basis, however, the crisis of an arrest might stimulate addicts to seek long-term care through the jails themselves.

Assuming that relatively large numbers of narcotics addicts can be persuaded or compelled to make their condition known to the professional diagnostic staff of the new jail, a number of valuable treatment services can then be provided for them at the pretrial stage. In the diagnostic wing, housing could be provided for those identified narcotics addicts who were ordered into preventive pretrial detention after a step 2 release hearing. Here methadone for detoxification could be dispensed on individualized schedules rather than on the standardized schedules now employed. For detainees who chose to undergo narcotic withdrawal without tapering dosages of methadone, other forms of assistance could be provided ranging from the dispensation of tranquilizing drugs to counseling by staff members. Another housing area might be set aside for voluntary detoxification patients—men and women who are eligible for pretrial release but who first wish to end their immediate drug dependency under specialized medical supervision.

Most of the addicts identified in the diagnostic wing of the new jail, however, would not be "detoxed" there. Instead, they immeditely would be placed in a public or private community drug-treatment program. For some, acquiring and honoring a treatment affiliation would be an administratively imposed condition of their pretrial release, which they would be able to challenge at the judicial release hearing. For others, treatment would be a voluntary option, proposed by members of the detention center's medical or counseling staff, and accepted by these arrestees because of its likely social and medical benefits, and not for collateral reasons.

Most of the addicts referred from the diagnostic wing to longer term addiction treatment will not be true volunteers. They will have been diverted with a promise that entry into treatment will earn them an initial deferred trial as a concession from the prosecution and that success in treatment could earn them the additional concession of a dismissal of charges. Working out a treatment placement for these addicts will not be a simple process. It will involve cooperation between the center's diagnostic and counseling staff, the administrators of treatment programs receiving referrals, the prosecutor's office, the arrestee's attorney, and the defendant himself.

One of the most significant practical limitations of many existing addict-diversion programs is that the crucial individuals who must make the decision to divert a defendant lack regular contacts and a routine meeting ground. The diagnostic wing, which would be designed to provide office space for treatment program staff and prosecutors, would serve this function. The diagnostic staff would have an opportunity to recommend placement gradually, they would acquire practical experience by which to test their theories of placement. The addict and the program each would have an opportunity to inspect the other critically before making a commitment. The rate of first-time diversion successes could be expected to increase as the decision-making bearing on diversion improved.

The success of a full-scale diagnostic detention facility could resolve the present debate over treatment alternatives for criminal addicts. The choice of program placements offered through the diversion on referral mechanisms of the facility would be as wide as the range of medical and nonmedical treatment services available in the community. Out-patient detoxification and supervision, the therapeutic community residence, methadone maintenance, and narcotic antagonist treatment all could be made available as alternatives to prosecution. The final power of choice or refusal would be with the addict himself.

The diagnostic wing could serve another important function. Some studies have indicated that addiction chemotherapy programs benefit when the patient can be stabilized on his new maintenance or blocking drug in a hospital setting. But few operating programs can call upon enough hospital beds in the community to allow for routine in-patient stabilization. For addicts about to be diverted into chemotherapy, the facilites of a diagnostic jail itself could fill this need.

For diverted addicts entering treatment programs that do not involve chemotherapy and for those who do not require or desire in-patient stabilization, the diagnostic staff could perform one additional service: Its members could take responsibility for referring these addicts from the detention center to the office, clinic, or residence where their treatment is to begin. Within a few days of entering the diagnostic wing for addiction screening, identified addicts could be on their way under professional supervision to a treatment program that they have selected for themselves with professional guidance.

When the prototypical jail population is deverted and located elsewhere in large enough numbers, the institution itself loses some of its problems (overcrowding, for example), and the treatment of remaining populations can be evaluated at different and more professional levels. The overused criminal justice apparatus, for which the jails are the dumping grounds, will be improved, as will the chances of those unfortunate jail citizens who could be diverted under such a reform program.

Wing 3: Dormitories for Community Correctional Programs

The third wing of the detention center should be dormitory for convicts working under correctional programs in the community. These programs could be expanded if they had the residential base that this wing would provide. Use of services in wing 2 would also be available where appropriate to residents of this third wing of the detention center.

The present system of jails does nothing for convicts. Convicted defendants should be kept either in real correctional institutions or in the community, whichever is best suited to each case. The future detention institution could service the correctional establishment without available community homes by providing dormitory services for certain individuals under its supervision. Convicts would not be imprisoned to serve sentences in this new facility. Those who would live in the wing would be convicts in partial release programs who do not have homes in the community.

The lack of available facilities and community hostility to correctional homes in its midst has limited the swing toward community correctional programs. This new public institution then could fill a void. It would allow more recourse to middle-ground treatment of offenders, between outright release and complete imprisonment. Presently men cannot go on parole status unless they can prove they have a job and home to go to. If a man is ready to return to the community but does not have either a job or home, this facility would provide a vital service. Furthermore, it could provide halfway-in alternatives for individuals who need some supervision short of prison. Youngsters and minor offenders could be sentenced to serve short or part-time sentences on work release. Their programs could be administered and housed in this part of the new detention facility.

Work Release

Work release is a widespread but underused practice that enables prisoners to be released during the working day to private employment, requiring that they return behind bars after work.[4] The technique also has been used to allow part-time release to participate in academic or vocational training programs or for voluntary service in the community.

The values of the work-release concept are obvious. Inmates are allowed to do a decent day's work in the free world to which they eventually must return. Inmates are relieved of the dreary, monotonous existence of correctional institutions for most of the day. They are able to earn a wage at prevailing civilian rates, adding to their feeling of self-esteem. They can support their families (and pay taxes) and pay their own way through correctional experience saving needless public costs. These programs involve the community in the resocialization of convicted offenders, a goal commonly espoused by the experts. While some correctional administrators dislike the administrative chores that work-release programs require, most jailers speak favorably of their experiences with such programs. Despite these benefits, few people have been given the chance to participate.

In various places, the correction system uses the work-release concept in different ways. A judge may sentence a minor offender to a work-release program instead of prison. Work release may be used as a pretrial condition of bail. In several places, work release is used as a prerelease technique to begin easing a person who has served most of his sentence in prison back into the community.

Halfway Houses

On the rise in this country is the use of the halfway house as an alternative between the free community and total prison. Typically, halfway houses are used for men who have served most of their sentences and are able to be released from prison early to ease their transition back into the community. Such men will ordinarily be in a halfway house for several months while they get a job, visit their families increasingly, and get assistance from staff in their transition to freedom.

Some judges have used a halfway-in as well as a halfway-out technique. That is, they sentence certain inmates to a halfway house, taking them out of the unsupervised environment they came from but at the same time not thrusting them into a totally closed prison system. This technique provides judges with a sentencing alternative for the many men for whom neither release nor imprisonment is appropriate.

Again, for the class of convict who would qualify for such programs, the metropolitan detention center could be the barracks. Supervision and control would be provided while an inmate worked his way back to freedom.

Furloughs

Inmates in prisons may be released to the community temporarily on furloughs. Sometimes this is done for extraordinary reasons like the death of a member of the family. At other times a furlough may be used as a reward, or an inmate will be released to spend a holiday with his family or to attend a special event.

The furlough concept should be expanded and used in nonemergency situations. It is an important technique to ease the ultimate transition of all prison inmates back to the community. The metropolitan detention center could be used to house men temporarily on furloughs under planned, short-term correctional programs (seeking a job to qualify for parole, for example) aimed at graduating the move from total incarceration to complete freedom.

Restitution Houses

An innovative feature of community-based correction would be to require men to work and make restitution to the victims of their crimes. While this idea has not been used in work-release programs to date, I view it as a promising technique for expanding the uses of work release.

Minnesota recently began a program employing this scheme that could be adapted more broadly. The fundamental idea behind the Minnesota program is that in the large majority of crimes (especially property offenses), restitution and reconciliation between an offender and his victim should be the key goals of correction. Once assuring that this process is completed, society has intervened appropriately and the inmate has been punished sufficiently, has proved his correction, and warrants release.

Part-time Prisoners

Other variations on the work-release theme might be suggested. In Denmark I visited one institution that held offenders only on weekends.

Certain offenders were allowed to work at their jobs and remain at home with their families all week, but were required to serve their sentences at the prison piece-meal and in a way that least destroyed their normal lives.

In England juvenile offenders are allowed to work off their minor sentences, and indeed to avoid prosecution completely in some cases, by reporting to the police for work assignments after school and on weekends.

All these community-based correctional schemes make sense. If the trend continues and more programs develop, there will be an even greater need for dormitories in the community to house convicts working in community programs. The metropolitan detention center of tomorrow could be a dormitory and administrative center for community-based correctional programs like these.

Conclusion

Changing the function and architecture and administration of jails from awful correctional insitutions to useful, helpful, social service agancies makes sense. There is ample evidence that the new detention centers would be cheaper, safer, and sounder than the present haphazard, onerous, counterproductive network of jails.

The services that would be provided by these detention centers would cost less than we presently spend for our counterproductive jails. The Vera Institute once did a cost-effectiveness study comparing the public costs of jailing defendants pretrial in New York City with costs of their supervised release project. They found their costs were one tenth of those of the city jails. And their flight statitistics were better than bondsmen's.

The right long-term investments in jail reform will eventually save society money. And public safety is more likely to flow from these reform programs than from our jails. We have ample, grim proof of the failure of our traditional jails to warrant trying reasonable alternative systems.

Notes

1. For a fuller treatment, see Ronald Goldfarb, *Ransom* (New York: Harper & Row, 1975), chap. 7.

2. Jones Blackstone, ed., Vol. 2, § 337, p. 2523.

3. Such a person might well be transformed to wing 2 of the detention facility for medical diagnosis and referral.

4. For a fuller discussion of this subject, see Ronald Goldfarb and Linda Singer, *After Conviction* (New York: Simon and Schuster, 1973), pp. 527–552.

Commentary

William G. Nagel

Ronald Goldfarb's paper is important. I enjoyed reading it for many reasons. Too often in meetings that I attend, people are unwilling to make recommendations. "All the information is not in." "We do not know what to do." "There are many reasons why we should not do this." And so on. Goldfarb made recommendations, clearly and understandably.

He makes an interesting proposal that the American jail as we know it today be abolished. I agree. I have talked with many men in many jails and testified in many court cases in which jails have been declared unconstitutional. How we are going to do it is of course another matter because there are between 5,000 and 10,000 inmates in jails—we do not know for sure how many—and jails are still being built. However, I think if we went to court on them tomorrow, many could be declared unconstitutional.

Goldfarb's proposal contains two elements. The first element is that most alleged defendants should be diverted from jail because there is no reason for them to be detained on either the grounds of public safety or economics. They should be released by a process of either police summons or police release on recognizance or through a court-ordered release (either on recognizance or under supervision). And with either of these two alternatives, there would be no money bail, and the bondsmen whose neon lights I see from many jail windows would be extinct. That is a good proposal. It has happened in Kentucky, as was mentioned. It has practically happened in Pennsylvania. Goldfarb suggests that these two release procedures would cover 80–90 percent of all criminal cases, and I suggest that they would.

The second element in Goldfarb's proposal would involve confinement, which would prevent detention. He says that such detention would take into account the need to prevent unnecessary and predictable crimes, especially crimes of violence. He suggests that this is already being done through the irrational or permissive money bail.

One of the areas in which he and I disagree was contained in his introductory remarks. I thought he tended to belittle what he called hortatory judicial pronouncements of constitutional principles and humanitarianism with respect to jails. I could not help but note that a little while later he quoted Blackstone's "least restrictive principle." These pronouncements of courts have done more to force counties to develop an alternative to confinement than any other single strategy that I know of.

I agree with almost everything Mr. Goldfarb says, but let me state a few reservations. I disagree that correctional reform must be sold to the public on the grounds of public safety and economics. Nor do I agree that the American public will never endorse and support jail reforms on the basis of inspirational churchly preachings or hortatory judicial pronouncements. I think many humanitarians seem eager to hide their sentiment behind or beneath the basket of cost effectiveness. I do not agree that the proposals Mr. Goldfarb makes should be described as cost effective. I suggest that they would be proper, humane, civilized, but I cannot be convinced that they would be cost effective.

Second, I am not quite able to agree with Goldfarb's recommendation that children and adults be confined to the same facility. I disagree with the premise that in the present detention situation, children receive the worst of both worlds. In our correctional architectural study of five or six years ago, we looked at thirteen brand-new jails, and we looked at twelve brand-new detention facilities. In each case the detention facility for juveniles was immeasurably more humanely designed, more adequately staffed, and more diversely programmed than was the jail. Even though the near savagery of some of our young people has reduced our benevolence toward the young, the fact still remains that our concerns for the welfare of the child offender far exceed our concerns for the welfare of the adult offender. When you confine children, even in separate sections of the same facility, they will indeed get the worst of the two worlds.

He seemed to anticipate my conflict with preventive detention without the right to bail. I know all the arguments about the misuse of bail, and I have a great deal of problem with that whole matter myself. But I have to tell you my biases. I am an unreconstructed civil libertarian. To me, the Bill of Rights is the foundation supporting all morality. One of those amendments happens to guarantee the right to reasonable bail. Though I know it is abused, and I do not know how to get around the abuse, I am terribly frightened about the erosion of those ten amendments. I think if the process of erosion of those first ten amendments ever begins, freedom as we know it in America will not survive. And so I am quite willing to take a stand on that. The Bill of Rights is designed to protect the minority, especially the despised minority of criminals, from the tyranny of the masses, and I do not want it to be eroded one iota.

However, there are certain things any jurisdiction can do toward achieving the aims, if not the substance of Mr. Goldfarb's proposals. First, mandate the use of summons, releasing on recognizance, and other diversion methods in the vast majority of arrests. Second, use medicaid, various forms of public and private insurance plans, public mental-health and addiction funds to contract with the local general hospitals and other facilities to provide for many of the services envisioned in his wing 2. Three, use correctional, vocational, rehabilitation, and public-assistance financing to contract with the private sector, especially places like the YMCA, Salvation Army, and so forth to provide the services as proposed in wing 3. Finally, by a formal or informal coalition of action by the state correctional agency, the state fire marshall, the state department of health, public law firms, and citizen–advocate groups, the counties can be required to provide humane, constitutional, and acceptable detention.

11 Community-Based Corrections: Theory and Operation

Richard P. Seiter

The treatment of criminal offenders in the United States has become the focus of controversy in the past decade. After almost two centuries of isolating offenders in prisons and jails, penologists began to discover the deleterious effects of imprisonment and argue for the use of community programs as alternatives. The extent of the utilization of community-based correctional programs has increased rapidly during the past decade. However, the growing realization of the egregious and dysfunctional effects of incarceration has failed to produce a systematic correctional process focusing on the use of community alternatives.

While there are several examples of well-operated and possibly effective community correctional programs, few communities have implemented programs with an overall correctional plan in mind. Programs are initiated where there is interest, talent, and financial resources rather than where there is need. This chapter emphasizes the need for a systematic design for the utilization of community-based programs in conjunction with the logical and humane operation of more traditional prisons and jails.

Defining Community-Based Corrections

Before any detailed discussion of the topic "community-based corrections" is possible, a common definition must be established. Although there has been considerable review of community correctional programs throughout the literature over the past two decades, an acceptable and comprehensive definition has yet to be determined. For most individuals with even a cursory knowledge of corrections, the meaning of community-based corrections is understood. In its simplest sense, it is an attempt to correct criminal offenders while maintaining them in the community rather than by isolating them in a prison. However, the philosophy, theory, and actual practice of community-based corrections are far more complex.

Community corrections is a concept that embraces several divergent programs. Most students of corrections would agree that the concept includes alternatives to pretrial detention, diversionary programs as options to prosecution and conviction, probation, halfway-in houses, work release or other furloughs from prison, parole, and the traditional use of halfway houses as a postrelease transitional residence. Some penologists would also argue that community corrections includes decriminalization of victimless offenses and a general reduction of the institution–community dichotomy by utilizing new physical designs and locations for prisons, the invovlement of the public in institutional programs, and expanded visiting and mail privileges for prisoners.

Community corrections encompasses several types of programs but has not yet been sufficiently developed to the point at which there is a systematic and integrated flow of programs throughout the correctional process. Planning and implementation of community-based programs has been haphazard, without a total regard for the needs and risks of the target population. Poor planning and piecemeal implementation have contributed to the lack of a comprehensive definition of community-based corrections that would highlight the general concept rather than specific action programs.

For purposes of this discussion, community-based corrections is conceptually defined as:

> Those programs focusing on the correction of offenders who attempt to minimize penetration into the correctional system, in which offenders either spend at least part of their time in the community or have the opportunity for extensive interaction with the community, and that involve community resources in the correctional process.

The concept of "minimum penetration" would suggest that there is a scale of intensity of involvement in the correctional system that can be gradated in terms of levels of supervision, stigmatization, and treatment. Under the minimum-penetration philosophy, an offender would be placed in the least secure program option to disrupt normal and positive community behavior as little as possible, while maintaining accountability and protection of society. The level of penetration is dependent on several factors: the risk the offender poses to society, the offense committed, prior offense history, and prognosis for success.

For a program to be termed community based under this definition, offenders must spend at least part of their time in the community and/or have the opportunity for interaction with community agents. In other words, a work-release program in which the inmate leaves the institution for work and returns at night would fit the definition. Even an inmate serving a sentence in jail could be classified as being involved in a community correctional program if allowed to interact with community resources to the point at which incarceration does not seriously damage current community ties.

Additionally, within this definition a community correctional program must also involve community resources in the correctional process. This involvement can be broadly defined and can include an offender working in the community, the use of community social service or educational agencies, the use of community volunteers, or simply the process of having offenders maintain themselves in the community. The emphasis is on linking the community to the correctional process in contrast to the isolation of offenders in a totally self-contained institution.

However, the fact remains that not all offenders should be involved in community programs, just as not all offenders should be incarcerated. The systematic and rational design of correctional programs to include various levels of control, both in the community and the institution, is a prerequisite for successful correctional program utilization.

There are four generally accepted goals of corrections: punishment, deterrence, protection of society, and correction of the offender. While there is little agreement on the degree of emphasis that should be placed on each of these goals, there is agreement that each does enter into the philosophies of sentencing and corrections. The concept of community-based corrections can be operationalized without circumventing any of these goals. By minimizing penetration into the correctional system, offenders are individually placed into a security level that will allow the maximum focus on correction while maintaining accountability (protection of society), punishment, and deterrence.

The Movement toward Community-Based Corrections

Prisons have been the predominant correctional tool since the American Revolution; ideally, they were designed to accomplish all the prescribed goals of corrections. Since World War II, opposition to the almost total reliance on imprisonment began mounting, and during the late 1950s and 1960s several factors served to motivate prison reformers and abolitionists. The inhumane conditions of many of the prisons came into the public eye, prisons proved ineffective at reforming offenders, and the cost of operating institutions rose to almost impractical heights.

Correctional theorists looked for a resolution to the problem. The task necessitated the reform or correction of offenders without increased spending on their upkeep while continually improving and humanizing prison conditions. However, it was still necessary to protect society, punish offenders, and deter them and others from further criminal acts. Treatment in the community, while maintaining an acceptable level of security, came to be perceived as a possible answer.

All prisons are not inhumane, nor is the act of imprisonment necessarily inhumane. On the contrary, several prisons have rapidly moved forward in the humane treatment of incarcerated offenders. Led by the innovations and examples set by the U.S. Bureau of Prisons in the construction of modern institutions offering inmates privacy and dignity, several administrators are abandoning the bastille prison architectural designs and realizing the positive potential of institutions constructed similar to the federal centers at Butner, North Carolina; San Diego and Pleasanton, California; and Morgantown, West Virginia. Imprisonment and isolation from family and friends in the community remains an obstacle to postrelease success and should be reserved for only those offenders who would continue to commit crimes or need a term of imprisonment as punishment and deterrence.

A second factor facilitating dissatisfaction with the emphasis on incarceration and the movement toward community alternatives was the realization that prisons have been ineffective in the correction and reformation of offenders. Estimates of recidivism among previously incarcerated offenders reach as high as 80 percent, and it is often cited that two thirds of any cohort group of inmates will be returned to prison after release. A more recent study of federal inmates indicated that approximately one third return to prison. Several studies have illustrated the ineffectiveness of imprisonment as a correctional tool and the potential for community programs.[1] The most damaging study for prison rehabilitation efforts was completed by Robert Martinson: "With few exceptions, the rehabilitative efforts that have been reported thus far (1945–1967) have had no appreciable effects on recidivism."[2]

A third factor facilitating the need for correctional alternatives to incarceration is the important pragmatic aspect of the high cost involved in building and operating prisons. As the prison populations throughout the United States continue to rise and institutions are holding many more inmates than originally designed, either additional prison beds must be built or alternative programs implemented. Since correctional agencies should avoid overcrowding and must often build new prisons to accommodate inmate numbers, it is incumbent upon local communities to develop community options to imprisonment and divert many offenders from incarceration who could remain in the community.

Correctional research findings have caused considerable consternation in corrections and forced penologists to attempt to determine what factors inherent in the incarceration of offenders cause the ineffectiveness of rehabilitation. A variety of theoretical analyses suggest that institutionalization, both during and after the fact, is often inimical to successful community adjustment.[3] The inmate moves from the impact of prison on the inside to stigmatization on the outside and faces an uphill battle in making the transition from the one status to the other. A strong need exists to tie the community into the correctional process, using community programs as alternatives to incarceration where possible, designing gradual reintegrative programs following release from an institution, and "blurring the lines" between the institution and the community.

Models of Correctional Policies

A visual illustration of the movement of corrections from policies focusing on the institution to policies focusing on the community has been structured by O'Leary and Duffee.[4] This model presents four practical policies on a scale plotting emphasis on community standards versus emphasis on the individual offender. As presented in figure 11-1, the models are reform, restraint, rehabilitation, and reintegration.

The reform model places maximum emphasis on community standards and low emphasis on the individual offender. It is a "compliance" model; the offender is expected to comply with community standards of behavior. The organization (prison) is designed to ensure that the offender does not cause the community any more inconvenience, expense, or injury. The restraint model is characterized by minimal concern for the community and the individual, focusing on the maintenance of the organization. The emphasis is on the organization's ability to run efficiently. In this model it is believed that people change only if they want to; therefore, there is little staff effort toward attempting to change anyone. Due process and other legal considerations are discouraged because adversary procedures disrupt the smooth, orderly routine. Community programs are not promoted as they are also too disruptive and controversial to be valuable.

The rehabilitative model places high emphasis on the individual offender but low emphasis on the community. This model emphasizes supportive control and punishment as therapy; the atmosphere sought approximates that of a hospital. In this medical model, the prison is a remote, independent unit free from contamination, where practitioners work with inmates in unique individualized programs. Community programs are

		Emphasis on the community	
		Low	High
Emphasis on the offender	High	Rehabilitation (identification focus)	Reintegration (internalization focus)
	Low	Restraint (organizational focus)	Reform (compliance focus)

Source: Adapted from Vincent O'Leary and David Duffee, "Correctional Policy: A Classification of Goals Designed for Change" Crime and Delinquency, 17, October 1971, pp. 373-386.

Figure 11-1. Models of Correctional Policies

neither encouraged, nor needed, due to the belief that the staff therapist can be most productive in assisting the offender.

The reintegrative model is characterized by high emphasis on both the community and the offender. The model attempts to reduce the stigma attributed to criminality, offering the offender alternatives to behavior, both while in the community and the institution. Emphasis on the community does not mean simply a stress on maintaining its values but on promoting changes as well within its institutional structure to provide opportunities for offenders and to reduce systematic discrimination based on economic and cultural variances. The reintegrative model does not exclude the use of prisons but acknowledges the problem of attempting offender correction in an isolated environment and therefore focuses on improving the ex-offender's ability to function in a community setting during the gradual reentry from prison to the community.

A Community-Based Correctional System

In response to the need for a total systems correctional plan, to include institutional and community programs, the following operational framework of current correctional programs is offered. This framework is structured to recognize the four goals of corrections, and is predicated on the utilization of resources, knowledge, and philosophies now available that simply need to be reexamined and coordinated.

The underlying philosophy of the framework emphasizes the correction of offenders as a method to reduce crime. In addition, punishment, deterrence, and protection of society are guiding objectives of the system. The operational philosophy is well summarized by the stated definition of community-based corrections:

> Community-based corrections are those programs focusing on the correction of offenders that attempt to minimize penetration into the correctional system in which offenders either spend at least part of their time in the community or have the opportunity for extensive interaction with the community and which involve community resources in the correctional process.

Whereas this framework is based on the reintegrative model of corrections, correctional practices range in gradations in terms of dispositional severity and isolation from the community. Gradated levels of dispositional options allow for the movement of the offender to the most severe option (imprisonment) with various options of severity intervals as well as providing options at various levels on an inmate's return to society. At each interval, the offender is allowed more (or less, depending on the direction of the movement) responsibility and freedom.

The framework (figure 11-2) illustrates the traditional correctional process on the left-hand side and includes community alternatives on the right-hand side. Brief descriptions of the elements within the framework are presented here. The numbered paragraphs that follow refer to the number of the programs presented in figure 11-2.

Utilizing the preceding definition of community-based corrections allows the introduction of community programs into the process model from the point of offense to final release from supervision following conviction. Some of the community programs can be used to supplement the traditional flows. This may be beyond what traditionalists feel as the role of "corrections"; however, there must be emphasis on correcting offenders at the earliest possible point.

1. The first possibility for utilizing a program of community-based corrections is the total diversion of an offender from the criminal justice system by decriminalizing certain offenses. Several victimless offenses (prostitution, gambling, drunkeness, drug use, homosexuality) can and are being decriminalized, eliminating criminal prosecution while treating the problem in the community. While some victimless crimes are only offenses against "public morality" and require little "correction" of offenders, others are simply deviations that should come under the realm of the medical and/or mental-health jurisdictions. Decriminalization of such offenses would avoid the inundation of police, courts, and correctional resources caused by processing such offenses and force a realization of the need to involve the community and its medical and mental-health resources in resolving these problems.

2. A second technique to divert "offenders" from the criminal justice system would be an increased use of summons and citations rather than arrests. Several minor offenses could be handled through simple citations and summons to court rather than an arrest and the resultant consumation of time and resources. Citations and summons could be used for several minor criminal offenses for which the offender poses no threat to society if allowed to remain in the community, just as they are now used for traffic violations.

3. Following an arrest an offender will usually be charged. There are other possible diversion programs that allow certain offenders to avoid prosecution and conviction and the corollary stigma. Recently, deferred prosecution programs have been instituted within several local jurisdictions. With such programs, minor or first-time offenders are provided the opportunity for release to the community and delay of prosecution should they commit no further offenses. If another crime is committed, the offender will be prosecuted for the original as well as the subsequent offense. Frequently these programs are termed "probation without adjudication," and the offender is supervised by either a professional or volunteer probation officer to monitor behavior and assist with problems.

4. A widespread practice in criminal justice is the detention of charged offenders awaiting trial. Many of these spend several days (even months) in jail without having been convicted of the offense. As a result several new and old methods are being utilized and expanded to allow a defendant to be released until trial.

Bail is an often-used alternative to detention, which allows an individual to deposit money as a guarantee to appear for trial. In itself, it is not an available option of many. Bail practices are often discriminatory against the poor and minorities. Programs providing for release on recognizance have recently been started, allowing good-risk individuals who cannot afford bail to be released on their own recognizance until their trial date.

Another option that expands the number of charged offenders eligible for release is "release on supervision." With these programs, offenders not otherwise eligible for release on bail or their own recognizance can be released under the supervision of a professional or voluntary officer of the court. The arrangement is then similar to someone on probation in that the offender reports to the supervising official who in turn maintains a minimum level of custody and may assist the offender with any emerging problems.

All the preceding programs have traditionally been under the realm of the courts and law-enforcement agencies. These programs are designed not only to alleviate management problems and improve the operating efficiency of the criminal justice system but are also intended to increase the possibility of an offender avoiding further criminal activity. The programs have become "correctional" programs aimed at assisting the offender to overcome problems caused by the stigma of criminality and the collateral consequences of arrest, detention, and conviction.

Historically, corrections begins after conviction. For years the only sentencing options have been imprisonment or probation. Over the last decade several community-based programs have been developed that provide judges with intermediate dispositions that may be more appropriate in relation to the legal and social needs of the offender.

For offenders who present no serious threat to society or themselves and for whom society does not demand severe punishment, imprisonment is an expensive, unnecessary, inefficient, and generally ineffective sentencing option. Other less serious sentences may fulfill deterrent requirements and be more effective in reducing recidivism. Sentencing options are determined after consideration of the threat to the community by the offender, the deterrent effect of the disposition, and the punishment demanded by society. As a general sentencing philosophy, I recommend that the least restrictive dispositions should be utilized (as punishment, deterrence, and protection of society might allow) to maximize the correctional and reformative effects on the offender.

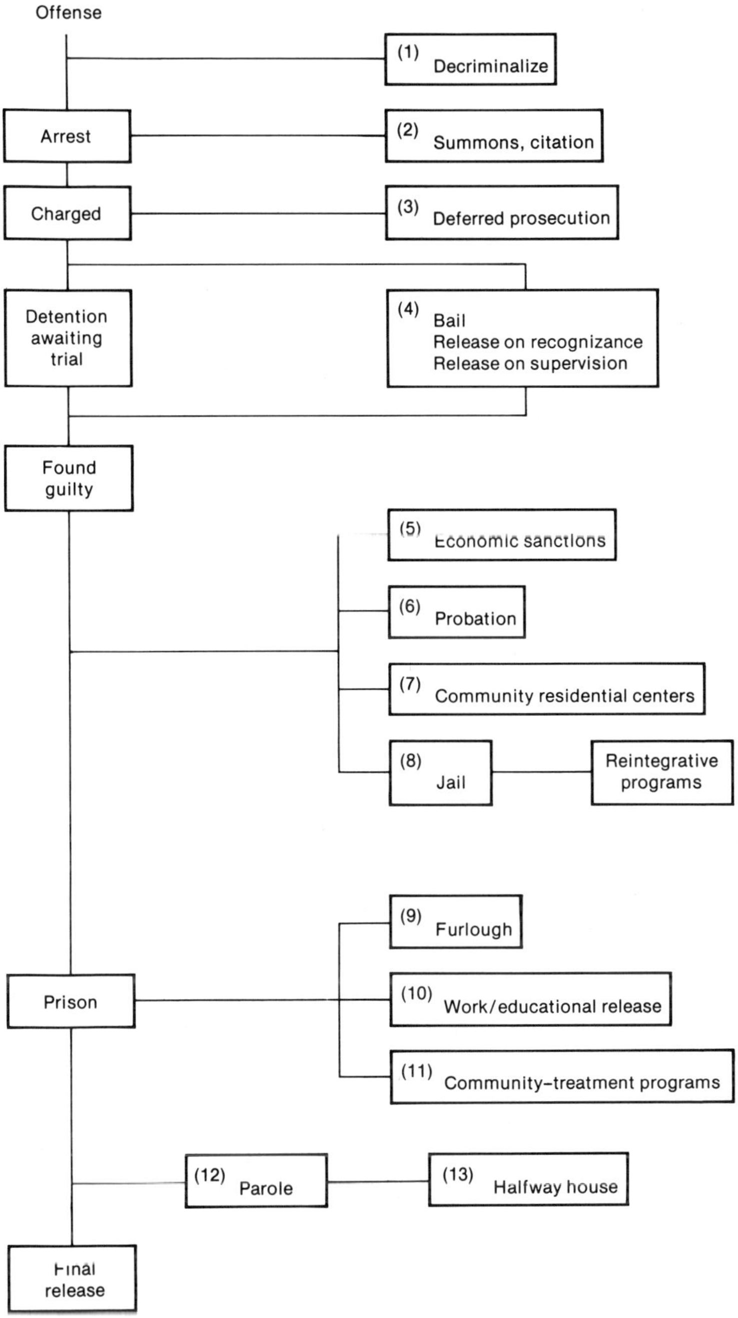

Figure 11-2. A Community-Based Correctional System

5. The least serious sentencing option (other than suspending a sentence) involves the use of economic sanctions. The use of an economic sanction as a disposition forces the offender to sacrifice for committing a crime. Economic sanctions are often used when the offender poses no risk to society if in the community or in conjunction with a more severe sanction. Although fines have historically been the most often-used economic sanction, the modern use goes beyond the simple fine for an offense and incorporates deterrent, punitive, and correctional goals. Sanctions may include graduated fines according to income or they may include using the offender's work or skill to perform a service to the community. Offender restitution to the victim has also received an increase in attention, and innovative programs for restitution are being initiated across the United States.

6. For the offender who may be seen as a minimum risk to society and who would require some community supervision, probation is an appropriate option. Probation is usually operated by the judiciary and is closely tied to the court to allow judges a flexible supervisory tool that can be designed to meet the needs of each case. Probation supervision includes scheduled dates for offenders to report to their officer and the opportunity for the officer to monitor offenders' behavior in the community while providing assistance in resolving problems that could inhibit adjustment. Many new supervisory methods such as specialized caseloads and decentralization of probation offices will hopefully improve the operation of probation programs.

7. A relatively new and highly welcomed correctional option is the community residential center. These centers are used as alternatives to incarceration, housing the marginal offender who presents too much of a risk for standard probation supervision but could benefit more by remaining in the community than by being incarcerated. This marginal offender probably does not present a sufficient risk to merit imprisonment but may be without community ties and support.

The residential center provides more supervision than probation as offenders live at the center and their activities can be restricted to the extent deemed necessary by center staff. During their stay at the center, offenders receive assistance in finding jobs, improving educational of vocational skills, and/or developing stable patterns of behavior to assist in adjustment.

8. For offenders who may need a period of incarceration (because of the risk to society or the demand for punishment), the oldest correctional mechanism (the jail sentence) is still a sentencing option. Jail sentences are for relatively short terms, generally less than one year. An advantage of the use of jail terms is that it allows the offender to remain in the community, close to family and friends. In addition, community-based correctional programs can be implemented within jails. Whereas jails used to simply

warehouse prisoners, reintegrative programs that allow the inmate to maintain ties with the community have been implemented in many localities. Visiting privileges have been expanded, social service counselors have been hired, and in some cases, inmates are allowed to leave the jail to go to work during the day and return to jail at night. These programs are designed to alleviate the deleterious effects of being locked in jails for months with little activity or contact with the community and can make the jail term a more positive experience.

Even though there are numerous community-base correctional sentencing options, there are still several offenders who will be sent to prison. These offenders present a risk to society if allowed to remain in the community or may have committed a heinous crime for which society demands the most severe punishment of imprisonment. In recognizing the problems in returning to society after a long term of isolation in an unnatural environment, correctional officials have attempted to change the structure of the prison. These efforts have resulted in changes in prison programs, architecture and operations, and the implementation of temporary-release programs to the community.

9. Several correctional systems allow inmates to leave the institution for short periods of time on furlough, usually to arrange for release but also to be with their families in times of crisis. Furloughs are generally allowed on an intermittent basis and only for specified activities.

10. Work or educational release is release from the institution to work at a job or attend a vocational or educational program not available in the institution. The inmates involved in these programs live at the prison but leave every day to go to work or attend classes just as a free citizen. When resources are not within a reasonable commuting distance to the institution, inmates may be allowed to live outside the prison in a designated facility.

11. A third community-based program of release from the institution is the utilization of community treatment centers. Such centers, originally implemented by the U.S. Bureau of Prisons, allow a prisoner to serve the final few months of his sentence in a residential center within the community. The inmate is still a prisoner but is free to begin a job, utilize community social service agencies, and work with center staff to ease the reintegration to the community. Under the Bureau of Prisons' operational policies, inmates are simply transferred from one institution to another (the community treatment center) to serve the remainder of their sentence in the community to take advantage of a gradual release transition.

12. The majority of inmates are still released from prison on parole. These offenders still have a portion of their maximum sentences to serve but are allowed to complete the sentence in the community under parole supervision. During parole, an assigned officer monitors parolees' behavior,

assists them with problems in adjustment, and can recommend a return to prison (following certain legal procedures) if they fail to meet the conditions of parole.

13. A popular supplement to the parole-release process has been the use of halfway houses as residential centers for parolees who leave the institution with a need for more intensive supervision or assistance than is available on regular parole. The halfway house is a transitional step from the totally structured institutional environment to relatively free societal living. The halfway house is similar to the community treatment center and in fact may serve the dual purposes of housing institutional prereleases and parolees. In this model there will be a distinction as the halfway house services paroled or released offenders, and the community treatment center is a community institution serving inmates still serving a sentence prior to a parole or release date.

All of the cited community-based correctional programs can be used to supplement traditional criminal justice practices while reducing criminal stigma, reducing loads on courts and corrections, lowering costs, and in several cases more effectively "correcting" offenders. Although all these correctional options are available and have been implemented in many jurisdictions, no carefully planned correctional systems have been developed with guidelines for maximum utilization of available options that offer the most promising possibilities for individual offenders.

Summary

This chapter has briefly presented a community-based correctional system and emphasized the use of the least restrictive program as a sentencing option to minimize penetration into the criminal justice system and maximize the utilization of community options. This philosophy incorporates the need to incarcerate certain offenders but emphasizes intermediate steps both before and after imprisonment. An offender should be initially sentenced to the least restrictive disposition and if the adjustment is not satisfactory, be gradually moved to more severe disposition. The same gradual process from the most restrictive dispositions through lesser restrictive programs should also be utilized.

While it is not possible to begin design of a correctional system from scratch with sufficient financial resources, the federal, state, and local governments must cooperate to develop as fully as possible a system that suits local needs. Historically, community-based programs have been developed as options from the furthest end of the correctional process as illustrated in figure 11-2. For example, the use of furloughs and postrelease halfway houses is more advanced than the use of release under supervision and deferred prosecution. However, the implementation of community options at the beginning of the continuum (arrest) would have far more effect on the overall criminal justice system.

By eliminating behavior that should not be considered criminal from the criminal justice system, the police and court loads could be reduced. Increased use of options to pretrial detention would lessen the overcrowding of jails and free some resources to implement community-oriented programs to jail inmates serving sentences. If more community-sentencing options were available and used by the local judiciaries, the prison populations would also decrease. Extensive use of community programs for the imprisoned would also assist in maintaining community ties and improve inmates' readiness for release.

The use of community-based correctional programs at the earliest time in the local areas is encouraged as a first priority. These local options have been the most neglected and can have the most impact on the overall criminal justice system. Since there are models of many programs in existence today, there is little innovation required, but a great deal of coordination and operation is necessary between levels and branches of government.

State legislatures must review and change laws prohibiting the use of community options and entrapping individuals into the criminal justice system who could be better treated by the medical or mental-health systems or left alone altogether. Correctional administrators must determine overall system needs and work to implement needed programs. The judiciary must understand and utilize options to sentencing and imprisonment.

Although the full implementation of a correctional system as advocated is an immense effort, it still deserves attention. The public demand for punishment, deterrence, protection, and correction will fluctuate over time, but there will always be a need to "skim off" offenders for whom deep penetration into the correctional process will have little positive effect. Without a firm commitment to the correction of offenders in conjunction with the need for accountability, the correctional process will simply continue to be a revolving-door warehouse, moving bodies efficiency, but with little effect on the long-term crime problem.

Notes

1. Examples include: Walter C. Bailey, "Correctional Outcomes: An Evaluation of 100 Reports," *Journal of Criminal Law, Criminology and Police Science* 57 (June 1966): 153; R.F. Sparks, "Research on the Use and Effectiveness of Probation Parole, and Measures of After-care," in the Council of Europe Report on *The Practical Organization of Probation and After-Care Services* (Strasbourg: Council of Europe, 1968), pp. 4–11

(unpublished). Dean V. Babst and John W. Mannering, "Probation Versus Imprisonment for Similar Types of Offenders: A Comparison by Subsequent Violations," *Journal of Research in Crime and Delinquency* 2 (1965): 60–71.

2. Robert Martinson, "What Works?—Questions and Answers about Prison Reform," *Public Interest* 35, Spring 1974, p. 25.

3. For examples, see Erving Goffman, *Asylums* (New York: Anchor Books, 1961), p. 4; Donald Clemmer, *The Prison Community* (New York: Holt, Rinehart, and Winston, 1966).

4. Vincent O'Leary and David Duffee, "Correctional Policy: A Classification of Goals Designed for Change," *Crime and Delinquency* 17 (October 1971): 373.

Commentary

Milton Rector

I would argue for a definition of "community corrections" as *sentencing alternatives to incarceration*. For convicted offenders, the range of alternatives should include, in amplification to those listed by Dr. Seiter,

1. Suspension of sentence when the offender does not require supervision and with the condition that the offender commit no further crime in a designated period of time.
2. Economic sanctions to include day fines where the monetary amount relates to the offender's daily earnings.
3. Restitution as a sentence whereby the offender contracts to pay for damages or injury to the victim.
4. Sentences ordering the offender to provide a specified number of days in the performance of a personal service for benefit of the victim and/or the community in lieu of imprisonment.

The narrower definition more appropriately would be called "community corrections" rather the "community-based corrections." The difference is important. Community-based connotes concrete foundations and buildings, small and large, open and secure buildings, in which offenders, juvenile and adult, will still be incarcerated. Temporary release for work, school, or other activities is an extension of institution control.

Regressive Community Corrections

Unless the designers of community corrections systems clearly intend that the goal of such a system is to phase out the use of incarceration as society's principal response to crime, it can become a regressive adjunct to traditional confinement institutions. There must be a total commitment by those who make public policy to the need to eliminate the destructive use of incarceration except for those who, because of violent and dangerous behavior, require confinement.

We have seen innovative programs to divert people from juvenile and criminal justice systems operate to extend the coersion of the justice system over people who otherwise would have been let alone. In much the same manner many correctional systems operate community corrections as new forms of institutional confinement for offenders who could otherwise conform with the law and sentence order without such confinement.

Another caution about regressive practices found in community corrections: Planning must include strategies to involve and train prosecutors and judges in the development and use of community corrections. Otherwise, the disproportionate use of such sentences will continue for white and middle-income offenders and thus increase the use of training schools, jails and prisons for the poor and minorities.

Construction Moratorium

The National Council on Crime and Delinquency and an increasing number of national, state, and local organizations are convinced that a halt to the construction of new institutions must be an ingredient of policy and planning for a community corrections system.

Consider the dilemma faced by today's directors of corrections system, especially those who would like to shift to a community corrections system. They could provide their criminal justice planning commissions the leadership in developing a base of informed public opinion by publishing regular analyses of the percentage of committed offenders who could better have been sentenced to a community alternative than to an institution. Such data are essential to system planning, but their compilation and publication require chief executives, judges, and legislators who seek a better system. Many a corrections administrator has been terminated for trying to lead his public policymakers in system change.

The excessive use of institution commitments for nondangerous offenders and excessively long court sentences have created severe institution-management problems. They force progressive corrections administrators to allocate a disproportionate share of the budget for both new and old institutions in a vain attempt to provide safe and humane housing for their prisoners. New institutions, originally planned as replacements, become instead overcrowded additions to the antiquated facilites. The more attractive the new prison, the more sentences it attracts. After custody is provided for, the residue of funds is too small for meaningful education, training, and industry programs for more than a few prisoners. Then to the administrators' dismay, the introduction of innovative programs attract still more sentences for offenders who could be more effectively and economically educated and trained for employment within a community corrections program.

Excellent examples of the importance of a construction moratorium to the development of community corrections occurred in Philadelphia, New York City, and Washington State.

In Philadelphia, a successful bond issue for a men's jail built the new jail. The bond issue for the women's jail failed to pass. Both the old and the new men's jail are overcrowded. Alternatives for male offenders are sparsely developed. Alternatives, on the other hand, have been developed to reduce the jailing of women offenders.

New York City Corrections, with a 1971 institution population of about 15,000, projected a prisoner population of about 25,000 by 1975. A bond issue for new institution construction was successfully opposed. Disturbances stemming from inhumane and overcrowded conditions accelerated the installation of tested alternatives. By 1978, the New York City corrections population was reduced more than half to 6,600 prisoners. Today New York City is trying to sell some of its underused institutions to the overcrowded state corrections system. This action ironically would further delay the development of a community corrections system by the state of New York.

The state of Washington had never imprisoned more than 50 women at one time. It built an attractive women's prison for a population of 185 prisoners before developing a statewide community corrections system. The new women's prison has been at full capacity or overcrowded since it was completed. There is still no pressure at the top policy level of the state for community corrections.

Commitment and Leadership of Top Government Officials

The commitment essential to the development of a community corrections system must come from the highest level of the executive, legislative, or judicial branches of government. But who will take the lead in a nation where crime and criminal justice issues have been so politicized? The abundant knowledge of the failure and exorbitant economic costs of institution systems is not given to the public for fear of not appearing tough on criminals. This occurs despite the fact that a wide range of community corrections sanctions are used daily and successfully in every city for criminal offenders of high social status.

The prospects of community corrections for juvenile offenders are currently brighter in the United States because of top-level federal support. The leadership for the Juvenile Justice Act of 1974 came from Congress, and President Carter has also given his support to this act.

There is at last top-level federal commitment to help states and cities dramatically reduce the institutional confinement of children in the United States.

Over seven years ago, the governor of Massachusetts and his youth service commissioner set the apex for how dramatic that reduction can be by closing its costly and destructive training schools for juvenile offenders.

Today only 70 security confinement beds are needed for dangerous juveniles in Massachusetts, a state of six million people. Projected nationwide where there are currently a total of 77,000 juvenile institution beds, the real need is for only 2,500 confinement beds when community corrections systems are in place for juvenile offenders, and nondelinquents are removed from the justice system. The question is whether the top-level officials of states will respond to federal leadership.

There has been no such federal leadership for a system of community corrections for adult offenders. To the contrary, the emphasis has been on institution construction with the federal prison system leading the way.

In the early days of the Nixon administration, the new chief of justice of the United States visited several federal prisons and spoke publicly of the need for prison reform; reform by improving the prisons, not by reducing their use. A presidential committee soon pointed to specific needs of the federal prison system. The new attorney general, John Mitchell, initiated the present mammoth construction plan that were intended to replace antiquated prisons with modern prisons of different size and design. The federal system was to serve as a model for the states to follow. And follow they did, to increase the imprisonment rate of the United States beyond every nation except Russia and South Africa.

All essential policy-level ingredients were present: The chief executive, the chief justice, and the Congress. Community corrections was not part of the plan even though the federal probation service is under the administration of the courts.

In 1973, the National Advisory Commission on Criminal Justice Standards and Goals recommended a ten-year moratorium on prison construction to permit the maximum development of community corrections. There was agreement in the commission that if nonconfinement alternatives were established in sufficient number and variety, every state would have more than enough security cells for its dangerous criminals. Only then should tax monies be appropriated to replace antiquated institutions with modern facilities. But the National Advisory Commission recommendations received no attention by federal policymakers and little by state policymakers. Our federal prison system best exemplifies the dilemma of corrections managers. To keep up with the prisoner population explosion caused by increased length of sentences and the absence of a community corrections policy, the old prisons that were to have been replaced are being refurbished.

Perhaps the greatest impediment to the development of community corrections in the United States will be the revised criminal codes pending in Congress and in most states. The essentials of community corrections are not included. Most to date have increased the length of sentences and mandate imprisonment for certain crimes. It is regretfully common to require a period of confinement even as a condition of a sentence to probation. The criminal codes continue to be the principal method of dealing with social and moral issues called victimless crimes. All promise to increase the overcrowding of our jails and prisons. At today's cost of about $50,000 per cell for construction and over $20,000 annually for total operating and care costs per prisoner, there will be nothing left for community corrections systems.

When Denmark in recent years adopted a new criminal code, that nation too shifted from the indeterminate to the determinate form of sentencing for most offenders. Policy for change carried a Parliament and executive mandate that the new sentencing laws must not permit prison population to increase. A blue-ribbon citizen committee was appointed to monitor the sentencing to see that that goal is attained. Denmark, Sweden, and many other countries have found, as we have in the United States, that imprisonment, except for dangerous persons, is too low in both economic and social cost benefit to merit continued public support. With few exceptions public policymakers in the United States have yet to acknowledge that fact.

Public Initiative and Support

The current national trend to even more severe sentences and higher rates of incarceration is said to meet public demand. To change the trend will require public initiative when public officials refuse to give leadership. There are many indications, however, that elected officials misjudge the support major changes in criminal justice policy would receive from a more accurately informed public.

Citizen committees studying the causes of prison riots over the past thirty years when informed of the true conditions within our prisons have consistently recommended greater changes than public officials themselves would have recommended. In many instances the recommendations were more progressive than those made by prison managers. The Massachusetts governor and state youth commissioner seven years ago could not have closed the state training school to initiate a statewide community corrections program for juveniles without a broad base of informed citizen support. They did so in the face of strong opposition from the legislative and judiciary. Citizen initiative, however, cannot bring about change without support of some top official.

Wisconsin has long been among the states making the broadest use of community corrections. It was also the first state to recommend phasing out most of its prisons in favor of an enhanced community corrections system. The recommendations were by a governor's citizen study committee.

Citizen support was not enough, however, when the governor withdrew his support, and there was no top-level support from any division of state government.

In Iowa and Minnesota, currently the leading states in the development of community corrections, there has been a happy combination of leadership from citizens, the office of the governor, the judiciary, and the legislatures.

The new state community corrections laws in Oregon and Kansas were attained through strong and well-informed citizen initiatives in concert with top state officials. In Kansas, however, citizen and legislative leadership succeeded without support of the governor or director of corrections.

It is doubtful that the federal community corrections initiative for juvenile justice would have succeeded without strong nationwide citizen support of the leadership in the Congress. The legislation initially was not supported by the executive or judicial branches of the federal government.

Commentary

Kenneth I. Schoen

The definition of community corrections should include the role of retribution and deterrence that Dr. Seiter's definition missed. Community corrections is not a program. It is a system of sanctions and criminal dispositions other than imprisonment. In establishing a desirable community corrections system, Dr. Seiter indicates that what we are missing is some confidence in the planning process, which should be required but is usually lacking. It is frankly the case all too often in corrections that we just do not plan.

We are also missing the means of developing a sense of local proprietorship so that the community feels that it owns what is going on in the community somewhat as it does the public school system.

The constituency is what corrections so frequently lacks. There are no points for a politician to support good corrections. Much more mileage is derived by saying that we should get tough and get these louts out of the community. In short, the thing we are lacking is a strategy to cause systematic reform to occur. Without one, the best intentions of many people are frustrated and lost.

In considering community corrections, one must examine the question of excessive social control. Are we destroying other alternatives to imprisonment and options to probation? Of course, I fully recognize that the basic purpose of corrections is social control, but the reference here is to excessive social control. I want to discuss the Minnesota Community Corrections Act of 1973, and its elements. The first element is a financial incentive to the local leadership, in this case the county commissioners, to elect to come under the act. Then the act calls for establishment of an advisory board to create a local constituency. This involves the participants in the criminal justice system and includes prosecutors, judges, law-enforcement representatives, and so on. Finally, there is built into the act a charge-back to the county to discourage inappropriate commitments.

The results thus far have been encouraging. We have reduced commitment rates to state facilities, and a good study has been done of comparative counties that are in the act and those that are not. As stated, commitment rates have been reduced significantly. Our jails and prisons are uncrowded. What has not happened is that the prisoners have not moved from the state prison system to the local jails. We are encouraged to see that. APT Associates just put out a study of the incarceration rates for both jails and prisons throughout the country. Minnesota again fortunately is at the bottom of the list.

Excellent alternatives have developed, including nonresidential programs for serious delinquents and serious offenders. There is an increased use of jails, which is not so bad. Furthermore, restitution and community service programs that tend to satisfy all the parties—police, prosecutors, defenders, and the public's pocketbook—are developing. We do not have them quite institutionalized, but we hope with our new law they soon will be.

The purpose of the Community Corrections Act is not to empty the prisons. It is a declaration by the legislature of the kinds of persons who should or should not be in a state institution. And it is done by the charge-back previously mentioned. So if you want to send a juvenile to a state institution, you must pay $50 a day. That is a discouragement, and you send fewer as a result. If you want to send an adult who has been charged with an offense that has a maximum of five years or less, you must pay $30 a day. The legislature is saying, in effect, keep those at home and reserve the state institutions for the people who have frightened us. The offenders that Wolfgang refers to who probably commit most of the crimes are the ones we want to have in our state institutions.

It comes back to the responsibility of correctional planning, programming, and monitoring. The only place we are going to be successful is in a partnership between the state and the community. Such a partnership creates a system wherein we can better eliminate forces conducive to crime.

There is a great difference between communities. And interestingly, the people that are offered the programs at the community level become rather enthusiastic. First of all, the financial crisis brings them together, the state is the enemy, and once you get beyond that, they pull together and really do a fairly decent job. The charge-back does speak to the issue of social control because the local community cannot move nondangerous offenders into expensive state programs. It also creates an atmosphere of shared responsibility for crime control as opposed to a simplistic one of crime and punishment. In many cases, responsibility is placed on the individual for commission of the crime he committed to make atonement in his own community level. Finally, we can involve the victim, if nothing more than by showing him the courtesy of informing him of what is going on in the system.

The program has been especially effective with juveniles. The results have been really quite startling, and it helps rationalize the overall system because if we operate the whole system as we can with juveniles, our adult system could be better.

In conclusion, three considerations must be given added emphasis. First, the cost effectiveness of new strategies must be considered a serious factor hereinafter. Second, the linkage between actors in the criminal justice system and scholars with knowledge concerning the system must be established if anything is to be accomplished. Third, these discussions and sessions must continue in the future.

12 The State's Strongest Medicine

John P. Conrad and
Simon Dinitz

We begin where our colleagues leave off—at a point generally considered to be at the end of the line. For all the reasons generally cited in support of alternatives to incarceration, we share the prevailing belief that any overhaul of any state's criminal justice system should concentrate on the creation of an effective array of community-based correctional services, beginning with a realistic administration of probation and parole, but going far beyond these traditional services to include innovations that will be discussed by our associates in this book. We confidently forecast that this shift to community corrections can and will succeed; in this cause the interests of public economy, good sense, increasing knowledge about human nature, and ordinary decency all converge.

Standing in the way is the ancient resistance to change of any kind in any public institutions, in this case reinforced by the community's natural anger against the criminal. Throughout history, that anger has called for vengence, for casting him out, not for reconciliation. The measure of our civilization is to be found in our power to convert unreasoning anger into intelligent concern. As we contemplate the shifting responses to the criminal throughout our history, we can see that perceptible movement toward that intelligent concern has been made in the countries of the West. It is for the Russians, heirs to centuries of incompetent and brutal tyranny, to sentence their citizens to long years of incarceration under conditions that have for generations been outlawed in Western penology. We have a long way to go before we match our practice with our aspirations, but there is a distance between the present conditions of our prisons and those prevailing in this country a century ago, or those prevailing now in the infamous Gulag Archipelago.

There is much to denounce in the American practice of corrections. We have begun this statement in an apparently self-congratulatory vein because we want to deal with a defeatist theme that prevails in contemporary comment about criminal justice. To sum up that theme in its simplest form, the argument runs that prisons are no good, never have been any good, never can be any good, harm everyone involved in them, and ought to be abolished. Not many advocates carry the argument to this extreme; the prevailing modulation is that prisons are no good, never have been any good, never can be any good, and only the most dangerous offenders should be confined to them. It follows from this position that no more prisons should be built, that those now standing are perfectly adequate to the needs of the foreseeable future, and that the state should use the money not spent on building and maintaining prisons for more socially constructive purposes.

This generous position rests on several perceptions of the state of criminal justice with which informed observers must agree. We do indeed confine many people in prison who could be punished just as effectively and at far less social cost in other ways. Many American prisons are terrible in the most literal sense of that adjective, physically dangerous to guards and prisoners alike. Finally, so long as we rely on prisons to dispose of offenders, they will be used for the punishment of men and women who could be sentenced to a more constructive penalty. Alternatives to incarceration are more plentiful than these advocates suppose, but there is still far too much use of prison cells for offenders who might just as well remain on the streets.

Our contention is that the advocates of deprisonization exaggerate, and to the extent that their exaggerations are taken seriously by the prison-reform movement, prisons will deteriorate, to the great disadvantage of the prisoners who have to be confined in them, the guards who have to control them, and the general public that relies on them—probably far more than it should—for protection. It is not true that prisons are no good, nor that they cannot be made better. It is not true that confinement in prison is irremediably destructive. The sweeping assumption that there is no important difference between an overcrowded, vermin-infested, "big house" of violence, and a competently managed, clean and safe prison supports an argument for the falsest kind of economy. It is an obstruction of humane change in criminal justice. By lending their voices to this argument, people with unimpeachable credentials for high-minded motives lend their standing to the ignoble position that nothing should be done to improve our prisons because nothing can be done and nothing is worth doing.

The evidence that this is the consequence of the prison moratorium movement is to be seen throughout the nation. With a very few distinguished exceptions, state correctional departments are drifting. The will to improve is corroded by the notion that nothing works, so why should any effort to improve be made? The best that can be done for criminals confined in prison is to keep them separated from the rest of society because, in the famous conclusion of Professor James Q. Wilson, we must recognize that "wicked people exist. Nothing avails except to set them apart from innocent people."[1]

That argument leads to the human rubbish heap, to the maintenance of human hells of abandoned hopes. That argument runs counter to the dominant theme of optimism that has always distinguished American culture from all others. We have been committed as a nation to the proposition that though man may not be perfectible, he is certainly improvable. Once we decide that "nothing avails" for any class or group or person, we deny the validity of that proposition and erode its meaning for everyone living in a country that has always nurtured hopes instead of denying them. Let those who consider this language to be rhetoric inappropriate for a logical disputation of the issues consider the contrast between the prospects of ordinary people in the rigidly deterministic society of the Soviet Union and the hopes and aspirations still entertained by ordinary people in this country.

We hold that prisons can and should be improved and that the state can and should make strenuous efforts to improve them. Their changed role in the criminal justice system calls for the reformulation of the principles governing their use and operation. A transformation is under way, whether we like what we see or not. It is urgent that thoughtful and informed leaders exert themselves to assure that these changes are reasoned, purposeful, humane, and carefully watched. If such an influence on change does not ensue from this colloquium, the changes in Indiana prisons will be the product of drift rather than intent. New York drifted into the disaster we remember as Attica. It is too soon to identify the forces that brought about the recent calamities at Pontiac State Prison in Illinois or at Reidsville Prison in Georgia, but certainly the state's inability to provide in advance for the cooling of hostilities was the product of drifting administration.

The changes in prospect must be recognized in advance. The good news is that there is reason to expect that some of the economic burden of incarceration can be relieved without increasing avoidable dangers to citizens from predatory criminals. We do not know how much the population can be reduced, and this is not the place to attempt an estimate. The fundamental principle is that the prison must be reserved as a last resort of the criminal justice system, to contain only those scoundrels for whom no other sanction will do. It is for the people to say what categories of scoundrels are to be contained. It does not seem that there is a consensus on this matter.

As informed advocates, we are certain that the number should be fewer than those now confined in Indiana. This opinion is partly based on the data furnished by our hosts, which tell us that Indiana locks up a lot of felons who are not violent or dangerous by any definitions of those loose terms. Over two thirds of the prisoners admitted to Indiana prisons in 1976–1977 had been convicted of nonviolent or victimless crimes.[2] It is difficult to believe that none of those thieves, burglars, drug addicts, and con artists could have been managed in the community had there been an adequate array of community correctional services.

We also base this opinion on the demographic statistics, which indicate that the boom times for crime are nearly ended. The babies born in the fifties are outgrowing their foolish and headstrong ways. The babies born in the subsequent decades were fewer in number, even if they have not grown up to be wiser or more restrained.

There is good reason to expect that prison populations will subside from their present swollen dimensions. The subsidence will be less noticeable in Indiana than in her neighbors to the north and east. This is a state that has somehow avoided the worst of the penal avalance of the middle seventies. Even now the prison population is less than the capacity of the prisons, a condition that is beyond rational aspiration in Michigan or Ohio. Consistently, the rates of incarceration for 100,000 inhabitants in Indiana have been well below the national average. In 1971 the earliest year for which the figures are readily accessible, Indiana confined 85 persons for each 100,000 of population; in 1975, this rate was 73. By contrast, the same rates for Ohio were 85 in 1971 and 107 in 1975. The national average in 1971 was 96; in 1975 it was 113.[3] Indiana's prison population can be significantly reduced, but we must keep in mind that Indiana is penologically trim.

The transformation of the prison will not be easy to accomplish. Its present mission is to restrain a general population of predominantly nonviolent felons. In the future, it will exclude that class wherever possible. The prison we foresee will house a much more specialized class, predominantly violent, somewhat younger than is now the case, and for the most part serving longer terms. Already we see in other states more advanced in this metamorphosis that a volatile, riotous, and intractable population is accumulating. One of us began work at San Quentin in the late forties. That prison, then the second largest in the land with a population exceeding 5,000, was the classic Big House of conniving, thievery, intimidation, snitching, and easy-going bumbledom. Nobody worked hard—staff or prisoners—and if nothing good ever happened, little that was very bad happened either. The evolution of the San Quentin climate of the forties to the present community of murder, rape, gangster intimidation, and extortion shocks those who can remember gentler days. It is easy to attribute the change to the prevalence of bad-check writers and thieves in the old prison, whereas in these more violent times the population is dominated by cut-throats and robbers. The statistics bear out this contention, but it is fair to say that the times are also different. The world of the late forties now seems to us like a period of halcyon placidity compare to the turbulence that we have lived through since. We have drawn on San Quentin for this comparison, but we have no doubt that the old-timers at Michigan City and Pendleton could make the same contrasts. Even as they are now, still diluted with nonviolent men, the prisons are more difficult to manage than they were; as the solution becomes more concentrated, the chemistry of the prison community will be potentially more explosive and dangerous.

As we consider the prospects for future prisons, we have to accept the likelihood that although less space will be needed for fewer prisoners, they will be more difficult to govern. In this contribution to these deliberations, we shall consider the principles for their governance in the context of a society with commitments to the present and expectations of the future that differ radically from those that prevailed as recently as twenty or thirty years ago. Our two essential concerns are easy to state: Whatever the numbers of men and women to be confined, what should be the conditions of their confinement, and what should we expect of the processes to which we subject them? Ultimately our answers to that pari of questions will lead to a series of resounding ukases, the sense of which we can sum up in one commodious sentence: *Prisons must be lawful, safe, industrious, and hopeful.* The rest of this paper will be devoted to outlining the means toward these four desirable, essential, and elusive ends.

The Legal Imperative

Above all, prisons must be lawful. We define the lawful prison as one in which it is the first goal of policy to prevent unlawful actions and conduct. Where violations of the law occur, they are punished appropriately under conditions in which the due process of the law prevails. If the prison is unlawfully administered or tolerates unlawful conduct by staff or prisoners, nothing else that it attempts will succeed.

This goal was easier to achieve in the old days. Wardens were full-fledged autocrats, endowed with unlimited powers and authority over all persons in their domains—guards or prisoners. Riots or spectacular escapes might topple them, but the accountability trail ran directly to the governor, who usually was interested in other things. It was acknowledged that wardens had a difficult task, and the courts consistently refrained from intervening between the keeper and the kept. They ruled as successful autocrats have always done from the time of the Caesars and before. They mixed terror, incentives, and favoritism as best they could to keep their prisoners fearful but not desperate, hopeful but always uncertain. The absolute power of the warden extended to the guards who were kept dependent on his favor for security in their employment and hopes for their advancement. A wise warden kept some of his powers in reserve, never depending on explicit intimidation alone.[4]

Whereas imperial conquerors from the time of the Romans to the height of the British Empire relied on the policy of divide and rule, the classic warden went further. He atomized the prison community. The formation of groups was never permitted. The lockstep and the silent system of control assured that solidarity was an impossibility in the era of the Auburn model of control. When the silent rule was relaxed, the warden instituted an intelligence system that increased his control. Stool-pigeons were everywhere; no one, guard or prisoner, could trust anyone else. Although uprisings occurred, the warden or his successor would regain control by the application of measures that were swift and none too scrupulous in the observance of due process in finding and punishing ring-leaders. As inevitable consequences of unregulated absolutism, there were grotesque abuses of power and privileges by wardens, captains, and con-bosses. These excesses increased fear and thereby increased the power of authority. When a captain boasted that he was represented whenever three were gathered together in the prison yard, he did not exaggerate. He had to know what was going on, and both the process of gathering information and the use of it for control assured the desired condition of atomization. The pervasive distrust assured the warden's power. Prisoners did their own time if they knew what was good for them.

The centralization of power in state prison systems has reduced the warden to a field manager and forced him to become accountable to a commissioner of corrections in the state capital and through him to the governor and the legislature. Courts have taken a vigilant interest in what goes on within those previously inviolate enclaves of untrammeled power. Many good things have been started as a result of this shift in authority, and many disgraceful practices have been stopped. But it is beyond denial that prisons have changed with the dispersion of coercive power and some of these changes have been for the worse. Violence has increased, contraband comes in freely, and the impression is far too general that the authorities are impotent. If in the bad old days the prison management used unlawful means to gain the end of control, it is evidence in the new times that control has been compromised, and unlawful conduct by the prisoners is carried out with impunity.

Lawful control must be achieved. That objective requires a reconstruction of the model. For the old prison of the lockstep and silence, any size would do. Enough strong-arm guards had to be on hand to keep the convicts in line and to punish those who got out of it, but not much training and less skill was needed. Where there were not enough guards, convicts could be found to help maintain control. The atomized prison of the snitch, the stoolie, and the omniscient captain called for more managerial skill but not necessarily more uniformed manpower. A prison housing thousands could be and was managed on these principles.

What we have described was a prison that achieved order through the application of methods considered intolerable in a free community. The prevention of free associations, the permeation of the entire population with distrust, and all the other devices of the autocrat were inescapably at variance with the freedom on which Americans place great value. Due process was ignored, equality before the law was irrelevant, and officials often and openly asserted that justice could not be administered in prison on the terms that are expected in the free community.

Everyone has a general appreciation that prisons could no longer be allowed to function as they did. The evolution has been swift and is continuing. We think the best statement of the principle that required the change is contained in the eloquent decision in *Morales* v. *Schmidt:*

> [I]f one of these rules of institutional survival affects significantly a liberty which is clearly protected among the general population, and its only justification is that the prison could not survive without it, then it may well be that the Constitution requires that the prison be modified.[5]

The modifications that the court had in mind do not allow the prison to be a lawless community in paradoxical surface compliance with society's requirement of lawfulness. The prison's disciplinary courts must not only administer due process; they must also assure that the laws and rules are enforced. Custodial officials must investigate infractions, and must take the steps necessary to prevent the commission of crimes. This is not the place to discuss the deployment of patrols, the proper methods for the interrogation of witnesses, the prevention of the introduction of contraband weapons and drugs, and the myriad other tasks that have to be done every day to maintain prison discipline by lawful means. However, two organizational innovations should ease some of the burdens of compliance with the demands of due process.

First, disciplinary proceedings will be more credible if they are administered by an official who is external to the prison. Ideally, this official should not be responsible to the system itself, but he should be at least independent of the warden. The administration of discipline in Minnesota seems to approach the objective of independence. There, all disciplinary proceedings are adjudicated by a hearing officer appointed by the commissioner of corrections. His decisions may be appealed by the prisoner but not by the warden. The commissioner may reduce the punishment, but he cannot increase it. Provision is made for the introduction and cross-examination of witnesses. It is understood that proceedings will be expedited, especially in cases when the prisoner is in detention awaiting his hearing.

This system is not without problems. The prison community is not the free community, and investigations cannot be carried out with the same approaches of confidence. The rules of due process that prevail in adversary proceedings in free society must be significantly modified. Nevertheless, it is a huge improvement over the typical disciplinary committee that achieves a pale simulacrum of due process by administering *Miranda* warnings but combines the functions of police, prosecutor, judge, and jury in a panel dominated by custodial officials and accountable only to the warden as the appellate functionary.

The second innovative support for the lawful administration of the prison is a properly designed and administered grievance procedure. Such a system might take many different forms; experience is insufficient to specify the minimum essentials for achieving a fair and free ventilation of grievances with assurance that steps will be taken to remedy them when they are verified without detriment to the complainant. Such a system should begin with the prisoner's complaint to the grievance officer, followed by a remedy where indicated or an explanation where no remedy is possible or appropriate. Appeals to a departmental chief grievance officer should always be available, and provision should be allowed for external review of rejected appeals and also of the entire system. In some state departments the whole system is external; the ombudsman concept is based on complete independence of operations, with the ombudsman himself reporting directly to the governor.

We prefer the combination of internal grievance resolution at the initial stages with external intervention of the final step for one compelling reason. The submission and resolution of complaints provides the warden and his supervisory staff with a gauge of the extent to which the prison is in compliance with regulations and expectations. It affords the warden an occasion to be seen as acting positively to improve the conditions in his domain. Further, the review of grievances provides the warden with a guide to the trouble spots, the points within his organization where timely action may avert serious trouble later. Nevertheless, it will be an unusual prison in which the warden enjoys the confidence of the prisoners to the extent that a grievance system will be credible without external audit. A committee of informed and disinterested citizens should be available to look over the shoulders of the grievance officers and assure that their actions are more than the window dressing that convicts will tend to believe them to be.

To sum up the requirements of the lawful prison, there must be a commitment to undeviating law enforcement supported by adequate patrol and inspection. The adequacy of these functions is readily determined. If contraband is coming in, if violence is occurring anywhere in the prison, neither inspection nor patrol is adequate. Either more diligence by the staff on duty or more staff is needed. When felonies are committed, the responsible prisoner must be prosecuted, and additional time must be added to his term. Rule infractions must be heard by an impartial and independent officer, whose decisions must be open to appellate review within the department. There must be an effective and credible grievance system to assure that as much trouble as possible can be forestalled by the redress of genuine complaints.

Finally, something must be said about the administration of good time, or as the Indiana statute has it, credit-time. Any administration of determinate sentencing must come to terms with the use of good time as an incentive for rule compliance and perhaps for other ends to be achieved in prison such as program participation and completion. The Indiana law provides for three classes of good time. Class I allows one day of credit-time for each day served. If a rule infraction is committed, a Class I prisoner may be reduced to Class II, in which he earns a day for each two days served. A class II prisoner may be reduced to Class III, in which condition he will earn no credit-time at all. Prisoners may be deprived of all or part of the credit-time earned after a hearing of the charges against them, and at the discretion of the commissioner, credit-time lost may be restored.[6]

There can be no doubt that a well-managed system of remission of time to be served is the most powerful incentive to order in the prison that can be made available to the authorities. It is an ancient practice going far back into the nineteenth century but falling into disuse with the advent of the indeterminate sentence. So far as we can tell, and information is sketchy and mostly oral, good time as administered in the old days was a complicated game of cat-and-mouse in which the role of prisoner-clerks to make calculations was a dubious wild card. There is not much to be learned from long past experience, but in states such as Texas, which make substantial use of the practice of remission, the managers believe its use does indeed influence the conduct of prisoners.

We believe that much more study would be given to the administration of credit-time in the interest of developing a model for its application. We believe that credit time should be vested, as provided for in the California law,[7] so as to increase the incentive for compliance. What can be taken away is not nearly so valuable in the earning as that which can be kept for certain. Other sanction available for misconduct can be and usually are sufficiently severe to deter infractions, and the loss of credit-time for the period in which the infraction occurred is one of the most powerful of such sanctions.

But even more important is the limit on the use of discretion. We are not informed on the rules that flesh out the application of the Criminal Code sections on credit time, but the law itself allows great discretion to the commissioner. A system of sanctions must be predictable if it is to be effective. The introduction of a much discretion as is provided in the Indiana law can serve only to reduce its reliability in the maintenance of discipline.

No one familiar with prison administration will claim that lawfulness is easily achieved by the methods that we have proposed, or by any others that are compatible with the laws of this democratic land. Order can be maintained by the imposition of official terror, and that was common in the bad old days. It is unacceptable now.

Safety

In the old days, prisons relied on unlawful procedures, but they were fairly safe. Riots occurred. Most of them resulted in a great deal of property damage, considerable rough handling of prisoners in retaliation, but infrequent personal injury to the staff. A veteran of those times once explained it to us this way: "Convicts wouldn't lay a hand on you. They didn't dare. They knew that if they did they'd be taken to a quiet place and beaten half to death. That's why we were safe then; we can't do those things any more, and that's why conditions are so dangerous now."

We do not assert that murders and assaults were unknown, but their incidence was certainly no more than in the deteriorated slums from which most prisoners came, and it was probably less.

The increase in prison violence has been most spectacular in New York, Illinois, and California. The murderous obligato of maximum-security life in those states may not be matched in Indiana, but we were reminded of the potential hostage at Michigan City. Indiana is not immune to the viciously circular fury that infests so many prisons elsewhere.

The increasing hazards of prison life have coincided with the increasing concern over due process and observance of prisoner rights. That coincidence leads to a common and serious misinterpretation. The recognition of the prisoner's rights to fair and humane treatment is thought by some to have caused the violence. There is a connection. The intervention by the courts required innovation at a time when young men with an unprecendented addiction to violence as a way of getting what they wanted were pouring into the prisons. Unskilled and untrained staff who often regarded the changes they had to administer as unwise and inappropriate were confronted with disciplinary problems that would have been hard to resolve in the old regime. These new prisoners were bringing in from the inner city streets the experience of gang organization, the mechanics of narcotics distribution, and an acceptance of violence at a level hitherto unknown in prisons. The new approach to discipline was designed to cope with old problems. Many adjustments must be made before the state's obligation to maintain safety in the cell-blocks is satisfied.

That obligation is unquestionable. In any situation the state must maintain its monopoly on the right to inflict violence and the means to inflict it. To yield that right to convicts in prison is a concession to anarchy. Further, the prisoner himself has a right to expect that if he conforms to laws and regulations, he will survive the unpleasant experience of incarceration. We have now to consider what the state must do to achieve the objective of safety.

First, we must recognize that we are changing the prison regime without changing the prison premises. The Indiana State Prison was built in 1859 during the age of the lockstep, the unskilled prison industry of hard labor, and the autarchic control that prevailed in prisons everywhere. The management was expected to do little more than prevent escapes and subdue the occasional mutinies. With a present capacity of 1,800 and a population that approaches it, this is the mid-nineteenth-century prison to be found in nearly every state in the nation; obsolete, decrepit, oversized, dangerous. It is unsuited to its function, and its replacement should be an item of urgent business.

Let us be specific about our reasons for this drastic prescription. What is needed is a small prison for a small population consisting mostly of violent men serving terms somewhat longer that the present average. They should be working hard in a prison industry—a topic that we will come to presently—but they will need close observation and control. The methods of the nineteenth century are no longer available. The solution is a reconstruction of the experience of incarceration that will depend on a social structure encouraging and requiring interaction between prisoners and staff. In the old prison these interactions were deemed unnecessary and were discouraged on both sides of the invisible boundary between guards and convicts. In the new prison interaction is the means of building trust and assuring the circulation of information with which control can be maintained without recourse to the surreptitious tidbits supplied by the unreliable and despised prison "rat."

That is the concept; how is it to be operationalized? We will accept the prevailing view of most authorities that prison populations should be held to a maximum of four hundred, divided into living units of no more than twenty. The design of the prison and its program should allow sufficient staff coverage during the day watches to assure that guards can be in daily close contact with groups in living quarters and at work assignments. The technology of television monitoring and turnstile counting should be strictly avoided; such devices are inefficient and contrary to the absolute necessity of human interaction. We do not mean that guards should think of themselves as therapists in any sense of that term. They are there to see and hear, to be seen and heard. The interests of order and predictability are served by the process of prisoners' knowing the staff well enough to achieve an easy-going trust. Information is to change hands without fear that it will be misused, without expectation of special favor, and under conditions of respect and responsibility. Those who believe that staff–prisoner interactions cannot be of this character are limiting their vision by reference to popular and untrue stereotypes.

What we have now in the typical large prison—and we do not know Michigan City and Pendleton well enough to generalize to Indiana—is the worst of both worlds. Because the traditional methods of control are impossible, guards have to double up on patrol in the large cell-blocks and around the yards in the interest of personal safety. Two guards working together all day will talk a great deal to each other and seldom to prisoners. Without that informal "rapping," no one really knows what is going on on the other side of that invisible boundary. Because no one knows, fear increases, and fear reduces the interactions even further. Demands for admissions to protective custody increase and cannot be responsibly denied. Guards are too preoccupied with their own security to know convicts well enough to separate them from hostile and vicious stereotypes. The same is true of the convicts themselves, except that in these large communities of fear, the convict cannot be sure which of his peers he can trust and which he must regard as a dangerous enemy. The safety of the prison depends on converting this anonymous mass of humanity of which the individual guard or prisoner can know so little into neighborhoods in which everyone knows everyone else. Human beings were not meant to live in swarms or anthills, and in no situation except the prison and the mental hospital does this condition occur.

More is required than a reduction of the size of the prison to human scale. There are small prisons in America that are gruesome in the violence that staff and prisoners inflict on each other. Brute force survives wherever skill in human relations is lacking. There was a time when all a guard needed was a ladder to climb to a tower and a rifle to fire at mutinees and escapers. No training was needed beyond qualification on a rifle range, and often not even that was available. We are now entering a period in which the guard must not only be confident of himself in the marital arts, but must also be easy and competent in human relations. The required skills call for extensive training in the vestibule, followed by regular and continuing training throughout the entire career. What is needed from the guard is a quality of service the intensity of which will put a heavy strain on his emotional stability. He will need the kind of refreshment that comes from regular exchange of experiences with others in similar situations. It is strange that in this country, where guards need this kind of support more than in prisons elsewhere, it is generally unavailable, whereas in the relatively peaceful prisons of northern Europe and Japan months of preparatory training are allocated to the recruit, followed by refresher courses along the way. It is no wonder that in so many maximum-security prisons many employees dread going to work in the morning and reach the end of the working day with relief that they have survived. In situations at that level of tension, the staff is understandably violent because they know of no other response in confrontations.

Work

Neither organization nor training will be of much use in reducing the violence of prison life if idleness prevails. It is a staple in the agenda of traditional prison reform that prison industries must be expanded to a level at which there is enough work for everyone to be fully and actively employed. Evidently no one listens to us. With rare exceptions, no more than two in this country that we know of, the goal of the industrious prison is as distant as ever.

The result is that idleness is the normal state of affairs. The work to be done is spread so thin that it is no longer work. Prisoners are assigned to school in which they doze through classes in which nothing more is expected of them. Inescapably the yards and cell-blocks are populated through the day with prisoners trying to cope with their ennui. Some play games, some lift weights, but all too many are scheming. It may be an avenue for escape, but more likely it is a deal for contraband or a gambling hustle. The vacancy of the day has to be filled somehow, and the satisfactions of outwitting the warden and the guards will fill it very well indeed.

None of this is news. The idleness of our prisons contrasts with the industry of prisons in other countries to our embarrassment. Our problem is partly political: The prison is an unwelcome competitor in any market and can be eliminated by legislation and administrative directive. Too often this result has been achieved by interests that begrudge prison industries the tiny share of the market they can hope to occupy. We have even seen the one industry on which prisons could count—the manufacture of license plates—severly curtailed by industrial invaders who have substituted stickers for annual replacement of metal plates. The economy of this innovation cannot be doubted, but the loss of work has been a severe blow to useful employment.

It is customary to deride such employment as license-plate manufacturing as useless and inappropriate because no similar work exists outside the prison. That is not true. Punch-presses, metal fabrication, and industrial painting processes are common in private industry. But even if it were true, work that fills the day usefully and at a fair rate of pay is preferable to the demeaning inactivity of the prison in which there is nothing to do but serve time.

Inveighing against the problem has not solved it and never will. Some states have succeeded in working out contract arrangements with private industries. Other states have aggressively and successfully carved off a large share of the state-use market. No doubt other arrangements have been negotiated; we do not pretend to have an encyclopedic knowledge of the state of prison industries. We have a modest proposal that has not, so far as we know, seen the light of day elsewhere.

We note the prosperity of the Federal Prison Industries which not only keeps federal prisoners fully employed at much better wages than prevail in state prisons but also manages to make a substantial profit on its operations. The base of the federal industrial operations is access to the entire market of the federal government for the production of goods and services. We suggest that it should be possible for Federal Prison Industries to contract with state prisons for production for the federal market. In this way some stability could be provided for the state prison's industrial base, and administrators would be relieved of the need for an incessant search for employment suitable for convict labor. No doubt formidable difficulties lie in wait for this solution, but it seems to us that the effort to surmount them will be worth the while of those who will have to be mobilized to make it.

To keep prisoners busy is an achievement of great value, but still not enough. Men and women in custody can be and are employed without pay other than in the coinage of credit-time. Such arrangements are hardly consistent with the assumptions of the market in which prison products are to be sold. In our culture, we cannot expect that a man will learn to gain satisfactions from his labor when it is not paid for, as is the case in some prison systems, or is paid for at the minute rates that are allowed in most systems. This basis for prison labor assures its inefficiency, justifies the resentment of competitors, and unfairly denies the worker the value of his labor. It is unlikely that the objective of wages paid at the rates prevailing in the free market will soon be realized; even the federal prisons have not managed to achieve parity. But sure progress toward this goal will produce benefits more than commensurate with the effort of making it. The incentives that motivate free labor to produce will operate in the captive society too. Prisoners could support their families, keep them together and waiting for the day of release, and save toward a less precarious situation than they now face in the first weeks after their return to the community. Prisoners who are fully occupied at serious employment and paid accordingly will have less time and energy to devote to the hustling and scheming that goes on so incessantly now. There can be little question of the transformation that would be achieved in prisons by the adoption of a policy of full employment, fully paid. The wonder is that the effort to reach this goal is so lackadaisical, so defeatist. Eventually the transformation will have to occur if the conditions of prison life are not to get even worse than they are now. The prospects are not going to improve with time, nor are the obstacles likely to diminish. This is a cause in which concerted action will be rewarded by early and tangible benefits. It cannot succeed without a major commitment to planning, negotiation, and appropriate legislation and administrative activity. That commitment cannot come too soon.

Rehabilitation

A criminal career is a desperate career, a career in which hope must be satisfied by transient scores, ultimately and inescapably terminated by the successive disasters of apprehension, prosecution, conviction, and incarceration. Anyone experiencing this sequence may well abandon hope of rejoining the conventional society, if he ever had any such aspiration. Most prisons do little to turn the convict from desperation to hope. What has been done has been in the name of the amorphous word, *rehabilitation*. Much has been said about the rise and decline of the rehabilitative ideal in recent years, and we do not propose to recapitulate a stale and meaningless argument based on almost completely false premises.

The point is that the commitment to the goal of rehabilitation in prison has been verbal, not substantial. Because prisoners could not be kept busy at work, they were sent to school, whether they like it or not, whether they learned anything or not, and whether competent teachers were available or not. The most that can be said for correctional rehabilitation is that, more by accident than by design, some good programs are offered, and some prisoners, not many, benefit from them. The notion is false that has been noised about so frequently in critiques of our penology, to-wit, that prisoners have been regularly detained for failure to become rehabilitated. Those who make decisions about release on parole enjoy hearing from a convict about the progress he thinks he has made toward self-improvement; this subject matter has endless possibilities for dialogue at a parole hearing. But decisions about release turn on a simple question: Has the man done about enough time? If he has not, no amount of demonstrated self-improvement will induce a parole board to release him. If he has done about the usual amount of time for the offense he has committed, he will be released regardless of whether he has profited from the meager opportunities available for bettering himself.

Much has been made of the widely heralded findings of Professor Robert Martinson to the effect that, "with few and isolated exceptions, the rehabilitative efforts that have been reported so far have had no appreciable effect of recidivism."[8] This cautious conclusion was widely translated into the firm proposition that no rehabilitative method "works." Although Dr. Martinson specifically rejected the imputation, the finding, if that is what it was, has worked its way into the generaly body of assumptions about penology. No one has calculated the damage that has been done by this oversimplification of a complicated and not well-understood situtation, but it must have been considerable. Prison staff have never been very confident of the value of what they were doing in the name of rehabilitation; neither have probation and parole officers. They got no reassurance from the news that rehabilitation does not work. Neither did prisoners and parolees. The motions are still gone through—what else is there to do? But we hear little of an innovating nature on the administration of services. The priorities in prison management go to meeting the exigencies of lawful control. We hasten to add that efforts in this direction are necessary and overdue. What we lack are the ideas and practice that afford the prisoner the reason to believe that there is hope for him in his desperate situation.

The point is that we cannot afford to convert our prisons into the kind of inferno that Dante conceived when he inscribed over its gate, *Abandon all hope, ye who enter here.* The words are carelessly quoted by many, but their meaning seldom sinks in. For what is hell but a place in which there is no hope? And what more cruel punishment can we devise than to deprive a prisoner of hope that through his efforts or those of someone else his condition may be better in the future than it is at present?

Hope for a reasoning man must have a basis. For most prisoners there is at least the prospect of release, but release without reliable employment, without qualifications for steady and attractive work, without the posibility of getting these qualifications leaves a man with a criminal record with only the hope that he may get lucky. And for most, getting lucky is going to mean getting away with a crime.

We believe we know that we cannot coerce people into self-improvement. What we know little about is the process by which self-improvement is initiated and proceeds, especially in the unpromising milieu of the prison. Here we can suggest only some principles that at least have the merit of general plausibility. First, there must be resources to choose from. From remedial elementary education to vocational training to group psychotherapy, believable programs offered by competent people have to be available at the option of the prisoner to be enrolled if he wishes. In a full-employment prison, there is no reason why the prisoner should not contribute toward the cost of the program. Until that goal is achieved, such an expectation is unrealistic.

Second, there must be some incentive to engage in the program. For educational and vocational training programs, the inducement of good time allowed for program completion may get many started who would not otherwise take an initiative, but the real incentive should be demonstrably increased employability. Much depends on the support of vocational training by employers and unions. Where this support is visible in frequent inspections by industrial and union personnel, where it is followed by placement on desirable jobs after release, no other incentive will be needed. We grant that the difficulties to be encountered in realizing this prospect are formidable in today's economic climate, but experience indicates that a persevering effort will be well worth making.

Third, there must be no penalty for failure to engage in a program other than not earning good time for participation. In the past wherever the indeterminate sentence prevailed, the penalty was seemingly formidable; not to be involved might be an embarrassment at a parole hearing. We have indicated our opinion that program participation had little to do with the length of incarceration, but the consideration that it might was certainly influential. In the new dispensation that we are now considering, we will do well to maintain the reality of choice.

But hope is not merely a matter of offering programs for prisoners to engage in as they please. The real hope for any prisoner should be an accepted place in the community. The reality of this acceptance has to be expressed in the interest and sustained involvement of the community. The activity of prison visitors, the participation of leaders in advisory committees, the presence of the community at religious and social events, all make connections that are essential to the maintenance of hope. Without these connections the only reality around the prisoner is what he sees of the cell-blocks, the yard, and the industrial plant where he passed the time. A prison in which outsiders do not venture is a prison with good reason to suppose that the outside world is indifferent at best and probably hostile.

In his recent and deeply provocative book, *Discipline and Punish,* the French historian and philosopher Michel Foucault suggests that the effect of imprisonment is to convert a man into a case, thereby depriving him of the animating relations with others that sustain us, enrich our lives with meaning, and make life worth living.[9] The intuitive nature of this contention makes it difficult for a reader to estimate its value in understanding the true impact of the prison experience. We may allow that conclusion to pend, but there can be no doubt that in this age of systems, systems analyses, and systems planning and management, the tendency to convert prisoners into items to be processed according to the rules of systems cycles, with "inputs," "outputs," and "feedback" (instead of arrivals, departures, and consequences) have unreal and inhuman qualities inappropriate to social institutions. In the real world nobody lives like that so long as he avoids becoming a "case," as most of us manage to do. Once the direction of a life is governed by standard decision-points at which judgments are made within guidelines based on an empirically derived theory, we become cases and irregularities of human existence are smoothed into data for a system. The student rebellions of the sixties made much of the unnatural effects of the computer on the nature of university life. Even more ominous for both the prison and the prisoner is the conversion of criminals into items for processing. A computer cannot allow for good luck, the interest of an altruistic counselor, the fortunate marriage to a supportive spouse, or the trust of an understanding employer. It can only make what it can of the masses of systematically coded data, very little of which offers hope to the prisoner of becoming anything better than he was.

Neither prisons nor prisoners can escape information technology. Unless the community can copiously add to it, the realistic hope for any prisoner's future is that it will be no worse than the dreary and unpromising past that led straight into the trouble in which he now finds himself. Hope must be made of better stuff than flowcharts and experience tables.

Recommendations

We are emerging from an era in which prisons were expected to be good for the prisoner and that the staff was supposed to be expert in providing whatever good it might be that the prisoner needed. It is a nice historical debate as to whether the Society of Friends, with the famous Pennsylvania System, or the English legal philosopher, Jeremy Bentham, with the Panopticon has the best claim to be the originator of the "treatment" prison, and we do not pretend to the historical erudition necessary to settle the question. But it is important to bear in mind that both the Quakers and Bentham were sure that what we now call a *total institution* (that is, an institution that totally occupies its resident's lives for months or years at a time) is good for people with social problems. In his important book *The Discovery of the Asylum,*[10] the historian David Rothman documents the belief on the part of our nineteenth-century forebears that not only were prisons good for prisoners but mental hospitals were good for the insane, orphanages were good for orphans, and poorhouses good for paupers. They even knew why: to separate the person in trouble from the influences on the streets that caused the trouble was a necessary step to his regeneration as a citizen. Jeremy Bentham was enthusiastic: He began with a design for a circular prison for English criminals to replace the practice of confining them in rotting old hulks of ships in the Thames. The circular prison was never adopted by the English, who considered the expense far too great for the treatment of undeserving malefactors, but was adopted a century later by the state of Illinois, to the subsequent regret of all recent correctional administrators in that state. But Jeremy Bentham was convinced that institutions are necessary if the way of life of the criminal, the psychotic, the pauper, or the orphan is to be changed. He was convinced that education, work, and good medical care, administered in such a setting, would transform the occupants of these truly Utopian facilities.

Later authorities took a different approach. Typical was the progenitor of the famous Auburn Silent System, Warden Elam Lynds, who was convinced that to reform a criminal, his spirit had to be broken. The great French observer of early nineteenth-century American institutions, Alexis de Tocqueville interviewed Lynds during his tour of this country and learned from Lynds that "it was necessary to begin by curbing the spirit of the prisoner, and convincing him of his weakness. This point attained, everything becomes easy... ."[11] In a very different sense than Bentham or the Quakers had in mind—or contemporary prison reformers—Lynds believed that it was the task of the prison staff to change the prisoner, whether he wanted to change or not.

Two centuries of experience have lowered our expectations of the prison. No one would suppose that a spell in prison would be beneficial to a person in difficulty unless he had been convicted of a crime; most would suppose that commitment to a prison would be a serious misfortune, a crippling experience from which full recovery, let alone "rehabilitation," would be at best unlikely. The damage wrought by prisons on those confined in them is probably overestimated. In a recent review of the evidence, Hawkins concluded:

> [T]he belief that all who enter prison are ineluctably doomed to deterioration proves, on examination, to rest on no more rational basis than the antithetical idea that, if only we knew how, panacean programs could be devised which would transform all offenders into model citizens.[12]

Nevertheless, the belief in doom persists. Sensitive men and women like the Quakers or the English Fabians in contemplating the modern prison are deeply disturbed at what their forefathers wrought two centuries ago. They now firmly contend that the prison can be no more than a necessary evil, to be used as little as possible. Their response to what they see is eloquent testimony to the indelible influence of the Golden Rule on our national conscience. Few can see a man sitting in a cell behind bars without empathy for him, without reflecting that the state is doing to him as we would not wish to be done to us. It does not relieve the conscience to hear that probably the convict will recover from his misery and in the meantime he receives his just desert.

The golden rule collides with the Mosaic law, whose actual severity will not be literally revived, but whose underlying philosophy is just as indelibly inscribed on our cultural consciousness. The vigorously punitive notions of Warden Lynds would find a receptive public today if he would omit the explicit references to the whip and the curbing of the prisoner's will. It is here that the smelly, unsightly, dangerous, and ugly world of the contemporary prison must be understood for what it is and will certainly continue to be if the curious alliance persists between those who would abolish it if they could and those who conceive it to be the only proper punishment for wrongdoers. At both ends of this continuum of opinion, there is indifference about what prison is to be like. We can be sure that that indifference, if it prevails, will lead us into the penological drift into conditions that no society can knowingly tolerate.

It is therefore essential that those of us who would prevent drift should set out a course for a reasonable and hopeful society to follow. The ukases that we would issue will lead to the lawful, safe, industrious, and hopeful prison we have specified in this contribution as the only kind of incarceration of citizens that the American culture can indefinitely tolerate. Toward this end our recommendations are:

1. The prison being reserved for the custody of serious violators of the law, it is essential that all persons abide by the letter and the spirit of all laws, rules, and regulations. Violations of the law will be prevented by all reasonable means, prosecuted when they occur, and punished when a conviction is obtained.

2. The prison being governed by bureaucrats and other fallible mortals, it is essential that all prisoners have redress of their legitimate grievances. The warden will institute a grievance system, taking care to assure that its actions are independently reviewed by disinterested persons.

3. The prison being a community of persons in involuntary and close proximity with each other, it is essential that it should be small. Therefore, all possible steps will be taken to build prisons of a size not exceeding four hundred prisoners and to demolish the existing facilities at Michigan City and Pendleton with all deliberate speed.

4. The prison being a community for the safety of which the state has direct and continuing responsibility, sufficient personnel will be provided and trained to assure regular and systematic control through observation of and personal understanding of all prisoners therein confined.

5. The prison being a facility in which citizens are restrained against their will, the right of the citizen to work at wages consistent with those prevailing in the free community will be recognized, and industrial employment will be provided for those whose services are not required for maintenance of the facility.

6. The prison being inhabited by persons who will eventually be released to free conditions, it is essential that provision be made for their survival in the conditions of freedom. It is therefore required that appropriate educational, training, and medical services be provided so that each prisoner can reasonably expect that his condition after release will be better than the conditions that occasioned his commission of a crime.

7. The prison being a repository for temporary detention of citizens, all measures possible will be adopted to assure their return to lawful civic life, including the encouragement of contacts with organizations and individuals in the outside world, furloughs for those who have earned trust, and programs of community education or service when opportunity exists.

Notes

1. James Q. Wilson, *Thinking About Crime* (New York: Basic Books, 1975), p. 209.

2. Indiana Criminal Justice System. Reference materials supplied by the Indiana Lawyers' Commission for its Colloquium, September 20, 23, 1978, p. v–13.

3. Michael R. Gottfredson, Michael J. Hindelang, and Nicolette Parisi, eds., *Sourcebook of Criminal Justice Statistics*, 1977, Washington, U.S. Department of Justice, February 1978, pp. 630–631.

4. Undoubtedly the most graphic written account in the recent penal literature is contained in James B. Jacobs, *Stateville: The Penitentiary in*

Mass Society (Chicago and London: the University of Chicago Press, 1977). There is an extensive literature to which the interested reader may wish to refer. Some of it is summarized in John P. Conrad, *The Control of Gang Violence in California Prisons: Who's in Charge?* in *Correctional Facilities Planning* eds. Robert M. Montilla and Nora Harlow (Lexington, Mass.: Lexington Books, D.C. Heath, 1979).

5. *Morales* v. *Schmidt,* 340 F. Supp. 544 (1972) at 554. [Reversed on other grounds, 489 F. 2d 1335 (1973)].

6. Ind. Code §§ 35-50-6-3 - 35-50-6-5 (Supp. 1977).

7. See California State Senate Bill 42 § 2931 (c) 1970.

8. Robert Martinson, "What Works? Questions and Answers about Prison Reform," *The Public Interest* 35 (Spring 1974): 22-54.

9. Michael Foucault, *Discipline and Punish* (New York: Pantheon, 1978).

10. David J. Rothman, *The Discovery of the Asylum* (Boston and Toronto: Little, Brown, 1971).

11. Gustave de Beaumont, and Alexis de Tocqueville, *On the Penitentiary System in the United States and its Application to France* (Carbondale and Edwardsville: Southern Illinois University Press, 1964), p. 165. For more about Warden Lynds, see also David W. Lewis, *From Newgate to Dannemora: The Rise of the Penitentiary in New York, 1796-1848* (Ithaca: Cornell University Press, 1965), pp. 86-89 *passim*.

12. Gordon Hawkins *The Prison, Policy and Practice* (Chicago and London: The University of Chicago Press, 1976), p. 80.

Commentary

George Beto

Conrad and Dinitz talk about the importance of public opinion and affecting change in the criminal justice system. They are right.

One of our problems today with presumptive sentencing, mandatory sentencing, the abolishment of parole and nonparole offenses, and the attitude on the death penalty is an indication that it is difficult to effect reforms. The general public likes those concepts, and it bothers me that some of my liberal friends go around the country selling extremely conservative legislators on the idea.

Conrad and Dinitz refer to the fact that our sanctions through the years in the United States have become more humane. And they are right. We do not torture people anymore, and even in my tenure as a prison administrator, I could observe that our treatment became more humane. Confinement in prison is not irremediably destructive. I would have difficulty defending the many years that I spent in prison administration if I really believed that prison is necessarily destructive.

They also discuss a moratorium on prison construction as not being realistic. I would like to agree with Nagel and with Rector. I do not like prisons. I wish we would not build any more. But I think we are going to have to build them as long as the public manifests this desire. I agree that prison must be reserved as the last resort of the criminal justice system. I think every method, particularly those used by Minnesota, should be employed to keep people out of prison and to use prison only as a last resort. I used to go around the state of Texas making speeches much to the dismay of the sheriffs' associations and the prosecutors that 75 percent of the people in Texas prisons did not need to be there. You could turn them loose. I was not saying that they should never have been sent, but our population could have been reduced by 75 percent, and there would not have been an appreciable increase in crime in our state.

Prison administrators frequently bring their problems on themselves. Recently they asked me to speak at their meeting, and I antagonized them when I told them, "You people are making a mistake when you say your problem is money. Give us some money, we will do a better job. Your problem fundamentally is faithfullness, imagination, and creativity in solving problems. It is not money."

As Conrad says, the prisons must be lawful, safe, industrious, and hopeful. I absolutely agree. If society is going to lock a man up, it has the highest obligation to protect him. Although I have been a reluctant and frequent litigant in the federal courts, I am enthusiastic about these suits, particularly against administrators for failing to protect inmates. Prisons should be industrious. That is self-explanatory because idleness is the bane of American prisons today. There are dangers involved in the complete abandonment of the treatment model. The fact that we have claimed too much for it in the past is no reason to abandon it completely.

I further agree there should be grievance procedures. But beyond that there needs to be informal communication between the people who are running the institution and the inmates. I kept trying to tell those young men, "No one on these units is so big or complex that you cannot visit every part of it every day... ." And if your communications with these inmates is adequate, your grievance procedure does not need to be so formal.

Now I should like to say something about discipline and due-process hearings. When this first became the fad—and American corrections is 150 years of undocumented fad—I bought the value of such hearings. A prison disciplinary hearing is not a due-process hearing. You are not trying to find the facts. In most cases you know them. The question is what is to be done with the prisoner? And the success of the management of those people is dependent to a large degree on the swiftness in disposition of those problems. Are you going to give him a written statement of what he allegedly did and twenty-four hours to summon witnesses? In Texas the inmates summon witnesses from the farthest unit. It would take two or three days to get all his witnesses together. There is no point in punishing him any more or trying to do anything about it. I know I am in a distinct minority. The only exception to this is that in good time removal, hearings should be held.

Conrad and Dinitz said no prison should be larger than four hundred. The Canadians say two hundred in their latest literature. National Standards suggest four hundred. I do not think it makes a whole lot of difference; the critical factor is prison management.

Conrad and Dinitz then talk about prison industry, suggest that perhaps prison industry could be developed, and I hope I understand what was said about contracting with the Federal Bureau of Prisons. I am still naive enough to think that a legislature, if approached properly, can be persuaded to pass a good state law that makes it mandatory that other state agencies buy from a prison system. Let me offer an admonition about prison industry. If you are going to have prison industry, good equipment is necessary. It has to be as good as equipment in the free world. And second, there must be quality control. Since the other state agencies are approaching your product with a bias to begin with, the quality of the product has to be not only as good as a comparable product on the free market, it has to be better.

I do not agree with Conrad and Dinitz about voluntary participation in treatment programs. I do not think inmates should have a choice whether or not they work. They should have a choice about group-counseling sessions, but they should be compelled to go to school. The state has a compelling interest in seeing to it that those people go to school, at least to the point that they are high school graduates. Shortly before I retired, I had our research section run a study for me on the complexion of our population. And at that time we had roughly 16,500 men and women in prison. Ninety-six percent were school dropouts. Fifty percent had no sustained record of previous employment, 18 percent were illiterate. That is a tragic commentary on a society that presumably has free, compulsory, and universal education. Fifty percent were under the age of twenty-five. I was absolutely amazed. They were boys with an average IQ of 80. They had a fifth-grade achievement level by tests. Ninety percent of them would walk the streets again as free men, so the need to do something about it is obvious. Some of my friends, former associates in prison administration, were highly critical of me when I went over to Alabama periodically to monitor Judge Frank Johnson's court order. They looked at me as sort of a traitor. They asked how could I do it? I replied, have you read the order? No, they had not read it. I said "When you wring the water out of this thing, it is a great order." He mandates really three items. One, he wants every able-bodied convict to work, and he believed in it. He wants it to be constructive work. Two, he says he wants controls, discipline. He says he is sick and tired of boys being raped down there, and he is sick and tired of all these killings. Get the knives out of the building, and see to it that a man can live safely there. Three, he mandated education. I agree with all three of those items.

When one looks at the complexion of that prison population, it is reflective of all the state population. I think that you can set a climate of constructive work, adequate control, and good educational programs.

For a good educational program, I recommend what we did in Texas and in several other states, that is, to create a nongeographical school district in the prison system. It is amazing what vistas open to a good educational program. And like industry, the educational program should be superior to that found in the streets, and it can be.

Commentary

Hans Toch

Rehabilitative goals cannot be legislated into or out of existence. It is not necessary to stipulate that prison exists for rehabilitation in order to have rehabilitation activity. Prison is a place in which you very rarely have individuals who are subjected to a neutral set of influences. Almost of necessity the prison experience has to be therapeutic or antitherapeutic, in a wide sense of those terms.

In talking with inmates, Daniel Glaser found that they pointed to foremen of prison industries, prison chaplains, and correction officers as having had significant impact on them, and I have no reason to question their judgment. I've also no reason to question their contention that counselors and other formal treatment personnel can be ineffective. I would argue that indeterminacy can interfere with the work of "rehabilitative" professionals. If I had a rehabilitative role to play, I should not want to be writing recommendations involving people's freedom (or any other consequences) that would make me exercise a judgmental role and would contaminate what has to be an uncontaminated relationship.

Of course the rehabilitative activities of prison staff are not found in job descriptions, but they are very real in day-to-day activities. Both staff selection and training and legislatively set minimum standards for treatment, training, and recreation might well be more important rehabilitation reinforcements than the sentencing process. There are rehabilitative activities in unlikely places in prison communities: You can get a lot of rehabilitation mileage by creating a self-governing community in prison.

A general point that strikes me as important is that nothing as complex institutionally as prison can have a dominant or single goal. That seems to me to create a need for defining the goals of prison separately for relatively autonomous parts of each megaprison.

We ought to understand that prison is a total sort of environment, and, therefore, the prison environment's potential for affecting the inmates is not to be underestimated. If we talk about rehabilitation having been killed, we ought to realize that what we are talking about is an abortion, because rehabilitation has not yet been tried.

13 Emerging Issues in Probation and Parole

Harry E. Allen, Evalyn Parks,
and *Eric W. Carlson*

Probation and parole assumptions, purposes, functions, and processes have recently joined the growing ranks of criminal justice system components that have been spotlighted by controversy and critical reassessment. Spurred by a number of widely publicized attacks on the prevailing theories and models that have directed criminal justice practices for the past quarter-century, policymakers and practitioners are no longer willing to continue to support certain current activities and programs simply because they are "traditional."

We have recently witnessed challenges in corrections to the medical rehabilitation and the reintegration models; we have seen devastating attacks on the effectiveness of correctional treatment programs; we have followed the recent trends in court decisions that challenge traditional practices by raising such issues as the constitutional right of convicted offenders, due process, and the right to treatment (or the right to refuse treatment); and finally, we are being asked to consider the implications of new or revived neoclassical concepts such as the deterrence model, the incapacitation model, the justice model, "just deserts," and even punishment.

Correctional administrators, policymakers, and practitioners reassessing the functions of their agencies have a critical need to know not only how their agencies presently operate, but also the strengths and weaknesses of those operations, operational costs, and the effectiveness of those operations. In addition, the experiences of other agencies that may have experimented with innovative or unusual programs or techniques, if assessed, can guide the administrator toward (or steer the administrator away from) alternative approaches.

In recognition of the need for a comprehensive compilation and analysis of available knowledge in adult probation, the National Institute of Law Enforcement and Criminal Justice awarded a grant to the Program for the Study of Crime and Delinquency of the Ohio State University for the purpose of collecting the scholarly and evaluative research literature on adult probation that had been produced since 1950. Our major tasks were to organize the mass of probation literature into appropriate issue areas, synthesize the research into statements accurately reflecting the current state of knowledge in each issue area, assess the adequacy of the research conducted in each issue area and, finally, provide a blue-print for identifying and addressing those areas in which future research is needed. The project ("Critical Issues in Adult Probation") was completed early in 1978. Nine major documents were written as final project reports.[1]

Immediately following the completion of the adult probation project, the National Institute asked us to conduct another nationwide study, of comparable size and scope, addressing the critical issues in adult parole. This study began in June 1978 and will require, in addition to the collection and assessment of available scholarly and research literature, an extensive survey of all parole boards and parole supervision agencies in order to permit description and analysis of current decision-making, supervision, management, and treatment practices.

Because the probation issues project has been completed while the parole issues project is just underway, this paper will be heavily weighted toward probation. We will, however, comment on issues in parole, particularly as they appear to be similar to or different from the issues that affect probation. The bulk of the material upon which our discussions, arguments, and conclusions are based is drawn from the above nine *Technical Issue* papers. To facilitate our discussions, we have eliminated the plethora of footnotes and citations that ordinarily characterize academic and legal writing. We assure our readers, however, that the support for our statements can be found in the individual volumes of the *Technical Issue Paper* series.

For ease of presentation and comprehension, we have organized the issues in probation into four rather broad areas: probation administration and management, probation prediction and treatment, presentence investigation reports, and innovations in probation. For each of these areas, we will discuss the issues involved, review the relevant research findings, and finally present some prescriptive statements that will, we trust, offer some food for thought, discussion, and debate.

Before discussing the various issue areas that we have identified, it might be helpful to give the reader a sense of the scope of contemporary probation activity. Recently a survey of probation and parole agencies was conducted by the Bureau of the Census for the Department of Justice.[2] Although the survey frequently mixed probation and parole data, it contains the only national probation data *currently* available.

The survey reports that on 1 September 1976, there were 923,064 adult probation clients under state and local supervision in the United States. Approximately 50 percent (455,093) of these clients had been convicted of felony crimes, and the balance had misdemeanor convictions. Eighty-six percent, or 795,231, were male. The rate at which the probation disposition is used varies widely from state to state. For example, Massachusetts reports

1,265 adult and juvenile probationers per 100,000 population, while Kentucky reports only 210. The rate for the entire United States is 583 per 100,000.

The number of offenders on probation, however, only tells part of the story. In 1976 there were 1,929 agencies that listed adult probation supervision as one of their functions. Fifty-six percent of these agencies operated at the state level, and 42 percent at the county or municipal level. Adult probation was listed as the only function by 340 agencies. These 340 agencies served a total caseload of 267,276, with a full-time counseling staff of 2,504, for an average client caseload of 107 clients.

The results of this survey emphasize the fact that the delivery of adult probation services is a big business, even though the individual probation agencies are often quite small. In the aggregate, probation touches more lives than any other area of corrections. The scope of probation activity alone warrants a careful study of the methods used to manage and deliver its services.

Probation Organization and Management

This section discusses the issues of the organization and management of the resources available for the provision and delivery of probation services. Here we will concentrate our attention on discovering what is known about the efficiency and effectiveness of various organizational and management techniques.

Historically, little discussion has appeared in the literature about specific organizational and management techniques that might affect the provision of probation services. This may have occurred because most probation agencies were relatively small and the administrative world of probation was fractionalized, resulting in a reliance by administrators on the traditional management strategies and techniques borrowed from business administration and other disciplines. In the past few years, however, there has been a noticeable emphasis in the literature on the treatment of management concerns and innovative strategies as an integral part of the probation function.

A significant amount of interest in the management and organizational problems of probation systems was prompted by the Comptroller General's Report to the Congress, entitled *State and County Probation: Systems in Crisis,* published in May 1976.[3] This report was critical of the performance of state and local probation agencies and stressed the positive role that could be played by the federal government, through the Law Enforcement Assistance Administration, by providing leadership, funds, and technical assistance to the states.

The importance of management concerns again was underscored by the October 1977 Comptroller General's Report to the Congress, entitled *Probation and Parole Activities Need to Be Better Managed.*[4] This report provided a detailed description of the shortcomings in the operation and administration of the federal probation/parole system.

The *Technical Issue Paper* on Issues in Probation Management runs almost five hundred pages and simply cannot be adequately summarized in a relatively short section. Our review of the available management literature emphasized the assumptions, rationales, operations, and research dealing with eleven separate management issues. Here, we can identify only the issues of interest and briefly state the conclusions about each which were supported by available research evidence.

Concerning the proper location for probation administration, we find that there are strong arguments for centralized administration, for decentralized administration, for placement in the executive branch of government, and for placement in the judicial branch of government.[5] It appears that this question is not amenable to a definitive answer; what is important is a thorough consideration of the tradeoffs that characterize each alternative. Neither is the question amenable to experimental research. But it is clear that comprehensive, descriptive studies of the experiences of agencies placed in different administrative locations could assist in accurately and completely delineating the advantages and disadvantages of each location.

The determination of which probation officer role is most appropriate has not yet been researched. Evidence does suggest that probation officers consider some activities to be more appropriate than others,[6] but that role perception has nothing to do with job satisfaction.[7] Research is also needed to determine whether role preference has any impact on client outcome indicators.

The caseload management strategies that are more effective or efficient has received too little attention by researchers. We know that some studies have determined that the level of supervision intensity can be varied, resulting in more or fewer contacts between the probation officer and the probationer; however, we still know very little about either an adequate procedure for classifying offenders by risk or need or about the nature and quality of the contacts.[8] Some research also suggests that specialized caseloads can be effective, as long as the cirteria for acceptance into the specialized caseloads are explicit.[9] Research cost of single officer versus team caseloads, the casework versus the brokerage approach to supervision and service provision functional specialization. We have examined several examples of workload derivation procedures, but research on the impact of the implimentation of such a system has not yet been done.

Are needed services being provided to probationers? Research has determined that they are not. Studies suggest that probationers who do receive needed services have a greater chance of successfully completing probation but that adequate needs assessments are not attempted, and consequently most probationers do not receive the services they need.[10] Several new and promising service provision strategies are emerging, but they have not yet been adequately evaluated.

Can paraprofessionals be effectively used in probation? The research suggests that they can be at least as effective as professional probation officers and perhaps even more effective with high-risk probationers.[11] This suggestion must be considered tentative, however, because of the small number of research efforts in this area. Can volunteers be effectively used in probation? The research produces mixed results. Some research finds volunteers having a positive effect on outcome indicators.[12] while other research finds neutral or even negative effects.[13]

How effective is the education and training of probation officers? In order to gauge effectiveness, we must first agree on a definition of probation officer competency. The little research available concerning education and training suggests that whatever value different educational backgrounds and in-service training experiences may have, that value tends to diminish relatively rapidly over time.[14] A review of the literature and research on education and training highlights the problem that we must first definitively agree on what it is that probation officers are expected to be able to do before we can decide what kind of educational background is required and what types of in-service training will be offered.

How do probation officers actually spend their *time*? They are most frequently in their own offices, alone, occupied with paperwork.[15] Since we have a fairly clear picture of the allotment of probation officer time to specific activities, we now need to link the achievement of those activities to the objectives of probation work. Research could also investigate the necessity of spending a significant amount of time on such activities as paperwork, travel, and administrative duties.

What kinds of probation information are currently available? We find that local and state probation departments keep a great deal of information, but it is seldom kept in systematic or comparable form. There is no national compilation of probation statistics. Research does indicate, however, that uniform data collection and statistics on a statewide, multistate, or national level are feasible.[16]

How does the cost of probation compare to the cost of alternative dispositions? We find that probation is considerable cheaper than incarceration, particularly when the benefits of allowing the offender to remain in the community are added in.[17] There are problems with the available cost/benefit research, however, because cost/benefit analyses are time-consuming and methodologically demanding.

What effect do the various sets of standards have on the management of probation? We do not know. Research looking at attempts to upgrade probation administration to meet standards would be productive, as well as research assessing the impact of meeting or exceeding standards on client outcome indicators.

As a general conclusion about the state of knowledge about probation administration, we find that current research in some areas *is* uncovering some answers to probation management questions, but there are still a number of critical, fundamental questions which have yet to be addressed. When that research is done, it is crucial that the research design and methodology be appropriate to ensure that the research findings will be of value and will add to our knowledge.

Although our research on parole has just begun, we might hazard a few guesses about which of these probation management issues will emerge as important parole questions. We suspect that the question of proper administrative location will be not especially relevant for parole, although the questions of whether the parole board should be independent of the parole supervision agency may be of some concern. It is more likely that the most hotly debated question will be whether the parole function should be located *anywhere.*

The issues of the proper role for parole officers and the various caseload–management strategies will undoubtedly arise, as will the question of service provision strategies. Paraprofessionals, ex–offenders, and volunteers have been used in parole supervision, although we may find that the assignments given to these individuals in parole supervision differ from their assignments when they are dealing with probationers.

With respect to the education and training of parole officers, we anticipate encountering the same problem we found in the probation study: Exactly what are the proper roles for parole officers, and what are they expected to be able to do? We will be most interested in seeing the results of parole officer time studies. Several time studies of probation officers indicated that as much as one fourth to one third of the probation officer's time is spent on the preparation of presentence investigation reports. Since this function is largely irrelevant for parole officers (with the exception of some agencies that require prerelease reports), we can anticipate that other functions such as supervision and investigation of possible violations will consume larger portions of the officers' working time.

Since virtually all parole supervision agencies are centralized, we know that the parole system will not experience the magnitude of problems of information collection and communication that plague the probation system, although those problems may still be present in a milder form. We know also that we have access to national aggregated parole data from the Uniform Parole Reports; we have yet to determine why a number of states require several years before reporting their annual statistics or decline to have their statistics made public.

We found rigorous cost analyses to be extremely rare in probation; we expect that to be the case with parole also, particularly with respect to cost/benefit analyses. Of special interest in parole cost studies will be comparisons of the costs of incarceration followed by parole with the costs of mandatory flat sentences (which will perhaps be of shorter duration than sentences followed by parole).

Probation, Prediction, and Treatment

This section, which addresses the provision of probation treatment, views treatment as a process. In this sense, probation treatment consists of three phases. The first phase is the prediction of an offender's expected future behavior. Prediction may occur both during the presentence investigation stage before the offender is placed in probation or immediately after the offender has been placed on probation. A great deal of probation prediction is intuitive; it consists of the investigation officer's best, subjective assessment of the likelihood that a particular offender will continue to engage in criminal behavior. In this section, however, we will focus on development of reliable and valid prediction instruments, which may have the potential for removing much of the guesswork from probation prediction.

The second phase of the treatment process is the classification of probationers. There are of course a number of ways of classifying probationers; however, the most common are classification by risk level and classification by level of need for service.

This third phase of the process is the treatment modality that is actually used for probationers. Our review of the available literature suggests that most treatment modalities currently in use can be classified into three broad groups: vocational counseling and employment, group and individual counseling, and drug treatment. We will discuss the research that has been conducted in order to evaluate the effectiveness of these different treatment modalities.

In criminology, prediction most commonly refers to forecasting a person's expected future behavior based on an assessment of present or past characteristics known to be associated with the behavior to be predicted. These characteristics (or "predictors") may be any attribute or quality ascribed to the individual. The future behavior (or "criterion category") is the particular type of performance we wish to predict. Prediction therefore can be expressed as an estimation of the criterion categories from the predictors, determined through previous studies of the relationship between the two.

Prediction instruments usually involve the combination of a number of predictor variables to estimate an expected outcome such as "completion of probation without any new convictions or probation violation." There are three types of methods for combining predictors: those that use all the predictors equally; those that employ some sort of differential weighting system; and configural methods such as Predictive Attribute Analysis and Association Analysis. Although empirical comparisons of these various methods of combining predictors are not common, several such comparisons support the view that the earliest, most simple methods of equal weighting for all predictors may provide prediction instruments equal or superior to those that require considerably more complex methods.

Most research on the use of prediction in criminal justice has focused on parole, which suggests the possibility of analogous applications in probation. Ohlin's work emphasized the ways in which prediction tables could be useful to parole administrators.[18] Gottfredson described a situation in which prediction tables were used as an aid to reduce confinement costs by securing early release for parolees, with no subsequent increase in parole violations.[19] The potential application of Gottfredson's findings to probation was noted by Frease.[20] A number of authors have also discussed the use of prediction tables as an aid in supervision practices. Suggestions have included their possible use: "as an administrative tool to equalize high-risk offenders among various caseloads"; "to focus services and attention on the probationers who need the most help"; and to "assist case managers in making decisions about how much time and effort to devote to working with certain groups of persons."

Unfortunately, there have been very few empirical attempts to explore the feasibility of these proposed applications of prediction methods in practice. A pilot study by Nicholson found prediction tables to be extremely useful in classifying "high," "medium," and "low" risk caseloads; the prediction instrument used was a version of a device originally developed for parolees.[21] The 1976 Comptroller General's Report also found prediction tables to be useful in establishing variable supervision caseloads, as did pilot studies by Frease and by Fiore.[22]

In summary, perhaps the most evident finding of this review of prediction as it relates to adult probation is that most of the questions that we can raise remain unanswered. We have seen that little work has been done in this area, and that which has been accomplished is not conclusive. The most pressing need in adult probation prediction seems to be for more emphasis to be placed on larger scale studies that meet stringent methodological requirements. On the basis of this future research, we may be able to validate and expand on the results suggested by the exploratory and pilot efforts that have already been done. Much of the groundwork for any such large-scale effort can be found in the pilot studies and from the extensive work done in the field of parole prediction.

An expectation of widespread use of probation prediction models in the future is not unrealistic; one only has to look at the progress made in parole to support such a prospect. The best example, perhaps, is provided by the U.S. Parole Commission which, as a result of a substantial research effort, now utilizes experience tables as guidelines for making parole decisions.[23] A research unit has been set up to periodically revalidate the tables, and as a result, the granting of parole has become a less arbitrary process. The federal parole commission now uses these tables to determine how similar offenders (similar to those who are being considered for parole) have performed on parole in the past. Using this information, together with mitigating or aggravating circumstances known to the parole commission members, the decision to grant or deny parole is now more consistent and fair, benefiting both the parole commission and the inmate, as well as serving the interests of the community. Analogous applications of prediction methods in probation may be well within reach and await only testing and implementation.

We have argued that the development of reliable and valid prediction instruments can be of value to a probation department in classifying probationers on the basis of risk. In this way, one could more accurately assign each probationer to the level of supervision that would be of the most benefit to both the probationer and the community. Another method used to classify probationers is by *need.* Under this method, the probationer is assigned to a caseload based on the offender's apparent level of need for services that can be provided by a probation officer or by referral to a community resource agency. A third classification method is to combine risk and need levels, yielding a classification system that would include, for example: high-risk-high-need probationers, high-risk-low-need probationers, low-risk-high-need probationers and low-risk-low-need probationers.

The Task Force on Corrections of the President's Commission on Law Enforcement and Administration of Justice (1967) summarized the situation with respect to classification efforts:

> A major requirement for using a differential treatment system is an adequate case analysis and planning procedure. Probably no deficiency is more universally apparent in current programs that the nearly complete lack of careful planning by probation officers, their supervisors, and clinical program consultants, including the active participation of offenders themselves.

Several considerations are deemed essential to the operation of the differential classification system. Accurate information and clear operational definitions must be available to ensure reliability, and the users of the system should be trained in the use of the classification form, which must periodically be revalidated and modified to reflect changes in clients and/or community.

Some sort of need classification system is clearly required if a philosophy of differential treatment is followed by a probation system, but it may also be justified on economic grounds. It is neither possible nor practical to provide all services to all probationers. The resources with which to provide services are limited and, logically, available resources should go to the areas of greatest need. This assumes of course that one can identify specific needs and those probationers most likely to respond to a particular type of service.

The research to date with respect to classification systems for adult probationers is inconclusive and somewhat poorly reported. It can be argued that a well-designed, well-administered classification system, which considers both the needs of the offender and the resources and limitations of the agency, will help to eliminate wasted time and effort on the part of both the probation officer and the probationer. What is needed is a careful study of available classification techniques and a comparison of the effects of alternative techniques on offenders, the resources of the agency, and the agency itself. From such a study, guidelines for the implementation of classification schemes could be developed.

Research into treatment modalities for probationers is relatively uncommon, and rigorous studies are rare. The entire area is as yet rather undefined and difficult to comprehend; however, a key element that does seem to emerge from the available research appears to be the development of a positive self-concept in the offender, if one could be a little reckless with concepts. This concentration seems to stem from the widely accepted belief that many probationers share a negative, "programmed for failure" self-concept. Many of the treatment techniques encountered in the research attempted to increase feelings of self-esteem and self-confidence in the belief that this would result in a reduction of the probationer's tendency toward criminal behavior.

Available treatment studies were categorized into: vocational counseling and employment, group and individual counseling, drug treatment, and voluntary versus involuntary treatment.

There is some indication that the effects of employment programs for probationers may be rather short lived, lasting approximately one year.[25] This is a question with policy implications and deserves a thorough research effort. Vocational counseling and employment programs can be very expensive on a per-client basis. If probationers do not maintain employment or improved employment status brought about by the program, the funds for the programs might be more effectively spent in some other area or program.

Poor research methodology inhibits a clear assessment of any of the counseling treatment modalities. Adequate definitions of the experimental treatments were not provided while even the traditional treatment methods were not defined, either operationally or in the context in which they were applied. Exactly what constitutes traditional probation was not defined in the studies; however, it was measured, criticized, and utilized as though it were a universally accepted and comprehensible entity. Until researchers come to grips with these evaluation problems, research utilizing such vague concepts may remain largely a waste of time and resources.

Our review of the probation drug-treatment literature revealed three basic models: treating drug dependence as a metabolic disease that requires methadone maintenance, utilizing casework techniques with a comprehensive referral system, and behavior-modification techniques. This was one area in which the research permitted some very positive conclusions.

Methadone maintenance was shown to be very effective in reducing arrests and incarcerations of persons following their treatment in a program.[26] Drug-treatment programs that utilize the casework model are also able to demonstrate success in inducing drug-free periods and in reducing crime and recidivism.[27] They were, however, unable to provide the dramatic demonstrations of success achieved by methadone programs. There is also evidence to indicate that behavior-modification programs may be more successful than traditional counseling when dealing with drug problems.[28]

More research and replication will be required to determine the most effective drug-treatment methods available for probation. Particular attention will also have to be paid to the negative effects of such programs, particularly methadone versus programs of abstention and supportive services.

In summary, treatment research in probation must be an increasingly important priority for the future. We were struck by the fact that once someone is placed on probation, we really are not at all certain of what to do with that offender. There are a number of probation officer activities that fall under the rubric of traditional probation supervision. In large measure, justification for performing them is just that: They are traditional. Future research must carefully examine not only these activities but also the decisions about which probationers should receive them. Probation has supported the notion of individualized treatment, but it may be that this support is not necessarily followed in practice. We were also struck by the recurring theme that runs throughout the treatment research that the "best" treatment for a large percentage of probationers may be no treatment at all; possibly even no probation. The time has come to determine if we can identify the persons who need no treatment and, if we can, to get them out of an already overburdened system.

Presentence Investigation Reports

Although the presentence investigation and report constitute only one of the major functions of probation, they can be quite demanding, both in terms of probation officer diligence in providing a thorough and accurate report and in terms of the amount of time necessary to perform the investigation. These demands are further heightened by the frequently court-imposed requirement that presentence investigations must be completed within a relatively short period of time.

The importance of presentence investigations to a probation agency can be seen in the data collected by a 1978 Census Bureau survey.[29] The data reflecting the situation in 1975, showed that 3,303 responding agencies reported performing probation functions. Of these 3,303 agencies, 2,540 agencies indicated that they conducted presentence investigations; almost one million (997,514) presentence investigations were performed by these agencies in 1975. In terms of the agency workload, almost one half (45 percent) of the agencies that conduct presentence investigations reported that more than 25 percent of their workloads were devoted to presentence investigations.

In recent years a great deal of space in the probation literature has been devoted to the subject of presentence investigation reports. The subject matter can be roughly divided into two target areas: the production of the presentence investigation (PSI) report, and the impact of the presentence investigation report.

In some localities, PSIs are mandatory in particular instances such as when the offense is a felony, before the defendant can be placed on probation, and for specific offenses. The degree to which these mandatory requirements are met and the effects on the probation agencies in meeting them are unknown.

Research suggests that, if PSIs were discretionary, they would be ordered for two reasons: (1) to provide time for the judge to evaluate potential sentences in light of community sentiment, and (2) to obtain additional data of a medical and/or psychiatric nature. These two reasons for preparation suggest reports that would have different content. The first suggests a long, detailed report that would require a large block of time to prepare; indeed, time is really what the report is intended to provide. The report would tend to be long and involved, possibly filled with superfluous, but difficult to gather information. The second suggests a very focused report aimed at a particular gap in the judge's knowledge of the offender. Although there is little empirical data, it is reasonable to expect that each of these aims might be achieved in better ways than the traditional long-form PSI.[30]

The optimal time during the presentencing process at which to prepare the PSI is a largely unsettled issue. It is apparent that most probation officers do not like to prepare a report before adjudication of guilt,[31] but this is probably to avoid unnecessary work rather than their possible objection to preadjudication preparation. We know very little about the effects of preadjudication reports on the guilt-determining process, nor do we understand their effects on plea bargaining or witnesses. The use of waivers to permit preparation of the preadjudication PSI is largely unexplored.

The question of who should prepare the PSI has been the subject of some research. It appears that both the background and experience of individual probation officers can affect their recommendations; that is, similar information given to probation officers with different backgrounds and experience will result in different recommendations.[32] There have been no concerted attempts either to understand or control for the effects of probation officers' experience and backgrounds on recommendations. The subject deserves study, however; if indeed the probation officer seems to function as a surrogate "sentencer" for the judge, this phenomenon could very well contribute to sentencing disparity rather than reducing it.

Some research indicates that the short-form PSI can be effectively used. Although court personnel tend to dislike and generally refuse to accept fill-in-the-blank type reports, they nonetheless rely on a relatively small amount of information included in the usual long form.

There is consistently a great deal of uniformity in the information used.[33] Offense, prior record, and various stability factors rank among the most frequently used and useful pieces of information, both for probation officers' recommendations and judicial sentencing decisions. Results indicate that these types of information are related to the recommendation contained in the report and to the ultimate disposition of the offender. What is unknown and should be addressed is how this material can be presented in such a manner that it can be uniformly interpreted by a variety of probation officers and judges to predict the probability of an offender's success on probation.

The PSI is of little use, at least in the traditional sense, if it has no impact on the sentencing process. Attempting to discern the impact of PSIs is extremely difficult, however, because these impacts are masked in the discretion that shrouds the sentencing process. Attempts to detemine those judicial characteristics that influence sentencing decisions have not been particularly fruitful and frequently contradictory except in demonstrating that judges can be inconsistent in their sentencing patterns.

The fact that an estimated 80–90 percent of the cases to be sentenced have entered guilty pleas means that judges have had, on average, little contact with the defendant prior to sentencing. This lack of information is regarded by many as one of the causes of uninformed, even inconsistent sentencing. Judges seem to at least partially accept this because they almost universally agree that the information in PSIs constitutes a valuable sentencing aid.

On the other hand, while judges and probation officers find it difficult to agree on whether a sentencing recommendation should be included in a PSI, they do seem to agree on the important factors in making sentencing decisions. The defendant's prior record and the facts of the instant case are most often cited as the important factors. It is possible that this consensus is responsible for the high levels of agreement between the PSI recommendation and the sentence imposed, which range from 72 to 96 percent.[34] To date, research has been unable to determine the causes of this high rate of agreement, although it is often attributed to judges' willingness to accept probation officers' recommendations. To resolve this issue, further investigation should be made to determine whether similar sentencing patterns would occur without the PSI.

There is also some evidence that PSIs do not serve to influence the nature of sentence disposition, but instead affect its length. This assumes that judges decide on the nature of the diposition prior to the PSI.

One area that is little researched is the relationship of other court personnel with the judge. The interrelationships among judges, bailiffs, probation officers, chief probation officers, and prosecutors should all be examined to determine their impact on PSI information and recommendations and sentencing patterns.

Finally, attempts should be made to develop and implement methods to reduce sentencing disparity. Guidelines for the granting and continuation of probation can be developed; the wider use of sentencing councils and the appellate review of sentencing could be encouraged. Each method should be carefully examined to determine the magnitude of its intended, as well as unintended, effects.

In summary, recommending research into PSIs leaves us in somewhat of a quandary. First, PSI research is so intimately tied to research into sentencing that a "chicken or egg" problem develops. We are inclined to recommend that general research into sentencing processes should come first because it is broader in scope. Second, we see little evidence that conclusively indicates that PSIs are worth their massive costs. The logic for using PSIs is persuasive; the demand of judges for them cannot be denied, but their actual impacts are not clear. We should also consider whether the move to more determinate sentencing patterns will allow the logic of PSIs to stand. Possibly it is time to consider a careful study to determine if PSIs are really worth their costs. If they do not impact on sentencing and serve only as light reading for judges and data for institutional personnel, locally funded probation departments should consider requesting that institutions themselves shoulder the cost of data collection.

Innovations in Probation

The use of probation as an alternative to incarceration evolved as an innovative means of avoiding or mitigating the harsh and lengthy sentences common in Britain and the United States in the seventeenth and eighteenth centuries. Since the mid-nineteenth century, when John Augustus began his "experiment" with probationers in Boston, probation has proven itself to be a fruitful field for program innovations. It is safe to say that the primary purposes of most innovations in probation have been to maximize the efficiency with which probation services are delivered, and to improve the rate of success for individuals on probation. To meet these ends, innovations can involve changes in the structure of probation, the emphasis on various probation activities, or in the delivery of probation services and treatment.

A wide variety of innovations have been tried in probation, some of which were highly successful and widely adopted and others that were implemented and quietly abandoned. The types of innovations that are encountered in any given period of probation history tend to be heavily influenced by dissatisfaction with the then-prevailing practices and philosophy of corrections and by the emerging shifts in philosophical and practical orientations. The emphasis on the changing purposes and goals of corrections cannot be too highly stressed since innovations, by definition, reflect new ideas and new ways of achieving new goals.

Our review of innovations in probation was not limited to only new programs and techniques developed in the United States. We also looked at a number of innovations used in other countries that use some form of probation or conditional sentence to widen the range of new approaches that might be of interest to American probation administrators.

Our review of the literature indicated that innovations in probation over the past quarter-century have tended to be of two fairly distinct types: broad, policy-level innovations and program-level innovations. Innovations at the policy level are those changes that affect the character or process of probation itself. Ordinarily, policy innovations tend to be implemented at the highest appropriate level, which may be the state or federal level. Occasionally, however, a policy innovation may also be made at the local level. Innovations at the program level are changes that introduce a new management or treatment technique aimed primarily at effecting an improvement in a local agency's capability for providing needed services to its clients.

The literature revealed five influential policy-level innovations in probation. Three of these were developed in the United States: "shock probation," which combines the increased use of probation with a short period of incarceration; probation subsidy, which combines a reduction in commitments to state correctional institutions with a new way of funding local probation activities; and restitution, both financial and symbolic, which is becoming a widely used condition of probation. The remaining policy-level innovations are used internationally: rehabilitation councils, which are used in the Netherlands and Sweden to coordinate the activities of a number of social service agencies; and volunteers, used extensively in Japan and Sweden.

Four program-level innovations were identified. Three of these program innovations (residential treatment centers and hostels, day training centers, and outreach centers) can be seen as representing varying degrees of control exercised by the local probation agency over the probationers. The Probation Employment and Guidance (PEG) program represents a concerted attempt to alleviate the serious unemployment, underemployment, and vocational guidance problems that are common among probation clients.

There are some important conclusions to be drawn from the research on shock probation. First, shock probation is in part based on the notion that the criminal justice system can equitably apply a sentencing alternative that combines both punishment and leniency. In practice, there is evidence that shock probation may be applied in a disciminatory manner.[35] Second, research indicating that persoms who were successful on shock were very similar to persons given regular probation raises questions about whether the shock probationers might have done just as well without the short-term incarceration.[36] Third, other research found that the variables associated with failure on shock were also associated with failure on regular probation.[37] Fourth, in theory, the value of shock probation lies in the "shock" impact of imprisonment for a short period which avoids the negative effects of longer term imprisonment. However, one study indicates that imprisonment of only thirty days, the minimum required by law, is sufficient for the negative effects of imprisonment to be felt.[38] This finding is, incidentally, consistent with international research data on the same issue.

In sum, the research to date has failed to clearly establish the outcome effectiveness of shock probation as compared to alternative sanctions. The research, however, has documented the difficulties of equitably applying shock to offenders, the possible negative effects of the prison sanction, and the possibility that shock may be an unnecessary sanction.

One major area of shock probation that seems to be untouched by research to date is the question of comparing outcome performances of shock probationers with (1) offenders placed on regular probation without the short period of incarceration, and simultaneously with (2) offenders who are incarcerated until they are granted parole or until expiration of sentence. In addition, it is assumed that the use of shock probation is less costly than longer periods of incarceration that are followed by parole supervision. A well-designed cost analysis comparing the costs and benefits (including performance on probation and parole) of shock probation with incarceration followed by parole would allow us to accept or reject this assumption, and would have considerable policy implications. We anticipate finding similar results in our study of shock parole.

The basic intent of *probation subsidy* programs is to reduce the overcrowded conditions in state penal institutions on the assumption that many offenders who would be committed to prisons could effectively function within the community on probation, thus reducing not only prison populations but also the costs to the state for expansion of correctional institutions. These prison cost savings to the state are used to make funds available to local probation departments for improvement of community probation services.

Probation subsidy, as an innovative means of providing financial assistance to encourage the expanded use of probation at the county level, appears to have accomplished its goals of reducing commitments to state correctional facilities (thus resulting in a substantial saving to the state) and of increasing the retention of offenders in the community under intensive supervision.[39] The goal of reducing recidivism among those offenders who would have been sent to state institutions but who were placed on probation was not met, although the recidivism rates of the subsidy probationers did not prove to be any higher than those of offenders released from state institutions on parole.[40]

There are a few areas of interest that have not been adequately covered in the available probation subsidy research. The first area touches on the question of individual probationer selectivity. Even though most researchers have assumed that, through probation subsidy programs, higher risk individuals were being retained in the community than before, we have no conclusive data to indicate that this assumption is actually true. Perhaps probation subsidy simply allowed local communities to place offenders on probation who should have been placed on probation before the advent of the subsidy program, that is, offenders who did not pose a serious threat to community safety but who would have been incarcerated because of a shortage of local probation officers. An elaborate analysis of the demographic and legal characteristics of pre- and post-subsidy probationers might reveal the accuracy of this assumption.

The primary treatment provided by local probation agencies following the introduction of the subsidy program was intensive supervision. We have no way of knowing, however, if the intensive supervision caseloads were actually composed only of those probationers who would otherwise have been incarcerated. Research utilizing controlled criteria for inclusion in such an intensive supervision caseload, to ensure that only those offenders who would otherwise have been incarcerated were included, would serve to demonstrate the impact of the subsidy program on the performance of the target population.

Another area of interest is the reported increase in costs to local communities caused by increased use of jail facilities. In light of the reported savings to the state resulting from the subsidy program, this increased cost to counties needs to be examined. A closely associated area of concern is the subject of cost analyses in general. In criminal justice, an important ingredient in cost analyses is the cost associated with various alternative sentencing dispositions. Our review of cost analyses, particularly with respect to determining the cost of probation and incarceration, revealed that these analyses have generally proven to be incomplete and poorly conceived, utilizing data of dubious quality and accuracy. Before claims of substantial savings to the state or increased costs to local communities can be accepted, we must be certain that the cost analyses upon which these claims are based are sufficiently complete and methodologically rigorous to sustain these conclusions.

Since probation subsidy payments were designed to encourage local communities to retain as many offenders in the community as possible, it has been assumed that only the serious, high risk offenders would have been sent to prison. It is possible, though, that state institutions received prisoners who were sentenced to serve longer sentences than the prisoners who were sent to state prisons before the subsidy program began. This might result in a prison population whose average length of sentence is considerably longer than in the pre-susidy period. The implications for institutional administrators of a prison population of more serious offenders serving longer sentences should be examined.

Finally, the research to date in probation subsidy has concentrated on the impact of subsidy on a state level and on performance indicators such as recidivism rates. Research might now begin to look at the effects on local probation agencies of the massive infusion of state money that has taken place for the past twelve years. As the local communities increasingly reduce their commitment rates, their share of state subsidy payments increases. It is possible that some local probation agencies are now relying quite heavily on state funding. It would be valuable to know whether this partial shift in the locus of probation funding has had any appreciable effects on the character of probation, on local probation personnel, or on the goals of local probation agencies. Finally, recent events have shown us the wisdom of anticipating the implications of a sudden cut-off of state payments to local agencies. It would be valuable to know what to expect before this possibility becomes a reality.

The principle underlying the use of restitution in criminal sentencing is that offenders should be held responsible to the victims of their offenses in some direct fashion, either through payment to the victim for losses sustained as a result of the criminal act or through participation in such symbolic restitution activities as working in mental-health centers, repairing houses of aged pensioners, working with children, working with juvenile offenders, doing charity work, or conducting community clean-up campaigns.[41] Restitution, whether financial or symbolic, is seen as contributing to rehabilitation by providing offenders with an opportunity to neutralize the damages done by their criminal acts.

While there is an abundance of theoretical and descriptive material about restitution, there is too little evaluative research on which to base any conclusions about the impact of restitution on the offender or the victim. No data is available on a systematic basis about the extent to which required restitution payments are actually made. Another area of evaluation almost completely neglected by restitution studies is the extent to which the laws requiring restitution are selectively enforced and offenders selectively ordered to pay restitution. Research might also attempt to calculate the benefits accruing to the victims of crime and to the community through restitution programs, as well as the additional costs (if any) to the probation agency of ensuring that restitution payments are actually made.

Although the rehabilitation councils that are currently in use both in the Netherlands and Sweden operate on what would generally be considered to be a local level, they are viewed as policy-level innovations because of their emphasis on tying together and integrating a wide variety of public and private criminal justice and social service agencies.

A recent (1976) report by the Council of Europe suggests that the needs of offenders cannot adequately be met by a legal, supervisory probation service but rather by general social welfare services.[42] The council believes it is important that the probation service draw on the wider resources of the community, both to supplement its own resources and, more importantly, because the ultimate object of reintegrating the offender into the community is achieved only when he is not isolated from using communtiy services provided for the public as a whole. In the future development of probation, its rehabilitative role with respect to bridging the gap to community resources in general will become of increasing significance. The rehabilitation councils in Sweden and the Netherlands offer an organizational structure for the gradual integration of probation work into the community services at large.

The rehabilitation councils originated in the Netherlands shortly after World War II.[43] At that time the ministry of justice considered it necessary to establish, in each court district in the country, a council with the specific purpose of coordinating the activites of the private rehabilitation agencies. When one looks at the present-day functioning of the rehabilitation councils in the Netherlands, it can be stated that serving as a coordination point between the criminal justice apparatus and the private rehabilitation agencies on the local and regional level is still their most important function. However, the scope of the rehabilitation councils has more recently been enlarged to accommodate the view now prevailing that a bridge has to be created between the criminal justice system and the population as a whole. Large social welfare bureaucracies such as social and health services, labor exchanges, and housing bureaus regulate vital areas in the existence of every individual's life. It is especially in these areas of assistance, finance, work, medical care, and accommodation that the offender encounters serious difficulties.

The rehabilitation councils in the Netherlands are thought to fulfill an important role in the development of alternatives to imprisonment. The rationale is that "offender integration" will have to be developed *with* the community, not only on a central level of government but also on the local or regional level.

The closest counterpart in American probation is the brokerage/advocacy approach to probation that has been adopted in some departments. Under this approach, the primary function of the probation officer is to link his probationers to resources already available in existing community social service agencies. When the probation officer determines that resources needed by probationers are not available, the officer assumes an advocacy role and encourages existing agencies to expand their services or develop new services. The brokerage/advocacy approach, however, is quite new and has generally been limited to the efforts of a single agency officer, or team of officers. It is clear that the comprehensive, highly integrated approach characterized by the rehabilitation councils, with their strong emphasis on participation by the community and the offender, has not yet developed in the United States.

Although the use of volunteers in probation has been increasing steadily in the United States during the past twenty years, the extent of use of volunteers, particularly in Japan, warrants inclusion in this section on policy-level innovations.[44] Volunteers are also used extensively in Sweden, however, Japan has perhaps the best known volunteer probation system, and the selection, appointment, and obligations of the volunteers are clearly defined in Japanese law.

The underlying assumption in employing volunteers is that probation is a treatment method designed to rehabilitate an offender in the community. Therefore, the understanding and cooperation of the community are indispensable. Volunteer probation officers in Japan thus have a special place in the administration of probation services.

The volunteer probation officers are part-time public officials appointed by the ministry of justice from among the residents of the area in which a probationer lives. These volunteers are appointed only after being recommended by the volunteer probation officers' selection council, set up in each district at the probation-parole supervision office. The candidates must be financially stable, command the confidence and respect of their community, and must be eager to help offenders rehabilitate themselves.

The system in Sweden represents a similar mixture of professional and volunteer services.[45] Probation is handled by the Swedish Prison Board, a separate institution from either the courts or the ministry of justice. Probation officers also handle parole cases and work within institutions.

Residential treatment centers, which have been used for a number of years for juveniles and adults released from institutions on parole, are now being used for community retention of probationers who would otherwise have been sentenced to imprisonment. The primary objective of these community-based, community-supported programs is to provide an alternative for those offenders who require more assistance and a more radical change in their lifestyles than would normally be possible through standard probation supervision. The underlying premise of these programs is that community supervision and assistance are more effective and cheaper than institutional commitment.

The available research indicates that residential program participants, who are generally seen as poorer probation risks, perform at least as well as regular probationers.[46]

It is clear that additional outcome research is needed to assess the effectiveness of residential treatment programs. Many of the programs, which are described in the literature, have been operating for a relatively short period of time, which is given as the reason why they have not yet been subjected to rigorous evaluation. It would appear, however, that an operation period exceeding two or three years would tend to preclude justifying a lack of research on the grounds that the program is too new to be evaluated. This situation again points to the wisdom of routinizing evaluative procedures into the operational process of any innovative program to accomplish a rigorous evaluation of the program at the earliest opportunity. More information about the costs and effectiveness of these residential treatment programs (particularly their effectiveness with high-risk offenders) would be of considerable value, since these programs tend to require large start-up investments. The best time to define outcome measures and create procedures for collection of pertinent data is the preoperational planning phase. It is strongly recommended that built-in evaluative procedures be a required precondition of programs of this type.

There are many probation clients who, while not requiring the structure and control that characterize residential centers, do require more assistance than could reasonably be provided by traditional probation supervision. When the needed assistance involves improvement of self-concept or upgrading of educational or employment status, required attendance at day training centers, developed in Great Britain, has been used.[47]

Many offenders, in particular, those who suffer from education shortcomings and lack work and other social skills, may be likely to continue in crime if the conditions of their lives are not changed. These needs can be met through the general services of the community, but there may be an advantage in meeting them directly through the probation system and possibly making use of them as a condition of probation. This approach is being tested in Britain in a number of experimental day training centers, which selected offenders attend for full-time but nonresidential) training for a period of up to sixty days. The experimental centers are testing, in their different ways, various methods of imparting social skills and broadening the experience of offenders sent to them. The program includes counseling by probation officers with low caseloads; other instruction is provided partly by probation officers and partly by employing other staff or using outside resources. Provisions were made for training centers in Britain in the Criminal Justice Act of 1972. Assessment of an offender's suitability for training is generally made during the presentence investigation process or directly by the court.

Other kinds of day-center provisions also exist, as yet on a small scale. Some of these centers are simply an extension of conventional probation office accommodations and thus provide some of the facilities of a recreational club. The objective seems to be to provide creative and recreational opportunities for offenders who fail to seek and use the ordinary community resources, and the creation of informal setting for individual counseling and group services of various kinds.

Some dissatisfaction, particularly on the part of probation clients, has resulted from the fact that most probation offices are located in downtown business areas (in county courthouses or municipal buildings), making it difficult for probationers to arrange transportation for their scheduled appointments with their probation officers. In addition to transportation problems, some probation offices have required their clients to report on weekdays during eight-to-five business hours. This has caused problems for probationers who are employed or are attending school full time. To make probation offices more accessible to clients, both physically and temporally, several agencies have developed decentralized satellite offices (called *outreach centers*) that are located in or close to neighborhoods in which probation clients live and are open evenings and on weekends.[48]

Like many new approaches to probation, outreach will ultimately be assessed in terms of client performance and impact on the probation agency. The results of studies of outreach efforts tend to indicate that they are effective in reducing client recidivism: however, more variables need to be assessed to determine whether outcome differences are actually a result of the special treatment sites and approaches. Other operational questions that have not been answered in the available material are whether problems exist in the management of the programs such as isolation of the professional and paraprofessional staff from the administrators in the central office, inaccessibility of client's records, increased staff turnover, and inability of professional probation officers to work effectively with the indigenous paraprofessional workers.

Probation officers and others in the criminal justice field have long been aware of a positive role of employment as a mechanism of social integration whereby offenders are provided opportunities to increase their commitments to conformity and reduce their reliance on criminal behavior. While many probation agencies have routinely included the search for employment in the treatment plans developed for probationers, innovative programs that focus exclusively on employment guidance and development have only recently become popular.

The PEG program is perhaps the most comprehensive attempt to focus probation resources on the problems of preparing probationers for suitable employment and of locating suitable jobs in an employment environment in which jobs are difficult to find even for nonoffenders.[49] It has been an article of faith for many years in correctional practice that adequate employment for an offender will contribute heavily to successful reintegration into the community and to decreased reliance on criminal behavior. The research available on the PEG program does not imply a causal link between employment and reduced recidivism but does suggest that there may be an association between program completion and reduced recidivism. This aspect of the program, along with the other costs and benefits accruing from the program, should be subjected to further study. Another interesting finding of the PEG literature was that the skills of job seeking and job retention that were taught by the PEG program appear to have a lasting effect. This fact should be taken into consideration when program benefits are calculated.

We can see that the underlying theme of most innovative programs is the need to avoid institutionalization and provide greater service to clients, thereby increasing their probabilities of adapting to society and ceasing criminal activity. It is generally assumed that community-based programs are better, from a humanitarian perspective, than incarceration.

In general, then, if one can achieve similar results with less psychological, emotional, or social damage than a more restrictic alternative, it should be tried. In studies where recidivism data are accurate, it can generally be concluded that, while probation may not have a better rate of success than incarceration, it certainly is not worse and is therefore at least as effective. As such, it may be financially less costly to the society and psychologically and socially less costly to the offender.

While recidivism rates reported from innovative programs may not be superior to prison, it should be remembered that many of the innovative progrms deal with a special clientele—those who, without the new program, would probably be incarcerated. This is a high-risk group and needs to be compared with a similar risk population. So, while the conclusions may be equivocal concerning these programs, their purpose may be unique.

There are, of course, factors beyond the scope of the programs that ultimately affect such programs. These factors are political, economic, and social, and transcend the organizational dimensions of the program or its intent. Probationers may fail for many of the same reasons they become involved in crime in the first place. Without going into a theoretical discussion on the etiology of crime, let it suffice to say that many of the problems facing probationers and other offenders are beyond the scope of the programs.

The general trend in innovative programs is a move away from supervision and control per se and toward more emphasis on general social assistance and guidance programs. The trend, thus, is away from the medical-model treatment modality and more toward improving social assistance. Most of the problems faced by offenders are problems in living, and probation as an institution may best serve the client and society by assisting in meeting these basic social needs.

Parole Issues

This chapter has, regrettably, been concerned primarily with defining the state of probation in the United States today. We have largely ignored the critical issues in parole since our assessment of the state of knowledge in parole has just begun. When completed, however, the parole study will provide a comprehensive view of parole by addressing the following issues:

The Legal Environment of Parole Decision Making and Operation: This environment includes the statutes, case law, administrative law, and historical practices that surround the parole process. This target area will be addressed from a legal viewpoint, with particular attention directed to the effects of the environment on the appointment of parole board members, offenders' eligibility for parole consideration, the decision-making process for granting parole, and processes for parole revocation and release from parole. Examples of items of interest that will be addressed include:

1. Statutory conditions for granting, continuing, and revoking parole.
2. Statutory conditions of parole, their application to specific cases, and the effect of "unofficial understandings" between parole officers, police, and parolees concerning conditions.
3. The major case law milestones which have affected parole practice:

Morrissey v. *Brewer*[50] and *Gagnon* v. *Scarpelli,*[51] and their effects on statutory law.

4. The extent to which parolees lose civil right and incur civil disabilities due to their status, and attempts to change this situation.
5. The effects of restructuring sentencing patterns on parole, for example, the change from indeterminate to determinate sentencing.

The Parole Board: Composition and Practices. This area will focus on research and commentary relating to the individuals who compose parole boards; their qualifications, compensation, duties, and methods of appointment; and the parole decision-making process as it relates to granting, revocation, and release from parole. Specific items of interest include:

1. The parole-granting or decision-making process, the variables considered by the parole board, the use of base expectancy scores, guidelines, risk tables, and problems in their utilization.
2. The environment of the parole decision-making process and its effects, particularly the use of board discretion to achieve policy aims such as institutional population reduction or mitigation of long mandatory sentences.
3. The effect of "contract" parole, mandatory release, and good-time provisions on parole.
4. The acitivities of parole boards in states in the process of abolishing parole.
5. The preparole setting of parole release dates contingent on institutional programs such as work release, furlough, and MAP and/or other specific conditions such as attainment of employment.
6. The policy-making parole board versus the operational parole board.
7. The use of hearing examiners to conduct board contact with parolees.
8. The effect of parole board policy on the relationship of time sentenced to time served.
9. Parole board responsibility for field-service provision.
10. Other functions of parole boards: clemency hearings, pardons, interstate compacts, revocations, and sentencing.

Contemporary U.S. Parole Practice. This area will focus on the management of parole operations, the supervision and treatment techniques utilized, and strategies used for service provision. Particular attention will be paid to the effectiveness and efficiency of various techniques and strategies of organization, operation and service delivery. Management will be dealt with at two levels. The higher level will address issues that directly affect components of the criminal justice system other than parole. Issues covered will include:

1. The effect of parole revocation practices on institutional population levels.
2. Parole as an institutional release mechanism to mitigate overcrowding.
3. Use of shock parole.
4. Reciprocal institution/parole effects that result from MAP, good-time provisions, furlough, work release, and the blurring of the traditional institution/parole dividing line.
5. Conflicts that arise when institutional personnel allow work release and furloughs, but parole is not granted.
6. Continuity of service provision from the institution to parole.
7. The effect of prerelease programming and prerelease requirements on field-service supervision.
8. The relationship of parole field-services personnel to courts, correctional institutions, and the police.

A second level of management issues deals with the provision of field services. Interest areas include:

1. Staffing and training of the field-service agency.
2. Caseload-management techniques.
3. The effectiveness and efficiency of various treatment techniques.
4. Provision of services through collateral service agencies such as education, training, employment, counseling, and halfway houses.
5. Balancing supervision and treatment services.
6. Usc of individual officers or a team approach.
7. Agency operating and planning information system.
8. Budgeting and financing parole field services.
9. Implementation of nationally recognized standards for parole operations.
10. Policies regarding parole officer duties vis-a-vis arrest, detention, release, and program planning for parolees.
11. Field revocation procedures and policies, written and in practice.
12. Use of uniform parole reports.

International Parole Practices. This area will attempt to identify foreign innovations and practices in prison aftercare services that appear directly or potentially applicable to parole practice in the United States. Also research that investigates the effectiveness of various parole treatment, supervision, and services delivery techniques will be revised.

The Effectiveness of Parole. The focus of this area will be an examination of research that purports to establish the overall effectiveness of parole versus alternative aftercare stategies, both supervised and unsupervised; and research that relates parole outcomes to sociological, psychological, and demographic variables.

The results of the study of these five target areas will be utilized as the basis for the comprehensive body of knowledge. The results will be used to produce (1) a technical issues paper and comprehensive bibliography for each of the five areas; (2) a treatment of selected critical issues in parole by target area; (3) an identification of the gaps in current knowledge regarding parole; (4) an agenda for future research and evaluation in parole; and (5) an identification and description of "successful" parole programs, processes, and procedures for consideration for national-level demonstration or replication purposes.

In closing, we wish to offer the following ukases:

1. For many standard-setting organizations, probation is the sentence of choice unless circumstances appear to require incarceration. In addition to endorsing this position, we suggest that many offenders who are currently placed on supervised probation be placed, instead, on unsupervised probation. From the available research, we have the strong impression that mandatory supervision for perhaps a large number of probationers is not only irrelevant but also constitutes a significant, unnecessary cost burden to most probation agencies.

2. We could find no conclusive evidence to show that special treatment programs have a significant beneficial impact on client outcome measures. We are particularly concerned with the prevalence of treatment programs described as "counseling," which appear (from totally inadequate definitions) to consist of intermittent, sporadic, and brief casework sessions. We felt that perhaps the "best" treatment for a large number of probationers is no treatment at all.

3. Another widely touted caseload-management strategy which has not been affirmed by conclusive evidence, is intensive supervision. We really need to ask ourselves what difference it makes to double the monthly contact time between probation officer and client if we are actually talking about the difference between ten minutes of contact time per month and twenty minutes per month.

4. We must stop preparing complete presentence investigation reports for a very large number of offenders. Research shows that both probation officers (in making their recommendations) and judges (in making their sentencing decision) tend to rely heavily on two factors: the offender's current offense and the offender's prior criminal record. We also know that

the preparation of presentence investigation reports consumes a significant amount of the probation officer's time. It would appear then that not only is most of the material contained in the PSI irrelevant and unnecessary but we are also wasting scarce time and manpower resources that can be used to greater effect for other probation functions.

5. If PSIs are not abolished altogether, their length should be limited to the standard short form. We might experiment with PSIs that would supply judges only with information that they specifically request rather than the commonly used comprehensive presentation.

6. All new or innovative programs in probation must be adequately evaluated by means of an appropriate, rigorous, methodologically sound research design. Operational definitions of all treatments, interventions, and critical variables must be provided. Too many examples of alleged "evaluations" are nothing more than descriptive narratives or management audits. And funding agencies have spent too much money on ill-defined, nonreplicable programs. Each newly funded program must have an evaluation component or capability.

7. We must take steps to compile a nationwide data base for probation for use by administrators, policymakers, and researchers. We know that information systems in probation are feasible not only on the local level but on the state, multistate, and national levels as well. Such systems, with appropriate guarantees for ensuring protection of the privacy rights of individual probationers, must be implemented.

8. With the spectre of Proposition 13 now a reality, we urgently need to examine the implications of sudden, drastic funding cuts for local probation agencies that depend on such funding. A state such as California, which is characterized both by the use of a probation subsidy and by a dramatically decreased tax base, should be carefully studied while the affected state and local agencies are in a process of transition.

9. We must increase the use of fines or community service orders as substitutes for probation. Fines or community service orders could appropriately be used with summary (unsupervised) probation.

10. One of the major thrusts in current probation literature is the critical need to ensure the delivery of services to probationers. A common thread of complaint in this literature is the confusion, disorganization, and duplication of effort involved in requiring each individual probation officer to deal with a bewildering number and variety of social service agencies—both public and private. In contrast to the fractionalized "jungle" typical in the United States, in the Netherlands, social services of all types for convicted offenders are coordinated by rehabilitation councils composed of representatives of all segments of the community. In the United States, we have only begun to approach this type of systematic, integrated service delivery; our use of specialist teams of probation officers is merely a rudi-

mentary step in the right direction. We must develop at least a modicum of coordination among our providers of critically needed social services.

11. Along with the rise of some of the new or revived correctional models, we are also seeing a move toward determinate sentences. A few states now have completely abolished indeterminate sentences (and at the same time have abolished parole). Other states such as Ohio, have decreed mandatory flat sentences for selected offenses. And still other states such as Indiana have significantly reduced flexibility in sentencing. We must determine the implications of determinate sentencing for the entire criminal justice system. For states that have abolished parole, consideration should be given to the development of parole-like aftercare services in which the released offender could voluntarily participate. Research must immediately begin to assess the impact of determinate sentences or relatively inflexible sentences on system costs, manpower requirements, and on client performance. We need to begin *now* to study those states in which statutory sentencing mandates have been changed.

Notes

1. Eric W. Carlson and Evalyn C. Parks, *Report #1: Critical Issues in Adult Probation, Summary* (Columbus, Ohio: Ohio State University, Program for the Study of Crime and Delinquency, 1978); Eric. W. Carlson and Evalyn C. Parks, *Report #2: Technical Issue Paper On Issues in Probation Management* (Columbus, Ohio: Ohio State University, Program for the Study of Crime and Delinquency, 1978); David A. Townsend, John W. Palmer, and Jennifer B. Newton, *Report #3: Technical Issue Paper of Presentence Investigation Reports* (Columbus, Ohio: Ohio State University, Program for the Study of Crime and Delinquency, 1978); Don M. Gottfredson, James O. Finckenauer, and Carol Rauh, *Report #4: Technical Issue Paper on Caseload Prediction and Treatment* (Columbus, Ohio: Ohio State University, Program for the Study of Crime and Delinquency, 1978); Paul C. Friday, *Report #6: Technical Issue Paper on International Assessment of the Use of Adult Probation* (Columbus, Ohio: Ohio State University, Program for the Study of Crime and Delinquency, 1978); Institute for Advanced Studies in Justice, *Technical Issue Paper on Legal Issues in Adult Probation* (Columbus, Ohio: Ohio State University, Program for the Study of Crime and Delinquency, 1978); Eric W. Carlson and Evalyn C. Parks, *Report #8: Technical Issue Paper on the State of Research in Adult Probation* (Columbus, Ohio: Ohio State University, Program for the Study of Crime and Delinquency, 1978); Eric W. Carlson and Evalyn C. Parks, *Report #9: Bibliography* (Columbus, Ohio: Ohio State University, Program for the Study of Crime and Delinquency, 1978).

2. U.S. Department of Justice, Law Enforcement Assistance Administration, National Criminal Justice Information and Statistical Service, *State and Local Probation and Parole Systems* (Washington, D.C.: U.S. Government Printing Office, 1978).

3. Comptroller General of the United States, *State and County Probation: Systems in Crisis, Report to the Congress of the United States* (Washington, D.C.: U.S. Government Printing Office, 1976).

4. Comptroller General of the United States, *Probation and Parole Activities Need to be Better Managed, Report to the Congress of the United States* (Washington, D.C.: U.S. Government Printing Office, 1977).

5. See, for example, American Bar Association, *Standards Relating to Probation* (New York: American Bar Association, Project on Standards for Criminal Justice, 1970); Council of State Governments, *Reorganization of State Corrections Agencies: A Decade of Experience* (Lexington, Kentucky: Council of State Governments, 1977); George G. Killinger, Hazel B. Kerper, and Paul F. Cromwell, *Probation and Parole in the Criminal Justice System* (St. Paul, Minnesota: West Publishing, 1976); National Advisory Commission on Criminal Justice Standards and Goals, *Corrections* (Washington, D.C.: U.S. Government Printing Office, 1973); President's Commission on Law Enforcement and Administration of Justice, *Task Force Report: Corrections* (Washington, D.C.: U.S. Government Printing Office, 1967).

6. Dale E. Van Laningham, Merlin Taber, and Ruta Dimants, "How Adult Probation Officers View Their Job Responsibilities, *Crime and Delinquency* 12 (1966): 97–108.

7. Timothy J. Mahoney, *Role Preferences and Job Satisfaction of Kentucky Probation and Parole Officers,* M.A. Thesis, Eastern Kentucky University, 1975.

8. See, for example, William P. Adams, et al., "The San Francisco Project: A Critique," *Federal Probation* 35 (December 1971); Jerry Banks, et al., *Issue Paper: Phase I Evaluation Of Intensive Probation Projects* (Atlanta, Georgia: Georgia Institute of Technology, School of Industrial and Systems Engineering, Draft, November 1976); Jerry Banks, et al., *Knowledge Assessment: Phase I Evaluation of Intensive Special Probation Projects* (Atlanta, Georgia: Georgia Institute of Technology, School of Industrial and Systems Engineering, 1976); Robert M. Carter, and Leslie T. Wilkins, "Caseloads: Some Conceptual Models," in *Probation and Parole: Selected Readings* (New York: Wiley, 1970).

9. See, for example, Thomas Kaput, and Michael Santese, *Evaluation of General Caseload Drug Unit* (Hartford, Connecticut: Department of Adult Probation, January 1975); James E. Olsson, *Final Evaluative Report: An Outpatient Treatment Clinic for Special Offenders* (Baltimore, Maryland: Maryland Governor's Commission on Law Enforcement and

Criminal Justice, 1975); Pima County Adult Probation Department, *Special Services for Mentally Deficient Probationers* (Tucson, Arizona: Pima County Adult Probation Department, 1975); Larry Yonemura and Dave Estep, *Evaluation Summary: Narcotic Treatment and Control Unit* (Los Angeles, California: Los Angeles County Probation Department, 1974).

10. Comptroller General of the United States, supra, 1976, n. 3.

11. See, for example, Peter C. Buffum, *Project Jaguar: Final Evaluation Report* (Philadelphia, Pennsylvania: Social Research Associates, 1974; A.L. Langbehn, G.E. Pasela, and P.S. Venezia, *Yolo County (California) Minority Probation Aide Project: An Evaluation of the Mexican-American Probation Case Aide Project (1971-1973)* (Davis, California: National Council on Crime and Delinquency, 1974); Ramon Priestino and Harry E. Allen, *The Parole Officer Aide Program in Ohio: An Exemplary Project* (Columbus, Ohio, Ohio State University, Program for the Study of Crime and Delinquency, 1975).

12. See, for example, Donald J. Amboyer, *Volunteer Probation Aides Project Evaluation of 1974* (Mt. Clemens, Michigan: Macomb County Probation Department, 1975); Rex D. Hume, et. al., *Evaluation of Probation Services and Volunteers in Probation Programs* (Bloomington, Indiana: Indiana University, School of Public and Environmental Affairs, Institute for Research in Public Safety, 1976); Richard Ku, *The Volunteer Probation Counselor Program, Lincoln, Nebraska: An Exemplary Project* (Washington, D.C.: Law Enforcement Assistance Administration, National Institute of Law Enforcement and Criminal Justice, 1976); Keith J. Lennhouts, "Royal Oak's Experience with Professional and Volunteers in Probation," *Federal Probation* 34 (December 1970): 45-51; Daniel W. Trexler, *Fourth Annual Report of Volunteers in Probation and Parole of Lancaster County, Pennsylvania* (Lancaster, Pennsylvania: Lancaster County Probation Department, 1976).

13. See, for example, Amboyer, ibid.; Hume, ibid.; Richard P. Seiter, Sue A. Howard, and Harry E. Allen, *Effectiveness of Volunteers in Court: An Evaluation of the Franklin County Volunteers in Probation Program* (Columbus, Ohio: Ohio State University, Program for the Study of Crime and Delinquency, 1974); Jack C. Sternback, *Evaluation Report: Community Resources and Volunteer Unit* Philadelphia, Pennsylvania: Philadelphia Probation Department, 1975).

14. See, for example, Arthur Miles, "The Reality of the Probation Officer's Dilemma," *Federal Probation* 29 (March 1965): 18-23; Jack C. Sternback, *Executive Summary of Evaluation Report: In-service and Graduate Training Project* (Philadelphia, Pennsylvania: Philadelphia Probation Department, 1975).

15. See, for example, Robert M. Carter, *Time and Motion Study of the Washington State Office of Probation and Parole* (Los Angeles, California:

University of Southern California, Public Systems Research Institute, n.d.); U.S. Federal Judicial Center, *Probation Time Study* (Washington, D.C.: Federal Judicial Center, 1973); Virginia Department of Corrections, *Results of Probation/Parole Officers Time Study* (Richmond, Virginia: Department of Corrections, Division of Probation and Parole Services, 1976); Albert Wahland and Daniel Glaser, "Pilot Time Study of the Federal Probation Officer's Job," *Federal Probation* 27 (September 1963): 20–25.

16. Peter S. Venezia and Alvin W. Cohn, *Uniform Probation Reports: A Feasibility Study* (Davis, California: National Council on Crime and Delinquency, Probation Management Institute, 1968).

17. Jeffrey I. Chapman, and Carol W. Nelson, *A Handbook of Cost–Benefit Techniques and Applications* (Washington, D.C.: American Bar Association Economics Center, 1975); Vincent Chitren and Regis Reynolds, *A Cost/Benefit Analysis of the Monroe County Pilot Program for Vocational Upgrading of Probationers* (Rochester, New York: Rochester-Monroe County Criminal Justice Pilot City Program, University of Rochester, Graduate School of Management, 1973). Robert L. Frazier, Charles M. Friel, Donald J. Weisenhorn, and John A. Cocoros, *Incarceration and Adult Felon Probation in Texas: A Cost Comparison* (Huntsville, Texas: Institute of Contemporary Corrections and the Behavioral Sciences, 1973).

18. Lloyd E. Ohlin, *Selection for Parole* (New York: Russel Sage Foundation, 1951).

19. Don M. Gottfredson, "Assessment and Prediction Methods in Crime and Delinquency," in *Task Force Report: Juvenile Delinquency And Youth Crime* (Washington, D.C.: U.S. Government Printing Office, 1967).

20. Dean Frease, *Probation Prediction for Adult Offenders in the State of Washington* (Olympia, Washington: Department of Institutions, Research and Program Analysis Section, 1965).

21. Richard C. Nicholson, "The Use of Prediction in Caseload Management," *Federal Probation* 35 (December 1968): 54–58.

22. Comptroller General of the United States, supra, n. 3. Frease, supra, n. 20; Nicholas Fiore, *A Statistical Examination of the Relationship between Base Expectancy Scores and Manner of Discharge from Probation and Recidivism,* M.A. Thesis, John Jay College of Criminal Justice, 1976.

23. Don M. Gottfredson, Leslie T. Wilkins, Peter B. Hoffman, and Susan M. Singer, *The Utilization of Experience in Parole Decision-making: Summary Report* (Washington, D.C.: U.S. Government Printing Office, 1974).

24. President's Commission on Law Enforcement and Administration of Justice, supra, n. 5.

25. See, for example, Chitren and Reynolds, supra, n. 17; James E. Phillips, *Report of the Probation Employment and Guidance Program: An Evaluation of Impacts on Employment and Recidivism* (Rochester, New York: Monroe County Department of Probation, 1975).

26. Vincent P. Dole and Herman Joseph, "Methadone Patients on Probation and Parole," *Federal Probation* 34 (1970): 42–48.

27. Seymour J. Rosenthal, *Report on the Evaluation of Philadelphia County Department of Probation Drug Unit* (Philadelphia, Pennsylvania: Temple University, Center for Social Policy and Community Development, 1974).

28. Robert L. Polakow and Ronald M. Doctor, "A Behavioral Modification Program for Adult Drug Offenders," *Journal of Research in Crime and Delinquency* 11 (1974): 63.

29. U.S. Department of Justice, supra, n. 2.

30. Robert M. Carter, *Prescriptive Package on Pre-sentence Investigations* (Washington, D.C.: National Institute of Law Enforcement and Criminal Justice, 1978); Lieberman, Schaffer, and Martin, *The Bronx Sentencing Project: An Experiment in the Use of Short-form Pre-sentence Reports for Adult Misdemeanants* (New York: Vera Institute of Justice, n.d.); U.S. Administrative Office of the Courts, Division of Probation. The Selective Pre sentence Investigation Report, (Washington, D.C.: Administrative Office of the Courts, Division of Probation, Publication N. 104, 1974).

31. Shapiro and Clement, "Pre-sentence Information in Felony Cases in the Massachusetts Superior Courts," *Suffolk University Law Review* 10 (1975): 49.

32. Robert M. Carter and Leslie T. Wilkins, "The Pre-sentence Report and the Decision-making Process, in *Probation and Parole: Selected Readings,* eds. Robert M. Carter, and Leslie T. Wilkins (New York: Wiley, 1970); Charles K. Eden and Harry E. Allen, *The Pre-sentence Report and the Decision-making Process: A Replication Study,* Paper presented at the 19th Annual Southern Conference on Corrections, Florida State University, Tallahassee, Florida, 1974.

33. Chester H. Bartoo, "Some Hidden Factors Behind a Probation Officer's Recommendations," *Crime and Delinquency* 9 (1963): 276; Carter and Wilkins, Ibid.; Eden and Allen, ibid.; J. Hagan, "The Social and Legal Construction of Criminal Justice: A Study of the Pre-sentence Process, *Social Problems* 22 (June 1975): 620-637; Robert O. Norris, *Decision-making in Probation: A Study of Pre-sentence Recommendations,* Ph.D. Dissertation, University of California at Berkeley, 1969; Shapiro and Clement, supra, n. 31.

34. Robert M. Carter, "It Is Respectfully Recommended...," *Federal Probation* 38 (June 1966): 38–42; Robert M. Carter, "Pre-sentence Information and Decision-making," *Trial Judges Journal*, 1969; City of Baltimore, *Pre-sentence Investigation Unit* (Baltimore, Maryland: Maryland Governor's Commission on Law Enforcement and the Administration of Justice, n.d.).

35. John R. Faine, and Edward Bohlander, *Shock Probation: The*

Kentucky Experience (Bowling Green, Kentucky: Western Kentucky University, 1976); David M. Petersen and Paul C. Friday, "Early Release from Incarceration: Race as a Factor in the Use of Shock Probation," *Journal of Criminal Law and Criminology* 66 (1975): 79–87.

36. Faine and Bohlander, ibid.

37. Henry Angelino, R. Fuller, J. Kishton, J. Waldron, and J. Zimbeck, *A Longitudinal Study of the Effectiveness of Shock Probation* (Columbus, Ohio: Ohio State University, Behavioral Sciences Laboratory, Organization Research and Service, 1975).

38. Faine and Bohlander, supra, n. 35.

39. Walter Corwin and Gary Lanstra, *Juvenile Probation Subsidy Program: An Evaluation* (Olympia, Washington: Department of Social and Health Services, Community Services Division, Bureau of Juvenile Rehabilitation, July, 1975); Travis Hirschi and David Rudisill, *An Evaluation of California Probation Subsidy Program,* 1, *Commitment Reduction and Probation Subsidy: A Summary of Available Data* (Davis, California: Center on Administration of Criminal Justice, 1977); Lowell Lyle Kuehn, *An Evaluation of the California Probation Subsidy Program,* Ph.D. Dissertation, University of Washington, 1973; Thomas Pattern and Christina Johns, *Michigan Department Of Corrections Special Probation Projects, Third Interim Report* (Lansing, Michigan: Department of Corrections, 1976).

40. Edward L. Barrett, Jr., and Lloyd D. Musolf, *An Evaluation of the California Probation Subsidy Program,* VI (Davis, California: Center on Administration of Criminal Justice, 1977); Floyd Feeney and Travis Hirschi, *An Evaluation of the California Probation Subsidy Program,* V: *Impact of Commitment Reduction on the Recidivism of Offenders* (Davis, California: Center on Administration of Criminal Justice, 1977).

41. Burt Galaway, and Joe Hudson, "Restitution and Rehabilitation: Some Central Issues," *Crime and Delinquency* 18 (1972): 403–410.

42. European Committee on Crime Problems, *Alternative Penal Measures,* (Strasbourg, Council of Europe, 1976).

43. N.W. deSmit, "Rehabilitation Councils in the Netherlands," in *Alternative Penal Measures to Imprisonment,* ibid.

44. Yasuyoshi Shiono, "The Use of Volunteers in the Non–institutional Treatment of Offenders in Japan," *International Review of Criminal Policy* 27 (1969): 25–31.

45. Patricia Elton–Mayo, *Probation and After–care in Certain European Countries* (Strasbourg: Council of Europe, 1964).

46. See, for example, Eric W. Carlson, *The Alvis House Probationary Diversion Program: A Second Year Report* (Columbus, Ohio: Ohio State University, Program for the Study of Crime and Delinquency, 1976); H. Richard Lamb and Victor Goertzel, "A Community Alternative to

County Jail: The Hopes and the Realities," *Federal Probation* 39 (March 1975): 34–39; Nathan G. Mandel, *Bremer House: An Analysis of Program Performance from March 13, 1972 through September 30, 1964* (St. Paul, Minnesota: Amherst H. Wilder Foundation, 1975); MetaMetrics, Inc., *Evaluation of the Residential Community Center, Philadelphia Adult Probation Department* (Washington, D.C.: MetaMetrics, 1975); Minnesota Governor's Commission on Crime Prevention and Control *Ramsey County Minnesota: A Report on Bremer House Community Based Rehabilitative Program for Male Adult Offenders* (Minneapolis, Minnesota: Governor's Commission on Crime Prevention and Control, 1973).

47. Douglas Payne, "Day Training Centres," in *Home Office Research Unit Report No. 4.*, eds. Andrew Crook and Nicholas Sanderson (London: Her Majesty's Stationery Office, 1977).

48. Pennsylvania Board of Probation and Parole, *Final Report: Establishment of a District Office and Out-reach Centers in the Philadelphia Area for the Pennsylvania Board of Probation and Parole 1975–1976* (Harrisburg, Pennsylvania: Pennsylvania Board of Probation and Parole, Research and Statistical Division, 1977).

49. Chitren and Reynolds, supra, n. 17; Phillips, supra, n. 25.

50. 408 U.S. 471 (1972).

51. 411 U.S. 778 (1973).

Part IV
Research

14 Future Perspectives in Research on the Criminal Justice System

Jerome Hall

Discussions of future perspectives in research, if they are to be something more than indulgence in Utopia, should be based on experience. I want to take advantage, if there is any, of having lived substantially beyond the alloted three score years and ten to share with you some of the things I believe I have learned about research on crime and criminal law.

In making my report, I accept Bertrand Russell's distinction between knowledge by acquaintance and knowledge by description. Knowledge by acquaintance is first-hand, direct knowledge, what I see or hear and what I discover about myself by introspection, while knowledge by description is knowledge based on what others say in describing their experience and discoveries, for example, regarding the distance of the moon from the earth, the cause of tuberculosis, and so on.

Convictions based on direct experience, knowledge by acquaintance, are difficult to avoid or to alter. For example, I firmly believe that living in Chicago fifty years ago was not the perilous thing it has become. I recall vividly that I went into parks late evenings, that sometimes, after theater or parties, I did not return home until one or two in the morning, did not fear other pedestrians, and that except for very few neighborhoods I did not hesitate to walk anywhere in the city, and in my experience the same was true of New York from 1932 to 1934. I need not describe the present conditions in Chicago and other cities. There are academics who say that I am mistaken if I think crimes of violence have increased. They say that only the publicity given crimes and the methods of compiling statistics have increased and improved; hence I was only lucky not to have been mugged or robbed since the same number of muggers and robbers were there fifty years ago. I can only say that far from being persuaded, I have not in the least altered my opinion regarding the change that has taken place regarding criminal violence in our cities. Without claiming to be "the voice of experience," I want to discuss salient features of three movements in criminal law with which I have had some contact. Then I shall say what I think might be learned from that experience, and I shall make some suggestions about research in the area of crime and criminal law.

Indeterminate Sentence

The first subject concerns the indeterminate sentence, my knowledge of which began in the early thirties, especially in my contact with Sheldon Glueck, who was a major architect of the philosophy of individualized treatment and its corollary, the indeterminate sentence.

The reasons that motivated Sheldon and Eleanor Glueck and the case they built were so persuasive that their views were universally accepted, at least in this country. In his book, *Crime and Justice,* published in 1936, Sheldon Glueck summarized those reasons. "'Individualization of punishment' has long been a slogan of reformers,"[1] he said. Indeed, he might have credited Plato and the Bible with its origin. But, continued Glueck, it has been restricted to distinctions drawn among crimes, not applied to the person of the actor or criminal. The then current mode of sentencing by judges was grossly inadequate. Judges are legally trained, not conversant with sociology and psychology; they cannot determine "the treatment best suited to various types of offenders."[2] Not only were judges ill-trained and ill-equipped, their opportunity to study offenders was also limited by the duration of the trial as well as by the restrictions of formal procedure. Moreover, since sentences were fixed by statute, there was a one-shot decision that ignored the individuality of the offenders and what could be learned about them, given additional time. What was plainly needed was a flexible procedure, time to study the offenders, and competent personnel to perform that function. This work "should accordingly be entrusted to a tribunal composed, say, of a psychiatrist or psychologist, a sociologist or educator and the trial judge."[3] "The treatment tribunal ought further to be implemented by appropriate clinics and means for forecasting...the probable subsequent behavior of various types of offenders... ."[4] He followed his argument to its ultimate conclusion by advocating "*wholly indeterminate* sentence... ."[5] I can think of no other words that would so clearly reveal how far current thought and law have moved in forty years from the perspective of one of our leading criminologists.

Of the postulates on which his thesis was based, two seem to have been decisive. First, punishment based on retribution is nothing but vengeance, a "scapegoat" theory.[6] Glueck borrowed this term from a book published in 1923 by Dr. W.A. White, a prominent psychiatrist, who said that man transfers his feeling of sinfulness by punishing the criminal, deluding himself and "bolstering up his own self-respect." "The principle is the same," said Dr. White, "as that by which an emotion such as anger is discharged upon an inoffensive lifeless object."[7] Glueck subscribed to that thesis and advocated treatment in terms of his criticism of the then-operative system that makes his perspective abundantly clear, indeed, obvious: It prescribes, he said, "*in advance* the length of time the *patient* should be kept in the hospital and then hold him there the full period or discharge him ahead of time, whether *cured* or not."[8] It is not my purpose here nor is there time to set Glueck's and Dr. White's view of punishment in the context of moral philosophy or to do more than note that the greatest moral philosopher of modern times, Immanuel Kant, is the principal advocate of retributive justice. I can only suggest that vengeance is an emotional reaction that bears no rational relation to the gravity of the offense and may even be directed against someone other than the offender, for example, his brother or father. It should therefore be distinguished from punishment that is imposed after very deliberate inquiry and is also based not only on the desert of normal adults who voluntarily harm persons but besides is proportionate to the gravity of the harm.

The other major postulate that supported Glueck in his advocacy of the indeterminate sentence was his faith in the social sciences and psychiatry, his confidence in the availability of the knowledge needed to carry out the individualization of treatment he advocated. He quoted with enthusiasm Holmes's statement, "An ideal system of law should draw its postulates and its legislative justification from science"[9] without, however, discussing the meaning of "science." Joining his two postulates, Glueck said, "The legal and institutional provisions for the protection of society should be based not so much upon the gravity of the act for which the offender happens to be on trial, as upon his personality and character that is, upon his social dangerousness... ." He added that "a relatively innocuous act may be, and not infrequently is, committed by one who in fact is a menace to society, while a relatively serious offense (even murder) may be committed by one who is fundamentally not dangerous."[10] Glueck was confident that psychiatry and sociology could supply the necessary knowledge.

In *Of Delinquency and Crime* published in 1974—almost forty years after he had expressed the preceding views—Glueck stood by his convictions, bolstering them by reliance on prediction tables. But by that time he had recognized the limitations, the failures of the indeterminate sentencing that had been adopted in the interim in many states. They were due, he said, to reliance on the probation officers' investigation report and on the "ripe experience" of the judge.[11] Sound individualization was much too complex for such a simplistic procedure; among many of its complications, "it involves the difficult art of prognosis." Glueck advocated the use of his carefully worked out prediction tables.

Despite Glueck's sustained and well-nigh heroic efforts to support the indeterminate sentence, we know that in the recent past it has been sharply curtailed or wholly repudiated in some states.[12] There are many reasons that account for this change. The abandonment of legality (*nulla poena sine lege*) in the dictatorships of Russia and Germany brought home the fact that unlimited discretion can lead not to wise, humane treatment but to gross injustice; appreciation of the rule of law, minimized in American Legal Realism, was restored. Great disparaties in sentences, not explained and probably not explainable on rational grounds, also gave rise to much concern. In the prisons that was aggravated by the grant of parole to some and its denial to others, again for no generally accepted reasons; and some riots seemed in part at least to be caused by such uneven–handed treatment. There was also, I think, much loss of confidence in the competence of parole boards, and for many there was the further implication that psychiatry and the social sciences could not provide the knowledge necessary to support a defensible system of indeterminate sentences, let alone complete individualization.

In my altered view of the indeterminate sentence, what weighed just as heavily was the statement by Professor Andenaes, the distinguished Norwegian criminologist, who wrote:

> At least in the Scandinavian countries the trend in recent years has been away from the sanctions of indeterminate duration back to the traditional system of fixed sentences meted out by the court. This change in the trend is not due to theoretical speculation, but to experience and research.[13]

If indeterminate sentencing failed in the small, homogeneous, wholly literate Scandinavian countries, how could it succeed in the United States? There was also a conversation I had several years ago with the head of the California Adult Authority. How much study do not make of the inmates of California prisons? I asked. Smiling, he said, in effect, there were 18,000 inmates in California prisons, and with our limited resources it is not possible to study them in any detail.

What a fall from the Utopian heights of the early thirties, when a thorough diagnosis was to be made of every felon, conjuring up the image of a medical and psychiatric clinic and a sociological institute that would spend months in the most detailed diagnosis of each inmate! The final blow was expressed in widespread depreciation of the rehabilitation movement in terms of almost universal criticism of prisons, and if one may judge from the paucity of recent essays in support of rehabilitation, the turnabout from the idealism of the early proponents of individualized treatment amounts to almost a complete reversal.

Juvenile Court

The other area where there have been major challenges, if not a complete turnabout, is that of delinquency and the juvenile court. Here again the origin of the relevant perspective goes back many years—to chancery and separate hearings and to institutions called "houses of refuge," one of which was established in New York City in 1825 and not much later in Boston and in other parts of Massachusetts in 1847. But the origin of the juvenile court as a distinct institution and the articulation of a supporting philosophy occurred in Chicago in 1899. Children were dependents or delinquents, not criminals; they were to be educated and rehabilitated, not punished. The judge was to be a wise and kind official, unhampered by a technical adversary procedure; his sole concern was the welfare of the child.

The first hard blow to that thesis, to my knowledge, was the publication in 1933 of the Glueck's *One Thousand Juvenile Delinquents* and their follow-up studies of the careers of youthful offenders after their release from correctional institutions. The Gluecks' earlier study was focused on the Boston Juvenile Court. This indeed was a court that met the highest standards of the proponents of the juvenile court idea. Presided over by a humane and thoughtful judge, a Cabot, it was aided by a clinic directed by Dr. Healy, a distinguished forensic psychiatrist, and by Dr. Bonner, a very able psychologist. Then in 1933 came the devastating report of the Gluecks. In their words:

> What was the conduct of our boys in the five-year post-treatment period? *Eighty-eight percent of them continued their delinquencies during this period.* ... The major conclusion is inescapable, then, that, *the treatment carried out by Clinic, Court, and associated community facilities had very little effect in preventing recidivism.*[14] (Emphasis added)

Indeed, many of the boys became recidivists on a much more serious scale than that of their earlier delinquency.

Between that hard blow to fond expectations and *Gault,* decided thirty-four years later in 1967, came a series of events that transformed disappointment into frustration and anger. In *Gault*[15] Justice Fortas tore the veil, as he saw it, from the pretensions of the juvenile court and its correctional institutions. Despite the propaganda and the soft talk, the process was in fact punitive; indeed, the correctional institutions were sometimes more punitive than the prisons in which adults were confined. The Court's judgment followed with inexorable logic; the child must be protected by the same constitutional safeguards that protect adults accused of crimes in criminal courts. It was emphasized that this should not affect the sentence or treatment of children; but Justice Stewart, in his dissent, spoke for many advocates of the juvenile court ideology when he said: "I believe the Court's decision is wholly unsound as a matter of constitutional law, and sadly unwise as a matter of judicial policy... ." And Justice Black, although concurring with the majority, said: "This holding strikes a well-nigh fatal blow to much that is unique about the juvenile courts in this Nation."[16]

The treatment of juvenile delinquents can easily be distinguished from juvenile court procedure. But regardless of the logic of the *Gault* opinion, its psychological affect cannot be ignored; certainly the experience of juvenile violence and the consequent attitude of legislators shown, for example, in pending bills in New York, support a very different perspective from that of the founders of the juvenile court. Indeed, the proposed severe penalization of children of fourteen and fifteen represents a complete turnabout from the idealism of the early supporters of the juvenile court. Again it is not my purpose to take sides, to intrude, however subtly, my own perspective on the problem of juvenile violence. My purpose is to discern the operation of divergent perspectives regarding the culpability of children and the competence of the juvenile court and its attendant institutions to cope effectively with juvenile violence and then later to suggest ways to study that and other major problems.

Victimless Crimes

I turn now to another area, that of the so-called victimless crimes, not because there has been a turnabout from earlier views but because it provides a good example of the need for analysis as an essential prerequisite of sound research. The current interest in this area was stimulated by the publication of the Wolfenden Report in 1957 and by many debates, notably those of Professort Hart and Justice Devlin. But the term "victimless crimes" seems to have been popularized by the publication in 1966 of Edwin Schur's *Crimes Without Victims.* Just as in the cases of individualization of treatment and juvenile delinquency, the origin of the thinking or, if one prefers, of the ideology supporting the current position regarding "victimless crimes" goes far back into the past. In 1935, for example, in an article published in the *University of Chicago Law Review* based on my experience as an assistant state's attorney and also as defense counsel, I said, "the vagrant, the drunkard (frequently a chronic alcoholic), the drug addict, the prostitute, the petty thief and others, should be separated in theory as well as in practice, from the truly criminal, and given treatment according to their needs."[17] But at least as regards alcoholism and prostitution, challenging voices were raised long before that, for example, almost two hundred years ago Bentham opposed the criminalization of "drunkenness and fornication" on the ground that that would do more harm than those vices left unpenalized.[18]

The Wolfenden Report, recommending the exclusion from the criminal code of homosexual practices among consenting adults, stressed the requirement of privacy. But "privacy" is obviously not limited to sexual conduct and cannot serve as a distinctive criterion of "victimless crimes." The criteria frequently used to distinguish so-called victimless crimes are consent of the parties[19] and lack of complaint to the police; but more insistently it is said that there is no victim in the sense that no particular person has been harmed.

That "consent," even if limited to normal adults, does not distinguish victimless crimes from universally recognized crimes is evident by reference to the limitations placed on consent as a defense, for example, consent to a public brawl, to mayhem, to aiding suicide. Indeed, as regards some of the most serious crimes, consent is simply irrelevant because no one can consent, for example, to treason.

The principal issue, however, has centered on the question of harm, and the polemic was unfortunately formulated in terms of harm versus the preservation of social morality. Those who espoused the harm thesis summoned the support of Mill who said, "the sole end for which mankind are warranted ... in interfering with the liberty of action of any of their number is self-protection."[20] This is not the place to discuss other statements by Mill that are inconsistent with the broad interpretation that was made of that statement, for example, Mill's views on roads, compulsory education, and defense of the country.

The use of "harm," meaning harm to specific persons, also encounters serious difficulties not only because "harm" is a vague concept but also because human beings are so interrelated that it is impossible to restrict harm to the person who harms himself. If a man incapacitates himself by use of alcohol or heroin, his family suffers, he may go on welfare, he may steal to support his habit. In every one of the practices called victimless crimes, because of the vagueness and ramifications of "harm," it is possible to present a defensible case that there are harms to other persons. When one turns to crimes like treason, the obstruction of justice, pollution, violation of zoning ordinances, and to carrying guns and driving recklessly or while intoxicated, it becomes quite clear that the assumption that every crime has a specific victim is fallacious.

A stronger case for victimless crimes might have been made if its proponents had focused on *mens rea* and causation. If *mens rea* were restricted to intention and recklessness, as has long been urged not only by me but also by Turner and Williams, it would be difficult, say in alcoholism or prostitution, even granting harm to others, to find the required *mens rea,* that is, to find that the resultant harm was sought or recklessly hazarded. Similarly, since proximate cause has been rejected in criminal law, notably in Pennsylvania and also in many other states, the eventual harm of alcoholism or prostitution is not the direct result of the relevant actions; hence it cannot be brought within the restricted, valid concept of causation in criminal law.

Instead of pursuing a vague and ill-conceived notion like victimless crimes,[21] we would do better, I think, if we approached the problem from the other end, that is, from that of the sanction. Since there may be both immorality and harm in the indicated activities, we should concentrate on the limitations, the crudeness, of the penal sanction, and seek more rational ways of dealing with those problems. My present purpose, however, is to emphasize the need for the analysis of concepts if we are to avoid the expensive detours that follow when vague, ill-defined concepts are accepted as valid.

There is a final point to be made in this context: The lumping together of vagrancy, alcoholism, gambling, prostitution, use of narcotics, adultery, bigamy, and others violates one of the principal findings of research that have emerged as sound, namely, the need to distinguish and divide if we are to control. Thus the study of addiction to alcohol or heroin may lead to a solution very different from that required for gambling or prostitution, and each of these may differ in important ways from the other solutions.

Conclusion

What can we learn from fifty years' experience with the indeterminate sentence, juvenile delinquency, and victimless crimes? Some may accept what Glueck called a "theory of maturation" which in plain language means that juvenile and youthful offenders slow up when they get to be twenty-five or thirty. Whether we agree with that sociology or take the chastened view of the historian of the annals of crime from Cain onward, the lesson is: Do nothing because there is nothing that can be usefully done. This was expressed in an epigram of unknown source that says that what men learn from history is that men do not learn from history. There may be more than a grain of truth in that aphorism, but I limit its relevance to the past that we only read about; it does not apply to the immediate past actually experienced by thoughtful people. Accordingly, we should not leap from the admission that perspectives are inevitable and that knowledge is difficult to attain to the conclusion that there is and can be no knowledge in the field of criminal law and criminology; instead, we should take reasoned steps to cope with perspectives and other difficulties.

If we are to learn from experience, we must recognize the barriers to the advance of knowledge of crime and criminal law. I believe there have been and are six principal barriers:

1. Innocence of the perspectives or convictions that influence researchers.
2. Lack of thorough analysis of basic concepts.
3. Misplaced reliance on authority.
4. Unwarranted confidence in the social disciplines and in the competence of personnel trained in those disciplines.
5. Lack of comparative studies especially of the criminal law of other countries.

6. Failure to study the relevant history and the consequently one-dimensional character of current research. One could easily find other limitations in much of current research, for example, carelessly drawn questionnaires, invalid sampling, and a superficial use of statistics; but I think these technical problems are subordinate to the preceding basic ones.

That knowledge of crime and criminal law can be discovered is shown by truths that all or most competent scholars would agree are known, for example, that the receiver of stolen goods is the core of the theft problems, that solutions should be based on differences among types of crimes and criminals, for example, the professional receiver as contrasted with the occasional buyer for his own consumption; that violence caused by passion in a sexual relation differs from the violence of a hired killer and that of a political terrorist; and no doubt these examples can be supplemented by many others that, even if they fall short of meeting the rigorous criteria of natural science, are, nonetheless, fragments of knowledge.

On the premise then that important discoveries can be made, what should be done about perspectives? First, in research especially on controversial questions, we should require the researcher to state in advance of his research, in a written statement to the director or dean, just what his conviction or perspective is. Then at the end of his research he should say whether he has changed his position in any important way. Second, if within a research institute there are individuals whose perspectives are opposed, for example, regarding the death penalty, the two researchers should proceed with the work simultaneously. Finally, able lay persons should not only serve on committees that evaluate the recommendations of the researchers, they should also be recognized as valuable sources of information.

With reference to the second barrier, the lack of analysis, it should be noted that there are several types of analysis. There is linguistic analysis designed to clarify ordinary language, limit vagueness, and remove ambiguities . There is legal analysis such as I have tried to exemplify regarding victimless crimes, and that sort of analysis depends on knowledge of criminal law. There is realistic analysis that is based on factual differences, understood in the light of a social discipline or a moral philosophy. All these analysts share one common goal—their problem is to determine exactly what is the problem.

The third barrier, unwarranted reliance on authority is, because of the nature of their profession, more common among lawyers and legal scholars than among others, although in the rigorously scientific community there is a parallel acceptance of established theories.[22] The barrier I have in mind consists of misplaced reliance. One of the best examples of that, known to me, was shown in Judge Kaufman's opinion in *U.S.* v. *Freeman*[23] where he said: "In 1953 ... the American Law Institute commenced an exhaustive study of ... criminal responsibility... . Nine long years of research, exploration and consideration culminated in the definitive version of Section 4.01... ."[24] In fact, ten years were spent on the entire Model Penal Code, and only a small fraction of that time was spent on mental illness.[25] I was a member of the advisory committee during the first year and a half of its work, and two very able psychiatrists, Drs. Friedman and Guttmacher, were also members of that committee. The plain fact is that they adhered to the convictions they had before they became members of the committee, and I must add that the same was true of me and my convictions. The principal point, however, is not Judge Kaufman's fantasy regarding nine years of research and exploration on criminal responsibility and mental illness but his reliance and that of many drafters in other states on the Model Penal Code without knowing even where the various members of the committee stood with reference to its provisions.

I must be equally brief about the fourth handicap—over-confidence in the social disciplines. I used to be very hesitant about challenging an expert, especially a psychiatrist, on any question that seemed to fall within his field, and I confined my critical discussions to legal issues about which psychiatrists forty years ago were ill-informed but regarding which some of them did not hesitate to express themselves emphatically. Then I read the work of some very able psychiatrists, for example, Dr. Frederic Wertham and Dr. Frederick Redlich, head of the Department of Psychiatry at Yale. Dr. Redlich said:

> I think we know what the seriously ill person in a given culture is. That we do know. In this respect we agree, incidentally, with policemen, with the clerk in the drug store. Our crude diagnostic criteria are reasonably similar.[26]

And later there was Dr. Szasz who went far beyond any criticism I had ever ventured. I am far from implying that there is no important knowledge in psychiatry or social science. I only suggest that lawyers and legal scholars should use those disciplines critically, and I have discussed some of the ways that can be done.

The fifth limitation of much of the research on criminal law and criminology is the lack of comparative study. That the experience of other countries should be studied is axiomatic; but at the same time it should not be assumed that because a law has worked well in another country, it will work well in the United States.

Finally, in speaking of the nonhistorical character of recent research, I am not referring only to long stretches of past history. I also have in mind not only neglect of the experience of older thoughtful layment but also the neglect of research groups to provide a detailed record of their inquiries and discussions. It is only necessary to compare the Model Penal Code and its tentative reports with the voluminous reports of German codifiers to realize that we in this country are unnecessarily handicapped because our predecessors did not leave a detailed record of their work and their proceedings.

I hope I have sufficiently discussed what I have tried to learn about research to delineate the main changes I would recommend in the future conduct of research on crime and criminal law. I refrain from characterizing the proposed reforms as "radical" or in any terms that might only praise my own perspective if ever so subtly. Although the articulation of a perspective is important, it is not a substitute for the careful analysis, study, and critical dialogue that are required to move nearer to the knowledge we must have if life in our cities is to become as secure as it was fifty years ago!

Notes

1. S. Glueck, *Crime and Justice* (Boston: Little, Brown, 1936), p. 222.
2. Ibid., p. 225.
3. Ibid., p. 226.
4. Ibid., p. 229.
5. Ibid., p. 228 (Glueck's italics).
6. Ibid., p. 227.
7. Quoted by Glueck, ibid., p. 217.
8. Ibid., p. 223 (Writer's italics).
9. Ibid., p. 207.
10. Ibid., pp. 214–215.
11. S. Glueck and E.T. Glueck, *Of Delinquency and Crime* (Springfield, Ill.: Charles C. Thomas, 1974), p. 190.
12. M. Zalman, "The Rise and Fall of the Indeterminate Sentence," *Wayne L. Rev.* 24 (1977): 45.
13. J. Hall, "Perennial Problems of Criminal Law," *Hofstra Law Review* 1 (1973): 26–27.
14. S. Glueck and E.T. Glueck, *One Thousand Juvenile Delinquents: Their Treatment by Court and Clinic* (Cambridge, Mass.: Harvard U. Press, 1934), p. 233.
15. In re Gault, 387 U.S. 1 (1967).
16. Id. at 60.
17. J. Hall, "The Law of Arrest in Relation to Contemporary Social Problems," *U. of Chicago L. Rev.* 3 (1936): 369. In later writing, I have also advocated the exclusion of inadvertent negligence from the criminal law. See J. Hall, *General Principles of Criminal Law* (Indianapolis: Bobbs-Merrill, 2d ed. 1960) pp. 315–139, and J. Hall, "Negligent Behavior Should Be Excluded from Penal Liability," *Colum. L. Rev.* 63 (1963): 632.

18. J. Bentham, *The Theory of Legislation* (London: Tribner & Co., 1882), p. 62.

19. "[T]his element of consent precludes the existence of a victim... ." E. Schur, *Crimes Without Victims* (Englewood Cliffs, N.J.: Prentice-Hall, 1965).

20. J.S. Mill, *On Liberty,* Currin V. Shields, ed. (Indianapolis: Bobbs-Merrill, 1956), p. 13.

21. I discussed this in "Perennial Problems of Criminal Law," *Hofstra L. Rev.* 1 (1973): 15. It has received much fuller analysis in Wertheimer, "Victimless Crimes," *Ethics* 87 (1977): 302.

22. J.Hall, *Comparative Law and Social Theory* (Baton Rouge, La.: Louisianna State Univ. Press, 1963), pp. 26–32.

23. T.S. Kuhn, *The Structure of Scientific Revolutions* (Chicago: Univ. of Chicago Press, 2d ed., 1970).

24. 357 F. 2d 606 (1966).

25. Id. at 622.

26. F. Redlich, "Definition of a Case for Purposes of Research in Social Psychiatry," in *Interrelations Between the Social Environment and Psychiatric Disorders* (N.Y.: Milbank Memorial Fund, 1953), p. 120. Quoted in J. Hall, "Science, Common Sense, and Criminal Law Reform," *Iowa L. Rev.* 49 (1963): 1049.

15 Conclusions

Cleon H. Foust and
D. Robert Webster

Action Proposals

One needs to approach the task of reporting colloquium recommendations with temerity. Recommendations are found in the formal papers and in colloquial exchange. Those reported here were derived from three sources: the material presented, the transcript of the final session, and staff notes. The second and particularly the third present unwanted opportunities for judgmental error or worse, reporting bias. As to judgmental error, one needs to decide in some cases whether the participant really intended what was said to be a proposal. As is true in all colloquia, in a very few cases an off-hand comment appears inconsequential or of such tenuous relevance that one believes it should not be mentioned. In cases of doubt, the doubt was resolved in favor of reporting. As to bias, it can be particularly suspect in the case of personal notes. Every effort has been made to let the participants speak and the writer report without bias.

Defense against and Prevention of Crime

Many times the suggestion was made that a substantial effort should be devoted to improve our capacity to predict crime and particularly violent crime. Can violent criminals and other criminals be distinguished other than by the crimes they commit? Once identified, can anything be done for the violence-prone criminal?

Perhaps a national coordinating agency for the study of violence is needed. Collateral to that, one participant, a psychiatrist, suggested that first a uniform set of descriptive behaviors should be agreed on before a thorough study of deviant behavior can become meaningful for all.

Has there been a well-planned and exhaustive inquiry into procedures, methods, or strategies designed to take the profit out of crime or, at least to minimize profits from crime? However the profit motive may affect the incidence of crime, it is bound to have a substantial effect, and even if that were not true, the reduction of criminal profit is good economics.

Victims

There was a general consensus that one of the priorities for those seeking to improve the criminal justice system is the careful development, preferably through the use of pilot projects, of a comprehensive victim/witness program. Inclusion of both is not dichotomous for, in a sense, any witness who is called is a victim of the offender. Indeed, if pressured or subject to intimidation, he is truly victimized.

It was also suggested that insufficient attention is being given the latter, a positive program to discover and thwart witness intimidation is obviously essential to a fair trial. But notwithstanding that, witness intimidation is apparently a fairly frequent occurrence, particularly in cases of urban crime.

Police

The debate between those who believe there is an inefficient proliferation of independent police agencies and those who oppose consolidation of agencies remained unresolved. There did seem to be agreement on a program that would tend to minimize duplication of expensive services such as sharing communication systems and sharing (by contract probably) of the special services (laboratory services, for example) of large agencies with small neighboring agencies or with overlapping agencies.

One of the recommendations was that since discretion is a system problem, the system should be supplied with checks and balances to make objective the discretion of police, prosecutor, and judge. To those might well be added correctional discretionary functions such as parole release or even prisoner classification. Standards and guidelines for the exercise of discretion would be the first step in that direction. Police discretion is the selective enforcement process, the most difficult of the system discretionary functions to make objective, nevertheless could be limited within broad administrative rules. (See ABA Standards 4-3, The Urban Police Function; N.A.C. Standard 1.3 Police).

Other suggestions were: (a) Police organization into miniprecincts similar to the Japanese model for more effective use of manpower resources; (b) more emphasis on citizen/police cooperative programs; and (c) organization within the police force of consumer protection units.

In connection with the general problem of apprehension of offenders and particularly in the shoplifting area, one significant comment was that through the use of self-service cashier stations at random points in retail establishment and minimal numbers of service employees even at cashier stations, the retail establishment may have succeeded in shifting substantial security functions and expense to local law-enforcement agencies.

Trial

It should not be surprising that most of the problems of the criminal justice system surface at discretion points within the system. The first of these discretion points is probably the decision whether to arrest, and from there they continue through the decision to release from parole.

Among those, a critical function involving discretion is that of pretrial release. In that regard there were two suggestions. One was that release on one's own recognizance with appropriate conditions attached might serve to prevent repeated crime. The second dealt with money bail. If it is true that the money bail system allows release of many who for the safety of the public should not be released and detains many of the indigent who should not be detained, what is to be done? The proposal: a second look at the money bail method of pretrial release and possible alterations to enable pretrial release and possible alterations to enable pretrial detention of the potentially violent and career criminals.

In addition to the general recommendation that the ABA Standards dealing with trial be implemented in the states, it was also suggested that: (1) Parallel prosecutor and defender systems should be organized on a district basis, and (2) the states should establish mechanisms to upgrade professionalism across the criminal justice system; that is, prosecutors, defenders, and judges.

Who should prescribe sentencing criteria-controls for judicial discretion? One argument made is that the formulation of criteria is not only made more flexible but also avoids transient emotion and political pressures if placed in the hands of a nonpolitical administrative board created for that purpose.

Sentencing and Correction

The Indiana Criminal Code that went into effect on 1 October 1977 provides the following presumptive determinate sentencing structure for felonies:

Class D: Two years plus a maximum of two years for aggravating circumstances.

Class C: Five years plus three for aggravating circumstances or minus three for mitigating circumstances.

Class B: Ten years plus ten or minus four.

Class A: Thirty years plus twenty or minus ten.

Murder: Forty years plus twenty or minus ten. Death sentence permissible for a limited group of murders.

Habitual offender: Plus thirty years.

In addition, sentences may not be suspended for felonies generally in cases in which a deadly weapon is used by the offender or serious bodily injury is caused to the victim.

This model came under criticism for its severity, a criticism with which an overwhelming majority of the participants seemed to agree. The criticism was: (1) that presumptive sentences generally are too long, (2) the ranges for increase or decrease for aggravating or mitigating circumstances are too great, and (3) there are too many mandatory sentences. One speaker characterized the possible sentence structure as a giant leap into the eighteenth century.

In that vein, it was suggested that there had been insufficient preenactment consideration of the impact of the sentencing structure, and since that deficiency could not now be remedied, the postenactment impact, fiscal and otherwise, should be closely monitored.

There was also general agreement that a harsh sentencing structure is exacerbated by the law that credit–time earned by an offender can be revoked at a departmental hearing, in other words, credit–time does not vest as earned.

Aside from the penological aspects of a sentence structure with long-term penalties, the impact on the courts and correctional system should be monitored. Some of the questions posed are: Will mandatory terms increase plea bargaining? What is the effect on population of correctional facilities? What is the cost of this structure? Can any deterrent effect of the long sentences be ascertained?

It is also fair to say that for the most part, the group was not satisfied with a position that would pose "just deserts" or "commensurate penalties" as the sole purpose of punishment. A continuation of dialogue and research to include deterrence and rehabilitation as purposes of punishment was deemed in order. It was argued that use of "commensurate penalties" does not necessarily foreclose efforts to change offenders' attitudes and responses. The evidence simply does not warrant abandonment of rehabilitation and deterrence as factors in punishment.

In any event, penalties must receive public acceptance which, in turn, mandates an informed electorate. The need to research public response to crime and the justice system for the purpose of education in the complexities of the system was mentioned several times.

Sentencing functionaries are rapidly becoming aware of the many alternatives a judge has in addition to, or better than, incarceration. For economic reasons, if for no other, the use of alternatives, when consistent with public safety, should be encouraged.

Persuasive was one argument that the system generally is not making sufficient use of fines as an alternative sanction.

As mentioned before under the police function, it was suggested that there should be standards for exercise of the sentencing discretion (and for parole).

Exemplifying a pervasive belief that rehabilitation remains as a viable objective of sentencing were suggestions that courts should make selective use of sentencing alternatives that do not require incarceration, that a sophisticated classification of convicted offenders is a prerequisite to constructive institutional programming, that educational and vocational opportunities for correctional inmates should be enlarged, and that prisoners should be encouraged and assisted in maintaining outside contacts.

The current trend to strengthen community correction by upgrading the quality of services and the skill of those who participate has many obvious advantages: reduction of pressure on state facilities and improved rehabilitation opportunities to mention only two. Without adequate local services and opportunities, sentencing options are closely restricted.

One intriguing suggestion was that pending more fiscal support for community correction and possibly to generate more support, the institutional population in Indiana (or any other state) should be carefully classified for possible transfer of those deemed fit into community correction centers. Only then could an economic assessment of the use of community resources be feasible.

Apropos of community correctional services, the current debate about the function of the local jail in any community program becomes relevant. One participant suggested that perhaps our intellectual approach to jails and jailing would be clarified if one could just eliminate the term "jail" from correctional vocabularies. It has acquired a substantial cluster of unsavory images. How to identify the local detention facility?; detention center?; criminal justice center?; community correction center?

In addition to the strengthening and expanding of meaningful prison industries and fair payment of inmates, it was recommended that states need to coordinate their manpower and criminal justice policies and to subsidize where necessary employment opportunities for the young and of releasees from prison in order to provide an economic alternative to crime.

There were also many suggestions for correctional institutions. Among them two had recurrent mention: On institutional administration, it was proposed that an independent, nonpolitical governing board of prestigious citizens produce an effective department of correction, and that correctional staffing both in quantity and quality remains a problem in most states, including Indiana. The root cause is, of course, lack of money.

Administration

The realities of systematic response require that those in responsible positions in the criminal justice system recognize the existence of a system that is affected as a whole by almost every decision. A police policy on selective enforcement affects the prosecuting, judicial, and correctional parts of the system. A legislative choice to raise penalties, to prevent probation or to decriminalize certain conduct affects almost every part of the system. One of the proposals most frequently mentioned was one to coordinate the various parts of the system in order that system dynamics could better be anticipated and controlled. Generally the proposal seemed to presuppose a more or less formal structure for planning, research, and coordination by those involved in the system.

Another prevailing concern was the lack of regular allocation of funds for research. It was believed that concurrent with the increased public concern about criminality, a well-developed and nationally coordinated program for criminal justice research should be launched.

Action Priorities

This allocation of priorities is by a perceived consensus rather than an explicit agreement or vote. There was not sufficient time for either of the latter. White-collar, juvenile early intervention, and priorities for proposed research will be developed at a later time. The five most repeated proposals are the following:

First, undoubtedly were concerns about the sentencing structure in the new Indiana Criminal Code: (a) The length of sentences should be recommended from time to time by a sentencing commission instead of the legislative, fixed terms; (b) the range of sentence choices for each class of felony, except Class D, is too broad; (c) the permissible sentences are much too long; and (d) mandatory sentences should be eliminated. While this multiple concern was expressed about only one state, Indiana, it may well reflect a concern about sentencing structures nationwide. Further, (e) a consensus that determinate sentencing by the judge within guidelines is the appropriate authority structure; (f) that with the exception of manifestly violence-prone criminals and career criminals, there is no dividend from long sentences; and (g) except for inmate classification and reclassification, which might affect the amount of future good time earned, there should be no administrative discretion affecting the release date such as discretionary parole. No direct reference was made to the impact, if any, of interstate disparaties in sentences and sentence structure. While disparate state tax structures may induce migration of wealth, there was no evidence of a like migration of crime and criminals because of disparate punishments. However, a modern study of comparative crime statistics and applicable penalties among states might be interesting.

The proposal was to change the Indiana sentencing structure. Some participants seemed to be saying it should be done as soon as possible; others only after careful monitoring has clarified the effect of long and mandatory sentences on the entire judicial/correctional structure.

The second proposal (a very close second), although couched in various terms, would provide mechanisms for coordination of planning and administration within the criminal justice system. While one is aware that the organization and effective operation of such an agency presents many difficulties involving "turf," competition for the tax dollar, and insularity, the general consensus was that the effort should be made to maintain and care for the total entity.

The third proposal, related as it is to alternatives in sentencing, to correctional costs, and to rehabilitation options, was to make much more use of community-based facilities and programs for offenders.

Fourth was the development of a comprehensive victim/witness program as discussed previously. Like community correction, one need not start with a full panoply of services. The program can be expanded as resources are developed. For example, immediate emergency services for victims could be provided very quickly without great expense and without legislation.

If it is fair to lump research suggestions together as an action proposal, certainly somewhere in the top five proposals would be the suggestion to devote much more money on an ongoing basis to research in the many areas listed hereafter. Concurrently, there is a need for more active coordination and clearinghouse services for research or for specific areas of research as has been done in the case of cancer research.

Research Proposals

Several participants in the colloquium touched on the need to increase research in various aspects of criminal justice. Participants in the colloquium and the audience heard Blair Ewing, director of the National Institute for Law Enforcement and Criminal Justice, discuss the research program and priorities of the National Institute. Jerome Hall devoted his address to research. On the final morning of the colloquium, each of those present was asked to specify the subject matter of any desired research.

Further, since several of the action proposals involved research or could be classified as research, there was not always a clear delineation between the proposals for action and proposals for research.

Even more difficult than in the case of the action proposals is an attempt to attach rough priorities to suggested research.

First, the most frequently mentioned concern was the Indiana sentencing structure and its impact on the entire Indiana criminal justice system. Assessment of the impact will require fact gathering, analysis, and conclusions, in short, research. It would be misleading not to list it as a research item and reluctantly, award it first place in priority. That reluctance is mitigated by the knowledge that a careful impact study in Indiana could be of comparative value in other states.

The second priority was in deterrence. Long-term rehabilitation research was also suggested. Consequently, one might like to suggest that the colloquium was moving toward its major research proposal, namely, in-depth research into the societal benefits from punishment, but had not had sufficient time to consolidate related suggestions into one umbrella proposal.

The third priority appeared to be research into criminal behavior. Suggestions like "more longitudinal studies of criminal career"; "research in prediction of behavior"; "three to five institutes for research in criminal behavior"; and "long-term study of cognitive development for early intervention" all deal with the general problem of prediction of deviant behavior. Prediction bears such a direct relationship to an effective sentencing and correction system that even though we may not be able to control criminal behavior as we may not now control the weather, accurate forecasting permits countermeasures in both cases.

The fourth priority moves from the strictly criminological to administration, that is, more efficient use of the courts. This entails elimination at the outset of those kinds of criminal cases that because of proof difficulties, offender/victim relationship, or for other reasons clutter up the justice system but never reach final adjudication. This was expressed as a "longitudinal analysis of offense mortality as cases move through the system." Another related suggestion was research "to find better means of what happens in case flow." Closely allied was a proposed "longitudinal study of victim processing through the system."

Several other suggestions for specific research should be listed here. The first group deals generally with preoffense concerns:

1. Public attitudes toward crime (presumably this is only a first step in a larger research project for public education).
2. The validity of competing juvenile court concepts (*parens patriae* versus criminal adjudication or a compromise?)
3. A comprehensive analysis of corporate crime.
4. Citizen involvement in law enforcement and particularly cooperation with police in high crime districts.

Two other research suggestions dealt with correctional research.

1. Research into ways to make prison industries more effective (presumably in their rehabilitative functions or as preparation for successful reintegration into free society).
2. A thorough study of costs and cost comparisons of various correctional measures.

Finally, so much has been said about the cost/benefit relationship in studies of the causes of crime that one is reluctant to raise that specter again. In the welter of cultural, economic, social, neurological, physical, educational, and familial hypotheses of causes of crime, one is inclined to accept the advice of some knowledgeable criminologists that there is no "payoff" in the research for causes of crime. Suppose that were said of the search for causes of other human oppressions such as cancer? Be that as it may, one brave participant did suggest further inquiry into crime causes.

About the Contributors

Harry Allen is a professor in the Department of Administration of Justice at San Jose State University.

David Bazelon is chief judge of the United States Court of Appeals for the District of Columbia.

George Beto holds the position of distinguished professor of corrections at the Institute of Contemporary Corrections and the Behavioral Sciences, Sam Houston State University.

Eric W. Carlson is an assistant professor in the Department of Public Policy, Planning and Administration at the University of Arizona, Tucson, Arizona.

John P. Conrad formerly was senior fellow at The Academy for Contemporary Problems in Columbus, Ohio, and presently is chief program analyst.

Philip J. Cook is at Duke University, where he is assistant professor in policy sciences and economics.

Simon Dinitz is senior fellow at the Academy for Contemporary Problems.

Ezzat Fattah is chairman of the Criminology Department of Simon Fraser University.

Edith Flynn is professor of criminal justice at Northeastern University.

Lucy N. Friedman is director of Victim Services Agency, Inc., New York.

Ronald Goldfarb, author of *Jails: The Ultimate Ghetto,* is an attorney in Washington, D.C.

Jerome Hall is professor of law at the University of California's Hastings College of Law.

Andrew von Hirsh is at Rutgers University where he is an associate professor in the Graduate School of Criminal Justice.

Nicholas Kittrie is dean of The American University Law School.

Terence E. MacCarthy is executive director of the Federal Defender Program in Chicago.

Kenneth E. Moyer is professor of psychology at Carnegie–Mellon University.

Patrick Murphy is president of the Police Foundation, Washington, D.C.

William G. Nagel is executive vice president of the American Foundation Inc., Institute of Corrections.

Evalyn C. Parks is a research associate and lecturer in the Department of Public Policy, Planning and Administration at the University of Arizona, Tucson, Arizona.

Roger B. Parks is associate director of the Workshop in Political Theory and Policy Analysis at Indiana University.

Milton G. Rector is president of the National Council on Crime and Delinquency.

Frank J. Remington is professor of law at the University of Wisconsin Law School.

Stanton E. Samenow is director of the Center for Responsible Living in Alexandria, Virginia.

Kenneth Schoen is former commissioner of the Minnesota State Department of Corrections.

Richard P. Seiter is executive assistant at the United States Penitentiary in Leavenworth, Kansas.

Earl J. Silbert is United States attorney for the District of Columbia.

Hans Toch, at the State University of New York at Albany, is professor of psychology in its School of Criminal Justice.

Ernest van den Haag is adjunct professor of law at the New York Law School.

Marvin Wolfgang is director of the Center for Studies in Criminology and Criminal Law at the University of Pennsylvania.

Eric E. Younger is a judge in the Los Angeles Municipal Court.

About the Editors

Cleon H. Foust received a J.D. degree from the University of Arizona College of Law. His professional life, other than several years of private practice and a like time as deputy attorney general and attorney general of Indiana, has been principally academic—twenty-nine years with the Indiana University School of Law, Indianapolis. Mr. Foust taught criminal law for eighteen of those years.

After serving as dean of the Law School from 1967 to 1973, he was loaned by Indiana University to the Indiana Lawyers Commission, Inc. The Lawyers Commission, a subsidiary of the Indiana State Bar Association, engages in criminal justice projects and programs. Currently, Mr. Foust is professor emeritus at the Law School, and executive director of the Lawyers Commission.

D. Robert Webster is director of Research for the Indiana Lawyers Commission. He received the A.B. degree from Indiana University and the J.D. degree from Harvard University. He is a trial and appellate lawyer in private practice, and is on the faculty of Indiana Central University. He is a member of the Indianapolis, Indiana, and American Bar Associations.